TOTAL VICTORY!

2ND EDITION

The Complete Management Guide to a Successful NLRB Representation Election

by Donald P. Wilson

Broken Arrow, Oklahoma

Copyright © 1997 by Labor Relations Institute, Inc.

Published by
Labor Relations Institute, Inc.
7850 South Elm Place
Broken Arrow, Oklahoma 74011
Phone: (918) 455-9995
Fax: (918) 455-9998

ISBN: 0-9638554-1-7

Printed in the United States of America

For information contact
Labor Relations Institute, Inc.
7850 South Elm Place
Broken Arrow, Oklahoma 74011
or phone (918) 455-9995

TABLE OF CONTENTS

FOREWORD

D onald P. Wilson graduated from Northeastern State University in Oklahoma in 1966 with a degree in psychology and business administration. He immediately joined Sperry-Rand Corporation where he began his career as Assistant Personnel Manager in a 300-employee division. Within a few years, he was promoted to Personnel Manager of an 1,800-employee plant, then designated Director of Industrial Relations for the Vickers Division of Sperry-Rand in 1972. Two years later, Mr. Wilson joined Kendavis Industries as Director of Industrial Relations. He entered private consulting practice in 1978 and founded the Labor Relations Institute, Inc., in 1980. Originally, LRI's objective was to offer management consulting services to assist employers in the maintenance of a union-free workplace. Between 1980 and 1987, members of the firm worked almost exclusively in guiding and directing management during National Labor Relations Board representation election campaigns.

In 1987, Don wrote the NLRB Representation Election Campaign Manual that provided management with the information and tools necessary to conduct a successful campaign. The following year, LRI produced the first generation of a video tape program designed to be shown directly to voters. These tapes convincingly explained the many disadvantages of union membership for employees. Since that time, the NLRB Representation Election Campaign Program has been used to assist over 3,500 employers of all sizes in winning their union representation elections. The program has become the industry standard and is considered by many labor attorneys and labor relations professionals to be an essential part of any employer's union-free strategy.

This book, based on the continuing development of the NLRB Representation Election Campaign Program and the experiences of LRI associates who have participated in these campaigns, is a clear and concise guide for any business owner, manager, or supervisor faced with an NLRB election.

ACKNOWLEDGMENTS

In writing this book, I have benefited from the contributions of many individuals, particularly the staff at the Labor Relations Institute. Bruce Smith was an invaluable help in editing and rewriting. Scott Carmichael made many important contributions. To each of them, I express my thanks.

During my career, I have received guidance and direction from many people. I'm sure Dave Acheson at Sperry-Vickers had serious reservations about promoting a 29-year-old to the corporate staff, but his faith allowed me to gain tremendous experience in labor relations. I will never forget what he said when I asked him for advice my first day in my new assignment. With a straight face and firm voice, he said, "Don't screw up."

I also learned a great deal from Archie Robbins. As he once told me, "You may have a degree in business and a masters in psychology, but you got your Ph.D. in labor relations from me." In retrospect, I believe he was right.

The National Labor Relations Board Election Campaign Process

Murphy's Law:
*Everything that can go
wrong will go wrong
at the worst possible time.*

Most business owners or managers faced with a National Labor Relations Board representation election campaign probably feel that Murphy is an optimist. No business can really afford the time, expense, and disruption of a representation election campaign. Management personnel usually have little or no experience running an effective campaign against a professional organizer who conducts perhaps five to ten such campaigns each year. Management must also compete against the financial resources of a huge international union desperate for new members. Nevertheless, an effective campaign must be waged within a short time, usually just a few weeks, while communicating information with which management is almost totally unfamiliar. That's the bad news. The good news is that the overwhelming weight of evidence is on your side. With a reasonably modest investment, you can inform employees of the many disadvantages of union membership. If you can persuade voters to make a rational rather than an emotional decision, you stand an excellent chance of winning your election.

Today's union organizers are becoming more adept at stealth campaigning, especially in the early stages. Still, most business owners or managers are usually aware of some union activity before an NLRB petition is filed. This knowledge, however, doesn't prevent the actual receipt of a petition from being a uniquely unpleasant experience. The form of the petition is foreign and you may not understand everything it contains, or your rights and responsibilities under the law. The first step should be to carefully examine the petition and determine if it is valid.

After receiving a National Labor Relations Board certification (RC) petition, first make sure your business is covered by the National Labor Relations Act. Although these guidelines are somewhat technical, you should become familiar with them. Many union petitions are ruled invalid because the business is not covered by the Act.

Which Employers Are Covered by the NLRA?

The National Labor Relations Board gets its authority from Congress by way of the National Labor Relations Act. (A copy of the Act is in Appendix A.) The power of Congress to regulate labor-management relations is limited by the commerce clause of the United States Constitution. Although Congress can generally declare what the rights of employees are or should be, it can make its declaration of rights effective only concerning enterprises whose operations "affect commerce" and labor disputes that "affect commerce." The NLRB, therefore, can direct elections and certify the results only in the case of an employer whose operations affect commerce. Similarly, it can act to prevent unfair labor practices only in cases involving labor disputes that affect, or would affect, commerce.

Although today the NLRA covers most organizations, smaller employers in particular should carefully review the Board's standards to make sure their businesses are covered by the Act. These standards are found on pages 42 through 46 of the publication "A guide to basic law and procedures under the National Labor Relations Act." (A copy of this guide is in Appendix B.)

Even if you believe your business is not covered by the Act, you should still prepare for at least a modest campaign to educate and convince your employees to reject unionization. If you don't, you could be in for a fatal surprise. Recently, the operators of a residential children's home in Indiana were convinced, after a review of the current NLRB standards, that the Board could not assert jurisdiction over their business. They were so certain of this they made no campaign preparations. Meanwhile, their attorney processed the case through the normal NLRB channels. After a lengthy delay, the Board ruled the business was correctly classified as a privately operated institution involved with the specialized care of children. The Board asserted its jurisdictional discretion and directed an election within 12 business days following the decision. Twelve days was insufficient time to convince employees of anything, especially since the union had been communicating with them about the progress of the case and the "advantages" of union membership, while the employer said nothing. The union won the election.

Always prepare for a campaign, even if you feel certain you will not be faced with an election. If the Board agrees with you, great. If, however, there is the slightest question about the Board's decision, planning in advance for a modest, ongoing campaign will give you at least an even chance of winning, should an election be held. More important, if the Board rules against you, you will be prepared to begin your campaign with a contingency plan already in place.

Which Employees Are Covered by the NLRA?

At a family-owned construction company in a rural Iowa town, I once came across a twist to that portion of the National Labor Relations Act that excludes family members from the voting unit. The construction company had been petitioned by the Laborers Union. The union's proposed bargaining unit included 35 employees, two of who were the owner's sons. Although under Board rules, individuals employed by a parent or spouse are generally excluded from any proposed bargaining unit, the owner quickly agreed to the union's proposed unit since he knew his sons would support the company and perhaps even be able to provide inside information about the union campaign. An election date was set and the campaign began. Toward the end of the campaign, I heard a supervisor claim that the owner's sons seemed to be the union's strongest supporters. Though this sounded impossible, I encouraged their father to question them about it. The sons admitted they were unhappy with the way the business was run and they believed the employees needed a union for a balance of power. Now aware of his sons' true feelings, the owner went to the Board and pointed out that according to the NLRA exclusions, his children should never have been included in the voting unit. The Board brought this to the union's attention, but the union asked to proceed with the unit as originally proposed. The Board concurred. On election day, the union won. I don't know if the sons have been put back in the will, but at the time of the election, their father was not a proud parent.

The National Labor Relations Act states that the term "employee" shall include any employee except the following:

- Agricultural laborers
- Domestic servants
- Any individual employed by a parent or spouse
- Independent contractors

- Supervisors
- Individuals employed by an employer subject to the Railway Labor Act
- Government employees, including those employed by the U.S. Government, any Government corporation or Federal Reserve Bank, or any State or political subdivision such as a city, town, or school district

Supervisors are excluded from the definition of "employee" and, therefore, not covered by the Act. Whether an individual is a supervisor for purposes of the Act depends on that individual's authority over employees and not merely a title. A supervisor is defined by the Act as "any individual who has the authority, acting in the interest of an employer, to cause another employee to be hired, transferred, suspended, laid off, recalled, promoted, discharged, assigned, rewarded, or disciplined, either by taking such action or by recommending it to a superior; or who has the authority to direct other employees or adjust their grievances; provided, in all cases, that the exercise of authority is not of a merely routine or clerical nature, but requires the exercise of independent judgment. For example, a foreman who determined which employees would be laid off after being directed by the job superintendent to lay off four employees would be considered a supervisor and would, therefore, not be covered by the Act; a 'strawboss' who, after someone else determined which employees would be laid off, merely informed the employees of the layoff and who neither directed other employees nor adjusted their grievances would not be considered a supervisor and would be covered by the Act.

"'Managerial' employees are also excluded from the protection of the Act. A managerial employee is one who represents management interests by taking or recommending actions that effectively control or implement employer policy.

"The term 'employer' includes any person who acts as an agent of an employer, but it does not include the following:

- The United States or any State Government, or any political subdivision of either, or any Government corporation or Federal Reserve Bank
- Any employer subject to the Railway Labor Act"

If, after careful review, you believe your employees are not covered by the Act, you should immediately contact your attorney or the Board. The Board is empowered to make a decision as to your status under the current standards.

Authorization Cards

By the time you receive a representation (RC) petition from the NLRB, the union's job of soliciting authorization cards will have been completed. However, it is important you understand the authorization card process and how it works before proceeding with an examination of the petition.

Whenever a union is seeking to become the representative of a group of employees, it is required by the NLRA to obtain signed authorization cards from at least 30% of the employees in the group it is seeking to represent. While 30% is the legal minimum required to petition for an election, unions will almost never petition with less than 50% signed authorization cards, and most unions require 60% to 65% as the minimum number to petition. (A typical union authorization card is shown as Exhibit 1-A at the end of this chapter.)

The solicitation of authorization cards is clearly the most critical part of the union's pre-petition activity. Virtually all of its efforts before filing a petition are directed at obtaining signed authorization cards. Most successful union organizers believe that the best barometer for predicting the outcome of an election is the degree of difficulty in obtaining cards. The more difficult it is to obtain signatures, the less likely the union will win the election, regardless of the number of cards finally signed.

The vast majority of authorization cards are "pure" authorization cards. This means that the signer of the card designates the union as his or her exclusive bargaining representative. Some unions may use a dual purpose card that both designates the union as the signer's exclusive bargaining representative and states the card may be used to demand an election. This type card is fairly rare. Some cards may include a "dues checkoff" provision authorizing the employer to deduct union dues from the employee's pay and forward that amount to the union. This card is also rare.

After a union has collected 50% or more of the cards in the group it is seeking to represent, it may mail the employer a letter stating it represents a majority of said employees and demand recognition. Usually, this letter is mailed at or about the same time the union files its petition with the Board. The union ordinarily does not wait for an answer, for it knows that either there won't be a response or the response will be negative. (An example of a union demand letter is furnished as Exhibit 1-B. If you wish to respond, a sample response letter is provided as Exhibit 1-C.)

During the initial card signing phase of the campaign, a union will attempt to keep its activities cloaked in secrecy. The motivation is to prevent the employer from launching a campaign to discourage employees from signing cards. However, when the union activity becomes general knowledge, it is not unusual for a union to correspond with the employer in the form of a letter. This letter will notify management that a campaign is underway, warn against unfair labor practices, and list the names of those on the employee organizing committee. The purpose of this letter is to attempt to inhibit the commission of unfair labor practices that could be detrimental to the internal organizers, as well as to prove that the employer is aware union activity has begun. During a union organizing campaign, management is restricted from many activities and a letter of this type from the union prevents management deniability.

The Petition

Exhibit 1-D is a reproduction of the NLRB petition form. There are several important pieces of information on this form you should carefully review immediately upon receiving the petition. Every petition filed with the Board is assigned a case number, located in the upper right hand corner of the form. The first one or two digits represent the number of the NLRB regional office responsible for processing the petition. There are 34 NLRB regional offices, so the first one or two digits of the case number will be a number from 1 to 34. This number will be followed by two initials corresponding to the box checked in Section 1 on the form. Since this book deals only with representation elections, we are only interested in the initials RC. This designates the petition is filed by a union seeking to represent the employees of a particular enterprise. The final four or five digits are the case number assigned to the particular petition. This number is followed by the date the union filed the petition.

Section 1 of the form states the purpose of the petition; in this case, RC petitions. Section 2 through 4b states standard information about the employer. Since this information is supplied to the Board by the union, it may not always be totally accurate. If inaccurate, it can be corrected by simply notifying the Board. However, there is another alternative you may wish to consider. Since it is often in your best interest to buy as much time as possible, you may want to force the union to refile the petition. This can delay the election by two weeks or more, giving you additional time to prepare.

In Section 5, the union must specifically state which groups of employees it is seeking to represent and which groups it wants excluded. *This section of the petition is very important and has often made the difference between winning and losing.*

Remember, not all employees are covered by the National Labor Relations Act. Anyone not covered is not an eligible voter. In addition, frequently a union will attempt to "carve out" a group of employees from a larger group of eligible voters. For example, assume that a company has 100 employees. Out of that group, 75 would be eligible voters under the NLRA. It is not necessary for a union to file a petition seeking to represent all 75 employees. Instead, it can try to "carve out" a smaller group. This strategy is based on the premise that if the union can get its foot in the door, it will have a better shot at going after the larger, more profitable group later. This process, while perfectly legal, can and often should be protested by management. That is why this section of the petition is so important.

Carefully examine the types of employees the union wants included in the voting unit. Are any of these employees ineligible based on the Board rules previously discussed in this chapter? If so, you will later protest their eligibility to the Board. Also, examine the types of employees to determine if the unit the union is petitioning includes all legally eligible employees or only a portion thereof. Many petitions filed by unions state under Included, "all production and maintenance employees," and under Excluded, "all supervisory, managerial, and confidential employees; all guards; all others specifically excluded by the Act." Basically, this means the union is seeking representation of all legally eligible employees.

Other petitions may list the job categories of the groups the union is seeking to both include and exclude. These petitions require especially close examination. If the description is broad, such as "all production and maintenance employees," you should determine if all these employees have a community of interest in their working relationship with the employer. For example, is the entire group covered by the same general wage and benefit provisions? The same supervision? Do they work under similar conditions? Is some of the group salaried while others are hourly? Do some employees report through the manufacturing organization while others report through the quality control organization? Do they work in different locations? All these considerations, plus many others, can determine whether the group shares a community of interest.

Why is this so important? A favorable determination of the voting unit has often meant the difference between winning and losing an election. For example, the union may specifically exclude groups of employees the Board would rule eligible voters because it believes that the particular group or groups does not support unionization. If you believe the union's proposed unit is incorrect, examine the proposed unit carefully. Would the inclusion of other legally eligible employees increase or decrease your chances of winning the election? Likewise, would the exclusion of particular groups of employees who do not share a community of interest increase or decrease your chances of winning? If you believe a redefined unit will improve your chances of winning, you should evaluate that option. Remember, however, that if you were to increase the size of the union's proposed unit and the union wins the election, it would become the bargaining representative of all employees in the larger, redefined unit. (Health care employers should refer to Appendix C for a description of appropriate bargaining units in the health care industry.)

Consider the case of a fish processing plant in Virginia that was faced with a petition from the United Food and Commercial Workers union. The UFCW was seeking to represent all 135 of the company's employees. The unit was defined as 15 captains, 45 seamen, five maintenance staff, and 70 processing employees. Management was certain the captains were opposed to the union, and certain they could be excluded from the unit as members of management. On the other hand, if the captains were included, the company increased its chances of winning the election. But if the union won with the captains included, it would surely have more negotiating leverage, as they were skilled employees who were essential to the business and could not be easily replaced during a strike. Management decided the risk of including the captains was too great and got them excluded from the unit. Fortunately, even without the captains, the company won, though by a smaller margin. The determination of which employees to include or exclude is not always this critical, but in all cases it deserves careful thought.

An interesting point to note is that a union's success rate in RC elections appears to be directly related to the size of the unit. The smaller the unit, the greater the union's chance of winning. Here is organized labor's success rate during 1995, based on unit size.

Unit Size	% of Elections Won by Unions
1-49	53.5%
50-99	44.3%
100-499	33.3%
500 or more	22.2%

The reason for a declining success rate as the unit size increases is because it is far more difficult for a union to make personal one-on-one contact with larger groups of employees. Conversely, management can continue to have close interaction with the voters through group meetings and supervision. Additionally, larger organizations typically spend more time, money, and effort on the campaign to defeat the union than smaller organizations.

It is important to note if you successfully argue to increase the size of the proposed unit, the union's eligibility to petition may be altered. The union must have signed authorization cards from at least 30% of the employees it is seeking to represent. Therefore, the inclusion of additional people in the unit may change the union's eligibility to petition. For example, if the unit for which the union is petitioning includes 100 people, only 30 signed authorization cards would be required to legally file a petition for election. But if the appropriate unit is actually 150 employees, the union would be required to have 45 signed authorization cards to legally petition. Including the additional 50 people could mean the union cannot legally file a petition at this time because of the 30% rule.

This scenario was recently played out at a rural electric co-op in Pennsylvania petitioned by the International Brotherhood of Electrical Workers. The petition called for a unit size of 33 employees. Since the management team had been involved in previous campaigns, it immediately started planning for the next one. Preparations for a campaign were well under way when a representative from the Labor Relations Institute discovered the company had a satellite facility that was just across the county line and that worked closely with the main office. On occasions, employees and equipment were even shared. Management had been so intent on responding quickly, it had failed to consider the community of interest these two groups of employees shared. After several meetings with the NLRB, the unit size was changed to include the additional 42 employees at the satellite facility. On the basis of this higher number, the IBEW could no longer meet the minimum 30% rule for authorization cards. The lesson here is to first explore your unit determination options before assuming you must run a campaign.

Next, examine Section 6a of the petition. The number found here represents the number of people the union believes are currently employed in the groups listed under "Included" in Section 5 of the petition. *The NLRA requires that a union have signed authorization cards from at least 30% of the employees it is seeking to represent.* If the actual number of employees is substantially different from the number listed by the union, you should notify the Board. This is particularly important if the union's number is lower than the correct employee count. *While the union may have 30% signed authorization cards based on its figures, it may not have 30% of the accurate, higher number.*

Remember, however, that while a union needs authorization cards from only 30% of the unit it is trying to represent, far more than that is needed if it hopes to have a good chance of winning the election. A recent survey conducted by the AFL-CIO Department of Organization and Field Services stated, "The number of authorization cards obtained has a direct relationship to the likelihood of the union prevailing. It is not until the union obtains signatures from 75% or more of the unit that the union has more than a 50% likelihood of winning the election." The survey then showed the following correlation between the percentage of employees signing cards and the likelihood the union will win an NLRB election.

Percent Signing Cards	Chance Union Will Win Election
75%+	60%
75%	50%
60% - 75%	49%
50% - 60%	45%
40% - 50%	33%
less than 40%	8%

When a union files a petition for representation, many employers honestly believe no more than the minimum 30% of their employees could possibly have signed authorization cards. But these figures from organized labor itself are convincing proof that a union is unlikely to file a petition without signed authorization cards from at least 60% of the employees it is trying to represent. *No matter what your opinion, the union almost certainly had at least that many signed authorization cards when the petition was filed.*

Section 6b of the petition form is simply the union's assurance to the Board that the petition is, in fact, supported by at least 30% or more of the employees in the unit.

Section 7a of the form refers to the possibility the union may be requesting recognition based on signed cards. As mentioned earlier, after a union has obtained authorization cards from a majority of individuals in the unit it is seeking to represent, it will normally send the employer a letter stating that fact and demanding recognition. (See Exhibit 1-B.) Sometimes, however, a union representative, after securing authorization cards from a majority of employees, will telephone or try to personally meet the employer. If contact is established, the representative will then try to discuss wages, hours, benefits, and working conditions in an attempt to engage in bargaining. If the union representative is successful, the Board often rules that negotiations have begun and will then certify the unit based on cards, rather than schedule an election. *Do not, under any circumstances, engage in any discussions with any representative of the union during this period. If it is necessary to communicate with the union representative, do so in writing through your attorney.*

Section 7b of the form is only applicable if the union is currently recognized as the collective bargaining representative of the employees, but has not been formally certified by the NLRB. For our purposes, this section of the form is not relevant since the assumption is that employees are not currently represented by a union. For the same reason, Sections 8, 9, 10, 11, and 12 are also not applicable.

The last section of the form is a declaration that must be signed by the person filing the petition on behalf of the union. This information is important, as you may want to determine the tactics of this particular organizer when planning your campaign.

When an employer receives a petition, the most frequently asked question is, "How do I know the union really has signed authorization cards from at least 30% of my employees?" In general, the determination of the extent of employee interest in being represented by a union is a purely administrative matter, wholly within the discretion of the Board, which has stated: *"While any information offered by any party bearing on the validity of the evidence offered in support of an asserted interest should be received, weighed, and, if appropriate, acted on, there is no right in any such party to litigate the subject, either directly or collaterally."* This means the Board has the absolute power to determine the validity of the cards submitted, and its decision regarding their number and validity is final.

After receiving notification of a petition for an election, one of management's first reactions is often to question the validity of the authorization cards. This is a normal, though emotional response. Unfortunately, it can cause valuable campaign time to be wasted. Before pursuing this tactic, you should try to look at the validity of authorization cards objectively. Any misleading tactics a union organizer might have used to secure signatures, or employees' ignorance of what they signed, is of no importance. Once signed, the cards are valid. If you suspect forgery, you must have solid evidence. Acceptable evidence would be expert signature comparisons or affidavits from employees stating they did not sign cards. However, it is not enough to question the validity of cards based on undocumented statements by employees denying their knowledge of union activities.

These denials are often made out of fear of retribution for associating with a union.

Union organizers seldom resort to forging authorization cards. The penalties are simply too great: a fine of up to $10,000 or imprisonment of up to five years, or both. The fact is that signed authorization cards are virtually always legitimate.

In the initial communications from the Board to the employer, a payroll list covering the employees in the alleged appropriate unit will be requested. The Board will require that this list, called an Excelsior list, be current on or about the date the petition was filed. To vote in an NLRB election, an employee must have worked in the unit during the eligibility period set by the Board and must be employed in the unit on the date of the election or have a reasonable expectation of re-employment or a continued working interest with the employer. The eligibility period set by the Board is usually a specific date. Employees hired after that date would be ineligible to vote. Employees who resign or are terminated by the employer before the election are also ineligible.

When you furnish the Excelsior list to the Board, the Board will verify that the names on the list correspond with the names on the cards submitted by the union. Although authorization cards are examined on their face (to check, for example, against signatures in the same handwriting), their validity will be presumed *unless called into question by the presentation of objective considerations.* This means if you have proof that cards have been forged, you should present this evidence to the Board. The Board will then conduct an investigation that may include attempts to obtain affidavits from the person or persons responsible for securing and submitting the cards, signature comparisons against the employer's records (such as W-4 forms), and questioning purported card signers. It is important to note, however, that this kind of thorough examination is not routine and will not be conducted unless objective evidence is presented that shows a reasonable basis for suspecting fraud or forgery has been committed. If, after examination, it is determined that the cards furnished represent at least 30% of the employees in the alleged unit, the case will proceed.

After the card check is completed, the Board will give a copy of the Excelsior list to the union. By using this list, the union can begin to conduct at least a portion of its campaign by mail. Prior to October 1994, most employers who submitted an Excelsior list to the Board identified the employees by first name initials only, for example: Adams, F.L. But in October 1994, the NLRB changed the rules. In *North Macon Health Care* (315 NLRB 50) the Board ruled that employers must include employees' first names on Excelsior lists. The Board stated, "we find merit in (the union's) objections with respect to the Employer's failure to include employees' first names on the Excelsior list. Therefore, we set aside the election and order that a second election be scheduled. Further, we hold that an employer's failure to provide the full first and last name of employees is a deviation from the Board's policy that an employer must 'substantially comply' with the Excelsior rule and tends to interfere with a free and fair election." (The text of this case is included as Exhibit 1-G at the end of this chapter.)

Often, employees will object to their names and addresses being given to the union. Therefore, it may be a good idea to post a notice or otherwise inform your employees how and why the union now has this information. For example, a notice might read:

> "On January 18, the company was required by the National Labor Relations Board to submit to them a list of the names and addresses of all employees the union is seeking to represent. The Board then provided the union with a copy of this list. We are required by law to comply with this request. We did not want to give out this information, which we regard as confidential. We did so only to comply with the law. We regret any inconvenience or annoyance this invasion of your privacy by the union may cause."

After submitting the Excelsior list to the Board, you need to keep abreast of any changes to the list. The names and addresses of anyone inadvertently left off the list should be submitted to the Board as soon as possible. If individuals whose names are included on the original list are no longer employed at the time of the election, the Board agent and the union representative should be notified of those changes at the time of the election. During the campaign, the union will probably make extensive use of this list. The following are suggestions for using the Excelsior list from the book Organizing and the Law, a handbook for union organizers:

1. Organizing campaigns must include planning geared to the availability of employee address lists after direction of election or employer consent. This planning should include extensive house calls, phone contacts, and home mailing campaigns in addition to other organizing methods. This should not be a "one-person show," but should be a cooperative effort, mobilizing as many key in-house people as possible.

2. All mailings should contain materials designed on a *positive basis.* Unions must realize that they are approaching the worker and the worker's family in their home and community environment rather than in the workplace. They should talk about what the union can accomplish in terms of security for the family breadwinner and economic benefits and protections for the family group. Name calling or attacks against the employer should be avoided. Mailings should be cleared with organizing directors before mailing.

3. These lists must be kept locked in a safe place always and never shown or given to outsiders. Misuse of such lists could jeopardize the communications gain made in the Excelsior decision.

4. The lists should be tested as soon as possible by mailing campaign literature and checking how many envelopes are returned. The employer may correct these errors, or the information may be used to establish a post-election objection to the accuracy of the list.

5. When an election is won, the list should be preserved. It can come in handy later.

6. If an election is lost, again the mailing list should be preserved. It may be invaluable for a later campaign.

Shortly after a union files a petition for representation, the NLRB's regional office will schedule a prehearing conference. The purpose of this conference is to obtain an agreement between the employer and the union on the required showing of interest, the appropriate voting unit, and the date, time, and place for an election. This prehearing conference may be a formal meeting or telephone conversations. If there are no major disputes over these issues, the Board agent will attempt to obtain an agreement between the parties. There are two types of election agreements. The first is a *consent election.* This agreement provides that all rulings of the Regional Director are final and binding on the parties on all questions relating to the election. These questions can include such issues as voter eligibility, challenged ballots, objections to the conduct of the election, and conduct affecting the outcome of the election.

The second type of election agreement is a *stipulated consent election*. This agreement permits appeal of the Regional Director's decisions to the NLRB in Washington for final determination of any disputes.

If no agreement is reached, there is a third type of election: a *directed election*. This is one in which the two parties are unable to reach agreement on the issues involved in a consent election. When this occurs, the Board will hold a formal hearing. At this hearing, the Board agent will listen to all evidence presented by the parties concerning their position on the issues in dispute. Following the hearing, a decision will be rendered and, if appropriate, an election directed.

If no dispute exists between the parties, or if a dispute can be resolved to your satisfaction, it is probably advisable to enter into one of the two types of consent elections. The stipulated consent election is usually preferable because it enables you to appeal any Regional Director's decision to the NLRB in Washington. Remember, a consent election simply means the employer and the union have agreed on the time and place of the election, the choices to be included on the ballot (generally for the union or against the union, meaning the employer will encourage employees to vote no), and a method to determine who is eligible to vote. The agreement also authorizes the NLRB to conduct the election. *A consent election is normally preferable to a directed election because the union generally will allow some flexibility on the day and time of the voting.* In later chapters, we will discuss the importance of selecting the proper day and time. In a directed election, the Board will arbitrarily set the day and time, which may not be in your best interest. Directed elections are usually set within 30 days after they are directed.

When a difference occurs that cannot be resolved informally as to the proper unit, the eligibility of specific individuals, the validity of cards, or any other matter, the NLRB will hold a hearing during which both parties will present their positions. The Board is empowered to render a decision in all of these matters. If, after reviewing the evidence, the Regional Director determines that an election is appropriate, he or she will direct an election to be held. During this stage of the election process, it is advisable to be represented before the Board by legal counsel that is familiar with NLRB procedures.

Following the establishment of the appropriate voting unit and the date and time of the election, the formal campaign will begin. Most campaigns in consent elections last approximately six weeks. In fiscal 1995-1996, for example, the median time to proceed to an election from the filing of a petition was 42 days. This is why a consent election is normally preferable to a directed election. Remember, a directed election usually takes place within 30 days of notification, while consent elections allow approximately 42 days to election. The additional 12 days of campaign time can be invaluable.

Normally, the NLRB will not be involved in the campaign phase unless one of the parties files an unfair labor practice charge alleging the other party has committed campaign violations. Obviously, management should avoid any conduct that could be viewed as an unfair labor practice. (A discussion of this subject is included in Chapter 3.)

If, during the campaign, the union determines it cannot win the election, one of three things will normally happen. The union may notify the Board it wishes to withdraw the petition. If this occurs, the Board will notify you. By withdrawing the petition "without prejudice," the union will be required to wait a specified period of time — usually six months — before filing a new petition. Reasons for withdrawal vary, but usually happen because:

- Union support has dwindled due to management's campaign
- The union needs additional time
- The unit appears inappropriate

The union's second option is to file an unfair labor practice charge to block the election. If this happens, the Board will determine the merits of the union's charge before conducting the election. These charges, known as "blocking charges," can delay an election for months or even years. Normally, if the union is simply seeking additional time, it will drop or settle the charge within two to three weeks.

The union's final alternative is to proceed with an election it knows it will lose. The strategy behind this option is that by losing the election, no other union can file a petition for representation for one year. This gives the union a full year to build the additional support it needs to win recognition. One of the sad facts of the NLRB representation election procedure is that a union can launch a petition drive year after year. There have been cases where a union lost 12 or more elections in a row before finally winning. But one victory is all it takes.

Shortly after a petition is filed, the Board will mail the employer a form entitled "Notice to Employees" and will ask the employer to post the document. (A sample of this form is shown as Exhibit 1-E.) The notice advises employees of their rights to organize under the NLRA and spells out certain types of employer conduct that is illegal. *The posting of this notice is NOT required.* While it is always a good idea to keep employees informed about what is happening with the Board, you should read this notice and determine if its posting will help or hurt your overall communications program.

Sometime before the election, the Board will mail several election notices to the employer. (A sample election notice is shown as Exhibit 1-F.) Each notice will contain a brief description of the employees who are eligible to vote, a brief description of the employees not eligible to vote, the time and place of the election, and a sample ballot. Also contained on each election notice is a section on the rights of employees, purpose of the election, secret ballot, eligibility rules, challenge of voters, authorized observers, and information concerning the election. *The Board requires that these notices be posted in conspicuous places in the work area(s) of all eligible voters. THE POSTING OF THIS NOTICE IS MANDATORY. IT MUST BE POSTED AT LEAST THREE DAYS PRIOR TO THE ELECTION.*

Though the notice of election contains a warning that it must not be defaced, management should examine the notice frequently to be sure union supporters have not turned it into a piece of campaign literature for the union. For example, many times employees mark the sample ballot on the notice. If this occurs, the notice should be replaced with a clean one. If possible, all election notices and other posted campaign literature should be placed in glass-enclosed and locked bulletin boards. The Board will notify you in a timely manner of all these requirements. You will find the Board instructions are clearly worded and easy to understand.

On the day of the election, an agent of the NLRB will arrive at the polls to begin preparing the election area and to conduct a pre-election conference. The Board agent is responsible for the arrangement of the polling area, including supplying the voting booth(s), ballot boxes, ballots, and all other material and equipment necessary to conduct the election. Approximately 45 minutes before the opening of the polls, the Board agent will assemble the observers, along with representatives of management and the union, for a pre-election conference. (See Chapter 15.) The agent will put "Voting Place" and "Warning" signs at appropriate locations.

Badges and instructions will be issued to the election observers. Outside representatives, including the management campaign director and the union representative(s) will be permitted to inspect the polling place and the sealing of the ballot box, and to participate in the final resolution of any Excelsior list questions. This will be the first occasion you will be required to allow the union representative(s) on company property. They will also be allowed to participate in any other pre-election conferences and to be present at the counting of the ballots. Though you are required to allow the union representative(s) on the premises during this phase of the election, you are not required to allow them on the premises unescorted. You may stay with them from your property line or front office to the voting area. After any conferences, you should escort them out.

Do not believe anything the organizer tells you. Get the facts before you let them do something that could give the union an advantage. Never forget a union organizer's job is to win elections, and they are good at what they do. (Additional information on the selection of observers and management conduct during this period is found in Chapters 2 and 15.)

Voters who arrive before the opening of the polls will not be allowed to vote before the scheduled voting time. They may, however, be permitted to line up outside the voting area. At the time the polls open, or shortly before, the outside representatives will be asked to leave the polling area and the election will then be under the complete control of the Board agent. If the agent does not ask these individuals to leave, you should ask the agent to ask them to leave. *No electioneering will be permitted at or about the polling place during the hours of voting, nor will any conversation be allowed between employees and agents of either the employer or the union in the polling area during this period.* Observers will not be allowed to wear campaign buttons, T-shirts or any other type of campaign material. If the union observers are wearing campaign material, bring this to the Board agent's attention and ask for appropriate action to be taken. Supervisors should refrain from observing or attempting to observe any activity in the voting area.

The establishment of voting times and places will vary from election to election, often depending on the size of the voting group. If the voting group is relatively small and works either one shift or two shifts that are consecutive or that overlap, the election may be conducted in a single voting period taking place near the end of one shift and continuing through the beginning of the next shift. In larger units or units consisting of three shifts, it may be necessary to have more than one voting period. For example, in many larger three-shift operations, it is normal to establish two voting periods, one beginning early in the morning to cover third shift and first shift, the second late in the afternoon to cover the second shift.

When establishing a voting schedule, the time just before and just after a change of shifts should be left open for those employees who wish to vote on their own time, either before or after work. The schedule should note employees may vote on their own time during the hours the polls are open, if they prefer. In many elections it is necessary for employees to vote in reasonably sized groups, rather than all at once. *If voting is to be done by employee groups, a releasing schedule needs to be established.* Releasing may be done by a public address system or by a traveling crew of observers (one representing each party) who may or may not be accompanied by a Board agent. If releasing is to be handled by a public address system, the announcement could consist of a statement such as, "Employees in department 501 are now released to vote." If the traveling crew method is used, the releasers should, if possible, stay together at all times. First, they should inform the appropriate supervisor of their intentions, then notify the employees, by word or by sign, that "You may go to vote now, if you wish." No one should be ordered to go to the polling place. *The releasing should be done by the releasing crew, not by a member of management or supervision.*

If any person or persons who are not eligible to vote attempt to do so, the Board has established a procedure for those votes to be challenged. Any observer or the Board agent may challenge a voter's eligibility. Any observer has the right to challenge a voter for cause. The Board agent must challenge anyone whose name is not on the eligibility list. Also, the agent must challenge a voter if there is reason to believe the voter is ineligible to vote. In this case, the agent should not challenge until and unless none of the parties voice a challenge. The Board agent will not make challenges on behalf of the parties. The reason for a challenge should be stated at the time the challenge is made. When a vote is challenged, the Board agent will normally allow the employee to vote, but will make a notation on the eligibility list that the vote has been challenged. The voter will then be given a ballot and instructed to enter the booth, mark the ballot, fold it to keep the vote secret, and return to the voting table. Upon returning to the table, the voter will be given a challenged ballot envelope that has been properly marked and identified by the Board agent. The voter will place the marked ballot in the envelope, seal the envelope and drop it in the ballot box. Following the election, but before the counting of the ballots, the Board agent will attempt to resolve any challenges.

If challenges are not resolved, the counting of the unchallenged votes will proceed. If the election is decided by a margin wider than the number of challenged ballots, those ballots become meaningless since even if all challenged ballots were cast for the losing party, the outcome of the election would remain the same.

The polls will close at the scheduled time, except that all persons in the voting line at the time for scheduled closing will be permitted to vote, even though this prolongs the election. If a voter joins the line after the polls are scheduled to close or arrives at the polls after they are closed, the Board agent may refuse to allow the employee to vote or may attempt to secure agreement from the observers as to whether the employee should be allowed to cast a ballot. If there is no agreement, the agent will normally allow the employee to cast a challenged ballot.

After the polls have closed, the ballots will be counted. The participants in the count are the Board agent and official observers. Others agreed upon by the Board agent, union representatives, and management may also be present. Normally, several representatives of the union and management are present. Voters, other than observers, are usually excluded.

The vote count will begin as soon after the close of voting as possible. The count may take place at any central location. Typically, however, the count is taken at the polling place. If a number of polling places have been used, the count will not begin until all ballot boxes have been collected. If the voting hours have been long, and if the count is expected to take some time, the Board agent may allow a rest period or meal period before the count. If this occurs, the agent will take extreme pains to preserve the intactness of the ballot box or boxes.

Before opening the ballot box, the agent will attempt to resolve any challenges that may have been made during the election. Normally, this is a simple procedure of explaining to the parties why the challenge was made and whether the challenged voter is eligible. The most common challenge that can be easily resolved is the challenge of a voter whose name is not on the eligibility list. The Board agent will call attention to those on the list who have been challenged. If it turns out — and all parties agree — the omission of a name was inadvertent and the voter in question is eligible in all respects, the challenge may be resolved.

Some challenges will simply be a mistake. Perhaps an observer makes the challenge without full knowledge or only "to be on the safe side." If facts can be quickly established that convince all parties that the voter is eligible, the challenge may be dropped. Any challenges cleared by this procedure will be handled in the following manner: The details of the disposition will be noted on the reverse side of the envelope stub; parties will signify their agreement by signing or initialing thereon; the stub will be removed and preserved by the Board agent; and the ballot will be dropped, still folded, into the ballot box with the other ballots.

The counting of the ballots will then begin. The Board agent will explain that a majority of the valid votes cast will decide the election and any ballot that clearly reflects the intention of the voter will be counted according to the apparent intention, even though the marking is unorthodox; for example, a check mark is made instead of an X; the word "yes" is written in the yes box, or the word "no" is written in the no box; the mark appears within the outer rather than the inner box; there are erasures; or there are markings in more than one box. *But a ballot, the intent of which is not clear, will be considered void. Also, a ballot that contains a means of identifying the voter will be counted as void.*

The Board agent will then announce the method of tallying the ballots. The ballot box will now be opened and the contents thoroughly mixed. The agent will remove the ballots and place them in piles according to the preference expressed on the ballot. The Board agent then counts the ballots in each pile. Elections with a large number of voters may require a more formal counting method, such as tally sheets and the packaging of ballots during the counting process.

The Board agent should rule on and count each ballot as it comes up; the interpretation of other-than-normal ballots should not be postponed. If one of the parties disagrees with the agent's interpretation of the voter's intention, the agent will segregate the ballot in a challenge envelope on which the circumstances will be detailed and the ballot will be counted as a challenged ballot. If the voter's intention is clear despite unorthodox markings, extra markings, or erasures, the ballot should be counted in accordance with the intention displayed, unless the voter's name, number, or other means of identification appear on the ballot. Void ballots will be counted as such and packaged separately.

After all ballots have been counted, the Board agent will announce the results of the election and serve on each party a Tally of Ballots form. A representative of each party is required to sign the form. The Board agent will then collect all election materials and leave.

If, in the unlikely event the number of challenged ballots could affect the outcome of the election, the Board agent will explain the challenged ballot resolution procedure to both parties.

If the election should end in a tie vote and there are no challenged ballots that could affect the outcome, the employer will be declared the winner of the election. Within five days following the election, a Certification of Election Results will be mailed to both parties, unless objections are filed.

Exhibit 1-A

(FOR THE UNION'S FILES)

Company _____

Address _____

Hourly Rate _____

Department _____

Length of service
with the company _____

Male _____ Female _____

Married _____ Single _____

Signature _____

Date _____

WORKING FOR LOW NON-UNION WAGES
IS WASTING YOUR REAL EARNING
POWER

SIGN UP TODAY FOR
PROGRESS AND SECURITY
STRICTLY CONFIDENTIAL

For Information
Rock Island 309 - 787-4456
Organizing Department

Phone _____

FOR THE INFORMATION OF THE NATIONAL LABOR RELATIONS BOARD

NAME _____ PHONE NO. _____
       (Please Print)

ADDRESS _____
       Street   City   State   Zip Code

I, the undersigned, employee of:

COMPANY _____

JOB CLASSIFICATION _____

of my own free will authorize the Teamsters Union, Local 371, their agents or representatives, to act for me as a collective bargaining agency in all matters pertaining to pay rates, wages, hours of work, and other conditions of employment. Affiliated with I.B.T.

DATE _____ SIGNATURE _____

(MAIL TODAY)
ALL APPLICATIONS STRICTLY CONFIDENTIAL

Exhibit 1-B

INTERNATIONAL REPRESENTATIVE

C͏ ͏ ͏ ͏ ͏nical & Atomic Workers
͏ ͏ ͏:rnat͏ ͏nal Union, AFL-CIO

M͏. ͏, 1992

The Oil, Chemical & Atomic Workers International Union and its Local 7-210 has of this date been authorized by the majority of the above referenced em loyees to be the authorized Bargaining Representative in the ͏ behalf.

I would l ͏e to take this opportunity to request that NSU offer automatic recognition of the Oil, Chemical & Atomic Workers International Union and its Local 7-210 as the Bargaining Representative of the above referenced employees and if not, then to please agree to a consent election.

Thank you for your attention and service to the foregoing. I can be reached at the address and telephone number listed below.

Very truly yours,

Oil, Chemical And Atomic Workers
International Union

Exhibit 1-C

Dear Mr.

I am in receipt of your letter of May 9 wherein you state that a majority of our employees have authorized your union to represent them for the purposes of collective bargaining. You further request that our company grant automatic recognition to your union.

The purpose of this letter is to inform you that we have a reasonable doubt as to the existence of these cards. However, even if the cards do exist, we have no way of knowing if employees were coerced into signing cards or whether the cards were signed as a result of misrepresentations as to their purpose.

We suggest that if you have a sufficient number of cards signed by our employees, you file a petition for an election with the National Labor Relations Board. We believe that a secret ballot election is the best way to determine whether your union has majority support.

Sincerely,

Exhibit 1-D

FORM EXEMPT UNDER 44 U.S.C. 3512

UNITED STATES GOVERNMENT
NATIONAL LABOR RELATIONS BOARD
PETITION

DO NOT WRITE IN THIS SPACE	
Case No.	Date Filed
	SAMPLE

INSTRUCTIONS: Submit an original and 4 copies of this Petition to the NLRB Regional Office in the Region in which the employer concerned is located. If more space is required for any one item, attach additional sheets, numbering item accordingly.

The Petitioner alleges that the following circumstances exist and requests that the National Labor Relations Board proceed under its proper authority pursuant to Section 9 of the National Labor Relations Act.

1. PURPOSE OF THIS PETITION *(If box RC, RM, or RD is checked and a charge under Section 8(b)(7) of the Act has been filed involving the Employer named herein, the statement following the description of the type of petition shall not be deemed made.)* **(Check One)**

☐ **RC-CERTIFICATION OF REPRESENTATIVE** - A substantial number of employees wish to be represented for purposes of collective bargaining by Petitioner and Petitioner desires to be certified as representative of the employees.

☐ **RM-REPRESENTATION (EMPLOYER PETITION)** - One or more individuals or labor organizations have presented a claim to Petitioner to be recognized as the representative of employees of Petitioner.

☐ **RD-DECERTIFICATION** - A substantial number of employees assert that the certified or currently recognized bargaining representative.is no longer their representative.

☐ **UD-WITHDRAWAL OF UNION SHOP AUTHORITY** - Thirty percent (30%) or more of employees in a bargaining unit covered by an agreement between their employer and a labor organization desire that such authority be rescinded.

☐ **UC-UNIT CLARIFICATION** - A labor organization is currently recognized by Employer, but Petitioner seeks clarification of placement of certain employees: *(Check one)* ☐ In unit not previously certified. ☐ In unit previously certified in Case No. _____.

☐ **AC-AMENDMENT OF CERTIFICATION** - Petitioner seeks amendment of certification issued in Case No. _____ *Attach statement describing the specific amendment sought.*

2. Name of Employer	Employer Representative to contact	Telephone Number

3. Address(es) of Establishment(s) involved *(Street and number, city, State, ZIP code)*

4a. Type of Establishment *(Factory, mine, wholesaler, etc.)*	4b. Identify principal product or service

5. Unit Involved *(In UC petition, describe **present** bargaining unit and attach description of proposed clarification.)*	6a. Number of Employees in Unit:
Included	Present
	Proposed *(By UC/AC)*
Excluded	6b. Is this petition supported by 30% or more of the employees in the unit? * ___ Yes ___ No *Not applicable in RM, UC, and AC

(If you have checked box RC in 1 above, check and complete EITHER item 7a or 7b, whichever is applicable)

7a. ☐ Request for recognition as Bargaining Representative was made on *(Date)* _____ and Employer declined recognition on or about *(Date)* _____ *(If no reply received, so state)*.

7b. ☐ Petitioner is currently recognized as Bargaining Representative and desires certification under the Act.

8. Name of Recognized or Certified Bargaining Agent *(If none, so state)*	Affiliation
Address and Telephone Number	Date of Recognition or Certification

9. Expiration Date of Current Contract, If any *(Month, Day, Year)*	10. If you have checked box UD in 1 above, show here the date of execution of agreement granting union shop *(Month, Day, and Year)*

11a. Is there now a strike or picketing at the Employer's establishment(s) Involved? Yes ___ No ___	11b. If so, approximately how many employees are participating?

11c. The Employer has been picketed by or on behalf of *(Insert Name)* _____, a labor organization, of *(Insert Address)* _____ Since *(Month, Day, Year)* _____

12. Organizations or individuals other than Petitioner *(and other than those named in items 8 and 11c)*, which have claimed recognition as representatives and other organizations and individuals known to have a representative interest in any employees in unit described in item 5 above. *(If none, so state)*

Name	Affilation	Address	Date of Claim *(Required only if Petition is filed by Employer)*

I declare that I have read the above petition and that the statements are true to the best of my knowledge and belief.

(Name of Petitioner and Affilation, if any)

By _____
(Signature of Representative or person filing petition) _____ *(Title, if any)*

Address _____
(Street and number, city, State, and ZIP Code) _____ *(Telephone Number)*

WILLFUL FALSE STATEMENTS ON THIS PETITION CAN BE PUNISHED BY FINE AND IMPRISONMENT (U. S. CODE, TITLE 18, SECTION 1001)

Exhibit 1-E

NOTICE TO EMPLOYEES

FROM THE
National Labor Relations Board

A PETITION has been filed with this Federal agency seeking an election to determine whether certain employees want to be represented by a union.

The case is being investigated and NO DETERMINATION HAS BEEN MADE AT THIS TIME by the National Labor Relations Board. IF an election is held Notices of Election will be posted giving complete details for voting.

It was suggested that your employer post this notice so the National Labor Relations Board could inform you of your basic rights under the National Labor Relations Act.

YOU HAVE THE RIGHT under Federal Law

- To self-organization
- To form, join, or assist labor organizations
- To bargain collectively through representatives of your own choosing
- To act together for the purposes of collective bargaining or other mutual aid or protection
- To refuse to do any or all of these things unless the union and employer, in a state where such agreements are permitted, enter into a lawful union-security agreement requiring employees to pay periodic dues and initiation fees. Nonmembers who inform the union that they object to the use of their payments for nonrepresentational purposes may be required to pay only their share of the union's costs of representational activities (such as collective bargaining, contract administration, and grievance adjustments).

It is possible that some of you will be voting in an employee representation election as a result of the request for an election having been filed. While NO DETERMINATION HAS BEEN MADE AT THIS TIME, in the event an election is held, the NATIONAL LABOR RELATIONS BOARD wants all eligible voters to be familiar with their rights under the law IF it holds an election.

The Board applies rules that are intended to keep its elections fair and honest and that result in a free choice. If agents of either unions or employers act in such a way as to interfere with your right to a free election, the election can be set aside by the Board. Where appropriate the Board provides other remedies, such as reinstatement for employees fired for exercising their rights, including backpay from the party responsible for their discharge.

NOTE:

The following are examples of conduct that interfere with the rights of employees and may result in the setting aside of the election.

- Threatening loss of jobs or benefits by an employer or a union
- Promising or granting promotions, pay raises, or other benefits to influence an employee's vote by a party capable of carrying out such promises
- An employer firing employees to discourage or encourage union activity or a union causing them to be fired to encourage union activity
- Making campaign speeches to assembled groups of employees on company time within the 24-hour period before the election
- Incitement by either an employer or a union of racial or religious prejudice by inflammatory appeals
- Threatening physical force or violence to employees by a union or an employer to influence their votes

Please be assured that IF AN ELECTION IS HELD every effort will be made to protect your right to a free choice under the law. Improper conduct will not be permitted. All parties are expected to cooperate fully with this Agency in maintaining basic principles of a fair election as required by law. The National Labor Relations Board, as an agency of the United States Government, does not endorse any choice in the election.

NATIONAL LABOR RELATIONS BOARD

an agency of the

UNITED STATES GOVERNMENT

THIS IS AN OFFICIAL GOVERNMENT NOTICE AND MUST NOT BE DEFACED BY ANYONE

FORM NLRB-5492 (8-95)

GPO: 1994 - 152-750

Exhibit 1-F

UNITED STATES OF AMER

NOTICE

PURPOSE OF THIS ELECTION This election is to determine the representative, if any, desired by the eligible employees for purposes of collective bargaining with their Employer. (See VOTING UNIT in this Notice of Election, for description of eligible employees.) A majority of the valid ballots cast will determine the results of the election.

SECRET BALLOT The election will be by SECRET ballot under the supervision of the Regional Director of the National Labor Relations Board.   Voters will be allowed to vote without interference, restraint, or coercion.   Electioneering will not be permitted at or near the polling place.   Violations of these rules should be reported immediately to the Regional Director or the agent in charge of the election. Your attention is called to Section 12 of the National Labor Relations Act:

ANY PERSON WHO SHALL WILLFULLY RESIST, PREVENT, IMPEDE, OR INTERFERE WITH ANY MEMBER OF THE BOARD OR ANY OF ITS AGENTS OR AGENCIES IN THE PERFORMANCE OF DUTIES PURSUANT TO THIS ACT SHALL BE PUNISHED BY A FINE OF NOT MORE THAN $5,000 OR BY IMPRISONMENT FOR NOT MORE THAN ONE YEAR, OR BOTH.

An agent of the Board will hand a ballot to each eligible voter at the voting place. Mark your ballot in secret in the voting booth provided.   DO NOT SIGN YOUR BALLOT.   Fold the ballot before leaving the voting booth, then personally deposit it in a ballot box under the supervision of an agent of the Board.

A sample of the official ballot is shown at the center of this Notice.

ELIGIBILITY RULES Employees eligible to vote are those described under VOTING UNIT in this Notice of Election, including employees who did not work during the designated payroll period because they were ill or on vacation or temporarily laid off, and also including employees in the military service of the United States who appear in person at the polls.   Employees who have quit or been discharged for cause since the designated payroll period and who have not been rehired or reinstated prior to the date of this election are not eligible to vote.

CHALLENGE OF VOTERS An agent of the Board or an authorized observer may question the eligibility of a voter. Such challenge MUST be made before the voter's ballot has been placed in the ballot box.

AUTHORIZED OBSERVERS Each of the interested parties may designate an equal number of observers, this number to be determined by the Regional Director or agent in charge of the election. These observers (a) act as checkers at the voting place and at the counting of ballots, (b) assist in the identification of voters, (c) challenge voters and ballots, and (d) otherwise assist the Regional Director or agent.

INFORMATION CONCERNING ELECTION The Act provides that only one valid representation election may be held in a 12-month period.   Any employee who desires to obtain any further information concerning the terms and conditions under which this election is to be held or who desires to raise any question concerning the holding of an election, the voting unit, or eligibility rules may do so by communicating with the Regional Director or agent in charge of the election.

WARNING: THIS IS THE ONLY OFFICIAL N

FORM NLRB 707 (8-83)

continued next page

Exhibit 1-F

EMPLOYEES OF
DAVIDSON TRUCKING, INC.
WEST SILOAM SPRINGS, MISSOURI

17-RC-10174
17-RC-10186

VOTING UNIT - 17-RC-10174

INCLUDED

All full time and regular, part time drivers and shop employees employed by the Employer at its West Siloam Springs, Oklahoma headquarters, who were employed during the payroll period ending March 3, 1989.

EXCLUDED

All others, including office clerical employees, guards and supervisors as defined in the Act.

VOTING UNIT - 17-RC-10186

INCLUDED

All office clerical employees employed by the Employer at its West Siloam Springs, Oklahoma headquarters, who were employed during the payroll period ending March 3, 1989.

EXCLUDED

All others, including truck drivers, shop employees, confidential clerical employees, guards and supervisors as defined in the Act.

DATE OF ELECTION   Wednesday, April 12, 1989

TIME   4:00 P.M. TO 6:00 P.M.

PLACE   Maintenance Shop, Employer's Headquarters, West Siloam Springs, Oklahoma.

UNITED STATES OF AMERICA
National Labor Relations Board
FORM NLRB-707HQ (AC. Am AO CASES; 11-84)

OFFICIAL SECRET BALLOT
For certain employees of
DAVIDSON TRUCKING, INC.

Do you wish to be represented for purposes of collective bargaining by -

GENERAL DRIVERS, WAREHOUSEMEN, DOCKMEN,
HELPERS AND TEAMSTERS LOCAL UNION 373,
AFFILIATED WITH INTERNATIONAL BROTHERHOOD
OF TEAMSTERS, CHAUFFEURS, WAREHOUSEMEN
AND HELPERS OF AMERICA, AFL-CIO ?

MARK AN "X" IN THE SQUARE OF YOUR CHOICE

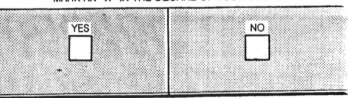

YES	NO
☐	☐

DO NOT SIGN THIS BALLOT. Fold and drop in ballot box.
If you spoil this ballot return it to the Board Agent for a new one.

Exhibit 1-F

?OR RELATIONS BOARD

?CTION

RIGHTS OF EMPLOYEES

Under the National Labor Relations Act, employees have the right:

- To self-organization
- To form, join, or assist labor organizations
- To bargain collectively through representatives of their own choosing
- To act together for the purposes of collective bargaining or other mutual aid or protection
- To refuse to do any or all of these things unless the Union and Employer, in a State where such agreements are permitted, enter into a lawful union security clause requiring employees to join the Union.

It is the responsibility of the National Labor Relations Board to protect employees in the exercise of these rights. The Board wants all eligible voters to be fully informed about their rights under Federal law and wants both Employers and Unions to know what is expected of them when it holds an election.

If agents of either Unions or Employers interfere with your right to a free, fair, and honest election, the election can be set aside by the Board. Where appropriate the Board provides other remedies, such as reinstatement for employees fired for exercising their rights, including backpay from the party responsible for their discharge.

The following are examples of conduct which interferes with the rights of employees and may result in the setting aside of the election:

- Threatening loss of jobs or benefits by an Employer or a Union
- Promising or granting promotions, pay raises, or other benefits to influence an employee's vote by a party capable of carrying out such promises
- An Employer firing employees to discourage or encourage union activity or a Union causing them to be fired to encourage union activity
- Making campaign speeches to assembled groups of employees on company time within the 24-hour period before the election
- Incitement by either an Employer or a Union of racial or religious prejudice by inflammatory appeals
- Threatening physical force or violence to employees by a Union or an Employer to influence their votes.

The National Labor Relations Board protects your right to a free choice

Improper conduct will not be permitted. All parties are expected to cooperate fully with this agency in maintaining basic principles of a fair election as required by law. The National Labor Relations Board as an agency of the United States Government does not endorse any choice in the election.

NATIONAL LABOR RELATIONS BOARD
an agency of the
UNITED STATES GOVERNMENT

MUST NOT BE DEFACED BY ANYONE

U.S. GOVERNMENT PRINTING OFFICE : 1988 O - 220-015

Exhibit 1-G

North Macon Health Care Facility, *and* **United Steelworkers of America, AFL-CIO.**
Case 10-RC-14442

October 26, 1994
DECISION AND DIRECTION OF SECOND ELECTION

BY CHAIRMAN GOULD AND MEMBERS STEPHENS, DEVANEY, AND COHEN

The National Labor Relations Board has considered objections to an election held December 8, 1993, and the hearing officer's report recommending disposition of them (pertinent portions of which are attached as an appendix). The election was conducted pursuant to a Stipulated Election Agreement, and the tally of ballots shows that of approximately 143 eligible voters, 57 cast valid votes for the Petitioner and 71 cast votes against the Petitioner. There were six challenged ballots, a number insufficient to affect the results.

The Board has reviewed the record in light of the exceptions and briefs and adopts the hearing officer's findings with recommendations only to the extent consistent with this decision.[1]

In Objection 10, the Petitioner contends that the Employer provided a "substantial number of incorrect and incomplete addresses for the eligible voters and refused to supply complete names of voters, thereby violating the intent of the *Excelsior*[2] rules which give [] the union an opportunity to communicate with eligible voters prior to the election. This act . . . destroys the laboratory conditions necessary for a free and fair election."

The hearing officer found that the Employer provided a list of eligible voters containing 33 incorrect addresses and with employees'. last names and first initials rather than their full names. In support of its objection, the Petitioner produced the Excelsior list provided by the Employer. The Employer submitted its own copy of the *Excelsior* list and a copy of the computer-generated payroll records of the unit employees provided it by a management corporation and based on the

Employer's records. The payroll records included employees' addresses and full first and last names. On the *Excelsior* list it provided the Union, however, the Employer had deleted the employees' first names and supplied only the first letter of the employees' given names. Further, nearly 23 percent of the addresses on the *Excelsior* list, or 33 out of 144, were incorrect.

The hearing officer recommended that the Petitioner's objection be overruled, noting that the Board has held that it will not apply the *Excelsior* rule "mechanically" to set an election aside on the basis of an imperfect list, in the absence of an employer's deliberate or grossly negligent attempt to avoid compliance with the *Excelsior* rule. The hearing officer found no evidence of such gross negligence or bad faith. With respect to the Employer's use of initials rather than first names, the hearing officer found that, although the Board does not condone the practice, this shortcoming does not rise to the level of a substantial failure to comply with the rule's requirements.[3]

In its exceptions, the Petitioner argues, in essence, that the Board's policy of not applying the *Excelsior* rule "mechanically" has allowed exceptions to its strict application effectively to erode the rule, that the spirit of the rule is violated where nearly 25 percent of the addresses provided are incorrect and the full names of employees are not supplied, and that no means other than an accurate *Excelsior* list exist whereby a petitioner can obtain such information.

For the reasons stated below, we find merit in the Petitioner's objections with respect to the Employer's failure to include employees' first names on the *Excelsior* list. Therefore, we set aside the election and order that a second election be scheduled.[4] Further, we hold that an employer's failure to provide the full first and last names of employees is a deviation from the Board's policy that an employer must "substantially comply" with the Excelsior rule and tends to interfere with a free and fair election. Although bad faith is generally not relevant in this area, under the particular circumstances of this case, we also find that the Employer's deliberate deletion of the unit employees' first names from the list provided by its management company is evidence of a bad-faith effort to impede the Petitioner's access to eligible voters and thus to avoid its responsibilities under *Excelsior.*

Our analysis begins with the Board's holding in *Excelsior* itself. In that case, the Board determined that objections based on the employer's denial of the petitioners' requests for the names and addresses of eligible voters raised grave questions respecting the administration of the Act. In response, the Board established

> a *requirement* that will be applied in *all* election cases. That is, within 7 days [after the approval of an election agreement or the direction of an election], an employer must file with the Regional Director an election eligibility list, containing the names and addresses of all the eligible voters. The Regional Director, in turn, shall make this information available to all parties in the case. Failure to comply with this requirement shall be the grounds for setting aside the election whenever proper objections are filed.[5]

The Board reasoned that the new rule was based on two fundamental bases: first, its recognition that Congress had entrusted to the Board alone the function of conducting elections

> free from interference, restraint, or coercion . . . [and] other elements that prevent or impede a free and reasoned choice. Among the factors that undoubtedly tend to impede such a choice is a lack of information with respect to one of the choices available . . . *[A]n employee who has had an effective opportunity to hear the arguments concerning representation is in a better position to make a more fully informed and reasonable choice.* Accordingly, we think that it is appropriate for us to remove the impediment to communication to which our new rule is directed.[6]

Second, the Board also perceived an intensely practical necessity for the new rule. It contrasted the situation of the employer,

which is assured of continuing opportunities to present its views respecting unionization to employees to that of a petitioner, "whose organizers normally have no right of access to plant premises,"[7] and therefore has no method by which it can be sure of reaching employees with its arguments in favor of representation, so that some employees might be unaware of them. The Board's express aim in promulgating the *Excelsior* rule was to ensure, as far as possible, the *all* employees be "exposed to the arguments for, as well as against, union representation."[8] The fact that unions might, by expending resources and energy in other ways, gain access to some, or even most, employees, was not sufficient; the Board explicitly discounted the availability of alternative means of communication with employees as a factor weighing against the requirement that employees provide a list of the names and addresses of eligible voters:

> This is not, of course, to deny the existence of various means by which a party *might* be able to communicate with a substantial portion of the electorate even without possessing their names and addresses. It is rather to say what seems to us obvious— that the access of *all* employees to such communications can be insured only if all parties have the names and addresses of all the voters.[9]

Nor was the Board moved by the arguments that requiring employers to provide such a list would be burdensome or would infringe on any employer rights. Rather, the Board reasoned:

> The arguments against imposing a requirement of disclosure are of little force especially when weighed against the benefits resulting therefrom. Initially, we are able to perceive no substantial infringement of employer interests that would flow from such a requirement. A list of employee names and addresses is not like a customer list, and an employer would appear to have no significant interest in keeping the names and addresses of his employees secret (other than a desire to prevent the union from communicating with his employ-

ees—an interest we see no reason to protect). Such legitimate interest in secrecy as an employer may have is, in any event, plainly outweighed by the substantial public interest in favor of disclosure, where, as here, disclosure is a key factor in insuring a fair and free electorate.[10]

The Board also rejected the argument that provision of employee names and addresses infringed on any rights of employees, e.g., their Section 7 right to refrain from union activities. The Board found that the Section 7 rights were exercised when the employee voted for or against union representation.[11]

The interpretation of the *Excelsior* rule adopted by the Board today with respect to employees' names derives from the Board's emphasis on the fundamental importance of the rule to a reasoned exercise of the Section 7 right and of the fundamentally practical nature of the rule. The *Excelsior* rule was not promulgated to test employer good faith, to augment other means of communication, or merely to "level the playing field" between petitioners and employers. It was imposed so that unions would have access to *all* eligible voters. As the Board stated, the prompt and complete disclosure of employee names and addresses is "necessary to insure an informed electorate."[12] Under *Excelsior*, an employer's failure to provide a complete and accurate list of eligible voters is an injury to *employees*, not just to petitioners; an incomplete or inaccurate list can effectively prevent employees from obtaining information necessary for the free and fully informed exercise of their Section 7 rights. The Board has long recognized that the rule is prophylactic, so that "[e]evidence of bad faith and actual prejudice is unnecessary because . . . the potential harm from list omissions is deemed sufficiently great to warrant a strict rule that encourages conscientious efforts to comply."[13]

Thus, we find that, in ruling that employers must provide the names and addresses of eligible voters, the Board intended that employers provide the employees' *full names*. There is no language in the *Excelsior* decision that even suggests that an employer has "substantial[ly] compli[ed]" with the rule where the employer has deliberately deleted the employees' first names in working up the *Excelsior* list from its payroll or other records. Consequently, we find

that the Employer here was not in "substantial compliance" with the *Excelsior* rule, and we clarify the "substantial compliance" standard accordingly. Further, although, as noted above, a finding of bad faith is not a precondition for the conclusion that an employer has failed to comply substantially with the rule, we shall view the submission of an *Excelsior* list containing only last names and first initials as evidence of a bad faith effort to avoid the obligations the *Excelsior* rule imposes.[14]

We further find that, based on our administrative experience in the area of representation elections, retroactive application of our clarification of the *Excelsior* rule will further the purposes of the Act. See *Deluxe Metal Furniture Co.,* 121 NLRB 995, 1006-1007 (1958) ("the judicial practice of applying each pronouncement of a rule of law to the case in which the issue arises to all pending cases in whatever stage is traditional and, we believe, the wiser course to follow"). See also *Iron Workers Local 3 v. NLRB*, 843 F.2d 770 (3d Cir. 1988) (per curiam) (approving retroactive application of *Deklewa* rules regarding 8 (f) collective-bargaining agreements), enfg. *John Deklewa & Sons*, 282 NLRB 1375 (1987), cert. denied 488 U.S. 889 (1988).

Contrary to our dissenting colleague, we find no circumstances here sufficient to overcome the Board's presumption in favor of retroactivity. As discussed above, application of the rule that an *Excelsior* list must include employees' full names serves important statutory goals by ensuring that all employees are fully informed about the arguments concerning representation. It would be anomalous for the Board to certify results of elections conducted without compliance with the *Excelsior* rule as set forth herein, after the Board has found that such elections do not ensure that employees are fully informed about the arguments concerning representation and thus are not able to exercise fully their Section 7 rights.

Nor do we agree with our dissenting colleague's argument that employers would be prejudiced by the retroactive application of our holding. In practical terms, retroactive application will require that a second election be held, and that the employer provide an *Excelsior* list containing full names prior to that election. Any burden imposed on the employer by this requirement is extremely slight. Thus, there is no indication that preparation of a list of employees which includes their full names will require employers to expend any additional time or effort.[15] Nor do we perceive any significant burden resulting from the mechanics of holding a second election. Although many employers accommodate Board elections by allowing them to be conducted on the employer's premises and by releasing employees from duty for appropriate periods of time so that they may vote, such accommodations involve at most a minimal burden and in any event are, of course, voluntarily assumed.[16]

Although it is true that a second election may result in a certification of representative, whereas the first election did not, we decline to find prejudice to employers on that basis. Any certification of representative that may result from the holding of a second election would occur only if a majority of unit employees currently desire representation. It would be inconsistent with the Act's animating principles to find that an employer is prejudiced by the Board's recognition of employee choice under these circumstances.

Thus, the Board finds that the election must be set aside and a new election directed.

DIRECTION OF SECOND ELECTION[17]

A second election by secret ballot shall be held among the employees in the unit found appropriate, whenever the Regional Director deems appropriate. The Regional Director shall direct and supervise the election, subject to the Board's Rules and Regulations. Eligible to vote are those employed during the payroll period ending immediately before the date of the Notice of Second Election, including employees who did not work during that period because they were ill, on vacation, or temporarily laid off. Also eligible are employees engaged in an economic strike that began less than 12 months before the election date and who retained their employee status during the eligibility period and their replacements. Those in the military service may vote if they appear in person at the polls. Ineligible to vote are employees who have quit or been discharged for cause since the payroll period, striking employees who have been discharged for cause since the strike began and who have not been rehired or reinstated before the election date, and employees engaged in an economic strike that began more than 12 months before the election date and who have been permanently replaced. Those eligible shall vote whether they desire to be represented for collective bargaining by the United Steelworkers of America, AFL-CIO.

To ensure that all eligible voters have the opportunity to be informed of the issues in the exercise of their statuary right to vote, all parties to the election should have access to a list of voters and their addresses that may be used to communicate with them. *Excelsior Underwear*, 156 NLRB 1236 (1966); *NLRB v. Wyman-Gordon Co.*, 394 U.S. 759 (1969). Accordingly, it is directed that an eligibility list containing the *full* names and addresses of all the eligible voters must be filed by the Employer with the Regional Director within 7 days from the date of the Notice of Second Election. The Regional Director shall make the list available to all parties to the election. No extension of time to file the list shall be granted by the Regional Director except in extraordinary circumstances. Failure to comply with his requirement shall be grounds for setting aside the election whenever proper objections are filed.

Dated, Washington, D.C.
October 26, 1994

_____

William B. Gould IV,   Chairman

_____

James M. Stephens,
Member

_____

Dennis M. Devaney,
Member

(SEAL)   NATIONAL LABOR RELATIONS BOARD

FOOTNOTES

[1] During the course of the hearing, the Employer objected to the hearing officer's evidentiary rulings

admitting into evidence P. Exh. 1 (a copy of the Excelsior list with annotations showing which of the addresses on the list were incorrect) and refusing to admit Emp. Exh. 1 (certain reports prepared by Petitioner after unsuccessful attempts to contact employees at the home addresses shown on the *Excelsior* list). However, we find that these issues are not properly before us, as the Employer has not filed exceptions to the hearing officer's rulings in this regard. Although the Employer notes in its brief that it filed motions for special permission to appeal these issues, the motions were denied on the grounds that the hearing officer's report had issued while the motions were pending, and the Employer was specifically advised that the appeals "are denied without prejudice to your renewing your arguments in appropriately filed exceptions." Nevertheless, the Employer did not file exceptions with the Board.

[2] *Excelsior Underwear*, 156 NLRB 1236 (1966)

[3] With respect to the number of incorrect addresses, the hearing officer noted that the list was based on the Employer's most recent records and that the Employer seldom had occasion to send mail to its employees

[4] Chairman Gould and Member Devaney would find also that the election should be set aside because of the large number of incorrect employee addresses on the Excelsior list submitted by the Employer. Member Stephens finds it unnecessary to reach this issue.

[5] 156 NLRB at 1240 (emphasis added and citations omitted).

[6] Id. (emphasis added and citations omitted).

[7] Id. This consideration has taken on even greater significance in light of the Supreme Court's recent decision in Lechmere, Inc. v. NLRB, 112 S. Ct. 841 (1992), in which the Supreme Court strictly interpreted NLRB v. Babcock & Wilcox Co., 351 U. S. 105 (1956), to limit further organizers' access to company property.

[8] Excelsior, 156 NLRB at 1241.

[9] Id. (emphasis in original). Thus, the fact that, as the hearing officer found, the Petitioner here was ultimately able to make contact with all but 12 of the employees is irrelevant.

[10] Id. at 1243 (citations omitted).

[11] Id. at 1244.

[12] Id. at 1242

[13] Thrifty Auto Parts, 295 NLRB 1118, 1118 (1989)

[14] Accordingly, we overrule the contrary holdings in St. Francis Hospital, 249 NLRB 180, 181 (1980), and other similar cases.

[15] In this case, for example, the Employer admittedly maintains lists of employees which include their first names; indeed, in the first election the Employer voluntarily assumed the burden of generating an additional list of employees for production to the Union from which first names had been redacted.

[16] In this case, the first election was conducted, by agreement of the Employer, on its premises during two 2-hour periods on December 8, 1993.

[17] We note that the language of the Direction of Second Election has been revised to reflect our holding here. We further direct that the Excelsior language set forth below, together with a citation to this decision, shall be used in all future election cases.

MEMBER CHOEN, dissenting.

My colleagues have made a change in the law and in established practice, and they have applied the change retroactively. In my view, assuming that the change is warranted-an issue that I do not reach in this case-this retroactive application is fundamentally unfair to the Employer who relied on then-extant law and practice. Accordingly, I dissent.

The Supreme Court has set forth three factors to be considered in determining the legality of a retroactive application of a change in law. *Chevron Oil Co. v. Huson*, 404 U.S. 97 (1971). These factors are: (1) whether the decision that is to be applied retroactively establishes a new principle of law, either by overruling clear past precedent on which litigants may have relied or by deciding an issue of first impression; (2) the effect of retroactively on accomplishing statutory objectives; and (3) the inequity imposed by retroactive application.

With respect to the first factor, the law was clear that an employer complied with *Excelsior* requirements even if the employer gave only first initials and last names of employees, rather than full names.[1] Indeed, my colleagues candidly concede that "the contrary holdings in *St. Francis*" are to be "overruled." Thus, the law was clear, and it is being changed.

With respect to the second factor, I do not believe that a "full name" requirement is a necessary ingredient for the accomplishment of a statutory purpose. My colleagues assert that a "full name" requirement will give unions greater access to employees and will result in a better-informed electorate. Assuming arguendo that the new requirement will help to achieve these goals, this is not to say that the statutory purpose has been unfulfilled in the past. There is no showing that the prior rule led to the destruction of "laboratory conditions" for the conduct of elections. Indeed, the Board has conducted elections, without the "full name" requirement, for 28 years under *Excelsior*. There is no suggestion that these elections have been invalid, i.e., that they have not been held under laboratory conditions.

Finally, as to the third factor, the imposition of the new rule is patently unfair to the Employer. The Employer relied on then-extant law, and the Petitioner lose the election. My colleagues now change the law and take that result away.[2] Moreover, my experience compels the conclusion that the Employer's failure to include full names was in no way determinative of the outcome of the election. Thus, even if my colleagues wish to impose a "full name" requirement, there is no reason to upset the election here. If my colleagues wish, as a matter of policy, to change the *Excelsior* rule by requiring full names, they could accomplish that change by other means. For example, in *Shepard Convention Services*, 314 NLRB No. 115, fn. 3 (Aug. 3, 1994), my colleagues denied as premature a preelection challenge to the use of initials. They could have simply included a "full name" requirement in their preelection order.[3] Instead, they now overturn an accomplished election result and put the parties and employees through another election.[4] I therefore dissent.

Dated, Washington, D.C.
October 26, 1994

Charles I. Cohen,
Member

NATIONAL LABOR RELATIONS BOARD

FOOTNOTES

[1] St. Francis Hospital, 249 NLRB 180 (1980). As that case made clear, the fact that the employer's records contained full names did not warrant a contrary result.

[2] Although Chairman Gould and Member Devaney would set aside the election on the additional basis of incorrect addresses, there is no Board majority for so doing. With respect to this issue, the hearing officer ruled, with appropriate case citations, that the incorrect addresses were insufficient to warrant setting aside the election. I would adopt this ruling. Thus, the dissent focuses on the "name" issue.

[3] A change could also have been accomplished by rule-making under Sec. 6 of the Act. Such a rule would, of course, operate prospectively.

[4] My colleagues assert that retroactivity will result only in a second election. However, the fact is that my colleagues take away from the Employer and employees a certification of the Petitioner's loss, and deprive the Employer and employees of 1 year's repose from the conduct of an election. See Sec. 9 (c) (3).

APPENDIX
(Hearing Officer's Report on Objections and Recommendation on Objections)

FINDING OF FACTS AND CONCLUSIONS

Objection 10:
During the period following the filing of the petition and until the election, the Employer provided a substantial number of incorrect and incomplete addresses for the eligible voters and refused to supply complete names of voters, thereby violating the intent of the *Excelsior* rules which gives the union an opportunity to communicate with eligible voters prior to the election. This act further destroys the laboratory conditions necessary for a free and fair election.

The issue, herein, is not controlled by credibility findings. Indeed, the relevant facts are not in dispute. Rather, the resolution of this issue is one controlled by Board law. In support of this objection, the Petitioner submitted the *Excelsior* list, provided by the Employer, as Petitioner's Exhibit 1. It is undisputed that the Employer used initials for the employees' given names. The Petitioner noted that of the 144 addresses provided theron, a total of 33 were incorrect. In further support thereof, the

Petitioner supplied copies of 19 returned envelopes, returned by the post office due to a variety of reasons, namely, insufficient address, not deliverable as addressed, no forwarding address and "attempt not know" (in evidence as Petitioner's Exhibit 2). The addresses on the 19 returned envelopes were taken from the list. The 19 returned envelopes are part of the 33 incorrect addresses in contention, herein, and not in addition thereto. A review of Petitioner's Exhibit 2 reveals that at least 9 of the documents were not mailed to the employees until well after the election. The remaining 10 were mailed and returned by the post office, or about December 1, and 4, 1993. Organizer Randal Rolen testified that the Petitioner made house calls to employees, based on the addresses provided on the list. According to Rolen, in several instances, the addresses did not exist or individuals other than the named employees lived at the addresses. According to Rolen, in some cases the individuals claimed to have resided at the address for extended periods of time. Additionally, Rolen testified that in several instances, addresses failed to include apartment numbers, further hindering the location of employees. Finally, Rolen testified that, while 33 of the addresses provided were incorrect he was able to make contact with all but 21 of the employees on the list, prior to the election.

The Employer submitted a copy of the *Excelsior* list as Employer's Exhibit 46. This document is the same as Petitioner's Exhibit 1, with the exception of the Petitioner's typed written notations regarding the incorrect addresses. The Employer also submitted a copy of the computer generated payroll records of all employees, including addresses department numbers (Employer's Exhibit 47). According to Administrator Doreen Hansard, the payroll listing was complied by the Employer's payroll department. Pruitt Corporation is responsible for managing the Employer's facility, including handling payroll matters. The addresses on the list were based on the payroll list provided to the Employer by Pruitt Corporation. An examination of Petitioner's Exhibit 1 and Employer's Exhibit reflect identical addresses. The payroll records, however, included the given names. In each instance, however, the initials on the *Excelsior* list correspond with the given names and addresses on the payroll records. According to Hansard, these are the same addresses used by the Employer during the campaign. Hansard also testified that normally, the Employer does not have a need to send mail of any kind to its employees.

The Board has repeatedly held that the rule, set forth in *Excelsior Underwear, Inc.,* 156 NLRB 1236 (1966), will not be mechanically applied where there is evidence that the employer has "made some attempt" to comply with the requirements thereof. Indeed, there must be evidence indicating a deliberate or grossly negligent attempt to avoid compliance with the rule, not merely the existence of an imperfect list, before an election will be set aside. The Board does not deem an insubstantial failure to comply with the *Excelsior* rule to be tantamount to gross negligence or bad faith. The evidence, herein, established that the Employer provided the Petitioner with the information in its files. There was no evidence presented to establish that the Employer was aware of the errors on the list or in some way acted in bad faith in the submission thereof. To the contrary, the evidence established that the Employer relied on the same list during the campaign. There was evidence offered to show that the Employer routinely sent mail to its employees, thus putting the Employer on notice of a need to correct its records. The Petitioner does not contend that nay names were omitted from the list. In this regard, it should be noted that the Board has drawn a distinction between the submission of incorrect addresses and omission of names from the list. The record evidence established that due to the errors on the list, the Petitioner was unable to contact 12 employees or less than 9 percent. While, clearly the inaccuracies in the list were largely the cause of the Petitioner's inability to contact these employees, it is equally clear that current case law does not support a finding of a substantial failure to comply. Similarly, the use of initials for given names, while not condoned, are shortcomings that do not rise to a level sufficient to warrant setting aside the election. Finally, the record is completely void of evidence warranting a finding of gross negligence or bad faith. *Fountainebleau Hotel Corp.*, 181 NLRB 1134 (1970); *Days Inn*, 216 NLRB 384 (1975); *West Coast Meal Packing*

Co., Inc., 195 NLRB 37 (1972); *The Lobster House*, 186 NLRB 148 (1970); *Kenftield Medical Hospital*, 219, NLRB 174 (1975). Accordingly, Objection 10 is overruled.

RECOMMENDATION

Having found Petitioner's Objection 10 to be without merit and having granted the Petitioner's request to withdraw Objection 1 through 9 and 11, I recommend to the Board that the objections be overruled in their entirety and that a Certification of Results issue.[3]

FOOTNOTES

[3] As provided in the Regional Director's Order Directing Hearing and Notice of Hearing either party may, within fourteen days from the issuance of this report, file with the Board an original and seven copies of exceptions. Immediately upon filing such exceptions, the party filing the same shall serve a copy with the Regional Director. If no timely exceptions are filed, the Board may adopt the recommendation of the Report.

Management Campaign Strategy

"Winning isn't everything,
it's the only thing."

VINCE LOMBARDI

That statement is particularly true in NLRB representation elections. If the union loses the election, it will try to keep the nucleus of its in-house committee together, collect additional information that may be useful in a future campaign, and prepare to come back for another try next year. If management loses, the union wins the right to represent the employees, and in the vast majority of cases retains that right virtually forever. Unlike elections for government representatives, a union, in most cases, never has to run for re-election. Its performance is rarely subjected to the scrutiny of another campaign. On the other hand, management can't realistically say "Wait till next time." Labor law is structured in such a way that usually there is no next time. To avoid a union representing your employees, you must conduct a successful campaign the first time.

Though an NLRB representation election campaign is not an exact science, there are a number of guidelines and techniques that have proven effective in past campaigns: 1) management stays in control of the issues, forcing the union to adopt a defensive posture; 2) management is aware of employee positions on unionization at specific points in the campaign and is then flexible enough to adjust to changing conditions to maximize results; 3) management is knowledgeable enough to know how to use the available information to the best advantage; and 4) management makes extensive use of its greatest campaign advantage, the captive audience meeting.

As with any election campaign, the side that is most effective in framing the issues, communicating those issues to the electorate, forcing the opposition to discuss those issues rather than its own, timing the campaign to achieve maximum voter support on election day, and getting out a favorable vote will be the winner. This book is intended to help you achieve each of these objectives.

It is possible to debate which side, the company or the union, has the advantage in the NLRB election campaign process. Both sides have certain advantages the other side does not. Therefore, it is incumbent upon management to fully understand and maximize the advantages it possesses. In a typical campaign, the union's primary advantages are home visitations and its ability to play upon employee desires for improved wages and benefits by using misleading information. Management's primary advantage is the captive audience meeting. These advantages and disadvantages are discussed in detail throughout this book.

Before beginning your campaign, you need to collect information about the opposition. Fortunately, this kind of material is readily available. Generalized information about unions can also be useful. However, the more applicable the information is to the union you are campaigning against, the more relevant it will be to the voting group.

Throughout the election campaign period, you will emphasize to the voting group the many disadvantages of union membership. This will be accomplished by video presentations and/or oral presentations, literature, postings, specialty items, and individual discussions with employees. Much of the information you will want to use is provided in this book or is readily available from the Labor Relations Institute. When determining which types of information would be most applicable and have the strongest impact on voters, the following choices, in order of normal preference, should be:

1. Same union, same location
2. Same union, different location
3. Different union, same location
4. Different union, different location
5. General union information

Deciding between selections two and three can be difficult. Try to put yourself in the place of a typical voter when determining what information would be the most meaningful or most persuasive. Perhaps there is a strong management supporter who is a member of the voting group who can help with these decisions. However, before using anyone from the voting group in this way, refer to Chapter 3 regarding what management can and cannot do during a campaign.

Campaign Research

The following kinds of information should be obtained before beginning your election campaign. (See the Research Resources list at the end of this chapter for information about ordering union data.)

1. A copy of the international union constitution and the bylaws, if applicable, of the local union — The union's constitution is an extremely valuable document for a variety of reasons. Most constitutions are 100 or more pages long and written in legal language that the average voter finds intimidating and difficult to understand. Union constitutions contain provisions concerning dues, fees, fines, assessments, rules and regulations, trials of members for violating the constitution, and many other provisions. Because it is so complex, most organizers do not show or explain the constitution to voters. But if management has a copy of this document and explains some of the provisions, voters will often think twice about committing to the union and all of its rules and regulations.

2. A copy of the international union's LM-2 and, if applicable, the LM-3 or LM-4 of the local union that is conducting the campaign — The LM-2, LM-3, and LM-4 are the financial disclosure documents the union is required to file with the Department of Labor each year. These documents are filed by any labor organizations that collected money during the fiscal year. The requirements for filing these documents are based on the labor organization's annual receipts and are as follows:

LM-4: Total annual receipts of less than $10,000
LM-3: Total annual receipts of $10,000 to $199,999
LM-2: Total annual receipts of $200,000 or more

This information can be vital to your strategy. Most of these documents show money being spent to maintain the union bureaucracy and pay for union salaries, but little if anything being spent on behalf of individual members. Also answered on these forms:

• Does the union have a PAC fund?
• Was an outside audit conducted?
• Was any officer paid $10,000 (or more)?

- Was any officer paid $10,000 (or more) as an officer or employee of another union or employee benefit plan?
- How many members?

3. A copy of the union's strike history — This will list all recorded strikes by union and by various criteria (i.e., local number, location, start and end dates, number of employees, length of strike, etc.). For example, you can obtain the strike history for the Teamsters union in the state of New York for the year 1995. Depending on the size of the union, you should obtain the strike history for at least one year in the case of a large union, or for at least three years or more in the case of a small union.

A typical strike history shows the company that was struck, the name of the union, the local number if available, city and state where the strike took place, the dates the strike started and ended, the number of days the strike lasted, the number of people on strike, and the total work days lost (number of people multiplied by number of days idled).

On the following pages are example of a typical strike history report, a detailed history of a specific strike, and a summary of all strikes within the selected parameters. These examples were generated through the LRI Online database.

Strike History Report

LRI Online Strike History Matches

Number of Records matched: **5 4**   Progress: **Done**   [**Print Listing**]

Double-click on a record to see a detail form.

Company	Union	Local	City	ST	Start	End	Days Out	Num. Idled	Total Lost
All Die Division of Great Eagle Enterprises	Machinists & Aerospace Workers	9	St. Louis	MO	1/23/95	9/8/95	161	10	1610
Rockwell International, Inc.	Machinists & Aerospace Workers	1293	Fairfield	IA	2/1/95	2/3/95	3	409	1227
Midway, Inc.	Machinists & Aerospace Workers	1363	Monroeville	OH	2/1/95	2/7/95	5	25	125
Lapp Insulator Company	Machinists & Aerospace Workers	1150	Le Roy	NY	2/13/95	2/14/95	2	14	28
Miller Brewing Company	Machinists & Aerospace Workers	2699	Albany	GA	3/6/95	5/21/95	55	500	27500
Silgan Containers Corporation	Machinists & Aerospace Workers	1528	Stockton	CA	3/27/95	4/24/95	20	90	1800
Bergen Machine & Tool Company, Inc.	Machinists & Aerospace Workers	677	Hackettstown	NJ	4/1/95	4/17/95	10	68	680
Chautauqua Hardware Corporation	Machinists & Aerospace Workers	1839	Jamestown	NY	4/3/95	4/10/95	6	255	1530
La France Corporation	Machinists & Aerospace Workers	98	Philadelphia	PA	4/10/95	4/25/95	11	90	990
Rowe Brothers Rebuilders & Equipment	Machinists & Aerospace Workers	1005	Portland	OR	4/13/95	6/14/95	43	12	516
Votator Division of Cherry Burrell	Machinists & Aerospace Workers	681	Louisville	KY	4/16/95	5/15/95	21	85	1785
Southtowne Machining, Inc.	Machinists & Aerospace Workers	9	Maryland Heights	MO	4/17/95	9/8/95	102	16	1632
Cowlitz Industrial Machine, Inc.	Machinists & Aerospace Workers	1350	Kelso	WA	4/21/95	9/7/95	97	37	3589
Arrow Gear Company	Machinists & Aerospace Workers	1202	Downer Grove	IL	5/1/95	6/12/95	30	159	4770
Simplex Filler	Machinists & Aerospace Workers	1327	Hayward	CA	5/1/95	1/19/96	184	8	1472
Hoover Precision Products, Inc.	Machinists & Aerospace Workers	2041	Washington	IN	5/3/95	5/5/95	3	93	279
Baldt Anchor	Machinists & Aerospace Workers	493	Chester	PA	5/22/95	5/30/95	6	26	156
Kennedy Valve Manufacturing	Machinists & Aerospace Workers	1379	Elmira	NY	6/3/95	7/1/95	21	450	9450
Great Bend Industries Division of Hein Werner	Machinists & Aerospace Workers	1989	Great Bend	KS	6/3/95	6/16/95	10	234	2340

Printed by: **RScott**
Title: **Strike History Detail**

Wednesday, September 10, 1997   9:55:16 AM
Page 1 of 1

LRI Online
Strike History Detail

Union: Machinists & Aerospace Workers
Local: 1202
Company: Arrow Gear Company
City: Downer Grove   **State:** IL

Start Date: 5/1/95   **End Date:** 6/12/95   **Statistics as of:** 8/1/97
Number Idled: 159   **Work Days:** 30   **Work Days Lost:** 4770

Industry: Manufacturing
Product or Service: Spiral Gears

Print Detail	Save Detail

Printed by: **RScott**   Wednesday, September 10, 1997   9:59:57 AM
Title: **Summary on: Machinists: start 1/1/95 to 12/31/95**   Page 1 of 3

LRI Online Strike History Matches

Number of Records matched: **4 3**		Progress: **Done**				**Print Listing**			
Double-click on a record to see a detail form.						Days Out	Num. Idled	Total Lost	
Company	Union	Local	City	ST	Start	End			

Total strikes: 54

Total Idled: 53642   Total Days Out: 1787

Total Days Lost: 3413257

Avg. Idled: 993   Avg. Days Out : 33

Avg. Days Lost : 63208

Continuing Strikes: 0

Top 3 Strikes - # Idled:

Company	Union	Local	City	ST	Start	End	Days Out	Num. Idled	Total Lost
The Boeing Company	Machinists & Aerospace Workers	824, 24, 70, 751	Seattle	WA	10/6/95	1/19/96	73	38000	2774000
The Boeing Company	Machinists & Aerospace Workers	70	Wichita	KS	10/6/95	1/16/96	70	7400	518000
Amana Refrigeration, Inc.	Machinists & Aerospace Workers	1526	Cedar Rapids	IA	9/24/95	9/28/95	4	2000	8000

Top 3 Strikes - Days Out:

Company	Union	Local	City	ST	Start	End	Days Out	Num. Idled	Total Lost
Simplex Filler	Machinists & Aerospace Workers	1327	Hayward	CA	5/1/95	1/19/96	184	8	1472
Auto Truck, Inc.	Machinists & Aerospace Workers	701	Chicago	IL	8/9/95	4/25/96	182	45	8190
All Die Division of Great Eagle Enterprises	Machinists & Aerospace Workers	9	St. Louis	MO	1/23/95	9/8/95	161	10	1610

Top 3 Strikes - Days Lost:

Company	Union	Local	City	ST	Start	End	Days Out	Num. Idled	Total Lost
The Boeing Company	Machinists & Aerospace Workers	824, 24, 70, 751	Seattle	WA	10/6/95	1/19/96	73	38000	2774000
The Boeing Company	Machinists & Aerospace Workers	70	Wichita	KS	10/6/95	1/16/96	70	7400	518000
Miller Brewing Company	Machinists & Aerospace Workers	2699	Albany	GA	3/6/95	5/21/95	55	500	27500

Strike History Summary

CA	3
GA	1
IA	4
IL	5
IN	2
KS	2
KY	1
MA	1
MD	1
MI	1
MO	7
ND	1
NJ	1
NM	1
NY	5
OH	6
OR	1
PA	3
RI	1
TN	1
TX	2
VT	1

Armed with this information, which is gathered by the Federal Mediation and Conciliation Service, you can make irrefutable arguments with rock solid documentation. It is also likely you can find one or more strikes that occurred in your area. By speaking with management from a company struck by the same union seeking representation, you may be able to obtain testimonials or other information that will further strengthen your position on the strike issue.

4. A copy of the union's election results — This will list all recorded elections by union and by various criteria (i.e., local, NLRB region, type of election, location, date, size of unit, winner, etc.). For example, you can obtain the election results for the Auto Workers for the year 1996 in units of 50 or more people in the state of Michigan. A report will show all elections the union won, as well as all the elections it lost. Most important, it will show all decertification elections. These are the elections where union-represented employees voted their union out.

An election results report includes company name, union name, local number if available, region and docket number, city and state of the employer, date the election was certified, the number of votes for each party, and the election winner.

As with union strike histories, you should order election results based on the size of the union. On the following pages are examples of a typical election results report, a detailed report of a specific election, and a summary of all election results within the selected parameters. These examples were generated through the LRI Online database.

Election Results Report

LRI Online Election Results Matches

Number of Records matched: **2 0 1**   Progress: **Done** | Print Listing |

Double-click on a record to see a detail form.

Company	Union	Local	Reg-Docket	City	ST	Date	Yes	No	Winner
International Multifoods, Inc.	Food & Commercial Workers	576	17 RC 11202	Bonner Springs	KS	1/3/95	27	61	Company
America's Catch, Inc.	Food & Commercial Workers	1529	26 RC 7679	Itta Bena	MS	1/3/95	52	100	Company
Howies Ranch Market	Food & Commercial Workers	770	31 RC 7253	Sierra Madre	CA	1/19/95	12	8	Union
Stevison Ham Company	Food & Commercial Workers	405	26 RD 948	Portland	TN	1/20/95	2	37	Company
RB Bruns, Inc.	Food & Commercial Workers	555	36 RD 1458	Eugene	OR	1/23/95	1	7	Company
American Drug Stores, Inc.	Food & Commercial Workers	881	25 RC 9431	Chesterton	IN	1/23/95	6	16	Company
Casey Care Center	Food & Commercial Workers	881	14 RD 1490	Mt. Vernon	IL	1/31/95	7	21	Company
Jerome Foods	Food & Commercial Workers	6	18 RD 2063	Fairbault	MN	1/31/95	42	62	Company
Safeway	Food & Commercial Workers	7	27 RC 7523	Englewood	CO	1/31/95	2	0	Union
Rainbow Foods	Food & Commercial Workers	653	18 RC 15707	Hopkins	MN	1/31/95	1	6	Company
Thrifty - Payless Drug	Food & Commercial Workers	1428	21 RC 19439	El Monte	CA	1/31/95	6	10	Company
Princeton Care Center	Food & Commercial Workers	576	17 RC 11189	Princeton	MO	1/31/95	1	19	Company
St. Elizabeth Hospital	Food & Commercial Workers	1	3 RC 10075	Utica	NY	1/31/95	47	49	Company
Carriage Hill Foods	Food & Commercial Workers	880	8 RC 15158	Salem	OH	1/31/95	183	254	Company
Thrifty Drug, Inc.	Food & Commercial Workers	1036	31 RC 7258	Wilsonville	OR	2/1/95	9	3	Union
Cinder Corporation	Food & Commercial Workers	653	18 RC 15694	Rochester	MN	2/2/95	6	0	Union
Falls Poultry - National Foods	Food & Commercial Workers	370	3 RD 1180	Livingston Manor	NY	2/3/95	12	1	Union
Sav - On Drugs, Store #3263	Food & Commercial Workers	324	21 RC 19444	Lakewood	CA	2/6/95	9	14	Company
Cottonwood Healthcare Center	Food & Commercial Workers	536	33 RC 3952	Galesburg	IL	2/10/95	25	28	Company

Election Results Detail

LRI Online
Election Results Detail

Certification Date: 1/3/95

Region Number: 17   **Type of Election:** RC   **Docket Number:** 11202

Union: Food & Commercial Workers   **Votes For:** 27

Company: International Multifoods, Inc.   **Against:** 61

                                                              Voters: 100

Local: 576   **Winner:** Company

Name: Mr. Dennis Winnett

Address: 2410 South Scheidt

City: Bonner Springs   **State:** KS   **Zip Code:** 66012

Telephone: 913-441-6310

| Print Detail | Save Detail |

Election Results Summary

LRI Online Election Results Matches

Number of Records matched: **4 9**   Progress: **Done** | Print   Listing |
Double-click on a record to see a detail form.

Company	Union	Local Reg-Docket City	ST Date	Yes No	Winner

Total Elections: 201

Number of Elections by
Type:

FC   1 6 8

FD   3 0

FM   3

Total Votes For: 6275   Total Votes Against: 6931

Number of Elections Won
by...

Company   1 0 7

Union   9 4

Number of Elections per
State:

AL   4

AR   4

CA   2 1

CO   7

CT   2

DE   2

FL   2

GA   7

IA   4

Election results information can often single-handedly turn a vast number of voters from union supporters to management supporters. You must have this information and use it effectively. As the summary shows, the union used in this example participated in 201 elections during the period selected. Of these elections, 33 or 16.4% were decertification elections where current members were trying to vote this union out. By narrowing the search slightly, even more startling information appears.

- In representation elections (RCs), the union won 51.8% of the time; 87 wins versus 81 losses.
- In decertification elections (RDs & RMs), the union won only 21.2% of the time; 7 wins and 26 losses.

Your point would be that though this union is very good at making people believe things will get better if it's voted in, the stark truth is that people who know how the union actually performs, vote it out over 80% of the time. Imagine the impact this information could have on a voting unit.

5. A copy of the union's organizing activity — This will show all petitions filed by a specific union within the selected time frame. It lists the name of the organization petitioned, location of this organization, the name of the union filing the petition, local number if available, region and docket number, date the petition was filed, and if withdrawn, the date that occurred. Additional detailed information is available that can be used to identify other union organizing activity undertaken by the same union and/or union organizer in the same area.

You can find the number of petitions that were filed by the union and later withdrawn. By comparing organizing activity with election results, there should be many examples of unions that file petitions but no election is conducted and no withdrawal is recorded. This could mean the union simply abandoned the campaign; it could mean that during the campaign one or more unfair labor practice charges were filed and remain unresolved; it could mean that an election was conducted but ballots challenged and the outcome of the election has not been certified. Whatever the reason, many petitions do not reach the point of an election being conducted or the results being certified for many years.

On the following pages are examples of a typical organizing activity report, a detailed organizing activity report, and a summary of all organizing activity within the selected parameters. These examples were generated through the LRI Online database.

Organizing Activity Report

LRI Online Organizing Activity Matches

Number of Records matched: **2 9 8**   Progress: **Done**   [**Print Listing**]

Double-click on a record to see a detail form.

Company	City	ST	Union	Local	Organizer	Reg	Docket	Pet. Date	W/D Date
Healthcare Services Group, Inc.	Milwaukee	WI	Service Employees	150	Elizabeth Levie	30 RC	5654	1/9/95	
St. Elizabeth Manor, Inc.	Florissant	MO	Service Employees	0		14 RM	698	1/11/95	
Foodlink, Inc.	Rochester	NY	Service Employees	1199		3 RD	1182	1/12/95	2/21/95
Blythe Ambulance Service	Blythe	CA	Service Employees			21 RD	2559	1/12/95	2/7/95
ARAMARK	Houston	TX	Service Employees	100	Orell Fitzsimmons	16 RC	9766	1/13/95	
Neighborhood Commons	Chicago	IL	Service Employees	1	Theodore	13 RC	19064	1/13/95	
Jones Creek Firestone Tire & Service Center	Baton Rouge	LA	Service Employees	100	Nina Schulman	15 RC	7883	1/17/95	
Plank Road Firestone Tire & Service Center	Baton Rouge	LA	Service Employees	100	Nina Schulman	15 RC	7884	1/17/95	
Florida Blvd. Firestone Tire & Service Center	Baton Rouge	LA	Service Employees	100	Nina Schulman	15 RC	7885	1/17/95	
Cortana Mall Firestone Tire & Service Center	Baton Rouge	LA	Service Employees	100	Nina Schulman	15 RC	7886	1/17/95	
Family Housing & Adult Services	Belmont	CA	Service Employees	535	David A. Rosenfeld	20 RC	17080	1/19/95	
Park Manor	Waterbury	CT	Service Employees	1199	Paul Fortier	34 RC	1316	1/23/95	
American Medical Response West	Fremont	CA	Service Employees	250	William A. Sokol	32 RC	3981	1/23/95	
Accurate Plastics, Inc.	Yonkers	NY	Service Employees	32-E	Scott P. Trivella	2 RC	21500	1/23/95	
Ogden Allied	New York	NY	Service Employees	32-E	Matthew	34 RC	1319	1/30/95	2/1/95
Charlestown Care Center	Catonsville	MD	Service Employees	1199-E	Debora Miller	5 RC	14147	1/30/95	
TUCS Cleaning Services, Inc.	Orange	NJ	Service Employees	32-BJ	James Fitzpatrick	2 RC	21501	1/30/95	
Kiel Center Limited Partnership	St. Louis	MO	Service Employees & Hotel & Restaurant Employees	50, 74	William Franz	14 RC	11503	1/31/95	
Cincinnati Classical Public Radio, Inc.	Cincinnati	OH	Service Employees	925		9 RD	1759	2/1/95	

Organizing Activity Detail

LRI Online
Organizing Activity Detail

Date Filed: 1/9/95   **Date Withdrawn:**
Region Number: 30   **Type of Petition:** RC   **Docket Number:** 5654

Employer Information

Name: Healthcare Services Group, Inc.
Rep: Mr. Paul Minear   **Rep Title:**
Address: 6925 North Port Washington   **Telephone:** 414-352-3300
City: Milwaukee   **State:** WI   **Zip:** 53217
Type of Establishment: Cleaning & Laundry
Unit Included: Service Employees

Union Information

Name: Service Employees
Local Number: 150
Organizer: Elizabeth Levie   **Unit Size:** 25

Print Detail	Save Detail

LRI Online Organizing Activity Matches

Number of Records matched: **3 3**   Progress: **Done**   [**Print   Listing**]

Double-click on a record to see a detail form.

Company	City	ST	Union	Local Organizer	Reg-Docket	Pet. Date	W/D Date

Total Petitions: 298

Number of Petitions by
Type:

RC	2 1 6
RD	7 2
RM	1 0

Number of Petitions per
State:

CA	4 1
CT	1 0
DC	1
HI	1
IL	1 8
IN	1
KY	7
LA	1 4
MA	1 0
MD	4
ME	2
MI	1 3
MN	5

This information can be a valuable networking tool that puts you in touch with other employers that have previously or are currently experiencing an organizing attempt by the same union or same organizer. By selecting additional details for each petition in your search area, you can obtain the name, address, and telephone number of the company representative.

The judicious use of organizing activity information can give you a huge strategic advantage over the union. If, for example, you find several campaigns conducted by the same organizer, you can contact representatives from the targeted organizations. They will usually be willing to share the tactics and strategies used by this organizer, as well as the union's campaign literature. Since most organizers utilize the same basic blueprint for each campaign, knowing how an organizer responds to certain situations or addresses specific issues can be a tremendous advantage.

6. A clipping file — This file contains newspaper articles about union plant closings, union violence, corruption, embezzlement of funds, and concessionary agreements. A typical online clipping file search will provide a list of newspaper articles about a particular union, the date the article appeared, the city and state where the newspaper is located, a search summary, and the text of any selected article.

Newspaper articles that are both union- and area-specific frequently show the side of unionization that organizers never talk about. Because these articles are taken directly from newspapers, they are usually accepted by the voting group as true without further explanation or documentation. If you know of specific incidents, contact newspapers likely to have covered the stories and request copies from their microfilm file. Though there are not always articles about every union in every region of the country, you should always check to see if you can obtain what is available.

On the following pages are examples of a typical clipping file report, a clipping file report summary, and the text of an article. These examples were generated through the LRI Online database.

Clipping File Report

LRI Online Clippings Matches

Number of Records matched: **4 5 8**   Progress: **Done**
Double-click on a record to see the text of the story.

Union	Date	City	ST
Teamsters	8/9/80	Philadelphia	PA
Teamsters	12/3/84	Atlantic City	NJ
Teamsters	12/3/84	Los Angeles	CA
Teamsters	11/1/85	Philadelphia	PA
Teamsters	1/25/86	Chicago	IL
Teamsters	5/17/86	Newark	NJ
Teamsters	6/28/86	Manchester, NH	NH
Teamsters	10/17/86	Pittsburgh	PA
Teamsters	12/15/86	New York	NY
Teamsters	1/17/87	Long Island	NY
Teamsters	1/31/87	Pittsburgh	PA
Teamsters	2/11/87	Milwaukee	WI
Teamsters	4/25/87	Newark	NJ
Teamsters	6/17/87	New York	NY
Teamsters	7/29/87	Cleveland	OH
Teamsters	12/1/87	Cleveland	OH
Teamsters	12/21/87	Cleveland	OH
Teamsters	1/23/88	Cleveland	OH
Teamsters	2/4/88	Washington	DC
Teamsters	3/29/88	Miami	FL
Teamsters	4/5/88	Los Angeles	CA
Teamsters	4/7/88	Cleveland	OH
Teamsters	6/29/88	Washington	DC
Teamsters	6/29/88	Washington	DC
Teamsters	6/29/88	Washington	DC
Teamsters	6/29/88	Washington	DC
Teamsters	6/29/88	Pittsburgh	PA
Teamsters	12/7/88	Cleveland	OH
Teamsters	12/8/88	New York	NY
Teamsters	1/18/89	Cleveland	OH
Teamsters	2/23/89	Kearny	NJ
Teamsters	3/20/89	Detroit	M
Teamsters	10/4/89	Binghamton	NY
Teamsters	11/21/89	Hartford	CT
Teamsters	1/18/90	Cleveland	OH
Teamsters	2/7/90	Morriston	NJ
Teamsters	3/5/90	New York	NY
Teamsters	3/28/90	Lansing	M
Teamsters	4/1/90	Boston	MA
Teamsters	7/11/90	New York	NY

Clipping File Summary

LRI Online Clippings Matches

Number of Records matched: **4 4**   Progress: **Done**

Double-click on a record to see the text of the story.

Union	Date	City	ST

Count of Records: 458

Number of Clippings per State:

	5
AL	1
AZ	2
CA	43
CT	3
DC	19
DE	1
FL	9
GA	5
IA	4
ID	1
IL	29
IN	10
KS	3
KY	7
LA	1
MA	14
MD	6
MI	19
Mi	1
MI	14
MN	5
MO	7
N	1
NC	1
ND	1
NH	2
NJ	49
NV	1
NY	41
OH	24
OK	5
OR	1
PA	96
RI	8
SC	2
TX	2
UT	1

Clipping File Text

DeskTop
Subject: Teamsters
Leader-Telegram

Back to work

Strikers return to jobs as negotiations continue

By Pat Adamson
Leader-Telegram correspondent

OWEN—Employees of Owen Manufacturing slowly are returning to work after putting down their picket signs Saturday and re-entering negotiations with the company.

Teamsters Local 662 Union Steward Kenneth Hansen of Owen said about 30 employees were back working at the custom wood manufacturing plant on Monday; about 40 were expected today.

The strike started Sept. 5.

"We were afraid that we'd be replaced by permanent workers," Hansen said about the decision to return to work.

He said the four union stewards had a meeting Saturday and voted to get people back to work.

"We didn't surrender. We are just going another way to get back to work. That was our goal—to get back to work," Hansen said.

Owen Manufacturing has been hiring employees to keep the plant running. Some employees of Master Package, which closed last week, were hired at Owen Manufacturing.

Hansen said workers who were on strike are going back to work only after they sign an agreement stating the employee is making an unconditional offer to return.

Owen Manufacturing President Richard Asdel was in a meeting and could not be reached for comment, but a company spokeswoman said he would have a statement later today.
Hansen said he is unsure when all the employees will be back.

Hansen said he is one of five workers who will not be hired back immediately because he has been accused of vandalism.

"That's what I understand. (The company) just said we're under investigation," Hansen said.

Hansen said contract negotiations are far from over, considering the meeting last Friday with a federal mediator did not go well.

"Both sides were really at each other's throats," Hansen said.

More negotiations are scheduled for Saturday.

Citations issued over alleged harassment

Clark County Sheriff's Department officials are investigating alleged harassment of Owen Manufacturing employees by striking workers, according to Sheriff Dale Olson.

A disorderly conduct citation has been issued to an Owen-area man in connection with an incident Sept. 19, in which the man allegedly drove his truck alongside another vehicle and threatened the driver, Olson said.

Another citation is expected to be issued against a striking worker who apparently tried to run a new company employee off the road the same day," Olson said.

Olson was not sure if it was the same striking worker, but initial reports indicate two different trucks were used in the events.

Olson said a woman notified the department that she had been followed for about 1-1/2 hours by a man driving a blue pickup truck, and that he attempted to run her off the road when she drove from Owen to Thorp. The woman's husband also was in the car.

The man making threatening remarks was driving a Dodge truck on Highway T. north of Withee.

"Both incidents were related and both have been resolved," Olson said.

7. A copy of all unfair labor practice charges filed by union members against the union conducting this campaign — Unfair labor practice charges, also known as C-cases, are formal documents filed by union members which state, sometimes in graphic detail, how the union has violated their rights. Available information will include case number, date the charge was filed, the union named in the charge, the local named, and location.

Many of these charges are incredibly damning to the union and make excellent campaign literature. Most union organizers try to persuade voters that they need a union to protect them from unfair or unreasonable actions by management. Imagine the effect of showing literally hundreds of charges filed against the union by members who state that they were not fairly represented when they had a work-related problem or were discharged. How might voters react when they learn the union failed to pay the required insurance premium for a member who is now stuck with thousands of dollars of medical bills? Would they be sympathetic to a union that required an employer to hold half of a member's pay until a union-imposed fine was paid? And these are not frivolous claims; they are documented charges filed with the National Labor Relations Board by actual union members.

On the following pages are examples of a typical ULP charges report and a copy of an actual charge. These examples were generated through the LRI Online database.

ULP Charges Report

LRI Online ULP Charges Matches

Number of Records matched: **2 6**   Progress: **Done**   **Print Listing**

Double-click on a record to see the download form.

Case	Date	Union	Local	City	ST
13-CB-14660	1/3/95	Electrical Workers	1031	Park Ridge	IL
14-CB-8405	1/4/95	Electrical Workers	1	St. Louis	MO
8-CB-7851	1/5/95	Electrical Workers	1996	Warren	OH
1-CB-8732-1	1/9/95	Electrical Workers	1505	Waltham	MA
15-CB-4052	1/10/95	Electrical Workers	11211	Gulfport	MS
13-CB-14664	1/10/95	Electrical Workers	336	Downers Grove	IL
19-CB-7692	1/11/95	Electrical Workers	191	Everett	WA
25-CB-7631	1/13/95	Electrical Workers	1393	Indianapolis	IN
25-CB-7630	1/13/95	Electrical Workers	723	Fort Wayne	IN
9-CB-9070	1/13/95	Electrical Workers	2287	Oxford	OH
3-CB-6732	1/13/95	Electrical Workers	2213	Syracuse	NY
17-CB-4650	1/17/95	Electrical Workers	304	Topeka	KS
3-CB-6735	1/17/95	Electrical Workers	1833	Elmira	NY
37-CB-1177	1/18/95	Electrical Workers	1260	Honolulu	HI
9-CB-9071	1/18/95	Electrical Workers	2331	Circleville	OH
30-CB-3735	1/19/95	Electrical Workers	2150	Waukesha	WI
31-CB-9483	1/20/95	Electrical Workers	428	Bakersfield	CA
8-CB-7857	1/23/95	Electrical Workers	998	Vermilion	OH
21-CB-11860	1/23/95	Electrical Workers	11	Pasadena	CA
17-CB-4654	1/24/95	Electrical Workers	1464	Kansas City	MO
25-CB-7636	1/24/95	Electrical Workers	723	Fort Wayne	IN
4-CB-7392	1/25/95	Electrical Workers	98	Philadelphia	PA
27-CB-3434	1/27/95	Electrical Workers	111	Denver	CO
2-CB-15556	1/30/95	Electrical Workers	3	Flushing	NY
1-CB-822	1/30/95	Electrical Workers	2222	Quincy	MA
1-CB-8522	1/30/95	Electrical Workers	2222	Quincy	MA

ULP Charge

FORM NLRB-508
(6-90)

FORM EXEMPT UNDER 44 U S C 3512

UNITED STATES OF AMERICA
NATIONAL LABOR RELATIONS BOARD
**CHARGE AGAINST LABOR ORGANIZATION
OR ITS AGENTS**

DO NOT WRITE IN THIS SPACE	
Case	Date Filed
4-CB-7392	1/25/95

INSTRUCTIONS: File an original and 4 copies of this charge and an additional copy for each organization, each local, and each individual named in item 1 with the NLRB Regional Director of the region in which the alleged unfair labor practice occurred or is occurring.

1. LABOR ORGANIZATION OR ITS AGENTS AGAINST WHICH CHARGE IS BROUGHT

a. Name
IBEW LOCAL N°98

b. Union Representative to contact
TIM BROWN

c. Telephone No.
?

d. Address (street, city, state and ZIP code)
1719 Spring Garden St
Phila Pa 19130

e. The above-named organization(s) or its agents has (have) engaged in and is (are) engaging in unfair labor practices within the meaning of section 8(b), subsection(s) (list subsections) (1)(A) of the National Labor Relations Act, and these unfair labor practices are unfair practices affecting commerce within the meaning of the Act.

2. Basis of the Charge (set forth a clear and concise statement of the facts constituting the alleged unfair labor practices)

ON OR ABOUT DECEMBER 13, 1994 AND AGAIN ON DECEMBER 19, 1994 TIM BROWN VISITED OUR JOB SITE. HE ASKED ONE OF CUSTOM ELECTRIC EMPLOYEES WHAT THEY WERE EARNING AND SAID "THERE'S GOING TO BE TROUBLE ON THIS JOB." BROWN ALSO SAID "WE ARE GOING TO BE ALL OVER YOU" AND ASKED "ARE YOU GUYS TOUGH?"

3. Name of Employer	4. Telephone No.
S. J. THOMAS CO	(610) 622-3720

5. Location of plant involved (street, city, state and ZIP code)	6. Employer representative to contact
MEDIA MUNICIPAL CENTER 3RD & JACKSON STS. MEDIA PA	GARY THOMAS

7. Type of establishment (factory, mine, wholesaler, etc.)	8. Identify principal product or service	9. Number of workers employed
CONSTRUCTION JOB SITE	GENERAL CONTRACTOR	x

10. Full name of party filing charge
GARY P. THOMAS

11. Address of party filing charge (street, city, state and ZIP code)	12. Telephone No.
3812 SCHOOL LN DREXEL HILL PA 19026	6102842311

13. DECLARATION

I declare that I have read the above charge and that the statements therein are true to the best of my knowledge and belief.

By (signature of representative or person making charge) — Gary P. Thomas — Carpenter (title or office, if any)

Address 3812 School Ln D. H. Pa 19026 — 610-282-2311 (Telephone No.) — 1/16/95 (date)

WILLFUL FALSE STATEMENTS ON THIS CHARGE CAN BE PUNISHED BY FINE AND IMPRISONMENT (U. S. CODE, TITLE 18, SECTION 1001)

---

8. Copies of all labor agreements currently in effect in your area — Obtaining labor agreements negotiated by the union seeking representation is a great opportunity to arm your campaign with devastating ammunition. The Federal Mediation and Conciliation Service reports all labor agreements in effect in the United States. Contract information will include the name of the employer, the city and state in which the employer is located, the name of the union, the local number, the name of the union representative who negotiated the contract, the size of the unit, and the date the contact expires. The name, address, and telephone number of management representatives are also available. By contacting an employer who currently has a labor agreement with the union, you can usually obtain a copy of this agreement.

Access to labor agreements that are union- and area-specific is critical. You may be able to find agreements that provide lower wages, fewer benefits, and less favorable working conditions than currently exist in your workplace. Even one will do. When you find an agreement like this, use it to drive a stake in the heart of the union's campaign.

If labor agreements consistently show union wage, benefit, and working condition levels that are substantially better than those in effect in your workplace, use this information in formulating a response to the union's argument, or better yet, make a pre-emptive presentation that negates the impact of the union's message.

On the following pages are examples of a typical labor contracts report and a contracts detail report. These examples were generated through the LRI Online database. When using this database, you may wish to limit your search in larger cities to specific zip code areas.

Contracts Report

LRI Online Contracts Matches

Number of Records matched: **5 6 2**   Progress: **Done**   [**Print Listing**]
Double-click on a record to see a detail form.

Employer Information Name	City	ST	Size	Union Information Name	Local	City	ST	Union Rep.	Unit Size	Exp. Date
Weinstock Bros (Brothers)	Valley Stream	NY	2	UAW	2179	New York	NY	Pablo Valcarcel	2	1/1/95
C M Products Company The (Cm)	Dayton	OH	9 4	UAW	888	Dayton	OH	Denni Whitey Jones	· 8 0	1/2/95
Hayes Track Plant Western Cullen Hayes	Richmond	IN	0	UAW	1244	Indianapolis	IN	Walter Gray	2 6	1/4/95
Mclaughlin Co The (Mc Laughlin)	Petoskey	MI	1 0 0	UAW	1669	Traverse City	MI	Richard Potrafke	8 0	1/5/95
Independent Steel Castings Company Inc	New Buffalo	MI	1 2 0	UAW	2076	Kalamazoo	MI	James Sanborn	6 0	1/6/95
Mcdaniels Ford Inc (Mcdaniel's)	Hicksville	NY	9	UAW	259	New York	NY	Carlo Oliveri	9	1/13/95
Hueller Hille Corporation	Pontiac	MI	0	UAW	155	Warren	MI	Herman Hageman	4 5	1/14/95
Ernst Enterprises Inc (2 Locations)	Cincinnati	OH	0	UAW	2029	Cincinnati	OH	Al Deboard	3 5	1/15/95
Dayton Walther Corporation	Carrollton	KY	0	UAW	1813	Indianapolis	IN	David Hutton	3 0 0	1/15/95
Almco Steel Products Corporation	Bluffton	IN	0	UAW	1888	Indianapolis	IN	Claudia D Campbell	8 5	1/15/95
Lefere Forge & Machine (Le Fere)	Jackson	MI	5 5	UAW	504	Jackson	MI	A J Smith Jr	5 5	1/15/95
Marine City Stamping	Marine City	MI	0	UAW	375	Marine City	MI	Bill Spencer	6 5	1/15/95
I & H Conveying And Machine Company (I&H)	Grand Blanc	MI	0	UAW	708	Flint	MI	John Schultz	0	1/15/95
Reynolds Metals (Formerly Miller Brewing Co)	Fort Worth	TX	1 0 0	UAW	129	Fort Worth	TX	Roy Hernandez	1 0 0	1/15/95
Diesel Technology Corporation	Rogers	MI	5 3 5	UAW	167	Wyoming	MI	Barry Baldwin	0	1/15/95
New S M Rose The (Sm)	Bronx	NY	2	UAW	259	New York	NY	William Pickering	2	1/19/95
Aurora Hydromatic Pumps Inc	Ashland	OH	3 1 1	UAW	1932	Ashland	OH	Larry Crain	2 3 3	1/19/95
Controls Inc	Logansport	IN	0	UAW	1954	Not Provided		Durward Fuller	2 0 0	1/19/95
Allied Bendix Corporation	Charlotte	NC	3 2 0	UAW	2081	Charlotte	NC	James M Voliva	2 4 5	1/20/95

Contracts Detail

LRI Online
Labor Contracts Detail

Employer Information

Name: C M Products Company The (Cm)

Representative: Gordon Jones	**Title:** Plant Mgr
Address: 6061 Milo Road	**Phone:** 513-898-4420
City: Dayton	**State:** OH **Zip:** 45414
Affected Location: Dayton	**State:** OH **Zip:** 45401

Union Information

Name: UAW   **Local:** 888

Representative: Denni Whitey Jones	**Title:** Intl Rep
Address: 1155 D Lyons Road	**Phone:** 513-433-1524
City: Dayton	**State:** OH **Zip:** 45458

Expiration Date: 1/2/95   **Bargaining Unit Size:** 80   **Establishment Size:** 94
Product: Auto Parts

[Print Detail]   [Save Detail]

9. The union's organizing tactics and literature, and if possible, the name of the organizer assigned to your campaign — If the union has recently conducted organizing campaigns elsewhere, it is likely that similar campaign literature and strategy will be used again. This type of information can be obtained from your local Chamber of Commerce or a local personnel association; it is also available from LRI Online in the Organizing Activity Library. You may also make a Freedom of Information Act (FOIA) request to your regional NLRB office. Request all RC petitions filed by the union for the last year or two. Copies of these petitions will include the organizer's name.

10. A list of all eligible employees, by supervisor, with the employees' home addresses — The current home address of all employees eligible to vote in the election is necessary for two reasons: First, you will need a list if you decide to conduct part of your campaign by mail, and second, a list must be given to the NLRB early in the campaign. This list, known as an Excelsior list, will then be given to the union, as discussed in Chapter 1. The list provided to the Board should not be divided by supervisor or in any other way that will make it easier for the union to contact employees.

If it is not economically feasible to order all the types of information available, you should still obtain as much as you can afford. It will prove invaluable as you conduct your campaign.

LRI Online

LRI Online is a database service developed by the Labor Relations Institute and offered exclusively to management-labor attorneys, consulting firms, and employers that need quick, precise information on union-related activity. Although LRI Online is highly flexible and can be used for a wide variety of purposes, here we will only review the labor libraries. LRI Online contains six labor libraries that are updated monthly. Each can be extremely valuable to anyone conducting an NLRB representation election campaign for management.

The system has been designed for ease of use and operates much like other online services. Users must have a computer, basic software, and a modem or access to the Internet. A start-up disk, instructional video, and one hour of complimentary online time are available by calling 1-800-888-9115. The six labor libraries and their contents are as follows:

ORGANIZING ACTIVITY LIBRARY

The LRI Online Organizing Activity Library contains over 34,000 records, including every NLRB representation (RC) petition filed since January 1, 1991. This library also contains all employer-filed representation (RM) petitions and all decertification (RD) petitions filed since August 1, 1993. Petitions can be retrieved according to any one or combination of the following data fields:

Union Name	*Type of Petition*	*City*
Local #	*Type of Establishment*	*State*
Region #	*Name of Organizer*	*Zip Code*
Docket #	*Unit Size*	*Date Filed*

ELECTION RESULTS LIBRARY

The Election Results Library contains more than 29,000 records of every NLRB election conducted since January 1, 1989. Information can be retrieved according to any one or combination of the following data fields:

Company Name	*Date of Certification*	*Winner*
Union Name	*Number of Voters*	*City*
Type of Election	*Votes For*	*State*
Region #	*Votes Against*	

STRIKE HISTORY LIBRARY

Over 3,900 strike records as reported by the Federal Mediation and Conciliation Service are contained in the Strike History Library. Records include strikes called by most unions since 1989, and all reported strikes called since 1991. Information can be retrieved according to any one or combination of the following data fields:

Union Name	*State*	*Number of Employees*
Local #	*Start Date*	*Length of Strike*
City	*End Date*	*Person Days Lost*

ULP CHARGES LIBRARY

The Unfair Labor Practice Charges Library contains over 31,000 charges filed against unions by their own members. These charges, also known as C-cases, can be retrieved according to any one or combination of the following data fields:

Case #	*Local #*	*Zip Code*
Date Filed	*City*	
Union Name	*State*	

CLIPPING FILE LIBRARY

The LRI Online Clipping File Library holds thousands of newspaper articles that document union strikes, violence, and financial irregularities, as well as plant closings and various other incidents unfavorable to unions. Articles can be retrieved according to any one or combination of the following data fields:

Union Name	*City of Article*	*Text of Article*
Date of Article	*State of Article*	

LABOR CONTRACTS LIBRARY

The Labor Contracts Library lists all labor contracts in effect in the United States and its possessions as reported by the Federal Mediation and Conciliation Service. Currently, this library contains over 151,000 contracts. Information can be retrieved according to any one or combination of the following data fields:

UNION INFO	EMPLOYER INFO
Name	*Name*
Local #	*City*
City	*State*
State	*Zip Code*
Zip Code	*Size of Establishment*
Contract Date	
Union Rep	
Unit Size	

Campaign Direction

Prior to beginning your campaign, an individual or small group of individuals should be assigned the task of directing the campaign. Obviously, it is preferable if the person or one of the people selected has had previous campaign experience. However, that is usually not possible. This book is intended to help management conduct a successful campaign, even without previous campaign experience. Most employers select the personnel director as campaign manager and, depending on the size of the organization, appoint others to assist. It should be remembered that in most cases, the campaign will be a full-time job for the entire campaign period.

Throughout the campaign, it is management's goal to direct the issues. You must determine, in advance, your campaign strategy and timetable, then focus on those issues that will convince your employees to reject unionization. Most important, you will attempt throughout the campaign to force the union to spend a majority of its time trying to counter management's arguments and issues, rather than focusing on its own issues.

In establishing your campaign calendar, increase the intensity of the campaign as you move closer to election day. You will notice that you are actually running several small campaigns, each covering a specific subject. In each of the segments, build to a climax. If you have a specific piece of literature that is topical by union or by area, consider using this to close the segment. If you have no topical literature, it is probably best to begin the segment with general literature and close it with a video presentation or speech.

A Word About the Family

The choice of how to vote in an NLRB election is often more that just an individual decision on the part of the employee. Sometimes, it is a decision in which family members have also played a part. Unfortunately, family members have not always been exposed to the employer's campaign message. This can be a particular problem if the union is engaged in home visitations. A union organizer who visits employees in their homes can appear to run unopposed as far as the family is concerned, and family pressure often influences how an employee votes.

When determining the direction of your campaign, the campaign director should consider what, if any, information will be mailed to the home. Generally, it is best to distribute literature at work so employees can discuss the issues between themselves. However, some employers elect to mail literature to the home so the family can also hopefully influence the employee to reject unionization. You might consider preparing a weekly summary in the form of a letter to employees highlighting some of the major points management made during the week. The campaign director needs to consider the circumstances of the voting group when deciding how to involve families.

Home visitations are probably the union's most effective selling tool. In a report on organizing, the AFL-CIO found that "personal face-to-face contact between organizers and the employees [is] the preferred method of communication during a union campaign. The most frequently cited reason for losing campaigns is lack of sufficient personal contact with employees, and insufficient staff. In 26% of the campaigns, there was no full-time organizer. In 55% of the campaigns studied, there was one organizer. House calls are an effective means of establishing personal communication. In cases where the organizer called on between 60% and 75% of the unit, the win rate was 78%. If the organizer made no home visits, the win rate was 41%."

Though management can do nothing to prevent home visits by the union, you may post notices to inform employees that they are not legally obligated to allow a union representative into their homes.

Planning the Campaign

Assess your current position honestly and realistically. Candidates for national political office spend millions of dollars each election season on polls that measure voter tendencies. This money is well spent; the data obtained is critical to a candidate's success. By knowing where the candidate stands with the voters, the campaign director is able to fine tune the campaign by increasing or decreasing the level of activity, targeting certain groups, identifying major issues, and structuring the remaining campaign time to the best advantage.

One of the most common problems of an employer confronted with an NLRB election is determining where they stand with the voting group. How many employees are for the union? How many are for management? How many are undecided? *Virtually every employer will overestimate their support among the voting group! For that reason, many NLRB election campaign experts suggest taking management's collective opinion of voter support, then reducing that projected figure by 15% and giving that number to the union. They believe this gives a more accurate picture of relative strength.*

The failure to honestly and realistically evaluate management's position with voters has caused many employers to lose elections they honestly thought they would win. Often, management will evaluate its position and decide to de-emphasize certain issues or hold back on literature in the mistaken belief that the union is falling behind. Remember though, at the time of the petition the union probably had signed union authorization cards from 50% to 65% of the voting group. All the organizer has to do is hold that strength and the union will proba-bly win. Management has to change minds and win back those employees who have already signed cards. *Even if your best information shows you are ahead during the latter stages of the campaign, stick to your game plan.*

Some employers, believing the election is won, stop campaigning during the last week or two and lose. This recently happened to an LRI client who began an effective campaign against the Teamsters. Before long, there were indications the vote was turning in the company's favor. Management was further encouraged when three strong union supporters came to the operations manager and said they had seen the error of supporting the union. One of them then produced sev-eral union authorization cards taken back from the Teamsters. Believing there was nothing more to fear from the union, management — against our advice — decid-ed to halt its campaign. When election day arrived, it was soon clear this had been a fatal mistake. The union's choice for observers were the three "converted" com-pany supporters who had so dramatically convinced management to suspend its campaign. Their story had been a lie and the returned union cards only props in a carefully staged play performed for management's benefit. Though the election was close, the Teamsters won by four votes — four votes that likely could have been converted to management, had the campaign continued. The moral of this story is that even though you believe you are ahead, and some voters may be com-plaining they are tired of the barrage of information, continue campaigning.

A word of caution: trying to convince voters that your organization has no employee problems or areas that could be improved is not a productive campaign strategy. *Rather, you should strive to convince voters that the union is not the solution to workplace problems.* Focus on aspects of employee relations where your organiza-tion has a strong record, and remind voters of benefits they currently enjoy with-out the presence of a union.

Using your employee list, ask supervisors to identify the entire voting group according to the following categories:

- union leaders

- for the union
- leaning towards the union
- undecided
- leaning towards management
- for management
- management leaders

(A Vote Projection Tally Sheet is shown as Exhibit 2-A.)

In making this assessment, be realistic. Keep in mind that very few union organizers will file a petition if less than a minimum of 50% of the eligible voters have signed union authorization cards. If the person responsible for conducting your campaign does not personally know the voters (and even if they do), first line supervision should also participate in compiling this information. It is important to begin this evaluation early in the campaign. Accurately assessing your position early enables you to time your campaign and obtain the greatest effectiveness. By knowing your relative position at the beginning of the campaign, you can better chart your progress against the various issues and identify your strengths as early as possible. Pinpoint certain groups, departments, or individuals where concentrated effort might shift the outcome of the election in your favor.

Another important aspect of accurate employee assessment is the allocation of valuable campaign time. Once you have correctly grouped employees according to the seven categories previously discussed, you can better manage campaign time spent with individuals or small groups. Many campaigns fail to reach their maximum vote potential because time is wasted on voters already converted to management's side, or voters who will probably never be converted. *While you should never ignore voters who are correctly identified as "management leaders" or "for management," neither should you spend a disproportionate amount of time on people correctly identified as "union leaders," unless there is a good possibility of converting them.*

In most elections, there is a segment of the voting population who will vote a certain way regardless of any information presented. There are people in this country who will always vote democrat, even if Attila the Hun was the candidate. Similarly, there are those who always vote republican, regardless of who is running. In NLRB elections there is usually a segment of the voting group who will always support the union regardless of the facts. The same holds true for management supporters. Most election experts agree that in any voting unit, approximately 25% to 30% of the voting group on each side is immovable. These employees will support either management or the union, without regard to the type of campaign waged by the other side. The reason for their unswerving support varies, but generally they take the position that their minds are made up, so don't confuse them with the facts. This leaves you with 40% to 50% of the remaining voters who will decide the election.

Do not make the mistake of believing everything an employee says regarding support for management. Many voters, when talking to members of management and supervision, will say what they assume their employer wants to hear. Because of fear of retribution, many employees will not tell their supervisor they are planning to support the union. Therefore, you must evaluate employees based on what they do or how they act, rather than by what they say. For example, employees who say they support management and are opposed to the union, but who spend a great deal of time with known union supporters, must be considered questionable management supporters at best. *Actions speak louder than words.* In addition, employees who have attended union meetings are often coached by the organizer not to say or do anything that would lead management to believe they are supporting the union.

As you evaluate your present position, the first objective is to move each of the groups one step closer to strong management supporters or union opponents. Specifically, plant enough seeds of doubt in the minds of those employees who are identified as "union leaders" or "for the union" to move them to a less rigid posture of "leaning towards the union." One benefit of this tactic is these individuals will often become less vocal and less persuasive around other employees. As the campaign progresses, try to move them even further. Begin to move those employees "leaning towards the union" to "undecided," "undecided" to "leaning towards management," etc. In an ideal situation, you would move a majority of those individuals supporting the union to an "undecided" or "leaning towards management" position by the latter stages of the campaign to convince them to vote No during the final week.

If you honestly believe that by working with some of the union leaders you can make a conversion, you will want to invest the time. Union leaders, by definition, will have followers. By *converting a union leader, it should be possible to convert followers, resulting in a major swing of votes to management.* But formerly strong union support converted to your side is often fragile. Once a union spokesperson has been converted, they will need frequent reinforcement to assure them they made the right decision.

From the perspective of the vote count, moving people from the union to the management side of the ledger is very rewarding. It really is a swing of two votes. One less vote the union can expect, one more for management. In assessing the present feelings of employees towards the union, you cannot use polling techniques or in any other way ask employees how they feel about the union. You can, however, poll supervisors about how they believe employees feel, based on their day-to-day contact, and how they believe individual employees would vote if the election were held today. *You should take at least a weekly reading of employee opinion.*

While determining the positions of the employee group, also develop a list of issues the union has used to entice employees to sign authorization cards. *It is a certainty that at least 30%, and probably more than half the employee group, was unhappy about a certain condition or conditions that existed at the time authorization cards were being signed.* Few employees who are happy about their employment relationship with management, and who are aware that management is opposed to unions, will sign a card. Most employees see unionization as a drastic step.

Generally, unions do not invent issues in an attempt to gain authorization card signatures. Instead, they exploit issues that already exist. These issues will likely become the framework for the union's campaign. Management should be aware of these issues as early as possible in the campaign process. Those members of management who are closest to the voting group — usually the first line supervisors — should list what they believe are the union's strongest issues.

The next step in preparing for the campaign is to conduct a vulnerability audit for both management and the union. This is simply a listing of the strengths and weaknesses of both sides. List the specific strengths and weaknesses in order of priority, with the greatest strength first and the greatest weakness first. The issues listed should not be guess work or personal opinions, but should be based on information from a variety of sources. If the person preparing the vulnerability audit knows some of the issues, list them. But also enlist the opinions of first line supervisors and other members of management who have direct contact with the voting group. If you have conducted meetings with the voting group where complaints or comments have been voiced, the notes from those meetings will be helpful. Any union literature distributed to date may be helpful, too. It may have already stated the campaign issues from the union's perspective. *It is important to know the union's issues so you can anticipate future literature and strategy. Never lose sight that your objective is to run the campaign based on your issues and timetable, forcing the union to constantly respond.*

Establishing a Tentative Timetable

You are ready to establish a tentative timetable for the campaign after collecting information about the specific union, evaluating the current positions of the employee group, identifying the major issues the union will probably try to develop, and conducting a vulnerability audit. *To establish this timetable, it will be necessary to work backward from the date of the election to today's date.* If a date has been established by the NLRB for the election, you already know exactly how much time is available. If a date has not been established, you should try to negotiate with the NLRB and the union for a six-week campaign period. Six weeks is sufficient time to get your entire message across, but short enough to avoid losing the employees' attention in the myriad of information they will receive during the campaign. If the election is more than six weeks away, there is no need to begin your campaign immediately, unless you feel the union is swaying voters in its direction and this movement needs to be stopped. Should the election be less than six weeks away, you will have to begin your campaign immediately, even if you have not gathered all the information you need. Put all the information you have available into a shorter space of time, or consider whether some information should be eliminated.

One of your primary objectives in putting together a timetable is to leave enough room to maneuver, should conditions warrant. As a rule of thumb, you need to plan some election-related activity two days a week at the beginning of the campaign, three days a week during the middle stages, and some campaign activity every day at the end of the campaign.

Always keep your voting group informed about what is happening. Be sure they receive correct information about election dates, eligible voters, or any other information from management first, not the union. This will help you establish and maintain credibility.

You should now have the following information available or on order:

1. Union constitution and bylaws
2. LM-2, LM-3, or LM-4
3. Union strike history
4. Union election results
5. Union organizing activity
6. Area labor agreements
7. Union organizing literature used in previous campaigns
8. Unfair labor practice charges file (C-cases)

9. Union- and area-specific clipping file
10. List of eligible voters with addresses
11. List of eligible voters by current position on election
12. List of issues

In this book, you have available the basic framework for an effective management campaign. Now you need to establish how and when you will communicate the information you have collected, by issue, to the employee group.

First, examine the issues you wish to address in the order they will be presented. These are the basic arguments against unionization, supplemented by specific examples, where possible, of a local or regional application of these arguments. Develop your strategy to obtain the greatest possible benefit from your single greatest advantage in the election process: the captive audience meeting. When a union holds a meeting with voters, it must rely on voluntary attendance. Employees cannot be forced to attend a union meeting. However, management can legally hold what has come to be called captive audience meetings. These are meetings with the voting unit held during regular work hours while employees are on the clock. Depending on the size of the voting unit, you can have all voters attend a single meeting or hold several meetings with smaller groups. Since there is no equal time requirement in NLRB election campaigns, management may hold as many captive audience meetings as desired, thereby presenting more information about the issues than the union can. By using the captive audience meeting to the fullest extent, you can gain a significant strategic advantage.

As mentioned earlier, your campaign will really consist of five mini-campaigns, each covering a specific disadvantage of union membership, and a preparation and training period. When scheduling these mini-campaigns, or campaign segments, keep in mind that the objective is to peak on election day. Resist the temptation to try and win the election the first week of the campaign. That strategy runs the risk of wasting your most powerful arguments too early and allowing the passage of time to dilute their effectiveness. Most campaigns should be structured as follows:

SEGMENT 1, Preparing for the Campaign
During this first segment, collect all the materials needed to conduct the campaign. In addition, assess your current position, establish your timetable, and train your managers and supervisors. Develop and distribute your first piece of campaign literature.

SEGMENT 2, How Unions Work — Big business, not charity

This segment concentrates on how unions in general, and hopefully this union in particular, actually operate. Discuss the decline in union membership nationally; how the union collects and spends dues money; how union organizers try to "sell" the idea of union membership to voters; and why unions are generally unsuccessful in gaining wage, benefit, and working condition improvements for their members.

SEGMENT 3, Collective Bargaining — The union gamble

During the third segment of the campaign, discuss the collective bargaining process and how it actually works. Among the voting group, collective bargaining will probably be the most misunderstood aspect of unionization. The union wants voters to believe that the collective bargaining process starts from a base of current wages, benefits, and working conditions and is always negotiated up from there. Of course, this is untrue. Use specific examples of employees who have lost wages and/or benefits during the collective bargaining process. Look for local examples to reinforce this point.

SEGMENT 4, Union Constitutions & Bylaws — Mechanisms of control

The fourth segment focuses on the many rules and regulations imposed on union members by the union constitution and bylaws. Discuss dues, dues increases, fines, assessments, discipline, trials of members, and other typical provisions. The constitution of the union seeking representation becomes an important document during this segment, as you will draw from it for actual wording when preparing campaign literature.

SEGMENT 5, Job Security & Strikes — Your future in the union's hands

As the campaign reaches its peak, discuss one of the most negative and emotional aspects of union membership: job security and strikes. Utilize a union-specific strike history and, if possible, local examples. Inform voters of how thousands of union members have lost everything and had their lives destroyed by union strikes.

SEGMENT 6, Election Day — Participation & choice

During the final segment of the campaign, address the union's weakest areas and management's strongest. Summarize the campaign, ending with the 24-hour presentation which will solidify your position with management supporters and hopefully convert the remaining union supporters. Work to create a bandwagon effect that convinces voters of management's popularity and certain victory over the union.

Preparing the Campaign Calendar

Careful development of the campaign calendar is essential for victory. When planning your calendar, there are several vital considerations: the campaign issues; an understanding of the information at your disposal; a reasonably accurate estimate of current support for each side and the strength of that support. In addition, your campaign must be structured according to the amount of time available. Remember that much of the information you wish to convey requires preparation time, as well as production time with a printer.

If two campaigns were run simultaneously, using identical strategy and information, but one was properly timed and the other was not, there is little doubt that the properly timed election would produce more votes for management than the poorly timed election. *In a close vote, campaign timing may spell the difference between victory and a union contract.*

Begin your campaign calendar by working backwards.

SEGMENT 6, Election Day — On election day there are no captive audience meetings. The day before the election may or may not be a heavy campaign day, depending on the time of the election. The National Labor Relations Board has established what is known as an "insulated period" that begins 24 hours before the polls are scheduled to open. For example, if the polls are scheduled to open at 7:00 AM, the insulated period would begin at 7:00 AM the previous day. During the insulated period, campaign activity should be seriously curtailed. *It is illegal to hold captive audience meetings during this period. It has been ruled that controversial literature distributed at this time, and which does not give the opposing party adequate opportunity to respond, could invalidate the election.* The best rule of thumb is to engage in non-controversial campaign activity during the insulated period. It is permissible for supervisors to answer questions on a one-on-one basis. Though it is permissible to engage in some mild campaign activity, refer to Chapter 14 before determining your course of action during this period.

The balance of the time remaining in this final campaign segment should be carefully structured. The 24-hour presentation should be scheduled as close as possible to the beginning of the insulated period. When scheduling the 24-hour presentation, remember the insulated period is the 24-hour period before the polls open, not the 24-hour period before an employee is scheduled to vote. For example, assume you have a three-shift operation. First shift hours are from 7:00 AM to 3:00 PM, second shift hours are from 3:00 PM to 11:00 PM, and third shift hours are from 11:00 PM to 7:00 AM. In order for all employees to have sufficient time to vote during regular work hours, the election is scheduled to be conducted in two segments, from 6:00 AM to 8:00 AM and from 3:00 PM to 5:00 PM on a Friday. Using this example, the insulated period would begin at 6:00 AM, Thursday. This means you have to make your 24-hour presentation to first shift employees before the end of their shift on Wednesday, second shift before the end of their shift Wednesday, and the third shift meeting must end before 6:00 AM, Thursday morning. Obviously, no campaigning is allowed while voting is in progress.

The 24-hour presentation should contain campaign highlights and make an impressive final appeal that can sway undecided voters to support management. This presentation can be a video or a speech delivered by your best spokesperson. It should be supported by one of your strongest handbills that may or may not be distributed at the 24-hour meeting. If not handed out then, distribute it on either the same day or the day before. Depending on the day of the election, you may or may not have time for another handbill. If there is adequate time, this handout should contain another powerful argument against unionization. Don't hold anything back. When selecting literature for the final segment of the campaign, identify your strongest issues and address them. You might also consider a powerful response flyer (see Chapter 14).

When scheduling the day for the election, never agree to a Monday or Tuesday vote. A Monday or Tuesday election forces you to make the final presentation to employees on Friday, giving the union the entire weekend to attempt to muster support. The union may hold a mass meeting, have a picnic or a dinner, or do any number of things to encourage employee attendance. Effectively, a Monday or Tuesday election gives the union the last word. The 24-hour insulated period does not apply to the union. The later in the week an election can be held, the better. If it is to your advantage to encourage a large voter turnout, payday is usually a good choice. If payday is also a Thursday or Friday, that would be preferable. (These rules may not apply if you have a continuous or seven-day-a-week operation.)

SEGMENT 5, Job Security & Strikes — This segment of the campaign is vitally important. Normally, it takes place during the last full week of campaigning and is the time when you should attack the union hardest on what you believe is your strongest issue. In most campaigns this will probably be the issue of strikes. *For a majority of employees, strikes are the most obvious and disturbing disadvantage of unionization.* Consider ending this segment with a comprehensive handout that describes in detail an unsuccessful union strike. This could be a situation where the union went on strike and the employer eventually closed, or where the union called a strike and the striking employees were replaced. Try to find a local or regional example of this type of strike. Perseverance and ingenuity are essential in obtaining information that makes a truly effective piece.

While conducting a campaign in Fayetteville, Arkansas, management learned of a great strike story that had occurred in Sapulpa, Oklahoma, about 150 miles from Fayetteville. The personnel director, unable to get enough information from the company that was the target of the strike, went to the Sapulpa newspaper that had covered the story extensively. The editor let her use the newspaper morgue to look up articles about the strike, but could not let her have the actual papers. She learned from the editor that the Oklahoma Historical Society maintained microfilm of all state newspapers. The society had the articles she needed and for a small fee would make copies. With these articles, she was able to develop a highly effective handout, though she had never spoken directly to any of the strikers. By combining a video presentation on strikes with the union's strike history and this handout, she presented voters with a solid body of information the union was never able to successfully refute. Incidentally, management won the election, 50 to 2. (This newspaper-based strike flyer is reproduced in Chapter 5.)

During the middle of this campaign segment, either show voters the *Job Security & Strikes* video presentation or deliver a speech on the subject during a captive audience meeting. Strike computers and other information that show what employees stand to lose during a strike are also effective. If a union-specific strike history has been purchased, a list of strikes recently called by the union makes an excellent handout early in this segment. (An example of a strike history flyer is shown in Chapter 12.) Statements from the union's constitution that show what can happen to employees who cross picket lines, as well as the limited amount of money the union provides to strikers, are also good.

SEGMENT 4, Union Constitutions & Bylaws — This is a transition time when you begin to intensify your communication with voters to at least every other day. In this segment, you concentrate on the union's constitution and bylaws. Union constitutions are wonderful sources for union-free literature. They spend pages talking about union dues, fines, special assessments, how members can be called up on various charges and put on trial, plus many other startling provisions. All constitutions contain very specific rules and regulations most people find distasteful. Union constitutions are often similar and their most incriminating sections are found in the table of contents.

The challenge in communicating information contained in a union constitution is the length of the document. Most are 100 or more pages long and written in legal style language. A few years ago, a company in Vermont found an effective way to discuss a union constitution with employees. First, the constitution was thoroughly examined. Those provisions that best illustrated points the company wanted to make were put into a four-page handout titled "Rules of the Road." Beside each provision, a brief explanation and/or comment was written. This proved to be a successful way for management to inform voters about the many negative aspects of the union's constitution.

End this campaign segment with a handout that contains statements taken directly from the constitution of the union seeking to represent your employees. Use the *Union Constitutions & Bylaws* video during the middle of the segment, or a speech. Begin Segment 4 with a general handout making employees aware of how union constitutions protect the union, not the union members. (Examples of effective constitution and bylaws handouts are shown in Chapter 11.)

SEGMENT 3, Collective Bargaining — Some experts contend this is the most important segment of a campaign. Many voters anticipate that union representation will automatically improve their working life in some tangible way. *Very few employees will vote for a union unless they believe representation will result in higher pay, better benefits, or improved working conditions. Even fewer will support unionization if they believe it could result in a wage, benefit, or working condition reduction.* During the third segment of the campaign, educate employees about the collective bargaining process and how it really works. While this process is the backbone of labor-management relations in a unionized workplace, it is also usually misunderstood. If a union wins a representation election, all it wins is the right to bargain collectively with the employer. Nothing more, nothing less. This is an extremely important point. You must discredit the idea that union representation is like a letter to Santa Claus. The voting group must be made to understand that in the collective bargaining process, everything it now has, such as wage rates, insurance, vacations, holidays, wage increase systems, would be subject to the collective bargaining process. While you cannot make the statement that employees will automatically lose anything, it is proper to make them aware that collective bargaining does not necessarily mean they will experience any gains, and that losses are a possibility.

During a captive audience meeting at a Wisconsin pizza factory, a strong union supporter objected to management's description of the collective bargaining process as a situation of give and take, and that all current wages, benefits, and working conditions are as much subjects for negotiations as are the things promised by the union. Another vocal union supporter stood up and stated the union organizer had promised better benefits and a fifty-cent-an-hour raise, and that management would be forced to accept these terms or there would be a strike. Management realized it had an opportunity to turn the situation into a positive company issue. The management representative thanked the speaker for her comments and asked if she believed the union had guaranteed these increases. She said yes. When asked if these guarantees were in writing, the employee said no, but was sure she could get them. Using examples from the warranty coupon booklet in Chapter 7, the manager wrote out a brief contract that stated the union guaranteed the things the employee had described, and if they were not achieved through collective bargaining, the union would make up the difference. The contract had a place for the organizer to sign. The company spokesperson then asked the employee to bring the signed contract to the next meeting so everyone could determine who was telling the truth. At the following meeting, guess who was absent? In fact, she was absent from work until election day. The company won by a wide margin. If the opportunity to gain a strategic advantage arises, always take it. If you are unsure of how to handle the situation, get advice, then take action.

The structure of Segment 3 will depend on the information you have been able to collect concerning unionized employers in your area. If you have specific examples of employees who have suffered decreased wages or benefits as a result of union contract negotiations, this would make an excellent handout. If this is the case, consider starting off with either the *Collective Bargaining* video or a speech, then follow up with the handout. If you do not have information of this type, distribute a handout similar to Exhibit 10-A in Chapter 10, then follow up with the video or speech during a captive audience meeting.

SEGMENT 2, How Unions Work — This segment of the campaign focuses on how unions actually operate. First, explain that a union is really a business — but a business very different from the ones with which most people are familiar. A union doesn't make or sell a product; it generates revenue by charging dues to the members it represents. Show voters how unions collect these dues and how this money is spent. Explain that union membership is in steep decline and today unions are unable to deliver on their promises of improved wages, benefits, and working conditions. Show how union organizers attempt to sell the idea of union membership to employees and how what they're selling often contributes to job insecurity.

Several years ago, during a Steelworkers campaign in Missouri, it was determined that job security was the predominant issue. Because of the employer's history of layoffs, it was clear the union would hammer that subject throughout the campaign. But if this one issue could be defused, the company stood an excellent chance of winning. Management learned of an incident in which the Steelworkers had caused over 2,000 members to lose their jobs at a company in Idaho. Newspaper articles and interviews from some of the affected workers were gathered. Armed with this information, a dramatic handout was produced that showed how the union had ignored the vote of its members and caused the facility to close, forcing over 2,000 employees and union members out of work. This single handout immediately put the union on the defensive and eliminated job security as a union issue. Most importantly, it allowed management to direct the campaign back to their issues. When the vote was held, the employer prevailed, 75% to 25%. (This handout is shown in Chapter 13.)

SEGMENT 1, Preparing for the Campaign — The first segment of the campaign is devoted to collecting information, handling the logistics of running the campaign, and training supervisors and managers.

Rational Decisions Versus Emotional Decisions

Since 1988, the *NLRB Representation Election Campaign Program* has been used in over 3,500 elections. Management has won over 90% of those elections. This has given the Labor Relations Institute the unique opportunity to evaluate election campaigns that have used basically the same information presented in basically the same way, but with differing results. In some elections, management wins by huge margins, a few even by 100% to 0%. In most, the margin of victory is about 70% to 30%. In some campaigns, the margin is narrower, and in less than 10% of the elections, the union wins. When this happens, what is the reason? Is it the size of the voting unit? No. Region of the country? No. Composition of the workforce?

No. Type of industry? No. Wage and benefit levels? No. The primary reason is the degree to which the voters base their decision on emotional rather than rational factors.

Our experience has proven that if the disadvantages of union membership are presented using the LRI program, approximately 74% of typical voters will vote against the union. In 1996, over 65,000 employees cast ballots in elections where management used the *NLRB Representation Election Campaign Program.* Over 48,000 of those individuals voted against the union. This means the vast majority — who were not predisposed to vote for management — voted against the union after being exposed to this program. Obviously, those who voted in favor of the union did so because of considerations that, to them, outweighed the facts. What kinds of emotional factors are strong enough to blind employees to overwhelming evidence that is well presented? Here are some of the most prevalent:

1. A strong dislike or fear of one or more members of management — For some voters, a union representation election involves more than just issues. They make up their minds based on what political experts term a "beauty contest," in other words, which person or side is the most superficially appealing. If a voter does not like or is afraid of their supervisor or some other member of management who is campaigning, it is likely the employee will vote not so much for the union, as against that manager or supervisor. The higher in the organization the person or persons disliked by the voting group, the greater the obstacle to winning the election.

Recently, an NLRB representation election was conducted on the east coast. There were 65 employees in the company; 47 were manufacturing employees and eligible voters. The owner of the company also served as president, but had very little contact with the voting unit. The manufacturing organization was headed by a plant manager known throughout the company for his autocratic management style and inconsistent administration of rules and regulations. Early in the campaign, it became clear the main issue was not the rational advantages or disadvantages of union membership, but rather the employees' emotional reaction to this particular individual and their perceived need for protection.

As the campaign progressed, it became clear the outcome would be decided on the single issue of the plant manager, not on the relative merits of union membership. The more the voters perceived the plant manager was opposed to unionization, the more they were in favor of it. The president faced a difficult decision. It seemed the only possible way of winning was to remove the plant manager from direct involvement with the voting group either through reassignment or termination. The president decided to reassign the plant manager, then took control of the election himself, including direct presentations to the voting group. The company won by a margin of 92% to 8%.

This is not meant to imply that you have to offer up a sacrifice to voters to win. In fact, this is rarely the case. It is only meant to show that when employees examine the issue of unionization rationally, management stands a good chance of winning. If, however, one or more emotional issues prevent a rational decision, then your chances of victory are substantially reduced.

2. Inconsistent administration — Some employees seek union representation simply because their supervisor plays favorites among the employee group by allowing certain individuals to violate employee rules and regulations, while forcing others to strictly adhere to those same rules and regulations. This is an open invitation for those less favored employees to react emotionally and seek union representation.

3. Sudden changes in working conditions — Employees develop a comfortable pattern of performing their job and interacting with co-workers. Frequent, unexplained, or radical changes in the work environment or relationships can cause employees to seek a more stable atmosphere through union representation.

4. Job security — This has always been a union's bread and butter issue because it addresses a sincere concern of the voting group. Employees who live in fear of being unfairly disciplined, discharged, or laid off are excellent candidates to become emotional union supporters.

5. Other inflammatory factors — These may include inadequate wages and benefits; an employee's strong pro-union background or ignorance of unions; lack of trust; lack of participation; lack of recognition; an employee's personal or financial problems; menial, repetitious work; and job safety.

Incidentally, unions agree. In a report on successful organizing drives, unions reported, "Where wages are the primary union issue, the win rate is only 33%. Other issues are associated with a much higher rate of victory. The three most effective union issues are: Working conditions — Where working conditions are a top union issue, the win rate is 69%. Grievance procedure — Where the desire for a procedure to achieve fairness on the job is a top issue, the win rate is

67%. Dignity — Where dignity on the job is a key issue, unions have a win rate of 55%."

Keep in mind that the greater the percentage of voters who cast their ballots based on a rational decision, rather than emotions, the greater the chance of a management victory.

The First Election Advantage

In all NLRB representation elections conducted in a given year, management will win over 50% of the time. If only first elections are considered, that number approaches 60%. However, management loses approximately 80% of all second elections conducted within five years of a first election.

The reason for this tremendous difference in win rates is that employees really do feel unionization is a drastic step. Some voters, particularly those who are undecided, often fall into management's camp at the last minute based solely on their resistance to change. Some may feel the devil they know is better than the one they don't. Most decide to give their employer a chance to correct those problems identified during the campaign. Their rationale is that if things improve, great, if not, they can always support the union later.

In second elections, not only does this situation no longer exist, but there is often the feeling among voters that management simply doesn't care enough to make corrections, therefore, the union is the only opportunity for change.

Labor laws prevent management from making major changes or improvements in wages, hours, or working conditions during an NLRB representation election campaign. However, if employees believe management has received their message and meaningful change will occur after a management victory, the first election advantage is not an unreasonable expectation.

Discipline During the Campaign

It is illegal to discipline or discharge any individual because of their union activity during the campaign period. That does not, however, prevent management from disciplining or discharging individuals for legitimate reasons. When making disciplinary decisions, you must consider the consequences. For example, even if you discharge a strong union supporter for a valid reason, will the union make a martyr out of that individual and increase its support among voters? During the campaign period, disciplinary decisions must be made very carefully. You must not only weigh the facts you would normally consider in deciding to discipline or discharge, but also the political consequences.

During a campaign, it is imperative that management demonstrate consistency, fairness, and sensitivity. Disciplinary actions that are not in keeping with past practices or established policy, or that are perceived by the voters as capricious or arbitrary, could have a negative affect on the outcome of the election. Such actions could also be the basis for the union filing an unfair labor practice charge. It is equally important that management not soften its policies, procedures, or disciplinary standards during the campaign out of fear of possible union reaction. The risk is that voters may perceive the union as a powerful force that can significantly alter management's actions.

A few years ago, a client's campaign was in full swing when the company's most ardent supporter — a former union member — got involved in a shouting match with the key union supporter. At the time of the incident, management believed the projected vote tally was tied seven to seven. Unfortunately, management took no action to prevent further trouble. Push came to shove and there was a fist fight sending the union supporter to the hospital with broken bones and multiple contusions. Management was then faced with a tough disciplinary decision. Its choices were to issue verbal or written warnings to both employees; suspend one or both with or without pay; or dismiss one or both of them.

The critical question was how the remaining voters would view management's response. A verbal or written warning was simply inadequate. Suspension offered management a response that did not jeopardize the company's most vocal supporter, but was risky because of how others might react to such a mild disciplinary action. Dismissing both employees had the advantage of not affecting the vote tally and would hopefully be seen as a fair response. However, after reviewing statements from witnesses who were both company and union supporters, it seemed clear that the company supporter delivered the first blow. Management was convinced this was the employee who had to be dismissed. The affect on the vote tally seemed obvious: the union would move ahead by one vote.

As expected, the critical issue was the voting unit's perception of the disciplinary action. A majority of voters saw management's response as fair and appropriate and rejected the union by a one-vote margin.

Research Resources

Labor Relations Institute, Inc.
One LRI Plaza
Broken Arrow, OK
(800) 888-9115

Department of Labor
Bureau of Information — Disclosure
Washington, DC
(202) 219-7393

Bureau of National Affairs
BNA Plus
Washington, DC
(202) 452-4323

Information on Local Unions, District Councils, and Joint Boards may be available from the Field Office of the U.S. Department of Labor, Office of Labor-Management Standards in your area. Often, this is a faster source than the Department of Labor in Washington.

Exhibit 2-A

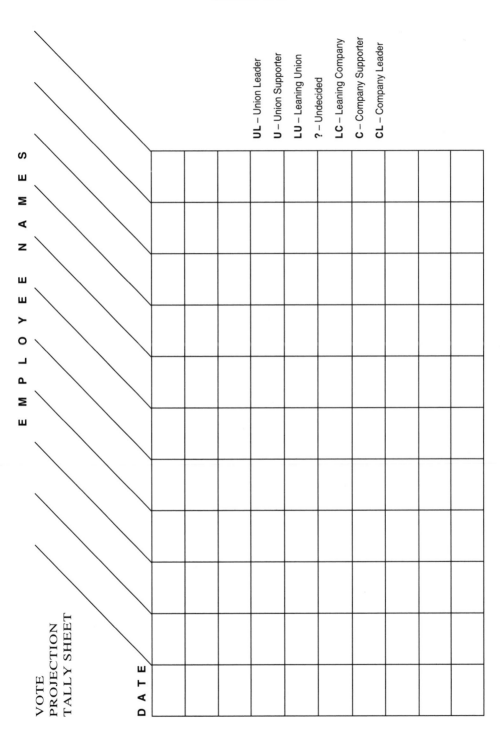

VOTE PROJECTION TALLY SHEET

EMPLOYEE NAMES

DATE

UL – Union Leader
U – Union Supporter
LU – Leaning Union
? – Undecided
LC – Leaning Company
C – Company Supporter
CL – Company Leader

Guidelines For
Supervisors & Managers
During A Union Organizing Effort

*"Never ascribe to malice
what can perfectly well be
explained by lack of direction."*

ANONYMOUS

In their day-to-day dealings with employees, both supervisors and managerial employees function as members of management. In that capacity, they have the duty and responsibility to implement management policies, interpret management plans, make decisions as they affect the employees who report to them, and accurately reflect the position of the employer. For these reasons, the attitudes, actions, and opinions expressed by supervisors and managerial employees regarding unionization and labor-management relations are of great importance.

The National Labor Relations Board and the courts have generally held that in these sensitive areas, supervisors and managerial employees are, in fact, management and that the employer will be held legally responsible for what they do and say. Supervisors and managerial employees can cause the employer to be found guilty of unfair labor practices if, in opposing unionization, they overstep the legal limitations, and equally if they engage in union organizing activities or render support to a union.

All members of management, both supervisors and managerial employees, need a thorough understanding of what they may and may not say, what they may and may not do, and how their statements and actions may be viewed by the NLRB.

Definitions of Supervisors & Managerial Employees

The term "supervisor" is defined in the National Labor Relations Act as follows: "Any individual having the authority, in the interest of the employer, to hire, transfer, suspend, lay off, recall, promote, discharge, assign, reward, or discipline other employees, or responsibility to direct them, or to adjust their grievances, or effectively to recommend such action, if in connection with the foregoing the exercise of such authority is not of a merely routine or clerical nature, but requires the use of independent judgment."

The term "managerial employee" is not defined in the Act, but two alternative tests have traditionally been applied by the NLRB in determining managerial status: 1) The employee is so closely related or aligned with management as to place the employee in a position of potential conflict of interest between the employer and his or her fellow workers. This test requires the employee be substantially involved in the employer's labor relations policy. 2) The employee formulates, determines, and effectuates the employer's policies or has discretion independent of the employer's established policy, in the performance of his or her duties.

The Employer's Position On Unions

Unionization is not solely a matter for unions and employees. Management has a proper and vital interest in any attempt to organize employees, and should feel a strong obligation to see that employees are aware of all the facts necessary to make a free, uncoerced decision.

Make your position on the issue of unionization very clear. Many employers would sum up their position along these lines: It is not in the best interest of either the employer or the employees to bring in a union to stand between them. Management and employees should continue to deal directly with each other, without the intervention of an outside third party. Employees do not need to pay union dues, fees, fines, and assessments to receive fair treatment. In short, the employer respects the employees' ability to act and speak for themselves.

Throughout the campaign, supervisors and managerial employees should not hesitate to communicate this position on unionization to employees.

General Standards of Conduct

Recently, I was managing a campaign for a company in Missouri. One morning, the personnel manager came to me with an envelope from the NLRB containing an unfair labor practice charge. The NLRB alleged that the personnel manager had conducted surveillance activities during a union meeting several days earlier at a motel next to a shopping center. He was accused of driving around the motel parking lot several times while attempting to determine the number of people at the meeting and, through identification of cars parked outside, the identity of those attending the meeting. I asked him if this was true and he admitted driving through the parking lot on the day in question, but said that he was only trying to find a parking space closer to the Wal-Mart store.

"OK," I said. "As proof, did you buy anything at Wal-Mart?"

"Yes," he replied.

"Did you get a receipt?" I asked.

"Yes."

"Great, what did you buy?"

"A pair of binoculars," he answered with a straight face. When I stopped laughing, I asked his suggestion for defending the unfair labor practice charge with those facts. He had none and neither did I. Fortunately, the Board only issued a cease and desist order and required that the order be posted for employees to read. We won the election.

Rules have been established by the NLRB for determining what actions by management are legal and illegal during a campaign. Though these rules are rather complicated, they can be summarized and easily remembered by thinking of the word TIPS. In the most general terms, the following actions by an employer would be ruled illegal:

T — THREATEN — You may not threaten an employee with any reduction of pay, benefits, or working conditions. You may not threaten an employee with the possible closing of the workplace or the loss of any other term or condition of employment as a result of supporting the union. You may not state that any employee or group of employees will suffer a reduction in pay, benefits, or position if the union wins.

I — INTERROGATE — You may not ask an employee about their views or activities in connection with unionization. In addition, you may not ask questions in an attempt to determine who is and who is not supporting the union.

P — PROMISE — You may not promise an employee any benefit for opposing the union.

S — SURVEILLANCE — You may not spy on union meetings or drive by a union meeting place to determine who or how many people are in attendance. Nor can you enlist any other person, including eligible voters, to do this on your behalf.

Other General Guidelines

In a campaign in Texas, I had worked closely with the supervisory and management group. During our meetings, I repeatedly advised them of their duties and responsibilities. I also encouraged them to be acutely aware of what was being done and said by their employees, particularly those who were supporting the union, for this would be an effective way to monitor the union's campaign and predict its future communications. With about three weeks until election day, we had done a reasonably good job and the campaign was progressing well. Then, on a Wednesday morning at our campaign headquarters, I received a call from a maintenance supervisor requesting an urgent meeting. He arrived shortly with another supervisor. For the next 15 minutes I sat flabbergasted as they laid out the entire balance of the union's campaign, including drafts of future handouts. Short of a total defection from a very high ranking member of the union's inner circle, I knew there is no way they could have acquired this information legally. I hesitated, but asked the question anyway.

"Where did you get all this?"

They told me I didn't want to know, which was right. However, the last thing a campaign director wants during the latter stages of a campaign is a major surprise, so I insisted. They told me that since the campaign had begun, the internal union leaders had been carrying around cardboard pocket folders that they left in their lockers overnight. The maintenance supervisor had seen one of the union leaders place his folder in his locker just before leaving the plant at the end of his shift the previous evening. Soon, the maintenance supervisor and the second supervisor devised what they thought was a brilliant plan. They would return to the plant around 2:00 AM, enter using the maintenance supervisor's pass key and access code, open the locker of the pro-union employee and find out what was in the folder. There they found the union's campaign calendar, the next three union handouts, drafts of the final two handouts, the schedule of union meetings for the remainder of the campaign, the union's list of supporters and possible converts, plus many other pieces of information. Copies of all this were made and the originals returned to the folder.

After a considerable amount of yelling and screaming about jeopardizing the campaign and the almost certain outcome of an unfair labor practice charge, I was able to convince the supervisors that the information, while interesting, provided nothing that should cause us to change our calendar. They had taken a huge risk, threatened the entire campaign, subjected the company to potential charges that would have cost tens of thousands of dollars to defend, and for what? Information that we did not use. And all of this after being told repeatedly of the necessity to conduct themselves within the restrictions imposed by the Act. Fortunately, the union never found out about the incident, no charges were filed, and we won the election. The only mystery during the balance of the campaign was why I kept calling these two supervisors Batman and Robin.

It is imperative that you consistently advise all supervisors and managers to conduct themselves within the confines of the Act. If they do not, you can be almost certain one or more of these individuals will say or do something damaging to your campaign. Other guidelines include:

1. Any decision made concerning an employee should not be influenced by his or her attitude or activities either for or against unionization. Such matters as promotions, work assignments, wage increases, discipline or discharge, and transfers must be decided strictly on merit.

2. To help employees make an informed choice, you should provide them with information about their employer and the union, as well as information about the processes and consequences of unionization. For example, you can explain your compensation, benefits, and other personnel policies, or correct union misstatements about these policies or actions.

3. You should accurately communicate to employees management's position on the matter of unionization.

4. You should continue to meet individually with employees in their work area to answer questions and to resolve problems and grievances according to past practice. However, you should not call individuals or small groups of employees into management offices for the specific purpose of discussing unionization. The Board has ruled that employees can construe this type meeting as being an "order" from management to vote against the union. This type meeting is not to be confused with a captive audience meeting that is not only legal, but is a fundamental part of management's campaign strategy. A prohibited meeting is one in which a manager calls a single employee or small group of employees into the manager's office and conducts a meeting the employees could interpret as an order to support management. The same information communicated to employees in their work area would be legal; it is the management office setting that causes the problem. Also, unlike the union, you cannot meet with employees in their homes.

5. The employer's supplies, equipment or services should not be made available to employees for the purpose of supporting or opposing the union.

The Most Frequent Violations

During a union representation election campaign, the most frequent management violations of the National Labor Relations Act usually center around these common statements and actions:

The statement or impression that collective bargaining "starts from scratch" — One of the keys to the outcome of a union representation election often involves the subject of collective bargaining. The union usually tells voters that their current levels of pay, benefits, and working conditions automatically become the starting point for negotiations and can only be negotiated up from there. Management frequently states that if the union wins, bargaining "starts from scratch." This implies that employees will definitely end up with reduced wages, fewer benefits, and less favorable working conditions. Neither statement is true. *Additionally, management statements that create the impression employees will automatically lose wages, suffer reduced benefits, or receive less favorable working conditions if the union wins will almost certainly be the subject of a successful unfair labor practice charge by the union.*

Collective bargaining negotiations begin with no fixed base or starting point. Many contracts negotiated in the United States result in improved wages and benefits for union members. But many others result in reduced wages and benefits. The outcome of the negotiation process is tied much more to the condition of the employer than to any other factor. Profitable employers typically agree to wage and benefit improvements during contract negotiations. Those that are less profitable, frequently negotiate wage and benefit reductions.

The key to winning the issue of collective bargaining is to make sure the voting group understands the process. Statements such as bargaining "starts from a blank sheet of paper" are permissible, but only if additional communications dispel any implication that wages, salaries, benefits, or other working conditions will be reduced if the union wins the election and collective bargaining begins. It must also be explained that any reductions will take place only as a result of normal collective bargaining negotiations.

The following definition of acceptable statements is taken from an NLRB decision. It is a helpful guide when preparing literature or discussion material for the voting group:

> "[S]tatements are objectionable when, in context, they effectively threaten employees with the loss of existing benefits and leave them with the impression that what they may ultimately receive depends in large measure upon what the Union can induce the employer to restore. On the other hand, such statements are not objectionable when additional communication to the employee dispels any implication that wages and/or benefits will be reduced during the course of bargaining and establishes that any reduction in wages or benefits will occur only as a result of the normal give and take of collective bargaining. The totality of all the circumstances must be viewed to determine the effect of the statements on the employees." (233 NLRB 155)

Following are four examples of permissible management statements made in previous campaigns:

1. "Unions often say that if they get in, employees would be guaranteed what they now receive. This is not the truth. The truth is, if the union should come in, all your present or future benefits are negotiable. Negotiations would start with a blank sheet of paper and each present wage and present benefit would be negotiated. Nothing is automatic. The NLRB and the courts have said you can lose wages and benefits in collective bargaining." (271 NLRB 1591)

2. "When you sit down to negotiate or to bargain, the contract you start with is a blank sheet of paper. There's nothing automatically on that paper. Everything that ends up in that contract is a result of negotiations. You may end up with what you started with, you may end up with less, you may end up with more. That's what negotiating is all about." (281 NLRB 54)

3. "Neither the company nor the union can predict what will be in the contract. Your wages and benefits could turn out to be higher, lower, or the same as they are now." (278 NLRB 85)

4. "These facts may seem harsh, but I think it's important that you know the truth about the collective bargaining process before you vote. Remember, bargaining means putting everything on the table, including the benefits you already have." (278 NLRB 85)

The key to winning the collective bargaining argument is to convince voters that collective bargaining is a two-way street, not a guarantee of wage or benefit improvements.

The statement or impression that strikes are an inevitable result of collective bargaining — The strike issue is one of an employer's strongest arguments against unionization. During most campaigns, the union attempts to convince employees that strikes are a rare occurrence and on those infrequent occasions when strikes happen, employees are well protected, receive adequate compensation from the union to prevent financial hardship, and gain enough improvements

---

through the strike action to make it worthwhile. Management tries to convince voters that strikes happen with relative frequency, are often beyond the control of the average employee, cause financial hardship, often turn violent, and can result in the loss of jobs though permanent replacements.

When dealing with the strike issue, management runs the risk of making predictions about what will happen should the union win the election. Showing the union's strike history, detailing strikes that have actually happened, documenting horror stories about how employees' lives have been adversely affected by strikes, all constitute legitimate management campaign tactics because they detail actual events. *Management can legally tell employees the cold, hard truth about what happens during union strikes. What management cannot do is make a prediction that the same thing will happen here.*

Discipline or discharge of active union supporters — Whenever an active union supporter receives any formal disciplinary action during the campaign period, particularly if that action is discharge, it is likely the union will file an unfair labor practice charge protesting the action. *It is perfectly legal to take disciplinary action, including discharge, against union supporters during the campaign period. It is not, however, legal to discipline or discharge individuals because of their support for the union.*

When making a decision concerning disciplinary action during the campaign, management must consider three separate but related factors. First, is the disciplinary action under consideration justified based on the facts and consistent with past practice? If so, the action is probably legal. Second, since management action in this case will almost certainly cause the filing of an unfair practice charge by the union, what will the effect of this charge be? If the charge will block the election at this time, is it in the best interest of your campaign? Finally, what will be the purely political effect of the action? Will management's decision cause the employee to become a martyr? Will it cause voters to feel insecure about their own jobs? Will it create an issue for the union that could distract voters from your message? All these factors must be considered when making disciplinary decisions.

What You Can & Cannot Do & Say

The following is a list of some of the things supervisors and managerial employees can do and say, followed by a list of some of the things they cannot do and say under the law. These examples are presented as guidelines for supervisors and managerial employees in their day-to-day dealings with employees. Remember, these guidelines cover particular situations in only a general way. They do not deal with every possible kind of permissible or impermissible conduct. If you are in doubt about a particular situation, or have questions concerning permissible conduct, do not hesitate to ask for advice. If employees ask questions and you are not sure of the proper response, tell them you will get the answers for them. Whenever you make a factual statement to employees, be sure your facts are accurate.

YOU CAN...

1. Tell employees that you or any other member of management are always willing to discuss any subject that is of interest to them, and they do not need to pay a union representative to speak on their behalf.

2. Tell employees that management prefers to deal with them personally and directly, rather than through an outside organization, a third party, or a stranger.

3. Tell employees that the union must be given the opportunity to be present whenever a grievance is settled, even if an employee wants to present their own grievance directly to the employer, and the settlement must be consistent with the union contract.

4. Tell employees about the wages and benefits they presently enjoy, and remind them these wages and benefits are provided voluntarily, without a union. (Avoid veiled promises of increased benefits or threats of loss of present or future benefits.)

5. Tell employees how their wages, benefits, and working conditions compare with those provided by comparable employers, whether unionized or not. (An excellent comparison would be with a union contract negotiated by the union seeking representation that shows lower wages and fewer benefits than you presently provide. Make sure you have all the facts and that your facts are accurate.)

6. Tell employees about the disadvantages that may result from belonging to the union, such as loss of income because of strikes, requirements to serve on a picket line and the expense of dues, fines, and assessments. If helpful, multiply the amount of monthly union dues by 12 to show employees how much per year they would pay, or multiply the annual dues each employee would pay by the number of employees to show how much money the union will make if it is voted in. (Avoid statements indicating there will be a strike or that employees will have to serve on a picket line; advise in terms of the usual disadvantages associated with belonging to unions in general.)

7. Tell employees that the law permits the hiring of a permanent replacement for anyone who engages in an economic strike.

8. Tell employees that, no matter what the union may promise, it cannot guarantee any changes in wages, benefits, or working conditions.

9. Tell employees that no union can make a company agree to anything it does not believe is right, or pay any more than it believes is fair. (Avoid any implication that management would not bargain in good faith or would arbitrarily refuse to consider a union's demands.)

10. Tell employees about any personal experience you may have had with unions.

11. Tell employees anything you may know about any union or its officers. (There are many published reports concerning union corruption. It is legal to show these to voters.)

12. Tell employees about any untrue or misleading statements or arguments made by a union organizer or by a union handbill or through any medium of union propaganda. You can always give employees the correct facts.

13. Tell employees your opinion about union policies and union leaders, even in derogatory terms.

14. Tell employees they are free to join or not to join any organization, without prejudice to their employment status.

15. Tell employees that signing a union authorization card or application for membership does not mean they must vote for the union if there is an election.

16. Tell employees about NLRB election procedures, the importance of voting, and the secrecy of the ballot.

17. Lay off, discipline, and discharge employees, so long as such action follows customary practice and is done without regard to union membership, activity, or sympathy.

18. Make job and work assignments, including assignments of overtime, so long as this is done without reference to the employee's participation or non-participation in union activities.

19. Enforce employee rules impartially and in accordance with customary action, irrespective of the employee's activity for or against the union.

20. Tell employees that you respect their right to do as they see fit, but you prefer not to have a union.

21. Tell employees that you hope they will not sign union authorization cards.

22. Tell employees if there is an election, you believe it is in their best interest to vote against the union.

23. Inform employees that unionization is usually a one-way trip. Once a union is voted in and gets exclusive bargaining rights, it is difficult for employees to have it decertified, even if they later decide they wish to be rid of it.

YOU CANNOT...

1. Promise or grant employees pay increases, promotions, improved working conditions, additional benefits, or special favors if they stay out of the union, do not sign an authorization card, or vote against the union.

2. Threaten employees with loss of jobs, reduction of income, or discontinuance of any privileges or benefits, or use any coercive or intimidating language to influence employees in the exercise of their rights to belong to or support a union (or to refrain from doing so).

3. Tell employees they would have received a wage increase or other benefits but for the start of the union campaign.

4. Threaten to or actually discharge, discipline, or lay off an employee because of activities on behalf of the union.

5. Threaten, through a third party, any of the above acts of interference.

6. Threaten to close down or to reduce operations if the union is voted in by employees.

7. Spy on union meetings. For example, attending a union organizing meeting or standing outside to watch employees entering or leaving would be improper.

8. Conduct yourself in a way which gives employees the impression that you are watching them to determine whether or not they are participating in union activities. For example, telling an employee that you understand they went to a union meeting would be improper.

9. Discriminate against employees who actively support the union by intentionally assigning them undesirable work.

10. Transfer employees because of their union activities or affiliation.

11. Engage in any activity that favors employees who oppose the union over employees who support the union.

12. Discipline employees who are supporting the union for an infraction that other employees are permitted to commit without being disciplined.

13. Make any work assignment for the purpose of causing an employee who has been active on behalf of the union to quit his or her job.

14. Take any action that is intended to impair the status of, or adversely affect, an employee's job or pay because of his or her activities on behalf of the union.

15. Intentionally assign work or transfer employees for the purpose of separating those you believe are interested in unionization from those who you believe are not interested in supporting the union.

16. Select employees to be laid off with the intention of curbing the union's strength or discouraging support for the union.

17. Ask employees about their personal opinions or the feelings of other employees concerning the union.

18. Ask employees whether they are for or against the union or how they intend to vote in the NLRB election.

19. Ask employees at time of employment, or thereafter, whether they belong to a union or have signed a union application or authorization card.

20. Ask employees about union activities, such as union meetings, the identity of union supporters, or the progress of a union organizing campaign. (Employees may, of their own accord, tell you of such matters. It is not an unfair labor practice to listen, but you must not ask questions to obtain additional information.)

21. Make the statement that management will not deal with the union or will only go through the motions of bargaining with the union.

22. Make the statement that present benefits will be reduced or taken away if the union is voted in.

23. Make the statement that employees will be discharged or disciplined if they are active on behalf of the union.

24. Urge employees to persuade others to oppose the union.

25. Give financial support or assistance to the union or its representatives.

26. Visit the homes of employees for the purpose of urging them to support or reject the union.

27. Call employees, individually or in small groups, into management offices or similar locations away from their normal work areas for private discussions concerning union matters. (It is not an unfair labor practice to hold large group meetings.)

28. Hold meetings with employees for the purpose of soliciting grievances and complaints, unless there has been a past practice of holding meetings for this purpose.

29. Sponsor or suggest a petition, or other written expression by employees, against the union, or encourage or take part in its circulation after being started by employees.

30. Solicit employees to request the return of union authorization cards they have signed. However, if employees ask whether they can get their cards back, you can advise them that if this is their desire, they should contact the person who solicited their signature.

Legal vs. Strategic Decisions

Throughout your campaign, you will be called on to make important decisions that can influence the election's outcome. First, you obviously do not want to do anything that's illegal under the National Labor Relations Act. Next, you need to consider not only the legal consequences of your decisions, but their strategic consequences as well. A decision or action that may be perfectly legal, could be disastrous from the standpoint of election strategy. For example, a strong union supporter violates an employee rule. You determine that disciplinary action, including discharge, is legal under the Act. Other forms of discipline, such as a written warning or suspension, are also legal and in keeping with past practices. Though you may terminate this individual, thereby getting rid of not only a union vote but someone who may influence others, should you automatically take this action? No.

You must consider all the possible ramifications. Would the union be able to effectively turn this person into a martyr or use them as an example of harsh, unfair, or inconsistent action? Could this incident be used to swing undecided voters to the union's side? If the answer to these questions is yes, you will probably want to consider an action that will not inflame voters during this sensitive period. On the other hand, you must not appear afraid to act because of the union's presence. These types of decisions require careful consideration. Sometimes, you may think you need the wisdom of Solomon; however, with all the information before you, you will likely make the right choice. Remember, just because something is legal does not automatically mean it is correct.

Can You Say It?

One of the more complex problems that faces supervision and management during a campaign is the question of what can be properly said to voters on the issue of unionization. The NLRB contends it tries to balance two highly valued rights: your freedom of speech and the freedom of employees to form, join, or assist a labor organization, or to refrain from doing so, without coercion or interference. This problem must be considered whenever a member of administration or supervision communicates with employees, either in writing or verbally, regarding the disadvantages of unionization.

We have just discussed many of the things management can and cannot say. Now, read each of the following statements and decide whether the statement is proper and legal. Indicate your answer by circling whether you think the statement is legal or illegal.

1. The election will be by secret ballot and no one will know how anyone votes.
   Legal   Illegal

2. Just because some of our employees signed union authorization cards does not mean they have to vote for the union.
   Legal   Illegal

3. Management will not permit a union here.
   Legal   Illegal

4. Under a union contract, your benefits may not necessarily continue as they are now. You could get more, you could get less, or you could continue to get exactly what you have now.
   Legal   Illegal

5. Let's take a look at this union's strike history over the last two years and see how many members have gone out on strike and how much time they have missed because of these strikes.
   Legal   Illegal

6. When you go into the voting booth, I want you to mark your ballot the same way I have marked this sample ballot.
   Legal   Illegal

7. No union — this one or any other — can get more than management is able to give.
   Legal   Illegal

8. The polls open at 8:00 AM tomorrow. I am going to assemble all the employees in my department just before they go home at 5:00 PM and give this union a parting shot.
   Legal   Illegal

9. The union talks about job security, but it cannot create or maintain jobs.
   Legal   Illegal

10. Our employees have better benefits than employees at XYZ Company, and those employees are represented by this same union.

                Legal   Illegal

11. The election will be decided by a majority of the employees who vote, not by a majority of those eligible to vote.

                Legal   Illegal

12. Anyone who signs a union card could lose their job.

                Legal   Illegal

13. Listen Gwen, if you make sure the union doesn't win this election, I will see to it you're made chairperson of the employee committee we plan to form after the union is defeated.

                Legal   Illegal

14. Linda, come into my office. I want to talk to you about this election.

                Legal   Illegal

15. Bill, I understand some employees signed union cards at a meeting last night. I want to talk to you about the signing of those cards.

                Legal   Illegal

16. This union has done a lousy job for the people it already represents.

                Legal   Illegal

17. My objective is to get you as much information about this union as possible.

                Legal   Illegal

18. Our employees haven't had a pay increase in over two years. I was thinking about giving them one anyway, so if I give it now it should help us win the election.

                Legal   Illegal

19. Personally, I think this union stinks.

                Legal   Illegal

20. I don't care what the union has told you. The law only says we must bargain in good faith, it does not say we must agree to any of the union's demands.

        Legal   Illegal

21. Did Scott go to the union meeting last night?

        Legal   Illegal

22. Tell the union to put its promises in writing with an accompanying guarantee that it will get you all the things you've been promised.

        Legal   Illegal

23. Karen, if the union gets in here there will be no more overtime.

        Legal   Illegal

24. The union isn't really interested in your welfare. It just wants your money.

        Legal   Illegal

25. If the union calls you out on economic strike, management can hire permanent replacements to fill your jobs.

        Legal   Illegal

26. If the union wins this election, I'm sure there will be a strike.

        Legal   Illegal

27. If the union calls you out on economic strike, you will receive no pay or benefits.

        Legal   Illegal

ANSWERS:

1. The election will be by secret ballot and no one will know how anyone voted.

        Legal   Illegal

It is perfectly acceptable conduct to explain the election process to the voting group, including the fact that all ballots are secret and contain no method of identification. The only exception to this is if the ballot is challenged.

2. Just because some of our employees signed union authorization cards does not mean they have to vote for the union.

Legal   Illegal

Once a union has petitioned for an election, a signed authorization card has little meaning. All eligible voters should examine the positions of both parties, then make an informed decision based on the facts. On election day, employees can secretly vote their choice, whether or not they signed a card.

3. Management will not permit a union here.

Legal   **Illegal**

A statement like this is considered a threat. If the union wins the election, the employer must meet with the union at reasonable times and reasonable places in a good faith effort to negotiate a contract. The statement that the employer will not permit a union implies that management would not meet these obligations, and is therefore illegal

4. Under a union contract, your benefits may not necessarily continue as they are now. You could get more, you could get less, or you could continue to get exactly what you have now.

Legal   Illegal

This statement is true and legal. Collective bargaining does not start at a base of current wages, benefits, and working conditions. Everything is subject to negotiations, including present levels of pay and benefits.

5. Let's take a look at this union's strike history over the last two years and see how many members have gone out on strike and how much time they have missed because of these strikes.

Legal   Illegal

It is perfectly acceptable conduct to point out the disadvantages of union membership to the voting group. The union's strike history is one of these disadvantages and it may legally be shown to employees.

6. When you go into the voting booth, I want you to mark your ballot the same way I have marked this sample ballot.

Legal   ***Illegal***

You cannot order a person to vote against the union. This statement could be construed as a direct order. When asking for a person's vote, you should do just that, ask.

7. No union — this one or any other — can get more than management is able to give.

Legal   Illegal

No matter what a union may say or imply, management is always free to reject any union demand.

8. The polls open at 8:00 AM tomorrow. I am going to assemble all the employees in my department just before they go home at 5:00 PM and give this union a parting shot.

Legal   ***Illegal***

The 24-hour period immediately before the polls open is considered an insulated period. Holding group meetings during this period is illegal.

9. The union talks about job security, but it cannot create or maintain jobs.

Legal   Illegal

Obviously, unions don't help an employer get additional business and therefore do not contribute to an employer's growth or stability.

10. Our employees have better benefits than employees at XYZ Company, and those employees are represented by this same union.

Legal   Illegal

Any comparisons you can make with other labor agreements negotiated by this union are perfectly acceptable campaign tactics.

11. The election will be decided by a majority of the employees who vote, not by a majority of those eligible to vote.

    Legal   Illegal

Not only is this statement true, the point should definitely be stressed to the voting group.

12. Anyone who signs a union card could lose their job.

    Legal   ***Illegal***

Obviously a threat.

13. Listen Gwen, if you make sure the union doesn't win this election, I will see to it you're made chairperson of the employee committee we plan to form after the union is defeated.

    Legal   ***Illegal***

Obviously a promise.

14. Linda, come into my office. I want to talk to you about this election.

    Legal   ***Illegal***

Borderline perhaps, but calling an individual into your private office to encourage them to vote against the union is generally not a good idea. The Board could rule that the employee might consider such encouragement to be an order.

15. Bill, I understand some employees signed union cards at a meeting last night. I want to talk to you about the signing of those cards.

    Legal   ***Illegal***

Obviously interrogation.

16. This union has done a lousy job for the people it already represents.

    Legal   Illegal

Derogatory remarks about the union are not illegal, as long as they do not violate any other standard. Perhaps this statement would be better if prefaced by "In my opinion."

17. My objective is to get you as much information about this union as possible.

   Legal   Illegal

   The more information, the better.

18. Our employees haven't had a pay increase in over two years. I was thinking about giving them one anyway, so if I give it now it should help us win the election.

   Legal   **Illegal**

   Improving wages, benefits, or working conditions during a campaign to influence votes is illegal; however, if you have a history of giving a 4% increase every March 1 and that date falls within the campaign period, granting such an increase is generally permissible.

19. Personally, I think this union stinks.

   Legal   Illegal

   No problem. Not a threat or a promise.

20. I don't care what the union has told you. The law only says we must bargain in good faith, it does not say we must agree to any of the union's demands.

   Legal   Illegal

   Absolutely true and perfectly legal.

21. Did Scott go to the union meeting last night?

   Legal   **Illegal**

   Not permissible; this is interrogation.

22. Tell the union to put its promises in writing with an accompanying guarantee that it will get you all the things you've been promised.

   Legal   Illegal

   Perfectly legal and often an excellent campaign tactic. Consider giving your employees warranty coupons and asking them to have the union guarantee certain levels of improved wages or benefits.

23. Karen, if the union gets in here there will be no more overtime.

           Legal   ***Illegal***

This is a threat.

24. The union isn't really interested in your welfare. It just wants your money.

           Legal   Illegal

Not a threat or a promise.

25. If the union calls you out on economic strike, management can hire permanent replacements to fill your jobs.

           Legal   Illegal

This is the law and therefore a legal statement.

26. If the union wins this election, I'm sure there will be a strike.

           Legal   ***Illegal***

No one can predict the outcome of negotiations, so no one can accurately predict a strike. This is also a threat. You can, however, show the union's strike history and let voters draw their own conclusions.

27. If the union calls you out on economic strike, you will receive no pay or benefits.

           Legal   Illegal

A statement of fact and therefore legal.

How Unions Organize Employees

Law of the Lie: "No matter how often a lie is shown to be false, there will remain a percentage of people who believe it true. And the great masses of people will more easily fall victims to a big lie than to a small one."

ADOLF HITLER

During a campaign, management often asks, "Why did the union do that?" or "What is the union going to do next?" There are no pat answers. Each union organizer will run a campaign based on their own successful experience and any training they may have received from the international union, as well as their own individual personality. For example, some organizers are effective public speakers and may hold many large group meetings. Other organizers may be more persuasive on a one-on-one basis and prefer extensive use of home visits. Still others may have excellent writing skills and prefer to conduct a majority of their campaign through handbills and home mailings. While it may not be possible to predict exactly how a particular organizer will conduct a specific campaign, almost every campaign contains similar elements. Knowing what unions do in certain situations can prove helpful for your campaign manager.

As discussed in Chapter 2 under the topic of Campaign Research, it is possible, through LRI Online, to determine if the union organizer has conducted other organizing campaigns in the area and, if so, the type of organizer this person is, including organizing methods and samples of previous literature. This information, combined with knowledge of standard union organizing techniques, should prepare you to anticipate and counter any union issue.

Occasionally, unions will publish handbooks for their organizers. These books review what the union considers to be its most effective organizing techniques. Their purpose is to serve as training manuals for the union's field staff organizers. While general in nature, these publications can help you anticipate union actions.

The type of organizing campaigns conducted by unions in the past may not be an accurate indicator of how they will conduct campaigns in the future. In December 1996, the AFL-CIO increased its 1997 organizing budget by 50%, from $20,000,000 to $30,000,000. In addition, the AFL-CIO is pushing its affiliated unions to increase their individual organizing budgets. Some of this additional money will be spent on future organizer training.

Following is a summary of several union publications devoted to organizing techniques, as well as some of the personal experiences of LRI consultants. This information may or may not be applicable to your particular campaign. A careful study of this section will give you a better understanding of the organizing process from the union's perspective.

Background

Until recently, union organizing wasn't a full-time job. In most cases, the organizer was a local representative of an international union and was responsible for activities that included negotiating labor agreements with employers, handling grievances and arbitrations for union members, conducting local union meetings, and representing the union at local and regional functions. Organizing was, at best, a part-time activity that the organizer usually didn't like to do, wasn't very good at, or both. Since organizing was such a small part of the local union representative's job, pay increases or promotional opportunities were almost totally unrelated to successful organizing.

This lack of emphasis on organizing became evident. Union membership rapidly declined as a percentage of the workforce, and during the last decade there has been a dramatic reduction in the number of representation elections. Unions now lose more of these elections than ever. But for several years, some labor leaders have spoken of the need for increased emphasis on organizing. Now it appears unions may have heard the wake-up call. Action, rather than rhetoric, is suddenly the order of the day. Unions are hiring professional organizers and embarking on extensive training programs for their field representatives. Organizing success is considered when determining pay increases and promotions. New strategies and techniques are being developed for organizing today's more diverse workforce. More sophisticated and persuasive campaign literature is being produced. Though some of the "old school" union representatives are still around, organizing has become a top priority. Today, when a union organizing campaign begins, it is likely the shots are being called by a trained professional using the latest organizing strategy.

Of the many phases of union work, the art and science of organizing is perhaps the most creative. While success in other areas of union activity depends on group coordination and detailed planning, organizing also depends upon the individual personality and initiative of the organizer. Organizing is creative in that it draws together people of various interests, aspirations, and social backgrounds and directs them toward a common effort: an election victory and a union contract.

Good organizers are really psychologists. The organizer's field is human relations. The employees the union attempts to organize are the raw materials, who are then refined through the group's effort to organize a union.

There is nothing static about organizing. It is an ongoing and constantly improving process. It means more than just getting a non-union worker to place their signature on a union authorization card. The act of signing the card is merely an indication the prospective union member is interested and prepared to keep an open mind. If maximum support is to be achieved on election day, a good union organizer must keep the core group of supporters motivated throughout the campaign, while constantly expanding the group to include additional voters.

The Preparation Phase

Contrary to popular belief, most union campaigns begin when a dissatisfied employee or group of employees contact a local union representative. While some organizations are union targets simply because of their size, location, or some other factor, most employers become the subject of an organizing effort because one or more employees volunteer to help the union. Also, unions do not target only large employers. In fact, unions now specialize in small employers. During 1996, the median size of employers petitioned by unions seeking representation was 24 employees. This means that half of the 3,046 representation petitions filed in 1996 were in units of 24 or fewer voters!

Once an organizer has been contacted by one or more employees, the preliminary organizing work begins. This work is divided into two parts. The first is the relatively routine task of learning as much as possible about the employer. Most of this information comes from the international union's research department, but some information may come from local sources, such as the public library or local newspaper. The organizer must also conduct a survey of the target employer. Every survey is based on the assumption that a campaign will be waged. Since an organizing campaign is in many ways like a battle, the organizer will assemble as many facts as possible before determining tactics. Background information is vital to a good organizer; unless there is a clear understanding of an employer's operations, the make-up of the workforce, and a thorough knowledge of wages, benefits, and working conditions, an intelligent appraisal of the organizing target is impossible.

The organizer will set up a file containing all pertinent information about an employer. With this, the organizer is in a better position to plan the campaign and to determine the techniques and tools to be used. This file will be kept open and continuously updated.

If the union representative conducting the campaign is a resident of the area and is conducting the campaign as a part of his or her regular duties, it is a relatively easy task to keep this work absolutely secret. However, if the campaign is conducted by an organizing specialist from the union's headquarters, and especially if the target employer is in a small community, remaining unknown may be much more difficult. Since secrecy is of the utmost importance, the organizer may use an assumed name or identity. It is highly unlikely that an out-of-town professional organizer will check into a motel in a small town and register as an employee of a union.

The first, and perhaps easiest, part of a survey deals with physical location. A few hours spent observing the targeted facility and talking with area service people, delivery people, or convenience store employees will usually reveal. . .

- Number and location of entrances and parking lots used by employees
- Starting times and quitting times for different shifts and types of employees
- Approximate number of employees per shift and their breakdown by sex, age, and race
- Eating and drinking establishments where employees gather
- Frequently-voiced employee complaints

A visit to the local library can provide information about the employer's operations. Libraries may also have special publications printed by the employer's public relations department. Back issues or clipping files from local newspapers can give the enterprising organizer additional information.

The next step in a survey usually involves contacting any other labor representatives in the community. These local union leaders can provide important background information on the community and the organizing target, including:

- Community reaction to organized labor
- The names of sympathetic public, civic, fraternal, veteran, and church leaders
- The local media's position regarding union representation
- The degree the targeted employer participates in community activities and the names of management officials who are considered community leaders
- The targeted employer's labor history
- A general idea of the targeted employer's wage rates and working conditions
- The names of employees who are active in the community through their church, civic leadership, sports, programs for children, fraternal organizations, and politics
- The names of employees who formerly belonged to unions in the area or are known to desire union representation
- The meeting dates of local unions and councils in the area
- Extent of the targeted employer's paternalism, such as softball or bowling teams, employee day care centers, etc.

The initial survey is now complete. The organizer has gathered vital information for the campaign, while remaining completely quiet. No employees have been approached except for the original contacts. The organizer has made promises to no one, and no overt campaign has been launched. While the survey is being conducted, the organizer will continue to learn as much as possible about the targeted organization from the initial contacts. Information received from these contacts, along with the survey data, will be instrumental in making a go or no-go decision.

The first and most important point the organizer will stress to the initial contacts is the necessity for secrecy. From now until the petition stage, the union will want to gain as much of a head start as possible. The longer the organizer can develop strategy and implement the early phases of the campaign without management opposition, the greater the likelihood of success.

If, after a discussion with the original employee contacts and a review of the survey information, the union representative believes a reasonable possibility exists for a successful campaign, the international union will be contacted and a possible campaign discussed. The initial amount and nature of assistance from the international will be determined at this time. If the unit size is large or the target considered important, one or more professional organizers may be assigned to the campaign. If not, the level of off-site international support will be determined. This could vary from minimum support, such as the preparation of literature, to additional personnel during the critical later stages of the campaign. Once authorization has been given by the international, the campaign begins.

The union's campaign can be divided into two segments: the preparation phase and the action phase. The preparation phase consists primarily of developing a complete list of the names and addresses of individuals in the proposed voting group and recruiting and training a group of employees who will act as internal organizers during the action phase. The voting group list is essential if the union plans to make home visitations, which are usually critical for success. This list can be extremely difficult to obtain or it can be fairly simple. The degree of difficulty depends almost exclusively on the management of the target facility. If a list of employee names and addresses is routinely published, or if the security of that list is less than adequate, it may be relatively easy for the union to obtain a copy. If this happens, weeks or even months of tedious, time consuming work for the union has suddenly been eliminated. If, however, this list is not available, the union must begin the process of developing such a list. During this period, many union organizing attempts flounder and eventually fail. People who first contacted the union begin to lose interest or become discouraged because of the lack of progress or because the organizer is not as readily available as the union supporters would like. If the union can obtain an employer document that provides employee names and addresses, this difficult part of the campaign is eliminated and the early union supporters will likely remain motivated and eager to proceed.

Assuming that a ready-made list is not available, the union organizer must begin the task of developing such a list. To obtain the names and addresses of the potential voting group, the union will need to build a committee of employee union supporters. The union organizer must carefully weigh how fast to expand the employee committee against the possibility that the greater the number of employees involved, the greater the chance of a leak. Most experienced organizers begin with the employee or employees who made the initial contact with the union and limit the first meeting to this person or group. The organizer will obtain as much information as possible from these individuals and will determine how much the committee needs to be expanded to acquire more information. Once the decision is made to expand the committee, the organizer must rely almost totally on the judgment of the initial contacts. The organizer will ask these individuals to recruit a small number of people, hopefully from different departments or areas of the facility, to widen the scope of the committee.

The most critical factor at this stage is still the need for confidentiality. The organizer will stress the recruitment of only those people who the initial contacts believe will strongly support the union and keep the activity secret. Any leaks to management that result in knowledge of the organizing campaign will almost certainly bring on a management response. At the least, such a response will be damaging to the union and perhaps fatal.

During the next several weeks of the preparation process, the employee committee normally meets once each week. To keep people interested and motivated, the organizer will try to make the meetings seem as much a social gathering as an organizing committee. These are the "dog days" of the campaign; some union supporters may think nothing is happening or that little progress is being made. But the successful organizer knows that as the committee expands and names are added to the list, the chances of a successful campaign increase. The organizer also knows that as acquaintances grow and trust develops, these individuals will be difficult for management to turn once the electioneering begins and voters are exposed to the disadvantages of union membership. Often the committee wants to move faster than is prudent. That is why the social nature of the group is important. It allows the organizer to train and educate the committee in an informal and relaxed environment, while keeping supporters from becoming too impatient.

Ideally, the organizer will grow the committee steadily, gaining representation from each department or division and from every ethnic group in the organization. The goal is for the composition of the committee to reflect the composition of the targeted employer. The eventual size of the committee will depend on the size of the target; it will be at least 10% to 20% of the voting group.

A recent AFL-CIO report underscored the importance of an effective committee. According to this report, "the most significant factor leading to union success...is active campaigning by an effective, representative committee (of employees). In the absence of an effective committee, the win rate is only 10%. Where the organizing committee does engage in active campaigning, the win rate is 62%. When the committee consists of 15% of the unit or more, the win rate is 61%. A committee of less than 5% of the unit correlates to a win rate of only 27%."

During this stage, the organizer faces the danger that the longer it takes to grow the committee and the more people who become involved, the more difficult it becomes to keep the process secret. The need for more information must be weighed against the possibility management will learn about the union's intentions. The organizer will constantly stress to the committee that campaigning must not start until the union is ready.

Since the primary purpose of this phase of the campaign is to develop a complete list of the names and addresses of individuals in the voting group, the organizer must decide when that goal has been reached. At this stage, the union will almost never obtain the names and addresses of 100% of the voting group, so the organizer must begin the next phase of the campaign. Most organizers feel if they can obtain the names and addresses of 60% of the voting group, this part of the campaign has been successful.

After the initial series of meetings which, besides list-building, are designed to increase the size and commitment of the in-house committee, the organizer begins to explain procedures that can be used to obtain recognition for the union, as well as the problems that might arise under each of these procedures. The employee leaders will be informed of the possibility of long NLRB delays and adverse decisions based on technicalities. The more the employee leaders understand about the union and the obstacles it will face during an organizing campaign, the better they will withstand future employer attacks on the union.

As these leadership meetings progress, the organizer will learn more details about specific working conditions. By this time, the organizer should know. . .

- Job classifications and wage rates, and how they compare with similar unionized employers
- The target employer's method of handling employee grievances
- Premium pay rates, pension benefits, and insurance coverage
- All other fringe benefits
- Any violations of state or federal laws regarding minimum wages, overtime, health and safety regulations, etc.
- Specific actions by management, including supervisors, that create hardships for individual employees or are considered unfair

By holding leadership meetings throughout this stage, the union organizer builds an organizing committee able to function as a team. This period is intended to add leadership to the committee so that it will parallel management's structure as closely as possible. By developing leaders in each department and shift, the union can quickly counter management's efforts to present the disadvantages of union membership to voters.

Employee leaders learn to articulate the benefits unions proclaim. They also come to understand the risks they will have to take. They gain an understanding of how the union's ideas are translated into action for the solution of particular problems. When this stage is reached, the organizer and the organizing committee are ready to begin a full-scale campaign.

Recently, a new union strategy has developed regarding the indiscriminate filing of petitions that are subsequently withdrawn before an election. When a union files a petition for election, the law requires management to furnish the union with a complete list of the names and addresses of all eligible voters (Excelsior list). It is very possible the union has only secured minimum support and filed a petition in order to obtain the Excelsior list. When this has been achieved, the petition is withdrawn and the union uses the statutory six month waiting period to prepare for the real campaign, now with the Excelsior list in hand. This tactic allows the union to obtain names and addresses of everyone in the voting group without the time consuming process normally required. The disadvantage is that management is alerted to the union's presence. If the union adopts this tactic, it is counting on management to halt all union prevention efforts based on the false assumption that the union did not have sufficient support and has abandoned the campaign.

When the organizer decides that acquiring the list of voter names and addresses has proceeded to the point where additional activity is not worth the chance of management detection, the official campaign begins. This may be done with great fanfare or to the other extreme with almost no outward display. It depends on the personality of the organizer and the nature of the campaign to date.

During the development of the names and addresses of potential voters, the organizer will also have made some basic decisions concerning the direction and implementation of the campaign. The most important is the selection of leadership and issues. Virtually every union organizing victory requires sincere, dedicated leadership that can carry the campaign successfully into the workplace. Since unions rarely attempt to invent issues, the organizer will determine the most effective existing issues and how to best develop them as the campaign progresses.

Selection of Leadership — The selection of the union leadership team is done with two basic objectives in mind. First, the leaders should be reasonably well respected members of the voting group. Articulate and respected leaders are vital to a campaign since it is assumed management will conduct its own aggressive counter campaign to discredit the union. While most people who initially support the union will be unhappy with their employer or with their particular job situation, the organizer must be sure the leadership does not consist exclusively of people who are widely known as chronic complainers or are viewed by the voting group as motivated solely by a desire for revenge. If the leaders selected are viewed by the voting group in an unfavorable light, voters may not listen to the union's story because of the image these leaders project. Second, the leaders should represent a good cross section of the voting group. In an ideal campaign, the union will have leaders for every subsection of the voting group: women for the female workers, men for the male workers, leaders within minority racial and national groupings, individuals for each department and shift, etc.

Selection of Issues — Unions do not invent issues; they exploit issues that already exist. During the preparation stage of the campaign, when the union is developing the voter list, the organizer will discuss with union supporters the basic issues that caused their initial interest in unionization, as well as other issues that might be exploited. As these issues are compiled, the organizer attempts to show voters that the union has been successful in helping other employees solve similar problems. For example, if one of the issues in the campaign is expected to be the employer's unfair discipline or termination of employees, the organizer may select a union contract with a relatively elaborate grievance and arbitration procedure to demonstrate how the union has been able to correct this "injustice." If the issue is wages and benefits, copies of labor agreements can be used that show higher rates of pay or better benefits for unionized employees doing similar work. It is rare that management is totally unaware of union activity at this stage of an organizing drive. However, many employers ignore the early signs of union activity and give the union a head start.

The Letter — The official kickoff of a union organizing drive usually happens in one or some combination of three ways. Frequently, the campaign will be launched when the union sends management a letter that announces an organizing drive has begun. This letter may also include the names of those employees who have already become members of the organizing committee and may even include the names of everyone who has signed authorization cards. The purpose of this letter is to put management on notice that the rules and regulations established by the NLRB are in effect. This prevents management from taking certain actions that, though normally fine, are prohibited during a campaign, such as granting a wage increase or terminating a union supporter with less than just cause. A second purpose of the letter is to gain some degree of protection for those employees identified in the letter as union supporters.

The Handbill — The union may elect to handbill the targeted employer. Handbilling means the union representative, assisted by members of the internal organizing committee, stand outside the target facility and distribute a piece of campaign literature to everyone entering or leaving. This handbill announces that a campaign has begun and usually lists one or more issues of concern to the employee group. It may include the names of those on the organizing committee and say something about the specific union. An authorization card is usually enclosed. During the work day, members of the organizing committee talk to their fellow employees about the benefits of unionization and encourage them to sign an authorization card.

The Blitz — In a dramatic effort to improve their poor win rate in NLRB representation elections, unions are trying the blitz organizing approach. Although this does not employ any revolutionary new organizing techniques, it does offer a blueprint for what unions always do during campaigns, but doing it faster. The blitz organizing manual contains this revealing statement: "In analyzing the reasons for winning or losing an election, generally we can track the outcome back to the early days of the campaign. Although organizers sometimes claim 'we lost the election in the last two days,' this is rarely the case. Since we know the company will unleash major issues in the last days or weeks of the campaign — strikes, plant closings, etc. — it is incumbent upon the organizers to build a foundation that will withstand this inevitable assault. This means building a strong committee, made of a representative group of key leaders, who can prepare their co-workers for the management campaign."

Blitz campaigns are divided into two phases: a preparation phase and an action phase. During the preparation phase, the union's emphasis is on list building and the recruitment of volunteer organizers. Though this phase may take several weeks or even months, the key to its success is absolute secrecy. Should management become aware of any union activity during this phase, the blitz program will probably not be successful. During this time, the union uses a small but constantly growing committee to compile the necessary list of employee names and addresses.

Once this list is as complete as possible, the union enters the action phase. The first step in this phase is to train as many people as necessary to make house calls on all eligible voters within a two- or three-day period. Because the internal committee will probably not be large enough to accomplish this alone, the union often uses paid "volunteers." These will usually be union members from other unionized facilities in the area, or union staff representatives.

During a typical blitz week, the union spends Monday and Tuesday training these volunteers and planning house call assignments. House calls are made on Wednesday, Thursday, and Friday. The goal is to speak with at least 60% of the workforce and to obtain signed authorization cards. On the following Monday, a petition for election would be filed with the NLRB. If a blitz campaign has been properly run, management is not be aware of any union activity until the house calls begin on Wednesday.

According to information made public by various unions, when the blitz organizing technique is used, the union win rate in NLRB elections has increased from 45% to better than 65%. Though the blitz isn't appropriate for every campaign — and unions know that — these kinds of results mean more future organizing campaigns will be based on this technique.

After the organizer has selected what he or she believes is the best way to launch the campaign, the employee organizing committee is trained concerning what they can and cannot do and say. The official campaign then begins.

The official start of the union's election campaign is the end of the preparation phase and the beginning of the action phase. During the action phase of the campaign, the techniques and strategy employed are in many cases exactly the opposite of those employed during the preparation phase. The hallmark of the preparation phase is absolute secrecy; during the action phase, the union's goal is to gain as much visibility and publicity as possible.

The action phase will begin with either the filing of a petition for election or an intensified effort to obtain additional signed authorization cards just before the petition is filed.

Every organizer knows there are several keys to a union victory: active and growing participation in open union meetings, effective campaign literature, and enthusiastic employee committees. As important as these things are, the organizer also knows the election will normally be won or lost in the workplace. If elections were held on the day the petition was filed, unions would win virtually every NLRB representation election conducted since a petition is almost never filed with less than 60% support. Union organizers know in virtually every election where the employer wages a serious campaign to convince the voting group to reject unionization, the union's support inevitably shrinks between the time the petition is filed and election day. According to a recent AFL-CIO report, in elections where the employer does not wage a campaign against the union, union win rates exceed 80%. In those elections where the employer wages a moderately serious campaign, the union win rate falls to just over 60%. When the employer mounts an intense traditional campaign, the union win rate falls to 35%. And when management uses the LRI Campaign Program, a union's rate of success plummets to only 10%. So by having a trained internal committee to help counter management's campaign in the workplace, a union dramatically increases its chances of winning.

A smart organizer will plan their campaign around those elements or options that he or she believes will be most effective in a particular situation. What worked well in one campaign may not be successful in another. This is a judgment only the organizer can make. Therefore, careful planning based on input from the employee committee will be extremely important to the outcome of the election.

Effective Organizing Committee — The most significant factor contributing to union organizing success is active and aggressive campaigning by an effective, representative committee of employees. When an internal organizing committee engages in active campaigning, the win rate is 62%. When the committee consists of 15% of the unit or more, the win rate is 61%. When the committee consists of less than 5% of the unit, the win rate falls to 27%. Without such a committee, the union win rate is only 10%. Obviously, during the preparation phase of the campaign, the organizer has attempted to build the committee to at least the 10% level. However, at the beginning of the action phase, when secrecy is no longer required, an active recruiting effort to expand the committee can be made. The success of this recruiting effort is one of the keys to a union victory.

Sufficient Authorization Cards — Though the union has solicited authorization cards during the preparation phase of a campaign, frequently the first stage of the action phase is to make a concerted effort to obtain additional signed authorization cards prior to filing the petition. The reason for this is simple: the more signed authorization cards the union obtains, the greater the chance of winning the election. Even in those cases where the union has collected enough cards during the preparation phase, it is highly unlikely every potential voter was contacted, so this final effort can pay handsome returns. The following shows the correlation between the number of employees signing authorization cards and a union's likelihood of success on election day.

Employees Signing Cards	Union Success
75%+	60%
75%	50%
60% - 75%	49%
50% - 60%	45%
40% - 50%	33%
less than 40%	8%

Mass Meetings — Mass meetings can be a highly effective campaign tool for a union, but only if they are well attended. This is true for two primary reasons. First, if a prospective voter is not present at a meeting, the voter cannot hear the union's message and therefore cannot be persuaded. Second, and perhaps more important, poor attendance creates the impression the campaign is failing and can cause even the most ardent union supporters to lose confidence and interest. The successful organizer will use mass meetings only if he or she believes they will be well attended. According to the AFL-CIO, "General or mass meetings offer opportunities as well as dangers. If less than 25% of the unit attend mass meetings, the win rate is 29%. But if more than 60% attend mass meetings on average, the win rate is 72%. This would suggest that unless the organizer expects to have at least 40% of the unit in attendance at a mass meeting, it may be harmful to call the meeting. This is consistent with other studies that suggest the importance of the employees' perceptions about the level of union support among their co-workers as a factor in their decision about whether to vote for the union. The use of mass meetings as the primary campaign tactic was related to a win rate of only 25%."

The survey report shows the correlation between attendance at union meetings and the chance the union will win the election:

Employees Attending	Union Success
More than 60%	72%
50% - 60%	67%
40% - 50%	55%
25% - 40%	33%
less than 25%	29%

Based on these numbers, the organizer would only want to use mass meetings if a substantial percentage of the voting unit will attend.

Shortly after a union files a petition for election, the employer receives from the NLRB a package of official correspondence about the petition and certain steps that must be taken concerning the election process. Included in this correspondence is a request for a list of the names and current addresses of all persons employed in the group the union is seeking to represent. The employer is required to provide this list to the Board on time. The Board then gives a copy of this list, called an Excelsior list, to the union. After receiving this list, the union can then add three other valuable elements to its arsenal of campaign weapons: the house call, the direct mail solicitation, and the telephone campaign.

There is no question that direct personal contact between voters and the organizer dramatically increases a union's chances of winning. The following statement is from a report titled *AFL-CIO Organizing Survey:* "The most frequently cited reason for losing campaigns is a lack of sufficient personal contact with employees, and insufficient staff. In 26% of the campaigns, there was no full-time organizer. In 55% of the campaigns studied, there was one organizer or less."

The survey indicates the importance of face-to-face contact between organizers and voters as the preferred method of communication during the union campaign. House calls are an effective form of personal communication. In cases where the organizer personally called on between 60% and 75% of the unit, the union win rate was 78%. If the organizer made no home visits, the win rate was 41%.

Letters and telephone calls do not constitute personal contact, according to the report, but they can be effectively used by organizers to supplement other forms of campaigning.

After receiving the Excelsior list, the organizer has all the available elements of a campaign. Now the job is to form a campaign strategy that retains the current level of employee support or, if possible, increases that level of support.

Typically, the union's organizing campaign uses several elements. The well run union campaign may look something like this:

Week 1 — A flashy full-color flyer introduces the union and a letter to the voters announces the filing of the petition. One or two major issues may be addressed.

Week 2 — A letter is sent to the homes of voters signed by the organizing committee. This letter announces a mass meeting later in the week. To encourage attendance at the meeting, refreshments may be served, including beer. The mass meeting is held at a local motel or union hall. The advantages of unionization in general are discussed, as well as how the union could assist employees in this particular instance. Voters' questions are answered.

Week 3 — A flyer attacking the early parts of management's campaign or reinforcing the union's strongest issue is distributed. Committees are developed to make home visitations and telephone calls during the last week of the campaign.

Week 4 — A flyer that shows one or more area union contracts with higher wages and/or better benefits than presently received by the voting group is distributed. Another flyer is distributed that illustrates cases of unionized employees who were fired, then reinstated with back pay by an arbitrator selected according to a union labor agreement.

Week 5 — A letter is sent to the homes of voters that announces a weekend family picnic. Telephone calls are made to encourage union support and extend a personal invitation to the union picnic. An issue flyer and picnic invitation are distributed.

Week 6 — The union picnic is held with intense campaigning. Home visitations are made. The union's final flyer is distributed.

During the entire campaign period, the organizer works continuously with the organizing committee to make sure an intensive word-of-mouth campaign supplements the formal activities. The union may also use cartoons that include characterizations of management personnel. Here is an example of such a cartoon:

Remember, a union's primary objective is to maintain the support it had at the time the petition for election was filed. It must try to keep attention focused on those issues that caused employees to sign authorization cards. Unions want to run their own campaigns and not respond to issues developed by management unless forced to do so.

From a Union Organizer's Manual

The following is an extended excerpt from a union manual designed to instruct organizers in campaign techniques and strategy.

The Basic Tools of a Union Organizer: The first basic tool is the capacity to like and to be able to work with and through people. Most union organizers, at least the good ones, are friendly and outgoing. Many are honestly concerned with the problems of others and truly believe union representation will bring improvements to the lives of employees seeking representation. These organizers are comfortable going into a bar and buying beer for everyone, or going to a church and making a formal presentation. Successful organizers are never uncomfortable or ill at ease with comparative strangers. Meeting people and exchanging views are enjoyable to them. *Perhaps most importantly, effective organizers do not attempt to invent issues, but rather they are able to skillfully exploit existing ones.*

The second basic tool is the ability to adapt to the immediate surroundings without appearing either superior or out of place. If an organizer cannot do this, they will certainly make prospective members uncomfortable and unwittingly create resistance to the union. Many employees have a deep "sense of kind" and a tendency to only warm up to those they consider "one of us." By adapting to this, the organizer puts employees at ease and makes them more receptive to the union point of view. Effective organizers are able to adjust their presentation to their audience, and can shift campaign styles according to circumstances.

Finally, the successful organizer must have patience. An organizer who shows impatience with prospective union members allows half of their effort to be lost. More than anything else, impatience on the part of an organizer can kill a campaign's effectiveness. After only the first discussion, it is unrealistic to expect non-union members to be completely sold on the idea of supporting a union. Therefore, it is up to the organizer to patiently bring people over to the union's side. Heated, rambling arguments are avoided, for the more intense the argument, the more resistant the prospective members become.

Though these personality tools are important to the success of a union organizer, this does not mean the organizer is only confined to the business of exuding charm and selling their public personality. Good organizers have a strong belief in the stated goals of unions. No doubt, they see what they are doing as a part of the same faith that has inspired workers to organize throughout the history of unions. Without that faith, the organizer runs the risk of being merely a 20-day wonder. It must be remembered that the American trade union movement sees itself as rich in humanitarian traditions.

Many of the best organizers once worked in a plant or factory, and through intelligence and political skill advanced to the position they hold today. Throughout their union life, they have been involved in elections in one way or another. Strictly from the standpoint of understanding the election process and how to motivate people to vote a certain way, they are far more experienced than the typical manager or supervisor.

Many of the most effective organizers are individuals who can, over a reasonably short time, cultivate the trust and confidence of the members of the organizing committee. During this period, the organizer becomes a good friend of the committee members. This personal relationship makes it hard for committee members to change their minds during the election campaign. Deserting the union is almost an act of betrayal.

Participation Pays Off: Remember, house calls during a campaign dramatically improve the chances of winning. When house calls are made on 60% to 75% of the voting unit, the union win rate is 78%. Every effort must be made to visit the home of each card signer as soon as possible after they sign a union authorization card. During the house call, the organizer should attempt to obtain the card signer's active support. Many organizers discover that once an employee participates in the union's cause, their sincerity and support are strengthened. Every good organizer knows that while employees fall into similar categories and may share common complaints, each is an individual with their own special desires and ambitions. No two employees are identical. Each will have their own reasons for accepting or rejecting the union. The house call eliminates the generalities of an organizing campaign, for it does not deal with the average employee or the average family, but deals with a single employee and their particular family.

In a union campaign there is always room for more help. Participation demonstrates to each supporter that they are important in building "their" union. Additionally, it generates enthusiasm for the union throughout the workplace.

As the organizer talks with card signers, each employee's potential value to the union's campaign is evaluated. If an employee is interested in helping, they may be of assistance in signing up others. They may be willing to serve on a general organizing committee, pass out handbills, work on publicity, or do detail work at campaign headquarters.

Before the organizer leaves the card signer's home, an attempt should be made to secure the names of other employees and the card signer's opinion of their union sentiments, as well as a description of the card signer's departmental conditions and major complaints against management. If possible, the organizer should try to obtain a list of potential union voters.

Once enough card signers have been contacted to establish committees, special meetings can be called and assignments made. Types of committees may include:

- *Membership* — to assemble the names and addresses of all bargaining unit employees, breaking names down by department, sex, age group, race, etc.
- *Publicity* — to discuss information included in material distributed during the campaign
- *Distribution* — to copy, help hand out or mail literature, and to maintain an accurate mailing list
- *Strategy* — to work with the organizer in planning campaign tactics and timing
- *Community* — to explain the union position to community leaders and to demonstrate that employees are actively participating in their own organizing campaign

While any or all of these committees are functioning, the leadership group maintains its key role as the on-site organizing committee. Without this committee, the campaign has little chance of success. Other committees play supporting roles by helping the organizer meet and talk with a wider group of employees, but they are not essential to victory.

In large facilities, area, floor, departmental, or other on-site organizing subcommittees may be formed. In these cases, subcommittees are headed by the proper representatives from the leadership organizing committee. The organizer in charge, or another union representative, will be present at all subcommittee meetings to give direction to planning and to avert actions that may endanger the campaign's progress.

If the organizer is fortunate enough to have several smoothly operating committees, he or she will be in a better position to spend time on house calls, preparation of leaflets, and the coordination of the campaign. By listening to these committees discuss their problems, the organizer can get an accurate picture of the union's strength.

Telephone Campaigning: In large voting groups or in situations where the organizer has limited time to spend on the campaign, house calls must be done on a selective basis, if at all. In these situations, large scale telephone calling may be used to increase awareness of the union message.

Telephone campaigns rely on volunteers who are given a short message or "approach." Calls are made directly to the homes of employees from lists assigned to each battery of callers. The Communications Workers of America used this device effectively in New York City during a successful campaign that involved 18,000 telephone maintenance workers scattered throughout the city's five boroughs and suburbs. The CWA installed a battery of phones in union headquarters and developed teams of volunteer callers who gave a few hours each week to the campaign. This kind of active involvement developed enthusiasm that paid off on the job, and the employees who were contacted liked the personal attention. It was discovered when employees were not at home, their spouses were interested in hearing the union's message.

Generally, telephone campaigns are used only when house calls are inappropriate or not possible. Telephone campaigns are not nearly as effective as house calls. According to the AFL-CIO, when the telephone is the primary means of campaigning, the union win rate is only 40%.

Publicity: Just as house calls and telephone calls are ways of communicating with employees, publicity is another communications tool. It is a weapon to be used in a campaign. Publicity alone probably never won any election for a union. By itself, the best handbill ever drafted never guaranteed a single vote. As one of many campaign tools, publicity is often a union's easiest way of reaching employees. It is nothing more than written organizing. Organizers who write well stand a better chance of communicating clearly to employees, thereby improving a union's chance of success. Written organizing may take the form of:

- Handbills given out at the employer's gate
- Letters to the employees' homes
- Advertising in the press, radio, and TV

- News releases that are pro-union and helpful to the campaign, but have the advantage of not being paid advertisements
- Billboards and union videos

Every organizer knows there are some things that can be more easily said than written. Certain words and phrases have more appeal to the ear than to the eye; and while certain combinations of words are easily understood when spoken, they are confusing when written down. In using publicity, the organizer remembers the campaign must be based on facts and it must also have an emotional appeal. Many words cause an emotional response, words such as:

- Security
- Freedom
- Dignity
- Respect
- Equality
- Justice

Handbills: The first union handbill is the easiest. In most cases, it is a leaflet that describes the union or discusses the general idea of unionism. This type of leaflet usually comes from the international union.

Future handbills, and the frequency of their distribution, are a different matter. After gaining an overall knowledge of the specific union, employees will no longer be interested in generalities; they will want to know "What does it mean to me?" As the campaign develops, union handbills will deal with specific situations within the workplace and the union's program to deal with these issues. Frequency of distribution will depend on the type of campaign, the number of employees, the use of other forms of communication, and the organizer's opinion of their need.

Basically, each union handbill consists of three main elements. It will have eye appeal to encourage employees to read it; it will present one, or at the most, two issues in understandable, brief language; and it will suggest means of dealing with issues. To have eye appeal, the handbill should use a large amount of white space. Eyes are lazy; the crowded, single-spaced page looks like too much work to read. Cartoons clipped from magazines or from union publications also help dress up a handbill. A humorous cartoon may get employees to read the text.

A good handbill is contained on one side of a piece of paper and uses its best paragraphs for the beginning and end. The first paragraph is thought provoking and encourages voters to continue reading. The last paragraph makes a voter say "That's right!" Finally, every handbill will probably be signed, not necessarily with the name of the organizer, but with the name of the union organizing committee (when they are willing), or the name of the union.

Letters: Letters are often used when longer messages need to be communicated, and when organizers want to involve the employees' families. While letters can be several pages long — although it is best to keep them fairly short — and do not usually have cartoons or eye catching headlines, their sentences and paragraphs will still be brief and to the point. The effective organizer will aim some remarks at the employee's spouse. Though the employee may keep working conditions or job-related problems private, the family knows about stretching the paycheck and is interested in pay, benefits, and security. Family members have also heard about strikes. If an employer is known to be paternalistic, the organizer will seriously consider the family's reaction to harsh words against management or against individual members of supervision. Like most handbills, letters will be signed, either by the organizer, a committee, or other employees.

While letters may be effective and certainly have their place in a union's campaign, the successful organizer does not rely too heavily on them or use them to replace more successful types of campaigning. The AFL-CIO reports that in campaigns where unions mainly rely on letters, the win rate is only 39%.

Advertising: An organizer's use of advertising is determined by the funds available. The impact of advertising on employees and the community is also considered. Newspaper, radio, and TV advertisements in large cities are not only expensive, but often are relatively useless. In a city where the general population is large and only the employees affected will be interested, the cost per voter is extremely high. In smaller communities, however, the situation may be different. Advertising may be relatively cheap and the organizer may feel public support is essential to the success of the campaign.

Generally, the most effective advertising with regards to both results and cost are billboards that feature the "Union Yes" message and logo. If billboard space can be purchased near the targeted employer, it is common to see this form of advertising. Today, some union billboards feature clever slogans, such as "You don't need to change jobs to get more money."

Newspaper ads are less frequently used, especially in larger cities where space is expensive and the effectiveness questionable. In smaller communities, however, newspaper space is far less costly and some organizers utilize this type of campaigning.

Radio and TV ads featuring the "Union Yes" message are reasonably effective, due to their use of famous personalities to convey the union message. However, this form of advertising is also expensive and is not used by most organizers.

Union organizers will think twice before going into paid advertising campaigns. Besides the need for expert handling, campaigns of this kind can kick back or have no measurable influence on either the community or the voters directly concerned. And the sustained use of these media is expensive. This is not to say, however, that unions never use newspaper ads or TV and radio spots.

News Releases: The objective of a news release is to be used as news, and in a form as close as possible to the way it was originally written. The release that is picked up as prepared by the organizer has the effect of free advertising for the union; but since it is not labeled as an ad, it carries the newspaper or TV station's reputation for authority and accuracy.

Again, the effectiveness of union news releases will depend on the community where the campaign is taking place. In a large city, the papers may announce that an election will be held, but the average organizing drive is not news and will not be given much space. In the small community, however, it is often very different. A union organizing campaign against an employer that provides a large share of the community payroll is definitely news and will be treated accordingly.

The organizer should not prepare a news release until local newspapers have been studied. By reading how they play local news, the organizer gets a feel for the best way to work the release. In writing a release, the most important information comes first. The lead paragraph will be dramatic enough to guarantee readership. The first few paragraphs must answer the questions: Who? What? When? Where? Why? and How?

Since newspapers, radio, and TV all shy away from outright propaganda, the organizer must be sure any emotional statements are written as quotations, either attributed to the organizer or to members of the on-site organizing committee. No newspaper story will say, "The management of company X is violently anti-union and has fired employees seeking to join Union Y." But a newspaper will print the statement if it reads, "Jane Smith, Union Y organizer, today charged that Company X is violently anti-union and has fired employees seeking to join the union."

One further point: newspapers, radio, and TV stations consider news to be especially worth using when it is happening or will happen soon. Stories talking about events happening a few days before the paper's publication are not news, they are history. For this reason, union news release should be written in the present or future tense, stressing action will take place or is happening today, rather than stating that something has happened.

Radio stations are given the same releases written for newspapers, but in some cases releases may be timed so the newspaper is on the street before the radio announcement, or vice versa. TV stations can also be given the same release, but an effort should be made, whenever possible, to include a picture. Since TV is mostly visual, inclusion of a picture (8 x 10) will help get the release broadcast.

The Issues, The Employer, and The Community: Every organizing campaign develops key issues that reflect the problems of major importance to employees and that are generally viewed as the reasons for joining a union. As the campaign gets under way, the organizer soon knows what these issues are and how to develop them. If enough employees can be convinced that the union, and only the union, has the remedy for these problems, the campaign to unionize will likely be a success.

Once these issues have been determined, whether they are wages, personal dignity, benefits, or working conditions, the good organizer uses all available organizing weapons to stress the union's solution. If the organizer can keep hammering on these issues, management will be forced to answer the union's charges. The theory that a good offense is the best defense holds true for the union, as well as management.

Handbills, publicity, letters to the home, meetings, house calls, and all other forms of communication are used to emphasize these issues. The smart organizer will stick to the facts, while varying the union's charges enough to maintain interest. Throughout the campaign, the strategy is to force management to answer the union.

Management, wanting to win the election, will also seek to take the offensive. While the union will usually answer those management statements that demand a response, the organizer tries to avoid playing into management's hands by becoming defensive. Whenever possible, management statements will be ignored or treated lightly, while union communications will continue to stress key issues. *This, therefore, becomes the heart of the campaign. NLRB elections are often decided by which side is forced on the defensive.*

Warning The Union's Supporters: Once management has indicated it is launching a full scale campaign, the organizer will warn union supporters of possible management actions. The leadership committee, as well as all other committees, will be advised of what management can do under the law and what the union can do.

In describing possible management tactics, the organizer will usually be candid with supporters. Committee members will receive no guarantee they cannot be fired for union activity. Every organizer knows that despite the language of the law, active union supporters are sometimes fired on other pretenses. Committee members will be told of management's right to hold captive audience meetings and the National Labor Relations Board's present interpretation of free speech. Other legally permitted management tactics will be described. Union supporters may be surprised and even dismayed by this information, but advance warning is considered better than last-minute disintegration of a campaign because of aggressive management tactics. During these discussions, the organizer attempts to predict what management will say over the course of the campaign. The organizer who correctly anticipates management's strategy will help prevent later defections. Every organizer knows the union will lose votes during the campaign. The job of the skillful organizer is to minimize those losses and retain the support of at least 50% plus one of the voting unit.

While management's attack against the union may be the greatest obstacle the organizer has to overcome, the attitude of the community is also important. In large cities, this attitude may be one of indifference and will have little bearing on the campaign's outcome; but in smaller cities and towns, public sentiment can be extremely important. Unions understand the effect of community sympathy and support for a well-respected employer. One response is for the union to try to win its own share of support within the community. In areas having little experience with organized labor, or where the targeted employer is large, such efforts may be worthless, but will probably be tried anyway. In other communities, union organizers may find strong support where they least expect it.

Once the campaign is in the open, the small community will know a union is trying to come in. Now, the organizer has nothing to lose by approaching community leaders and finding where their sympathies lie. House calls on community leaders can be as effective as house calls on unorganized employees. Other unions in the community might suggest which people to visit. If there are no other unions, the organizer might start by visiting municipal officials and church leaders. A pro-labor clergyman or a sympathetic elected official can be the source of other influential contacts.

If other unions are active in the community, the organizer will want them involved in the campaign. Local union leaders, business agents, and council officials will be urged to speak to friends who work for the targeted employer, as well as to employers and community leaders with whom they have a personal acquaintance. Union officials and members living in the area can be of assistance by speaking at campaign meetings or supplying the organizer with needed volunteers for distributing literature.

In speaking to community leaders, the union representative should appear as objective as possible and avoid personal attacks on the employer being targeted. Instead, the main point stressed should be the right of working men and women to seek self-organization and to vote in a union election. If community leaders are impressed by this message, the organizer may win valuable allies. Should community leaders be willing to support the union openly, the organizer will quickly take advantage of the situation. A community committee might be formed — just as management often does — with letters mailed to employees, as well as news releases and ads in newspapers. The more prominent the community leaders, the more helpful they will be to the union. When the organizer finds a community leader who is on the fence, an attempt will be made to find literature that quotes others in the leader's same occupation or profession who support trade unionism.

Although most organizers will find it difficult to form a community committee that speaks out openly for the union, personal contact may at least succeed in neutralizing management's possible use of the same people. The organizer can achieve an important union goal if the community takes the position that the decision to be represented by a union should be left up to the employees involved. In dealing with the community, the union organizer's personal behavior is extremely important. Because all the organizer's actions will be closely watched, behavior that could reflect badly upon the union must be avoided.

Timing: The timing of an election campaign is critical for both management and the union. Both are seeking to maximize their support on election day. Of course, only one side will accomplish this. Normally, during the latter stages of a campaign, the winning side is talking about the issues it has selected and the losing side is responding to those issues.

Like a battle, an organizing campaign depends on strategy, tactics, and timing. If both strategy and tactics are properly developed, the union's campaign can still falter should the organizer fail to time the drive so that it reaches the high point on election day. As with every other part of an organizing effort, the timing of each campaign is different, but the final objective is always the same. The organizer wants pro-union sentiment to reach its maximum strength on the day voters go to the polls.

During the 1960 national elections, many political experts claimed the closeness of the result was due to the Kennedy campaign peaking too soon. Some believe Kennedy reached his high point, or maximum votes, ten days to two weeks before election day, and had the election been held one week later, Nixon would have won. If this analysis is correct, what happened during the 1960 presidential election often happens during organizing campaigns: The union uses up all its ammunition, has the drive running at full speed, but active interest cannot be maintained through election day.

Even worse for unions are the campaigns that reach their peak before the NLRB sets an election date, then dwindle in interest as the Board permits management-requested delays. Because of this, many organizers hold back until the election date is set and then plan their publicity and other activities to reach a climax on the eve of the vote. These organizers have learned that when the final union message contains nothing more than balloting instructions, last minute management appeals can have a devastating effect.

The final 24 hours before the polls open is a critical time for the union campaign. Management has wrapped up its own campaign and cannot hold any more captive audience meetings. If the union stages a rally, meeting, or some other function during this period, it may be able to gain an advantage, particularly with undecided voters. The danger in holding a meeting at this time is the risk of poor attendance. The attendance goal should be 50% of the eligible voters; however, successful meetings have been held with far less. The purpose of the meeting is to whip up as much emotional support for the union as possible. A discussion of issues is far less important than a "win one for the Gipper" type speech. During these meetings, it is not uncommon for the union to conduct a practice vote and announce the results.

Aiming For Election Day: In many campaigns, the organizer finds peak support has been reached well before the election. If the projected vote count shows a union victory, regardless of how narrow, efforts will be concentrated on maintaining existing support, even to the point of ignoring non-union and on the fence employees. Such action may force the union to take a defensive posture in the last days of the campaign, but if votes can be held, the organizing effort may still be successful. Usually, though, the organizer is fighting a lost battle. This defensive position allows management to concentrate on the undecided and hard-core union supporters. Usually a number of votes will switch.

As some campaigns progress, the organizer may believe there are grounds for unfair labor practice charges. Yet, the union will probably question whether the filing of charges and a delay of the election are in its best interest. If the union's strength is sufficient, the organizer may push on toward an election. At this point in the campaign, the strategic advantage probably lies with management. Since the union and its key supporters have been working on the campaign much longer than management, and have probably been communicating with certain groups of employees much longer, it may be difficult for them to maintain the necessary momentum.

Election Day Planning: Election day marks the conclusion of every campaign. The importance of the union showing its strength, and thereby creating a bandwagon psychology, should not be underestimated. Some organizers work hard up to election day assuming everything possible has been done and then sit back to wait for the vote count. They follow the theory that "if employees don't know about the union by now, they never will."

Politicians have long known that while this may sound logical, it does not take into account the sometimes strange behavior of human beings. For this reason, both major political parties work long and hard on election day. Surveys show the work produces extra votes.

Long before election day, most organizers have selected observers chosen for their leadership and respect in the workplace. Although the NLRB has rules governing activities at the polling place, the organizer can still generate a bandwagon atmosphere by getting pro-union supporters to wear buttons, caps, T-shirts, etc., thereby voicing their voting intentions and talking up the union and the election away from the polls. The organizer will likely follow the political precinct practice for turning out the vote. A committee of union supporters check off those employees who have voted and contact those who have indicated pro-union sentiments, but have not cast their ballots. Vacations, time off, and shift schedules are analyzed by department to make sure transportation is available when needed. In addition, employees not reporting to work on election day are contacted during voting hours to be sure they plan to cast their ballots.

Organizing headquarters is often used as the union's election day center. Employees working late shifts might be asked to make phone calls, while others provide cars. Every effort will be made to transport any union supporters who are sick to the polls. While the organizer will not waste time trying to turn out the non-union vote, it is not unusual for friends of on-the-fence voters to drive these undecided employees to the voting place. It will be left up to their friends to determine, ahead of time, whether these employees represent potential union votes.

Assuming the organizer or the leadership committee have a list of all eligible pro-union voters, every effort will be made to get each of these voters to the polling place. Often, union supporters fail to vote because they are convinced the election is won, only to find the union has lost. If the organizer and the various committees work hard to obtain the maximum union vote, they know they have done everything possible to secure a victory.

When it comes to successful union organizing, there are no absolute formulas. Each campaign will be planned and carried out according to the circumstances that present themselves. Tactics vary and those proven successful in one campaign may fail in another. The experienced union organizer recognizes the need for planning, but also knows plans must be flexible and tactics often need to be changed as events dictate.

There is no substitute for the on-site leadership organizing committee. The more these committees are built and spread throughout a targeted employer's facility, the greater the union's chance of success. Neither is there a substitute for face-to-face contact with employees. This means going where the targeted employees go, especially into their homes. In large campaigns, house calls may have to be selective, but they can only be ignored at the risk of failure. In smaller campaigns and communities, unions understand how much can be gained by visiting each employee at least once.

Never underestimate a union organizer. Good ones are constantly benefiting from common sense and experience. Most will run a well-planned campaign that requires management to make a serious and equally well-conceived response.

Literature Distribution & Development

*"Let thy speech be short,
comprehending much
in a few words."*

<small>ECCLESIASTICUS</small>

The distribution and development of effective campaign literature during a National Labor Relations Board representation election campaign often spells the difference between winning and losing. Fortunately, this is one area where management enjoys a distinct advantage over the union. When the union decides to distribute a piece of literature, it is immediately faced with several problems. First, the methods of distribution are restricted. Basically, unions have four primary methods of distributing literature to the voting group:

1. Handbilling
2. Mail
3. Distribution at union meetings
4. Distribution on-site

A union usually distributes literature by handbilling. An organizer stands just beyond the employer's property where employees must pass going to and from work. As employees go by, the organizer hands out literature. There is usually no time for any discussion of campaign issues. Not all employees will accept union literature. Perhaps they are supporters of management or strongly oppose the union; maybe they are just tired of the campaign and in a hurry to get home. And many who accept literature never read it. Finally, handbilling allows no opportunity for follow-up or for answering questions raised by the literature.

Distribution by mail insures 100% coverage, assuming the union has the Excelsior list. However, this method also has many of the same inherent disadvantages of handbilling. There is no way to tell if voters have read the literature, no way to measure its effectiveness, and no adequate way to follow-up or answer questions.

Distribution at union meetings solves many of the problems associated with handbilling and mail distribution, but this is somewhat like preaching to the choir. Generally, only strong union supporters regularly attend meetings. Though an undecided voter may attend, union meetings are usually structured to be strategy meetings rather than campaign events.

Distribution on-site is legal if it takes place during non-work time in non-work areas. On-site distribution usually takes the form of handbilling and has the same disadvantages.

Management, however, has few restrictions placed on how campaign literature is distributed. You can distribute literature to voters while they are at work and during working hours. This enables you to easily confirm that each employee received a copy. Employees can be asked to read the literature, and may even be given time to stop work to do so. Later, you can go back to each employee and ask if they read the handout and if there are questions. If an employee has not read the handout, you may ask them to please do so. There is absolutely no way any union can compete with the effective distribution and follow-up network enjoyed by management. With these advantages, plus the wealth of union-free information available, no employer should ever lose the literature battle. Unfortunately, however, many organizations fail to effectively use this campaign advantage.

Obviously, it is impossible to force employees to read your literature; but if it is attractively designed, grabs attention, and does not look as if it will take all day to finish, many people will take the time to read the material. Distributing literature just before a scheduled break or lunch period, for example, encourages employees to look over the material during their free time. There is, however, a danger in distributing literature just before the end of the work day. Employees with other things on their mind may ignore the handout or plan to read it later, then simply forget.

Restrictions On Union Literature Distribution

Before going further, let's review the restrictions placed on literature distribution by the union or by employees who are union supporters:

1. Under normal circumstances, union organizers who are not employees *are not* allowed to distribute literature on an employer's property. Although it is not illegal for management to allow them to do so, you *are not* required to permit this. If a union organizer (non-employee), is distributing literature on your property, you may ask them to leave. If they refuse, you may call the police and force them to move. This is seldom necessary since union organizers are aware of the law and will usually move voluntarily.

2. Employees who are supporting the union *can* distribute union literature on your property under certain circumstances. The literature can only be distributed during non-work time and in non-work areas. Non-work time means any time the employee is not scheduled to be on the job. For example, time before the start of a shift, any authorized break, lunch periods, and time after the end of a shift would all be considered non-work times. A non-work area is any place where work is not being carried on. For example, the employee parking lot, rest rooms, and lunch room would all be considered non-work areas. Under certain circumstances, places normally considered work areas may become non-work areas. For example, if no work was being done in a plant, and no work was scheduled during an authorized break or lunch period, the plant would be considered a non-work area during the authorized break or lunch period only.

Management Literature Distribution

Whenever management distributes a piece of literature, certain rules should be followed:

1. For most pieces of literature, distribution should be handled by the employees' immediate supervisor. Generally, the supervisor will know the employees better than any other management representa-

tive. His or her chance of engaging employees in conversation about the literature is better than someone the employees do not know as well or do not feel as comfortable with.

2. Before literature is distributed, supervisors (or whoever will be responsible for the actual distribution) should be called into a meeting to discuss the contents of the literature. Management should share as much information as possible about the specific handout, including background information so supervisors can answer as many questions as possible on the spot.

3. The distribution should be timed to achieve maximum readership. Generally, the end of a shift is not a good time. Employees who are leaving work are eager to get home and may not read what they are given. Even if they do, it is more difficult to engage them in a conversation the next day. Some employers want employees to read the literature on their own time. If this is the case, the distribution should be made before a scheduled break or before lunch. Others may want employees to read the literature on company time. If this is the case, the distribution should be scheduled to allow sufficient time for discussion before employees leave for the day.

4. When possible, the distribution should be done at the same time throughout the facility. If literature is distributed at 10:00 AM in one department and at 2:00 PM in another department, there is a good chance employees in the later group will have heard about it and perhaps even formed an opinion before ever receiving a copy. This will cause the handout to lose some or all of its value.

5. After each distribution, the supervisor (or other designated individual) should attempt to engage each employee in a brief discussion about the literature. A good opening line would be something like, "Sue, have you had a chance to read the literature I gave you?"

Remember, the critical factor in literature distribution is to make sure all employees read the material. The only literature guaranteed not to be effective is the kind that is never read.

Literature Development

Management campaign literature comes in a variety of formats and sizes. It may contain a great deal of information, just a few sentences or, occasionally, just a few words. All literature, however, should be attention getting, easy to read, informative, and relevant. Cosmetically, the best general purpose literature tends to meet these criteria:

1. The size is 5 and 1/2 inches by 8 and 1/2 inches (an 11 by 8 and 1/2 inch sheet of paper folded in half), or a single sheet of 8 and 1/2 by 11 inch paper.

2. The cover or some part of the sheet should contain a large headline with a bold statement or question.

3. The cover or some part of the sheet may also contain a cartoon or other graphic that grabs attention.

4. The message should be restricted to the amount of information that can be comfortably included on the inside of the document or the single sheet.

5. The back should be left blank or include no more than a campaign slogan or employer logo.

6. The paper should be a color other than white to generate attention. Unless your literature will use corporate colors, you may want to change the paper color for each handout. Neon colored paper available from most office supply stores is excellent for campaign literature.

Let's now develop a couple of pieces of general literature. First, you need to become familiar with the subject you will address. In this case the subject is job security. Examine the labor contracts you have obtained to see what job security issues in those contracts would make good campaign material. One of the many topics available under this subject is super-seniority. Many union contracts have a provision or provisions that grant super-seniority (or preferential seniority) to union officers, committeepersons, stewards, and other individuals. Super-seniority artificially gives these individuals more seniority than other employees if there is a workforce reduction. In other words, during a layoff, employees who are also union officials would retain their jobs, while those employees who have more seniority, but are not union officials, could be laid off. A provision like this proves that under a union contract, union officials protect themselves at the expense of ordinary union members.

To begin, you need a cartoon and a good title page; a union contract, preferably from the union you are campaigning against and that contains the appropriate language; and you need text for the flyer. You should prepare the text first since that will dictate the cover and title. Examine the contract language you will use as your example. Will you quote the language exactly or paraphrase it? How will you make your points most effective in the space available? Don't, however, make the process more difficult than it is. Good pieces of campaign literature almost write themselves.

Here is an example of a short and simple super-seniority provision taken from an OCAW contract in Memphis. The provision says simply:

"Section 10: Employees occupying the following positions in the Local Union shall be considered the most senior employees during their tenure in office:

1 President

1 Vice president

1 Financial Secretary

2 Grievance Committee

1 Recording Secretary

* Up to Six Stewards

"*When the bargaining unit workforce exceeds one hundred (100) employees, the Local Union may notify the Company of their desire to add up to six (6) employees to the Steward list."

That is the actual language. Based on this, it should be easy to develop a good flyer that explains super-seniority. Since the text of the language in this contract is short, it should be used exactly as it appears in the contract. Before we quote the language, we need a brief explanation of the super-seniority process and how it works.

Let's start with a headline like, "Does Super-Seniority Sound Fair To You?" Then we can follow with a brief paragraph: "Seniority is an important employee benefit each of you has earned. It is a benefit that must be protected and not compromised by provisions in union constitutions and collective bargaining contracts. The union talks about job security, but really is only interested in its own security."

The sub-headline "Did You Know?" is followed by a brief explanation of super-seniority: "Union officers and stewards want super-seniority no matter how short a time they've worked. Union leaders promise you seniority, but give themselves super-seniority. Under super-seniority provisions, employees are laid off first. Union leaders are laid off last. Super-seniority undermines the job security you've worked for and deserve."

We can now go to another headline: "In The OCAW's Own Words." This is followed by a strong message: "If the workforce at Velsicol Chemical Corp. in Memphis is less than 100 employees, 12 people have super-seniority. If the workforce is over 100 employees, 18 people have super-seniority. That's great if you're one of the select few who kiss up to the union. If not, you're screwed. The OCAW contract with Velsicol Chemical Corp. contains this super-seniority clause. Read it for yourself."

We then quote the actual contract language.

After you have written the text, select a title page and cartoon. If someone in your organization has artistic abilities, you may wish to have them create a cartoon. If not, there are many clip-art software programs available. Or, you can purchase copyrighted cartoons published by the Labor Relations Institute. Perhaps you don't want a cartoon, and instead prefer just a title page set in large letters. The important thing is to be sure the title and/or the cartoon are relevant to the flyer's message.

Exhibit 5-A is an example of the super-seniority flyer we just developed. An attention grabbing cover clearly introduces the subject. The text is simple, easy to read, and takes less than two minutes to get through. It starts with a summary of the disadvantages of super-seniority and includes the direct quote from the local union contract and a list of people under that contract who have super-seniority. As you can see, effective handouts are not hard to create, if you have the right information.

It is also easy to create simple, yet effective, handouts that contain more technical information about the particular union attempting to organize your employees. For example, let's assume you have the union's strike history. With this information you can create a dramatic and thought provoking handout, even though you don't really expect your voters to read the entire document. First, decide what time period you want to present. Always use at least one year, but no longer than five years. After developing your headline and any additional text, which should be brief, list each employer that experienced a strike, their location, the number of employees affected, the length of the strike, the number of work days lost (number of employees multiplied by the number of days the strike lasted), and the dates the strike began and ended. You may also wish to show the approximate amount of money the members of this union lost as a result of these strikes. To determine this approximate amount, take a sample wage — usually the average hourly wages your employees earn — multiply by eight, then multiply by the total number of days lost due to strikes. Since this number is arbitrary, you may decide not to include it in the handout. (An example of a strike handout is shown as Exhibit 5-B.)

If the union you are campaigning against is large and has called many strikes, you may not be able to fit all of them on a single page. This is fine. Voters are not expected to examine every strike; but page after page of statistics graphically shows that the union *does* call strikes that cost some of its members a great deal of money.

Possibly the best piece of campaign literature I ever saw was a strike history. In one of its flyers, the union had stated: "About 98% of all our contracts with companies are negotiated without a strike — A record to be proud of in any league." The targeted employer, who had purchased a five-year strike history on the union, decided this statement could be used for a piece of campaign literature. Management designed a flyer that folded to 11 by 8.5 inches for distribution. A bold headline stated, "The union tells you they have a record to be proud of in any league." The flyer unfolded at the top, to become an 11 by 17 inch sheet with another headline that said, "Here it is...in their words." Below was a reproduction of a small portion of the union handout. The flyer unfolded again to its full 22 by 17 inch size. The final headline said, "Here's that record they're so proud of...506 strikes in 5 years." The balance of the sheet contained a listing of all 506 strikes, in very small print.

The dramatic impact of this handout was unmistakable. It killed the union on the strike issue and resulted in a huge management victory. Obviously, this flyer was expensive to produce. A five-year strike history was required, as well as custom printing. But it worked and management felt it was money well spent.

There will probably be times during the campaign when the message you want to communicate to employees will not fit in a small flyer. It is always best to increase the size and number of pages, rather than force the material to fit in as small a space as possible. Effective handouts can be several pages long, or even in a booklet format. The cardinal rule is that to be effective, the material must be read by the voting group. If it isn't read, no matter how important the information, it won't do any good. The only exception to this rule is when the information is mostly for effect, such as a long list of strikes.

To develop another flyer, we will use a union strike that happened in Oklahoma a few years ago and was thoroughly covered in local newspapers. After reviewing all the stories, we select those that are likely to have the greatest impact with the voting group. We then build the flyer using these newspaper articles as documentation. By using large headlines on each page that sum up the accompanying articles, it is not necessary that all the stories be read for the handout to be effective. If you start with the right information, little or no campaign experience is needed to develop a dynomite handout. (A copy of this flyer and another newspaper-based strike flyer are shown as Exhibit 5-C and Exhibit 5-D.)

Several other examples of effective management literature are included in Chapters 9 through 13. Many of these may fit your needs, but if you wish to develop literature specific to your own campaign, you are encouraged to do so. The more sharply focused the information you communicate to the voting group, the better.

Using the information you accumulate, you should be able to create union-specific literature that produces positive, dramatic results. If, however, you do not have the time or the expertise to develop this literature in-house, it is available for purchase from the Labor Relations Institute.

If you have acquired the campaign research materials suggested in Chapter 2, an abundance of information should be at your disposal. Selecting the right information for distribution at the right time will be more of a problem than finding enough information. Before developing any campaign literature, examine all the materials you now have. Working with your campaign calendar, the videos or the suggested captive audience speeches, and the literature samples provided in Chapters 9 through 13, decide what you want to communicate to the voting group. Organize this information by category, which will generally be the same categories discussed in the chapters covering each of the five campaign segments.

You are now ready to prepare your first handout. This will either be an introduction to, or a summary of, the first video presentation or captive audience speech. If you have a piece of information dealing with a topic covered in the video/speech captive audience presentation, but you have no other place for it in your projected calendar, you may want to use it here. If not, you may want to consider a handout like the samples shown in Chapter 9.

While writing the handout, remember your audience. Consider their backgrounds and levels of education. Tailor your presentation to the voting group. You are not trying to win the Pulitzer Prize for literature; you are trying to make a specific point to a specific group of people.

Consider whether the handout will be distributed before or after the video/speech captive audience presentation. Before this presentation, most employees will have only a general knowledge of the subject of unionization, but after the presentation they will be better informed.

Have someone who has not assisted in its preparation read the handout, preferably someone with the same general background as the voting group. A strong management supporter could fill this role. Keep in mind that you are only attempting to learn if the handout clearly conveys the message you intended. If a management supporter wants you to move faster or hit harder than your strategy dictates, don't let that opinion change the course you have charted unless there is a valid reason to do so.

After the handout has been prepared, a printer must be selected. This is an important decision. You need to be sure company literature is not leaked to the union before it is distributed to voters. As the campaign progresses, you might have several handouts at the printer at the same time; should the union get advance copies, it will have gained a distinct advantage. If you operate an internal printing department, consider having the material printed in-house. But be sure none of the voters or union supporters have advance access to the literature. If you decide to use a commercial printer, be certain it is a non-union company. Union printers have often given copies of union-free literature to organizers. If you use a word processor to generate literature, you may choose to simply Xerox the flyers. This has the advantages of quick turn around and good security. However, there will probably be some pieces you wish to have professionaly printed, so a printer should be selected at this time.

Once campaign literature has been printed, you must decide the best method of distribution. It can be handed out during meetings, included in pay envelopes, or mailed to the home. Though it is not necessary to distribute every piece of literature the same way, experience has shown the best way to distribute most kinds of campaign handouts is to employees individually through their immediate supervisor. This is not to say you should reject all other methods, but under normal circumstances this has proven the best way to distribute most handouts. Campaign material distribution through supervisors assures management that every employee receives a handout, is personally encouraged to read it, has time to read it, and that a supervisor follows up each handout.

When planning a handout, it is wise to bring supervisors together to discuss its content. If the handout is related to a video/speech captive audience presentation, that material should also be reviewed. Give your supervisors as much information as possible about campaign literature so they are prepared to talk intelligently and answer employee questions. In political terms, a supervisor can then "press the flesh." By seizing opportunities to talk to employees individually about issues presented in a handout, the supervisor can further persuade them to reject the union. If you are using the training program discussed in Chapter 8, your supervisors should be well-prepared.

When distributing a handout, supervisors should make some comment to each employee, such as, "I have some information that I think you will find interesting. I would appreciate your taking a few minutes to read this handout, then I will get back with you to answer any questions." After giving the voting group enough time to read the literature, the supervisor should return to each employee and ask if he or she has read it. If the answer is yes, the supervisor should ask the employee if they have questions or if there is anything the supervisor can explain further. Should the employee have no questions and not ask for a further explanation, the supervisor can still continue the discussion by asking a question, such as, "What did you think about the part where it said..." By making supervisory discussions part of the literature distribution process, supervisors will develop a feel for how each worker stands on the subject of unionization in general, as well as their specific areas of concern. This information can be extremely valuable during the final stages of the campaign.

Good campaign literature is important. Though the captive audience presentations are usually the most essential elements in a campaign, properly constructed literature can dramatically reinforce the points made in the captive audience presentations and can give management supporters ammunition for persuading others to vote No.

Posters & Cartoons

An often overlooked type of campaign literature is the poster. A poster is a public piece of literature displayed in conspicuous locations in the workplace. A poster should contain no more than a few words, be easily seen and understood, and require only a moment to read. Cartoons fall into the same category. There are, however, a few general rules about posters and cartoons.

1. If possible, a poster should be displayed in a locked, glass-enclosed bulletin board. Without protection, union supporters can deface a

management poster, turning it into an embarrassing piece of union propaganda.

2. Posters should be left up for only a short time, usually no more than 48 hours. It does not take long for a poster to lose its impact.

3. While it is not necessary to immediately replace one poster with another, if you plan to use posters, you should try to post a new one each week. The anticipation of the next poster is often a positive factor for your campaign.

4. Material originally used for the cover page of campaign literature can be enlarged to create posters that reinforce your handouts.

5. If you use cartoons, do not use copyrighted characters without permission. For example, using Peanuts characters can be very expensive if Charles Schultz or the union representing his cartoonists finds out. Someone in your organization who has drawing skills could be a source for cartoons, as could students in local high school or college art departments. Cartoons and posters can also be purchased from the Labor Relations Institute. On the following pages are examples of effective cartoons and posters.

Cartoons

ANOTHER ⚠
D A N G E R
of
COLLECTIVE
BARGAINING

Your benefits can be used as bargaining chips.

Unions have a record of giving away benefits that employees already enjoy in exchange for something that's only important to the union, such as dues check-off, a union security clause or super-seniority. **DUES CHECK-OFF** is the way a union makes sure members pay dues – by having them deducted directly from a person's paycheck. A **UNION SECURITY CLAUSE** requires all employees to belong to the union and pay dues or lose their jobs. **SUPER-SENIORITY** provisions give artificial seniority to union officials so that in case of a layoff, those union officials keep their jobs while other employees with more service are let go first.

NO

Vote ✓

Q. and A. about the union

QUESTION

Why is management against unionization?

First, we are **pro-company** and **pro-employees.** But the union does not understand our business; and it does not understand the present economic conditions in our industry. The union seems to think that all we have to do to raise wages and increase benefits is to pass those increased costs on to our customers. If it was that easy, we would have done it already. We believe that **a rise in prices at this time will only result in less business and perhaps fewer jobs.**

ANSWER

Exhibit 5-A

UNION SUPER SENIORITY IS A THREAT TO YOUR JOB

Exhibit 5-A

The union probably hasn't told you about super seniority—here's why

△ Super seniority means that employees are laid off <u>first</u>.

△ Union officials are laid off <u>last</u>, no matter how <u>short</u> a time they've worked.

△ Super seniority <u>undermines</u> your job security.

Does super seniority sound fair?

This union member didn't think so. Here's an unfair labor practice charge recently filed with the National Labor Relations Board.

[NLRB Charge Against Labor Organization form — FORM NLRB-508, Charge Against Labor Organization or its Agents; Case 4-CB-7888, 6-13-97; Labor Organization: Warehouse Employees Union, Local 169, affiliated with I.B.T.C.W.&H. of America; Employer: Americsource Corporation; declaration signed Joseph J. Nugent, 6/11/97]

In a union's own words...

Many labor agreements negotiated by unions contain super seniority clauses like the following:

ARTICLE III, Section 4

"Stewards and members of the Grievance Committee shall be given seniority preference in their classification with respect to layoffs."

Employees working under this contract are laid off first, before any of these 59 union officials:

President	Sentinel
Vice-President	Grievance Committee (3)
Recording Secretary	Chief Steward
Secretary-Treasurer	Assistant Chief Steward
Conductor	Stewards (45)
Trustees (3)	

Seniority is an important employee benefit that each of you has earned. It needs to be protected and not compromised by provisions in union constitutions and collective bargaining contracts.

On election day, protect yourself and your future...

Vote NO

Exhibit 5-B

ONLY THIS KIND OF STRIKE IS FUN

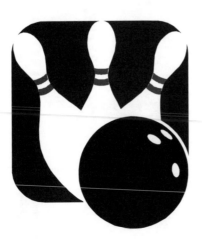

Exhibit 5-B

NOT THIS KIND!

The UNION kind of STRIKE can cost you money, even your job.

Union organizers want you to believe that strikes are rare. THIS ISN'T TRUE. Figures from the Department of Labor prove that strikes still happen. In fact, the total number of union members affected by strikes has recently increased.

Year	Members on Strike	Year	Members on Strike
1996	120,753	1997	333,832

During these two years, striking union members were out of work an average of **34 DAYS — 34 DAYS WITH NO PAYCHECK OR COMPANY BENEFITS.**

One of the strikes that ended in 1996 had gone on for 635 DAYS.

Members who follow their union out on strike can lose more than their wages and benefits—sometimes they lose their jobs. **EMPLOYERS CAN LEGALLY HIRE PERMANENT REPLACEMENTS FOR ECONOMIC STRIKERS.**

Good customers often stop doing business with companies that have gone through a strike. Once a strike is settled, the result can be a need for fewer employees. We aren't saying that a strike will happen if the union is voted in, but we are saying that strikes would always be a *possibility*

Who doesn't lose during a union strike?

Union bosses and other union officials continue to draw high salaries and receive lavish benefits, while union members and their families are expected to sacrifice for as long as a strike continues.

Protect your future and your economic security...

Vote NO

Exhibit 5-C

PICKETS • VANDALISM • VIOLENCE • HARASSMENT • FINES • LOST WAGES

PICKETS • VANDALISM • VIOLENCE • HARASSMENT • FINES • LOST WAGES

Exhibit 5-C

THIS IS THE TRUE STORY OF A UNION STRIKE

IT HAPPENED IN SAPULPA, OKLA.

READ THE FACTS BEFORE THE SAME THING HAPPENS HERE!

THIS IS HOW IT ALL BEGAN...

DURING NEGOTIATIONS, THE UNION MADE DEMANDS

BUT THE COMPANY SAID NO

Exhibit 5-C

SO THE UNION CALLED EMPLOYEES OUT ON STRIKE

Workers place picket at Liberty Glass

By R.B. ROBBINS
Herald City Editor

Glass workers early today staged picket lines in front of the Liberty Glass Co. plant as the first full day of a strike for improved benefits began.

A federal mediator today said a renewed bargaining effort may begin next week to resolve the contract dispute. However, Liberty Glass Thursday filed a complaint alleging unfair practices with the National Labor Relations Board.

About 350 members of the Glass, Pottery, Plastic and Allied Workers, Locals 185 and 138 are involved in the strike, which began at midnight Thursday when the union's contract with Liberty Glass expired.

Wayne Buckley, president of Local 185, said negotiations over the company's benefit package, not wages, had prompted the dispute.

Exhibit 5-C

Liberty Glass sets hiring

By GLENN C. McCASLAND
Herald Managing Editor

Liberty Glass Co. officials Saturday announced plans to employ people to replace some 320 striking union workers on Monday.

The company authorized placement of display advertisements in the Herald and Tulsa area newspapers seeking new employees as the strike entered its third day today.

The union workers walked out Friday morning, complaining they are worked too hard and get inadequate benefits.

The advertisment released by Liberty Glass Co. officials said the company is "now taking applications for permanent positions" and listed openings for qualified personnel including forming machine operators and upkeep, electronic and mechanical maintenance,

forklift drivers and utility workers.

Liberty Glass job applicants join strikers

By R.B. ROBBINS
Herald City Editor

Glass workers walking picket lines today were joined by a second group outside the doors of Liberty Glass Co. — dozens of job seekers hoping for the positions the strikers had left last week.

The job applicants, waiting outside the glass company personnel office in the wind and light rain, were responding to advertisements for employment which ran in area newspapers over the weekend.

While there were no reports of confrontations between the applicants and picketers, the move replace striking workers has angered union members.

Exhibit 5-C

THE STRIKE GOT OUT OF CONTROL WHEN MASS PICKETING & DEMONSTRATIONS STARTED

Liberty Glass demonstration planned today

By R.B. ROBBINS
Herald City Editor

A demonstration of support for striking glass workers at Liberty Glass Co. will be held today near the glass plant despite allegations by a company spokesman the protest march constitutes a violation of a temporary injunction.

Wives, family, friends and community members — but no union members — planned the march to protest the hiring of replacement workers at Liberty Glass, organizers said today.

Attoney William Toney, who represents the glass bottle manufacturer, said today the demonstration was "mass picketing" and would interfer with the free movement of trucks from Liberty Glass, thereby violating picketing prohibitions contained in a temporary injunction granted by District Judge Don Thompson.

The planned two-hour march, which will begin at 4 p.m., will be conducted on a sidewalk on the east side of Mission Street in front of the glass plant, said Sandy Sutton, one of the demonstration organizers.

Liberty Glass demonstrators do their thing

More than 100 people protesting the hiring of replacement workers marched for two hours Friday afternoon in front of the Liberty Glass Co. plant in support of striking glass workers.

Wives of strikers and strike supporters carrying makeshift signs paced the sidewalk across Mission Street from the glass plant as union members stationed at the strike headquarters cheered and company officials, security guards and Sapulpa police officers looked on.

The march ended peacefully and company officials, who earlier claimed the march was a violation of a judge's ban on picketing activity, apparently made no attempt to block it.

The march was an effort to rally public support and convince Liberty Glass to meet with union officials to end the five-week old strike, said Sandy Sutton, one of the protest organizers.

Union spokesman Cliff Tyler declined to say what effect the march would have on a settlement effort, but said the protest was "a good thing" regardless. "If nothing else, it will help lift people's spirits," he said.

Attorney William Toney, who represents the glass bottle manufacturer in the labor dispute, said Friday the march constituted mass picketing, prohibited in a temporary injunction issued by District Judge Don Thompson.

Toney also indicated the company's position in contract negotiations would remain firm.

Members of the Glass, Pottery, Plastics and Allied Workers Union say a proposed contract they have refused to sign would weaken benefits and seniority rights won in earlier contracts.

Toney said the union was trying to impose an industry-wide contract package that did not "take into account Liberty Glass' age, size, product, and its circumstances in Sapulpa."

The attorney said the company's position "has hardened" after the

See LIBERTY, Page 2

Exhibit 5-C

NEGOTIATIONS CONTINUED, BUT FAILED TO BRING A SETTLEMENT

Strike talks fizzle

By R.B. ROBBINS
Herald City Editor

A new round of negotiations between union members and Liberty Glass Co. ended Friday with no apparent progress as a strike at the Sapulpa glass plant entered its second week.

Representatives of the Glass, Pottery, Plastics and Allied Workers International Union and the glass manufacturer halted negotiations in Tulsa after several hours at the bargaining table with federal mediator Hugh Collett.

A new date for resuming talks has not been scheduled.

Exhibit 5-C

THEN THE VIOLENCE BEGAN

Glass worker's car destroyed by bomb

By GLENN C. McCASLAND
Herald Managing Editor

An automobile owned by a Liberty Glass Company employee was destroyed today in what police say was an early morning firebombing incident.

The incident was the latest in several reported acts of violence involving Liberty Glass Company employees since the company was struck by members of the Glass, Pottery, Plastics and Allied Workers Union April 1.

The 1972 blue Gremlin owned by Daniel Diaz, 23, was found gutted by fire when police and firemen arrived at Diaz's house, located at 721 S. Linden, about 3:30 a.m. today.

Police Detective Lt. Tom Clark said a quart-sized beer bottle with the remains of what appeared to be a cloth wick was found inside the automobile and fire department officials said the vehicle "appeared to have caught fire after an explosion of some type."

Diaz, who was home at the time of the apparent firebombing, told Clark and Patrolman Steve Tolliver he felt his car was burned because he had recently went to work at Liberty Glass and that several of his friends were on strike.

Diaz said he had been followed home "several times" since he had been employed at Liberty Glass and that he felt the persons who had followed him were strikers.

Clark said no suspects had been identified in the firebombing as of mid-morning today.

Two witnesses to the firebombing were able to contain the blaze in the car and by the time Sapulpa fire trucks arrived, the fire was out, Assistant Fire Chief Leon Smith said.

Agents with the Alcohol, Tobacco and Firearms division of the U.S. Treasury - Department arrived at noon today to assist Sapulpa police with the investigation.

The federal agents were brought into the case at the request of Police Chief Jack McKenzie to assist with specialized arson and bomb investigation procedures.

The firebombing is the latest in similar incidents reported to police that involves either Liberty Glass Company security guards or employees. Four bottles, believed filled with gasoline, were thrown into a parking lot across from Liberty Glass in April, damaging the windshield of a car, but causing no fire.

No arrests have been made in that incident.

A spokesman for the glass workers' union, who declined to be named, said the union "would cooperate in any investigation" concerning the firebombing incident.

"We don't like that sort of business and don't condone it," he said.

Both Wayne Buckley and Louis Hood, presidents of the two union locals involved in the strike, could not be contacted for comment. Both

See GLASS, page 2A

Firebomb attempts probed by police

Attemped firebombing of automobiles in a parking lot at Liberty Glass were under investigation Saturday by Sapulpa police amid reports of additional violence at the labor-troubled manufacturing company.

Tight-lipped city police took statements before noon from at least two persons believed to be Liberty Glass officials regarding the incidents which began Friday morning.

However, shortly before press time Saturday night no formal reports concerning the difficulty had been filed at police headquarters.

Police said four glass bottles filled with what is believed to be gasoline were thrown into the parking lot at Mission and Haskell Streets about 5 a.m. Friday, one bursting into flames, a second shattering and the other two failing to break on impact.

The windshield of an automobile parked in the lot was smashed by one of the bottles, Patrolman Mike Romine said.

Witnesses Lynn Sherron and Randy Coyle, both security guards at

See FIREBOMB, Page 2

Police seek warrant for firebomb suspect

Sapulpa police today were searching for a suspect in connection with the early Wednesday firebombing of a car owned by a Liberty Glass Co employee.

Assistant Police Chief Johnny Moore said information supplied to investigators in the incident that destroyed Daniel Diaz's auto as it sat parked in front of Diaz's home, 721 S. Linden, had 'developed leads to a suspect."

Moore said detectives were "trying to develop those leads today," in an attempt to "put us in a position to obtain a warrant."

Diaz's vehicle was gutted by fire believed caused by a homemade firebomb tossed into the front seat of the vehicle about 3:30 a.m. Wednesday.

The incident marked the first major damage in several reported acts of violence that have occurred since the glass company was struck by union employees April 1.

Diaz had been employed at the labor-troubled glass company two weeks when the firebombing happened, authorities said. The 28-year-old man told officers he had been followed home several times after he was employed by Liberty Glass and he felt those who followed him "may have been strikers."

Union spokesmen said the Glass, Pottery, Plastic and Allied Workers local would cooperate with police and federal authorities, who entered the investigation at mid-day Wednesday.

"We don't condone that kind of thing," an unidentified union spokesman said. "If it is related to the strike, it isn't something we will put up with."

Moore said agents of the Alcohol, Tobacco and Firearms division of the Treasury Department had assumed investigation of the arson and firebombing aspects of the case.

"They are running tests on the bottle and cloth wick we found in the automobile and also are checking for fingerprints," Moore said. "The ATF people are better equipped for that kind of investigation that we are and besides they have jurisdiction under federal law."

Police Chief Jack McKenzie said

See POLICE, page 1

Literature Distribution & Development • 175

Exhibit 5-C

SEVERAL EMPLOYEES BECAME DISSATISFIED WITH THE UNION & RETURNED TO WORK

HOW DID THE UNION RESPOND?

7 workers file dispute against union

A determination in several grievances filed by several parties in the six-week-long Liberty Glass Co. labor dispute may be forthcoming, a National Labor Relations Board investigator said today.

Frank Molenda, resident investigator with the NRLB office in Tulsa, said he hoped for decisions in "at least one and possilby more grievances as soon as the beginning of next week."

The most recent grievance was filed by seven glassworkers who broke ranks with union and returned to work at the glass plant.

The workers — Dennis Houser, Norman Cook, Earl Hankes, Bobby Hurt Jr., Jackie Peck, Ramona Hurt and Ina Rice — claim they have been threatened with fines by the Glass, Pottery, Plastics and Allied Workers Union for resigning from the union and returning to work, Molenda said.

Exhibit 5-C

SEVERAL STRIKERS WERE ARRESTED

Arrest, tire cutting mars Liberty calm

Arrest looms in strike incidents near Liberty

Judge orders striker arrested for contempt in Liberty Glass case

Exhibit 5-C

FINALLY, THE SITUATION GOT SO BAD, SECURITY GUARDS HAD TO CARRY GUNS

Sapulpa Daily **HERALD** Thursday

25¢ DAILY 50¢ SUNDAY   A Park Newspaper   Sapulpa, Okla. 74066   June 2, 1983

Liberty security guards may arm selves

Violence brings warning to union, Creek County sheriff

By GLENN C. McCASLAND
Herald Managing Editor

Members of a striking glass workers union were told Wednesday that increases in violence at Liberty Glass could result in arming of security guards.

The warning came during a meeting between the glass workers union president, company security guard officials and Sheriff Bob Whitworth.

M. Kent Bretz, president of Security and Investigations, Ltd., of Tulsa, said a decision to arm the some 60 guards at Liberty Glass "would be made only as a last resort" if vandalism and acts of violence continue.

At the same time, Bretz presented 61 complaints alledging acts of vandalism and violence to Whitworth for investigation by the sheriff's department.

Union President Louis Hood of Sapulpa, one of four union representatives present during the 90 minute meeting held at Whitworth's office, said afterwards the union "would do all in our power to prevent further problems. We feel many of these incidents are acts of persons who are not union members nor employees of Liberty Glass. However, we don't want guns and the possibility of injury to happen here. We will police our people as best we can."

Whitworth called the meeting "very cooperative and peaceful."

"Everybody understood the seriousness of the situation and seemed willing to work to the problems at Liberty Glass," Whitworth said.

Bretz said that the 61 incidents were presented to Whitworth over a wide period of time, but in the several days — a week or so

See LIBERTY, Page 2

Exhibit 5-C

BUT THAT DIDN'T STOP THE UNION...IT EVEN STARTED SHOOTING RIFLES INTO HOMES

New violence erupts in Liberty dispute

Several bullets were fired into the mobile home of a Liberty Glass Co. employee late Thursday, narrowly missing two children.

The incident was one in a number of acts of violence reported at the Liberty Glass plant or to employees of the Sapulpa glass manufacturer and being investigated by area law enforcement agencies.

Jerry Shipman, a former union member who returned to work at Liberty Glass, reported the gun shots were fired at his trailer shortly after 10 p.m. Thursday.

Capt. Jerry, Siler with the Creek County Sheriff's Office said 36 holes were found in the trailer.

Shipman and two of his children were in the trailer, located in the rural Mounds area, at the time of the incident, Siler said.

Siler said the bullets apparently missed hitting Shipman's children by about two feet.

Shipman today said his children, a 19-year-old daughter and 13-year-old son, were watching television when the bullets ripped through the trailer. Another son was at work at the time, he said.

Siler said the pattern of bullet holes did not resemble those left by a shotgun, and speculated the projectiles could have been fired from a .22-caliber rifle.

An investigation is being pursued by Deputy Leroy Harrison, Siler said.

About 90 minutes later, Liberty Glass employee Gavin Punch was threatened by an unknown person who threw a pallet through the windshield of a small service vehicle Punch was driving, Siler said.

Punch apparently was filing bottle with propane near Liberty Glass

See NEW, Page 2

Exhibit 5-C

STRIKERS WEREN'T HELPED MUCH BY THE UNION STRIKE BENEFITS

THEY EVEN HAD TO ACCEPT CHARITY

Strikers receive food gifts

By R.B. ROBBINS
Herald City Editor

"Solidarity" was the word Saturday when striking glassworkers in Sapulpa received truckloads of material and emotional support from fellow union members in Ada, Okla.

Representatives of two Glass, Pottery, Plastics and Allied Workers locals from Ada brought an estimated $1,000 of food to strike headquarters in Sapulpa in a show of support for the Sapulpa unions' 114-day-old strike against Liberty Glass Co.

The two Ada unions — Locals 183 and 187 — also donated $1,200 in cash to the strikers, and a state AFL-CIO official donated a fishing boat that strikers will use in a fundraising drive.

The assistance effort was decided at a union membership meeting in Ada, said Wayne Bradley, president of Ada's GPPAW Local 187. "We decided to pitch in to help the guys out in Sapulpa. We thought food would be the best thing."

Food collections began about two weeks ago, Bradley said. By the time union officials left Ada at 9 a.m. Saturday, they were hauling three trucks and a trailer load of potatoes, vegetables, fruit, can goods, soda pop, beans and other commodities.

The Ada unions also handed Sapulpa officials checks totaling $1,200. Ross Williams, state AFL-CIO secretary-treasurer hauled in a new bass boat and trolling motor he recently had won.

GPPAW Local 125 President Louis Hood of Sapulpa expressed appreciation for the donations. "It will really pick them (the strikers) up knowing somebody else is

See STRIKERS, Page 2

Exhibit 5-C

BUT THE VIOLENCE STILL CONTINUED

Sapulpa Daily

HERALD

25¢ DAILY 50¢ SUNDAY

A Park Newspaper

Sapulpa, Okla. 74066

Monday, July 25, 1983

Liberty Glass fire called possible arson

By GLENN C. McCASLAND
Herald Managing Editor

Fire that damaged a large metal warehouse at Liberty Glass early this morning has been termed "possible arson," by investigators.

Firemen battled smoke and flames inside the 180 by 700 foot building for five hours before controlling the fire shortly before dawn at the violence-plagued plant where union members began a strike 116 days ago.

Sapulpa Fire Chief Tony Woodall said a bottle containing a liquid believed to be gasoline was found along the east wall of the warehouse. He said the blaze began apparently along that wall, about three feet from the concrete floor.

The warehouse, located just south of the Liberty Glass Company's main plant on North Mission, is used to store flat cardboard boxes and some glass bottle products, Woodall said.

Woodall said the fire was being listed a suspicious and probably was set by an arsonist. One metal wall was found pushed open in two places, he said, allowing access to the building.

Nearly everything in the structure was damaged by fire or sustained smoke and water damage, Woodall said. A sprinkler system inside the giant facility activated and helped keep fire damage down, the chief said.

Liberty Glass spokesman Alan Will said shortly before noon today that no damage estimates would be available until mid-afternoon at the earliest or early Tuesday.

Will said company officials were attempting to gather the information than this morning and did not feel they should comment until "we have all the facts possible."

State Fire Marshal Shelley Phillips was on the scene at midmorning along with Sapulpa Fire Marshal Ed Dorrant and Woodall. The fire investigators were meeting with Liberty Glass officials at press time.

Daryl Rector, business representative for the striking Glass, Pottery, Plastics and Allied Workers Local 185, denied union involvement in the fire.

"We are certain it's none of our people," Rector said this morning. "The more of that stuff (violence) that goes on, the more hard feelings there will be on down the road. We will have to work in that building one of these days."

Woodall said all 32 members of the Sapulpa Fire Department responded to the alarm received at 12:30 a.m. after plant security officers smelled smoke and investigated the source.

Firemen climbed atop the roof of the building and cut ventilation holes to allow smoke to pour from the metal structure.

"This allowed the men to find the fire and start putting water on the blaze," Woodall said. "They did a bang-up job of it."

No one was injured while fighting the fire, Woodall said. The building

See LIBERTY, Page 2

Sapulpa Daily

HERALD

25¢ DAILY 50¢ SUNDAY

A Park Newspaper

Sapulpa, Okla. 74066

Friday, August 19, 1983

Five injured in Liberty Glass violence

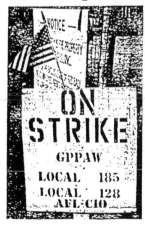

Strike investigation

THE LIBERTY GLASS labor dispute zone marked by pickets and protest signs (left), erupted into violence Thursday. Local and county law enforcement officers investigated the scene of the struggle that left five people arrested and two men in custody. (Herald photos by Curt Reed)

See related photo, Page 2
and Editor's Corner, Page 4

By GLENN C. McCASLAND
Herald Managing Editor

Armed security guards ringed Liberty Glass Co. facilities today after violence erupted Thursday that ended with injury to five persons, including four guards.

Two persons were arrested and later freed on $1,000 bond set by Special Judge Clyde Patrick pending filing of charges in the incident as police pursued investigation of the incident.

Sheriff Bob Whitworth identified those arrested as Danny Ray Collins of Sapulpa and Medaline Radford of Tulsa.

The two men have been employees of Liberty Glass for 16 years and 18 years respectively and are members of the striking Glass, Plastics Pottery and Allied Workers Union. Whitworth said.

More arrests were expected today as investigators met with Assistant District Attorney Luther Cowan to seek both formal charges against Collins and Radford as well as obtain warrants for several additional suspects.

Injured in the melee that Whitworth called "a near-riot" were security guards Russ O'Brien, Mark Chew, Danny Sayliers and Jack Cantrell, former Creek County deputy and son of Oklahoma Highway Patrol Supervisor Weldon Cantrell of Oklahoma City.

The sheriff said the guards were struck over the heads, body and arms by union members swinging baseball bats, bedslats and hammer handles. Several weapons were seized at the scene of the fight.

Whitworth said one Liberty Glass employee was believed injured, but the name of the employee was not known to investigators and Liberty Glass spokesmen were not available to identify the worker today.

Shortly after the melee, Kent Brentz, president of Serratto and Investigations, LTD, of Tulsa, the security firm guarding Liberty Glass, instructed his men to arm themselves with shotguns and more.

"I am directing my men to fight back if attacked. I am sorry we are being forced to do this, but I have no choice but to see my men are protected," Brentz said.

Brentz turned a video tape recording of the fight along Mission Street over to Sapulpa police detectives and officers were meeting the films in an attempt to identify others involved in the fight.

As the investigators worked, heavily armed city police and county deputies appeared at Liberty Glass Company gates this morning at the 6 a.m. shift change in case additional violence erupted.

"The shift change was peaceful enough, but you could feel the tension," Lt. Don Jones said after the officers returned to police headquarters.

Assistant Police Chief Johnny Moore said officers would continue heavy patrol of Liberty Glass and strike headquarters, located just a block from each other, as a preventative measure "until things cool off."

See FIVE, Page 2

Exhibit 5-C

AFTER 21 MONTHS OF AGGRAVATION, VIOLENCE, NO PAY, & NO BENEFITS, THE STRIKE FINALLY ENDED

Liberty strike over

Exhibit 5-C

HOW DID THIS STRIKE END?

Liberty workers vote union out

By TERRY HULL
Herald Staff Writer

TULSA — The union has been voted out at Liberty Glass Co.

The only step left in ending a strike which began in April of 1983, a federal official said, is a "really clerical" certification of the vote.

"The employees' wishes have been published with this vote and it's over," Liberty Glass attorney Bill Toney said after the ballots were counted. "We just hope that everyone now will get on with their lives and this will be a chapter in history that they'll all forget."

Liberty Glass replacement workers voted to decertify the Glass, Pottery, Plastics Allied Workers union as the collective bargaining agent of plant workers. If the vote is certified — which is expected — and the GPPAW is ousted, the 22-month-long Liberty Glass strike will be over.

Workers in the "cold end" of the plant voted 222-4 to oust the union. In the "hot end," the vote was 47-0 to decertify the GPPAW. Votes were held to individually decertify the two locals which had served the plant.

The National Labor Relations Board opened the ballots Thursday afternoon in its Tulsa office, in the presence of company and union representatives. NLRB official Frank Molenda said action on certifying the results will be taken by the end of next week. Once the vote is certified, continued picketing by union strikers will be illegal.

This morning, the picket line was still up at the glass plant. Union attorney Robert O'Brien in New Jersey said he would fly to Oklahoma early next week to confer with GPPAW local presidents Lewis Hood and Wayne Buckley about what action to take.

O'Brien said the election outcome "was not unexpected," since the NLRB decided not to count the votes of strikers.

Both strikers and replacement workers cast ballots in the June decertification election. But none of the ballots was opened until Thursday, while the NLRB heard arguments from both groups on which ballots should be counted.

After months of wrangling, the NLRB in Washington, D.C., last week upheld an earlier decision not to count strikers' ballots. The NLRB declared that strikers had been permanently replaced for more than 12 months and therefore had no say in whether to decertify the union.

After Thursday's vote was counted, union representatives Hood and Pete Dodson left the NLRB office without meeting with the press.

Hood's only comment referred to the decision not to count strikers' ballots.

"I'd like to be a politician and count only one side of the ballot," Hood said.

Company men Toney, Alan Will and Ralph Moore did linger to talk.

Toney said the vote "reflects the employer's right to replace striking employees and operate its facility."

For the first time, Toney commented on the issues underlying the strike, which began April 1, 1983.

"The major issues were costly items in pension improvements, vacation imrpovements, benefits in hospitalization," Toney said.

Wages were not an issue, according to Toney: "We met the so-called industry wage package and actually granted wages over the industry rate for certain (skilled jobs)."

Toney said that on March 18, 1983, just two weeks before the strike, the company offered "an excellent wage package. It was second to none in the Tulsa metropolitan area.

"We did it in an effort to avoid a strike."

Toney said, "The international union had goals of its own."

He said the union demanded that Liberty Glass follow suit with contracts negotiated with larger glass manufacturers, but "they ignored the fact that this was a small, one-product manufacturer."

Dodson of Tulsa said today he and other union representatives had no comment on Toney's comments or on Thursday's ballot-counting.

The Glass, Pottery, Plastic Allied Workers union was voted in at Liberty Glass Co. in the early- to mid-40s, according to Will.

Exhibit 5-C

THOSE PEOPLE DIDN'T THINK IT COULD HAPPEN TO THEM

BUT IT DID!

THINK!

DON'T LET THIS SAME THING HAPPEN HERE

VOTE NO!

Exhibit 5-D

ON STRIKE
at
Buck Creek
A sad, but true story

Exhibit 5-D

April 1, 1993 The union-represented employees of Buck

Creek Coal in Sullivan, Indiana, go on strike. None of the striking union members could guess they would be out of work for **19 months**, or that the normally quiet rural community would be nearly **torn apart**.

Like most strikes, this one begins with the union and the strikers confident of victory.

All fine as clock strikes 9

This group of striking Buck Creek miners — and one wife — were night shortly after erecting one of three picket sites at Indiana's large found on County Road 50W in front of the Buck Creek office.

Ally Pittman

Mine struck despite 'idle' order

By RICH AZAR
Times Staff Writer

Union miners streamed down a darkened stretch of highway to set up picket lines outside the Buck Creek Mine Wednesday night in spite of a company announcement that the mine would be "idled" through Sunday.

About 25 members of United Mine Workers Local 4538 were split among three pickets just off old State Route 54. The first was erected at the employee gate shortly before 8 p.m., another soon sprouted to the east at a truck entrance and a third formed outside the Buck Creek Mining Co. office on County Road 50 West, dubbed "Scab Road" by miners who huddled there sipping coffee.

Other miners were set to arrive with makeshift shelter, fire barrels and plenty of wood, a portent of what some miners privately concede could become a protracted strike over alleged unfair-labor practices.

Buck Creek's announcement earlier Wednesday that the mine would be idled caught some union members by surprise. Included in that group was UMW International Board Member Roger Myers, who also serves as chief negotiator for the Buck Creek miners.

"I didn't know a thing about it until I got here tonight," said Myers, who darted from one picket line to another during the early hours of the strike.

Striking miners who worked their shift earlier Wednesday said the company claimed the shutdown was to repair a hoist that lowers men into Indiana's largest underground mine and to perform needed electrical work.

Myers said company officials suggested to several miners that they would not get strike benefits from the union while the mine was idled.

"I can tell you straight up that these men will be compensated as of tonight," Myers said of strike benefits that average about $150 per week.

The strike followed 16 months of negotiations that ensued after the 45-38 vote in November 1991 that established union representation at Buck Creek. A tentative contract was voted down the following February; subsequent negotiations have yielded little fruit.

Exhibit 5-D

ON STRIKE Page 2

April 8, 1993 Only eight days into the strike, violence
erupts at the entrance to Buck Creek Coal Mine. A driver hauling coal for an
independent trucking company is **attacked** and **beaten** by strikers when he steps
from his truck. A union official calls the attack a **"declaration of war."**

Melee erupts at Buck Creek Mine

By CYNTHIA MOFFATT
Times Staff Writer

The confrontation at rural Sullivan's
Buck Creek Mine escalated today with a
melee sparked by fisticuffs between a striking miner and a truck driver. A top union official characterized the incident as a declaration of war.

Today launches the second week of a
strike that followed 16 months of failed contract negotiations at Indiana's largest underground mine. United Mine Workers International board member Roger Myers predicted
today's incident "will start a war in Sullivan
County."

Sullivan County special deputy Doug
Inman is investigating the incident that occurred shortly before 7 a.m. in front of the
mine on Route 54 that involved striking
miner Terry Simmons and truck driver Jay
Vela. Inman said both union and company
officials captured the incident on videotape.

**Responding to the strike
violence, a judge issues a
protective injunction to limit
the number of pickets, but it
does little good. Through the
spring and summer, property
damage and harassment
continue.**

Jack rocks are thrown in the path of cars and
trucks entering and leaving the mine. **Bullets**
are fired at vehicles. Buck Creek employees
who continue working, as well as employees
of companies doing business with Buck
Creek, are verbally **harassed**.

Exhibit 5-D

ON STRIKE Page 3

August 23, 1993 A security guard working at the

mine is **hospitalized** when bricks are thrown through his windshield as he drives home. The Sullivan County sheriff and Buck Creek management ask Indiana's governor for state troopers to help control the strike violence; the request is denied.

Mine guard hurt as bricks flung down 41

By RICH AZAR
Times Staff Writer

A security guard at the strikebound Buck Creek Mine was hospitalized early Sunday morning after he was struck with "brick bats" while motoring down U.S. 41, according to the Sullivan County Sheriff's Department.

Richard J. Jones, 22, Terre Haute, was treated for neck and head injuries at Mary Sherman Hospital and later released, according to the incident report.

Jones was northbound on 41 near Farmersburg shortly after 4 a.m. when a dark-colored pickup pulled alongside and someone hurled two bricks, shattering the windshield, deputy Gerald Mize wrote in his report.

Jones skidded off the road and struck a fence row, the report said.

Buck Creek employees who have crossed the picket line to support their families are the targets of more union harassment.

Pen from funeral home reportedly sent to strikebreaker

By CYNTHIA MOFFATT
Times Staff Writer

A Buck Creek miner who reportedly crossed the picket line last week told sheriff's deputies he found the word "scab" spray-painted on his car hood and door late Tuesday night.

Meanwhile, a hearing to overturn a judge's decision limiting the number and movements of striking miners was in progress this afternoon in Terre Haute.

Regarding the alleged vandalism, Ray Taylor, 39, New Lebanon, said his car was parked in the garage behind his residence when the vandalism occurred, according to the Sullivan County Sheriff's Department.

The garage was locked but entry was gained through a back door that appeared to be pushed in, according to the report.

Taylor said he found the damaged car about 2 a.m. Two tires on the leased 1993 Pontiac were also slashed, the report said.

Union workers called their strike at Sullivan's Buck Creek mine last Wednesday following 16 months of failed contract negotiations. About 16 miners have crossed the picket line to continue working at the mine, according to United Mine Workers officials.

In a separate incident, Buck Creek Mining Vice President David Steele told sheriff's deputies that several miners who have crossed the picket line have allegedly received threatening letters.

Steele claimed the letters contained ink pens from Newkirk's Funeral Home, Dugger, with a warning that "if they continued working that they would need Newkirk's services," Deputy Jerald Mize wrote in his report.

Exhibit 5-D

September 16, 1993 Rocks and hardware are

reportedly **hurled** by strikers at truck drivers and others entering and leaving the Buck Creek Mine. The owner of a local trucking company calls the rock-throwers "a bunch of hoods."

Owner of trucking company blames 'hoods'

Charges, rocks fly at Buck Creek

By MARK STALCUP
Times Staff Writer

Truck drivers and others entering the strikebound Buck Creek Mine Wednesday are claiming that picketers used slingshots to hurl a torrent of rocks and hardware their way, according to the sheriff's department.

The first stone was reportedly thrown at 8:20 a.m. and struck a car driven by Ewing C. Tipton, Vincennes. Tipton alleged that a striker from Sullivan hurled the rock, according to the incident report. The report did not indicate whether Tipton is a strikebreaking worker.

Moments later, four Energy Hauler Inc. trucks were reportedly dented by metal nuts and other objects as they entered and exited the mine, the report said.

A truck driven by Billy W. Smith, Lewis, was reportedly struck upon entering the mine in the morning and again when he exited in the early afternoon, the report said.

Smith gave police the name of two suspects, both union picketers.

In a related matter, Smith is scheduled to appear Oct. 5 in Sullivan Superior Court regarding a charge of criminal recklessness that stemmed from a July incident in which he allegedly ran over a union tarp on the

strike line, the record shows.

Also Wednesday afternoon, Buck Creek mine superintendent Ray Taylor, rural Sullivan, reported he was struck in the leg by a nut allegedly fired from a slingshot by a striker from Dugger, according to police reports.

No arrests have yet been made in any of the alleged incidents occurring Wednesday, but they remain under investigation.

United Mine Workers officials today denied that union strikers were responsible, and claimed that mine management is behind death threats leveled at a UMW picketer.

"These allegations are just more of the company trying to make us look bad," said United Mine Workers International board member Roger Myers. "I spoke to (Buck Creek Mine co-owner) Walter Pieper yesterday, and told him if he had all the evidence he said he had, he should file charges."

Meanwhile, Myers said picketers plan to file several reports today, including allegations of a top mine official telling a striker, "You're dead meat." Myers claimed strikers also videotaped management hurling rocks at them.

Buck Creek representatives declined comment on the developments. However, Terry Jarvis, co-owner of Energy Haulers

Inc., said even if he pursues charges against those who allegedly struck his company trucks, he believes he'll get nowhere.

"This has been going on since April 2," Jarvis said. "You can't get anybody arrested in Sullivan County.

"I think it's political — everybody down there wants to keep their jobs and elected offices."

Classifying stone-throwers as "a bunch of hoods" and "nothing but a bunch of malicious people, a bunch of criminals tearing things up," Jarvis said he had spoken to strikers the first day of the strike and declared himself neutral.

"I told them we didn't want any trouble, and if we didn't haul the coal, somebody'd be in there the next day to haul it," Jarvis said. "We don't have a thing to do with their wages. That's mine management."

But Sheriff John Waterman, who denies union claims that he is biased against them, similarly discounted the suggestion that his department has not responded to complaints.

Waterman said reports are forwarded to the county prosecutor's office to determine if probable cause exists for any arrests.

"My understanding was there will be arrest warrants issued for what happened yesterday," said Waterman. "Of course, we've been told that before."

By November 1993, 179 acts of violence have been reported at the strikebound company.

December 1993 A suspicious **fire** destroys a house

owned by Buck Creek and used to house security guards. By now, permanent employees have been  hired to **replace** the strikers and keep the mine open.

Exhibit 5-D

ON STRIKE Page 5

A major stumbling block to settling the strike is the union's demand for a closed shop that would force all employees to join the union and pay dues. Buck Creek management has resisted this because an employee committee to get rid of the union has been active since before the strike began.

March 10, 1994 The president of United Mine Workers

District 11 sends a letter to union members asking them to urge Buck Creek's largest customer **not to renew** its contract with the coal company.

William H. Yockey, President

United Mine Workers of America

P.O. Box 904, 9 N. 5th Street • Vincennes, IN 47591
1-800-831-UMWA-8692
PHONE: (812) 882-1085 • Fax (812) 882-1586

March 10, 1994

Dear UMWA Member:

As your District President, I write to you asking for your assistance on behalf of the striking brothers at the Buck Creek Mine located in Sullivan County. Local Union 4538 was certified in December of 1991, after a lengthy organizing drive that resulted in two elections being held. After certification by the National Labor Relations Board, the Union attempted to negotiate a contract with Buck Creek Coal Inc. for 15 months until April of 1993 when we began a strike over violations of the National Labor Relations Act as well as unresolved bargaining issues.

The letter concludes with this request:

I ask you to contact Mr. Burnett Carrithers, Sullivan County REMC representative on the Hoosier Energy REC, Inc. Board. Mr. Carrithers can be reached at 812-398-3493 or by mail at RR 2 Box 22 AI, Carlisle, In 47838. Please express to Mr. Carrithers your concern over Hoosier Energy's support for BCCI's business philosophies. Further express your desire to see Hoosier Energy extract itself from its contract with BCCI at the earliest possible moment and refuse to extend or sign anew at the 1994 termination date, taking only the minimum amount of delivery till such time. Also request that you be informed when the next Board meeting is scheduled so that you or your representative can attend.

As your District President, I am asking you to help us fight for Justice, Corporate Responsibility, and Our Way of life.

In Solidarity,

William H. Yockey
United Mine Workers
President, District 11

Exhibit 5-D

ON STRIKE Page 6

April 1, 1994

The strike against Buck Creed Coal enters its **second year**. Some members of the local union are beginning to criticize the international leadership for what they see as a lack of commitment. Also, the recent **conviction** of the district union's president for his part in the **theft** of $720,000 in union funds has distracted union officials from the Buck Creek strike.

Negotiations are at a standstill. A Buck Creek manager tells the press, "It's very, very hard to sit down and negotiate with someone who you know has vandalized your home and threatened your wife."

Buck Creek strike enters second year

Photo By MARK STALCUP

Miners who have crossed the picket line leave the Buck Creek mine after Thursday's shift. UMWA Local 4538 employees have been on strike for the past year, claiming company officials have used unfair labor practices to discourage union participation.

Company says jobs are gone

By MARK STALCUP
Times Staff Writer

Recalling a year of strike-line violence, Buck Creek Coal Inc. officials declared contract talks at an impasse Thursday and said strikers won't have jobs to return to.

Regardless, few see an end to the strike.

"When our best offer was rejected Dec. 7, we began hiring permanent replacements for these workers who are out on strike," said mine owner Walter Pieper. "Now we are employing more workers than we were before the strike."

Annual mine production, at 1.5 million tons prior to the strike, fell to 800,000 tons this year. However, Pieper said production is increasing.

"We're not at 100 percent yet," he said. "But we're getting close."

The hiring of permanent strike replacements could be prohibited should the strike be declared based on unfair labor practices, as United Mine Worker officials contend.

But regardless of the outcome of a June hearing of union allegations by a National Labor Relations Board judge, Buck Creek Vice President Mike McDowell said current employees likely will stay on the job.

"Whatever the outcome of that hearing, whichever side which doesn't get what they want will most certainly appeal to the full NLRB board," McDowell said.

"That could drag out for months or years, and essentially renders the decision null and void until the hearing."

Only a handful of issues remain unresolved in the strike. Mine management strictly opposes UMW demands for a closed shop, where all employees would be required to belong to the union.

"That was strictly on behalf of the Buck Creek 'Vote No Committee,' " a coalition of employees who oppose a union shop, said Pieper.

Striking miners blame national leadership

By MARK STALCUP
Times Staff Writer

When you've been on strike a year like the union men at the Buck Creek mine, you tend to have some time on your hands. Some draw. Others read. Sullivan's Cary Laughlin writes poetry — including four pages some on the strike line believe sums up the way they feel on this anniversary.

"What happened to leadership?
"Seems our officials lost their grip ...
"Time has come to send a message!
"Does (United Mine Workers President Richard) Trumka have any courage?
"To clear our hopeless passage!"

The poem, written in mid-January, stems from a winter of discontent picketer Nicholas Reynolds said began with a Thanksgiving Day standoff over a court-imposed ban on the strikers' shack.

"Our leadership said there was no way that shack was coming down," said Reynolds. "Everybody here was ready to go to jail except (UMW District 11 president) Bill Yockey."

But strikers sitting in the relocated picket shack on County Road 50W Thursday said they still strongly believe in the strike. They'd just like to see more commitment from those higher up.

"The problem isn't with Local 4538's

leadership," said Reynolds. "It's with the ones higher up, the ones who make the real money."

Laughlin concurred, adding "the local's stronger than ever, thanks to everybody getting to know one another."

The men say they're willing to stay on strike as long as it takes to achieve a fair contract. But some here feel they've been forgotten by the national and district leadership.

A demonstration to commemorate the anniversary of the strike was originally scheduled for today, but was canceled due to Good Friday, Reynolds said.

Continued on Page 5

Exhibit 5-D

ON STRIKE Page 7

July 1, 1994 Strike violence returns, this time to the home of
Buck Creek's president. Walter Pieper, his wife, and their 11-year-old son are
sleeping when a **bullet is fired** into their home. "I can't prove anything," says Mrs.
Pieper, "but we've had other disturbances. We never had this before the strike."

Shot enters home of mine chief

By Paula Baughn
Staff reporter

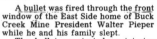

A bullet was fired through the front window of the East Side home of Buck Creek Mine President Walter Pieper while he and his family slept.

The bullet penetrated an interior wall and lodged in a bookshelf in a downstairs room.

Walter Pieper, his wife Susan, and their 11-year-old son were at home when the shot ripped into the house early yesterday morning. No one was injured, but Susan Pieper said she had almost gone to sit in the room the bullet traveled through because she couldn't sleep.

"It's scary," she said. "What's even scarier yet is our son doesn't understand what's going on and someone has invaded his home, and it's not safe anymore."

Mrs. Pieper filed a complaint with Evansville Police in which she indicated the incident might be related to a 15-month-old United Mine Workers strike against Buck Creek Mine near Sullivan, Ind.

UMW District 11 President Bill Yockey denied union involvement in the incident, suggesting the shot could have been an effort by the coal company to deflect attention from an ongoing federal investigation of alleged safety violations at the mine.

Yockey said the union is conducting an internal investigation, but "I'm confident none of our people did it." All striking miners have been accounted for at the time of the incident, he added.

Union miners picketed the Pieper home from July to November last year, but have been prohibited by a court order from continuing, Mrs. Pieper said.

Both union and mine officials have accused each other of threats, intimidation and slander during the strike.

In the police report, Mrs. Pieper states she heard a noise, possibly a "bang," between 1 and 1:30 Thursday morning while the family slept at their Bellemeade Avenue home. When she got up later in the morning, she discovered the shot had been fired through the front window of a downstairs room.

Police indicate a "limited" chance of determining who fired the shot.

"I can't prove anything and never will be able to, but we've had other disturbances," Mrs. Pieper said. "We never had this before the strike."

Buck Creek has been under scrutiny of federal mine officials and the U.S. attorney's office, which are investigating alleged safety violations.

November 3, 1994 After 19 months, the strike
finally ends. Under the contract, all current Buck Creek employees will be required
to **join the union** within two years. Both
management and the union call it a
"good contract," and express the hope
there will be no further strikes in the
future.

But the Buck Creek story wasn't over...

Strike finally over

By MARK STALCUP
Times Staff Writer

The often-bitter 19-month strike at Buck Creek Coal Co.'s Sullivan mine ended Thursday in smiles and handshakes, as union and company officials signed a five-year contract.

"We're glad this at an end, as it's been a long, hard struggle," said United Mine Workers International Executive Board member Roger Myers as he and mine owner Walter Pieper signed the pact.

The pair also promised new negotiations will begin long before Thursday's pact expires in 1999, a move they said hopefully will prevent further strikes.

"When Buck Creek prospers, the UMW prospers — we have jobs," Myers said, adding he thought this contract proved problematic since it was the first the company had negotiated with the UMW.

All of the nearly 60 strikers will be offered their old jobs back, Pieper said, while the mine's current 70-man workforce remains intact.

Strikers are expected to return within the next 30 days, Myers said. Some were reportedly undergoing pre-work physicals even as the pact was signed.

"If there is a current worker in their old position, then that worker (current employee) will be moved to a new job," said Myers. However, he added not all strikers will return, noting some have found other work during the strike.

"It'll all be up to them as to whether they come back," he said.

The final handshakes came almost a week after the union's initial announcement that 89 percent of UMW Local 4538 membership had ratified a tentative agreement with the company.

Further talks with the company resulted after Pieper said he hadn't been notified of the UMW plans, but remaining issues soon were settled, both sides said.

Myers said the two issues that provided breakthroughs at the negotiating table were concessions by both sides on the status of a union shop and whether five workers — three initially fired by the company for alleged strikeline violence, two let go for alleged pre-strike absenteeism — would be allowed to return to work.

Under the new pact, all current mine workers will be required to join the UMWA within two years.

Exhibit 5-D

December 9, 1994 Hoosier Engery, Buck Creek's

biggest customer before the strike, considers switching its business to a **cheaper** and more dependable **non-union** supplier. Hoosier Energy is the same company that 9 months before had been **pressured by the union not to renew** its contract with Buck Creek.

Buck Creek bosses say mine will close if contract with HE not renewed

By JEFF SALYERS
Times Staff Writer

Buck Creek Coal Inc. and United Mine Workers of America Local 4538 officials — at odds with each other during a recently-ended and often acrimonious 19-month strike — find themselves on the same side of the fence this morning: fighting for survival.

Mine officials met this morning with miners — both union and non-union — and told the workers that if Hoosier Energy does not renew its contract with Buck Creek the Sullivan mine will close.

Rudy Riva, financial secretary for UMWA Local 4538 at Buck Creek, said mine Vice President Mike McDowell and mine Superintendent Travis Wellman told workers Buck Creek delivers coal to Hoosier Energy for $17.50 a ton. He said mine officials said Triad Mining Co. has submitted a bid to provide Hoosier Energy coal for $15 a ton.

Hoosier Energy officials are expected to make a decision on the contract Monday, Riva said.

After a long and violent 19-month strike – after struggling to live on union strike benefits – after seeing friendships torn apart – the returning union strikers face a still uncertain future.

December 12, 1994 Buck Creek loses the

Hoosier Energy contract. A spokesperson for the Indiana utility notes that Buck Creek had **difficulty delivering coal** during the 19-month strike.

Buck Creek loses out on HE contract

By JEFF SALYERS
Times Staff Writer

Buck Creek Coal Inc. and United Mine Workers of America officials are studying their options today in the wake of Hoosier Energy's rejection Monday of Buck Creek's bid to supply the company's Merom Generating Station with coal for the next three years.

"We're looking into getting verification from whoever regulates utilities that Buck Creek was given fair consideration," Bill Yockey, UMWA District 11 president said this morning. "The company tells me they still believe they were the low-cost supplier. Buck Creek may be looking at legal action."

Mine officials told union and non-union miners Friday that the mine might close if the

mine did not win the Hoosier Energy contract. Hoosier Energy currently purchases 600,000 tons of the 1.4 million tons mined annually at Buck Creek. That contract expires Dec. 31.

Buck Creek officials did not return calls this morning seeking comment on their current plans.

Hoosier Energy awarded three fuel contracts Monday to supply a portion of coal for the company's Merom Generating Station. Two of the contracts were awarded to Triad Mining in Knox County and Solar Sources in Daviess and Pike counties. Triad will supply 480,000 tons of coal per year from Jan. 1 through Dec. 31, 1997. Solar Sources will furnish 300,000 tons annually during the same period.

Hoosier Energy also agreed to purchase 120,000 tons of coal in 1995 from Cyprus/Amax Coal Co.'s Chinook Mine in Clay County.

Chris Tryba, Hoosier Energy communications manager, said each bidder was given a fair chance to develop its best offer. He said the process is designed to prevent discrimination or treating any one supplier uniquely.

"It's not true," he said of claims made by mine officials and relayed by union miners Friday that the bidding process gave non-union mines preferred treatment. He said the final decision was one based on economics. He did not note that the company had trouble receiving coal shipments from Buck Creek before and during the recently resolved 19-

month strike by UMW Local 4538 members.

"The coal quality and delivery problems were only two factors in the decision-making process," Tryba said. "Overall, economics was the major consideration."

Exhibit 5-D

ON STRIKE Page 9

December 22, 1994 Only days after the loss

of its largest customer, Buck Creek management announces that the number of both salaried and hourly employees will be **reduced to 15**. Before the union was voted in and a strike began, Buck Creek employed over 100 people.

Buck Creek cuts back to 15 employees

Times Staff Report

Buck Creek Coal Inc. announced today it is reducing the work force at its Buck Creek mine from 132 salaried and hourly employees to 15.

No date was given for the layoffs, but the mine has been closed for the past week. Monday mine officials said the mine would remain closed until the end of the year.

"Plans have been submitted to the owners which may allow the mine to activate coal production on a 'restricted basis' in January 1995," Mike McDowell, Buck Creek vice president for human resources, said in a press release faxed to the Times by the United Mine Workers. "We regret such actions are necessary, but have no choice in light of recent events."

Buck Creek had hoped to sign a new coal contract with Hoosier Energy to provide coal for the utility's Merom Station generating plant, but Hoosier Energy awarded contracts to three other coal suppliers on Dec. 12. Buck Creek's current contract with Hoosier Energy expires Dec. 31.

UMW District 11 President Bill Yockey said the layoff will be conducted in accordance with terms of the recently signed 5-year labor agreement between the union and Buck Creek that utilizes seniority and skills as a determining factor.

"No fairer procedure exists," he said in the press release. "Management and labor continue on the harmonious path that was laid with the signing of this agreement.

"This is a tough, skilled group of workers and managers. Don't count this mine out."

McDowell said the union and management will work together.

"Our workforce has faced adversity before and survived," he said. "We have no reason to believe otherwise now."

Neither Buck Creek nor UMW officials could be reached this morning for comment.

December 14, 1995 What was once one of

Indiana's largest underground coal mines prepares to **close**. Buck Creek's new owner says the company was never able to recover from the **crippling** union strike.

Mine shutdown

Miner fears layoff may be permanent

By JEFF SALYERS
Times Staff Writer

For 19 months, Rudy Riva walked a picket line outside Buck Creek Coal, improving mine safety his main concern. This morning the mine mechanic is out of a job — maybe permanently.

Riva got official word of the layoff of 36 of Buck Creek's 37 miners as he completed the midnight shift this morning.

The reason, owner Chuck Schulties said, is the mine's inability to recover from a crippling strike by the United Mine Workers of America.

The 19-month strike ended in November 1994 with the signing of a five-year contract. In December, Buck Creek failed to win a contract with the Hoosier Energy generating station at Merom. That forced a four-day mine shutdown and the layoff of all but 15 of the 132 union miners employed at that time.

The coal market worsened, and the mine has struggled to sell its coal. Schulties said the final blow came when the mine lost a 250,000-ton-a-year contract

with Central Illinois Public Service.

"It's a shame," Schulties said. "At one time, this mine employed 120 people. Now we're down in the 30s and conceivably we could be done completely."

Shulties purchased the mine from Walter Pieper in May. Some workers eventually returned, but he cited poor market conditions when announcing the layoff of about 30 union miners in October.

Riva said he agrees with Shulties that the strike contributed to the mine shutdown.

That's a shame, he said, because "the strike did what it was supposed to do," improve safety at the state's largest underground mine.

He said his future — and that of other Buck Creek union miners — is up in the air right now.

"We're just going to hang around and see what happens," he said.

Riva said he thinks the strike was a contributing factor to Hoosier Energy's decision not to renew its coal contract

Even a local union official and former striker agrees that the strike contributed to the shutdown.

The End

Captive Audience Meetings

*"It is a wonderful feeling
when you discover some evidence
to support your beliefs."*

ANONYMOUS

S everal years ago, by accident, I discovered video's powerful advantages while conducting an NLRB campaign for a client. Halfway through the campaign, the company's general manager suffered a stroke. He was hospitalized and the prognosis was he would be unable to resume campaigning. Besides being a personal tragedy, his illness dealt a serious blow to the company's chances of success. He was the only effective speaker we had available. His second in command, the plant manager, was one of the reasons the employees were seeking union representation, so we couldn't use him. For a variety of reasons, the personnel manager was not acceptable either. It appeared we would be conducting an uphill campaign without our most effective weapon, the captive audience meeting. While reviewing the alternatives, the personnel manager suggested taking a video crew from the local college to the hospital to tape the general manager's final presentation to employees. After receiving permission from the family, the doctor, and the hospital, we shot the video. It was shown during a captive audience meeting and the impact was overwhelming. The company won by a wide margin. After the election, I evaluated the campaign and its individual elements. The video had clearly made the greatest impact. But was this due to the general manager's illness, or the way the message was presented? Obviously, both factors played an important part. That day, I became aware of video's power to communicate management's message, and the dramatic and positive effect it can have on the voting unit.

During the NLRB representation election campaign process, each side has advantages the other does not enjoy. The union's most effective campaign tool is the house call or home visit. It is illegal for management to engage in this activity. However, management has one advantage that, if used effectively, can tip the scales in your favor: the captive audience meeting. A captive audience meeting is a meeting scheduled by management during paid work hours. The exclusive purpose is to inform voters of the disadvantages of union membership and to encourage them to vote against the union in the upcoming election.

The union has nothing in its arsenal that competes with captive audience meetings. Although it can make home visits, in most cases the union cannot reasonably expect to make more than one visit per employee during the campaign. Management, though, can hold as many captive audience meetings as it wishes. When the union calls a meeting, it must be during non-work hours, and attendance is voluntary. If 45% to 50% of the eligible voters attend, that will be considered a good turnout. Management, however, can have multiple meetings with 100% of the eligible voters attending. This is a sizable initial advantage. But it's an advantage that often is not fully utilized. Sometimes management holds only one or two meetings during the course of an entire campaign.

Research by the Labor Relations Institute has shown there is a direct correlation between the number of captive audience meetings and the likelihood management will win an NLRB election.

Number of Captive Audience Meetings	Chance Management Will Win Election
5+	92.7%
4	79.6%
3	69.5%
2	58.9%
1	45.2%
0	32.1%

Captive audience meetings work. Additionally, the more frequent the meetings, the greater the chance of victory.

Since captive audience meetings are so effective, why aren't they used more extensively? First, management is often unaware of the relationship between captive audience meetings and election victories. Second, these meetings are expensive. To hold a captive audience meeting, the voting group must be taken off their jobs for between 30 and 45 minutes per meeting, or longer. If five or six meetings are held during the campaign, up to eight hours of work time may be lost. However, when the much higher cost of dealing with employees through a union is considered, lost work time is a small trade-off. Third, a traditional speech or oral presentation is difficult and time consuming to prepare. The presenter must develop a long and complex program about a subject with which he or she is not familiar, and deliver it in a compelling manner. Consequently, only a limited number of traditional captive audience meetings are usually held. Finally, the messages must be diverse enough and the presentations interesting enough to hold the voters' attention throughout the campaign. Creating several effective 20- or 30-minute presentations is a difficult, if not impossible, task.

These are the common reasons management usually limits itself to only one or two traditional captive audience presentations. Unfortunately, this neutralizes management's most effective communications tool. As the statistics prove, employers that hold no more than one or two captive audience meetings can expect only a slightly better than average chance of winning their election.

In 1988, the Labor Relations Institute introduced the *NLRB Representation Election Campaign Program,* consisting of a series of video presentations designed to be shown to the voting group during captive audience meetings. Except for the expense of taking employees off their jobs, these video presentations have solved most of management's problems in holding multiple captive audience meetings. Now used in more than 3,500 representation elections, the program has achieved a management win rate of over 90%, versus a win rate of less than 50% for management in campaigns where the program has not been utilized.

Captive audience meetings need to be the backbone of your campaign. Whether you choose to use video or oral presentations, the content of these meetings should be the same. For the balance of this chapter, it is assumed that you will use video for your captive audience presentations. However, if you elect to use oral presentations, the fundamental points made in this chapter still apply.

Using Video

Today, people are so accustomed to getting most of their news and information from television, it has become the preferred means of communication. Information received through the audio-visual medium is retained better and is more credible than information received through any other source.

Videos shown during captive audience meetings must be properly presented. Showing videos in a dark or partially darkened room will add to their visual impact and help focus a viewer's attention. Make sure all employees can clearly see the screen and hear the audio. Under normal circumstances, with controlled seating arrangements, approximately 20 people can easily view a standard size TV screen. With controlled seating arrangements, 60 to 75 people can easily view a large screen or projection TV. Depending on the size of the voting group, you should plan enough meetings to comfortably accommodate all voters. If you do not have video equipment, regular size TV monitors or projection TVs and video cassette players are available for rent in most areas.

Information gathered from thousands of video-based campaigns shows that, if possible, small groups of between four and eight employees are ideal for captive audience meetings. A group this size is more likely to discuss the videos and thereby internalize the union-free message.

The viewing schedule must also be considered. Once presentations of a particular video begin, they should run consecutively so that employees attending the first presentation will not have time to discuss the video with those attending the last presentation. Though it is not always possible, your goal should be to allow the video to deliver the message, not word of mouth.

Though presentations can be made at all times of the day and night, you might want to consider using the following strategy: If union support among the voting group is strong, or if you have more outspoken union supporters than management supporters, schedule your presentations near the end of the work day. This way, union supporters have no opportunity to voice their opinions to the undecided voters until the next day. The undecided group has 16 hours to think about your message without rebuttal. If, however, there are a large number of vocal management supporters, you may want to show the videos early in the day so those individuals can use the information they have just received to sway the undecided group. Another consideration is the attention span of employees during the latter part of the work day. If you believe fatigue could prevent full attention to the presentation, consider showing the videos earlier in the day.

You can control the mix of employees attending a captive audience meeting. Vocal union supporters who could disrupt a presentation for undecided or pro-management voters can be grouped together in their own meetings, or they can be disbursed in meetings of predominantly management supporters.

Because LRI videos are structured to be self-contained, the need for a formal introduction or conclusion delivered by the campaign director or other member of management is eliminated. However, if an introduction or conclusion is desired, this is fine.

Some employers have used captive audience meetings to conduct a question-and-answer session following the video presentation. This is acceptable campaign conduct as long as the meetings are not used to solicit employee complaints or grievances where this practice has not previously existed. Simply providing voters with additional information or answering campaign-related questions is acceptable. However, there is always some danger in opening meetings for employee participation. Union supporters can seize this opportunity to voice their opinions about campaign issues. Sometimes a management spokesperson can successfully turn these situations around and gain support. Often, however, the union gains a platform that is counterproductive for management. You must evaluate your own situation, including your ability to persuasively counter union issues, before deciding whether to include other activities when presenting the videos in a captive audience meeting.

Regardless of how you structure these meetings, always remember that they are the cornerstone of the campaign. All literature topics and distribution schedules should be planned around the captive audience presentations. Distributing literature at the end of captive audience meetings can produce excellent results, especially if the literature relates directly to information presented in a video. For example, the *Job Security & Strikes* video documents an actual union strike. Reproducing and distributing the handout in Chapter 5 that parallels this presentation helps to reinforce the video's message about one of the greatest potential dangers of union representation. And research has proven that many voters will keep and read campaign literature if they believe it is especially relevent. Linking literature to video presentations provides relevancy.

While many employers rely exclusively on captive audience presentations to encourage voters to reject unionization, the best way to secure maximum employee support on election day is through a combination of captive audience presentations, issue-specific literature that supports your position, and active supervisors who can articulate the Vote No message for employees.

Gimmicks & Gizmos — Pizzazz with Purpose

*"Persistence is what makes
the impossible possible,
the possible likely,
and the likely definite."*

ROBERT HALF

I t began when I was involved in a very tough campaign for a large employer in Tucson, Arizona. After a long day of campaigning, the management committee decided to call it a night and go to a Chinese restaurant for dinner. When the meal was finished, the waiter brought out the traditional fortune cookies. Everyone opened a cookie and read their fortune aloud. I don't remember what my fortune said that evening, but for some reason, when it came my turn to share my fortune with the group, I said, "Union dues buy no shoes." Almost in unison, everyone started demanding that I show the fortune. I had to confess I had made it up. Soon, everyone was making up their own non-union fortune. Within 30 minutes, we must have written 25 or 30 fortunes and decided to include fortune cookies as part of the campaign. Thus another gimmick — the union-free fortune cookie — was born.

Specialty items have a place in almost every campaign. Used by both management and the union, they are a simple way to get across a difficult message, or to inject humor into a rigorous campaign. Some campaigners use them to help create a bandwagon effect and as a subtle reminder to voters. While it is hard to determine exactly what impact specialty items play in persuading employees to vote a certain way, there is no question that they help keep people involved and aware of campaign issues.

There are many kinds of specialty items; they range from buttons and T-shirts to strike computers and fortune cookies. Specialty items are suggested and briefly discussed in each of the campaign segment chapters that follow. You need to be aware of the different types of specialty items available and how they can be utilized. Basically, there are two categories of specialty items: informational and bandwagon. Informational items make a simple point or statement; bandwagon items are intended as a public display of support.

Informational Items

Specialty items that are informational also make excellent handouts. These items include strike computers, warranty coupon booklets, question-and-answer flyers, and any other items making strong, relevant points without using formal litera-ture. In addition, since these items are not usually viewed by voters as literature, they can be distributed in conjunction with traditional campaign handouts and at captive audience meetings.

The strike computer is an excellent example of this type of specialty item. It is designed to work like a simple slide rule. An employee sets the computer on the amount of money he or she makes per week and the number of weeks a union strike might last. The computer shows the amount of money the employee would lose as a result of a strike and how long it would take to recover their losses based on the amount of money struck for. Strike computers make excellent handouts during the strike segment of a campaign.

Another good example of an informational item is the warranty coupon booklet. Many voters mistakenly believe a union victory would automatically translate into higher pay, better benefits, or improved working conditions. An organizer may have made statements or implied that if the union wins, these improvements will occur. Giving voters an opportunity to hold the union's feet to the fire quickly dispels the idea the union can guarantee anything.

A warranty coupon booklet is simply pages of written guarantees to be signed by the union organizer. Guarantees might read: "I GUARANTEE: You will get a raise of _____ per hour in the first contract my union negotiates with your employer. If you don't receive this raise, my union will pay you the difference"; or: "I GUARANTEE: My union will never fine you or make assessments against you. This promise supersedes any language to the contrary found in the union constitution"; or: "I GUARANTEE: You will not be held back from pay increases or promotions because other union members have more seniority than you."

Obviously, no union organizer will sign these statements. When voters see for themselves that the union cannot guarantee anything, it often helps change their minds, particularly those who honestly believed the union could make a positive difference in their working lives.

Other items we call informational may actually contain no information at all, but still make an important point. For example, one LRI client developed a 20-page booklet titled *What The Union Can Do For You!* The inside pages of the booklet were blank except for the inside back cover which contained a large red dot and said, "Blow on this dot. When it turns blue, union promises will come true."

Bandwagon Items

At some point in your campaign, you may decide to whip up a bandwagon atmosphere by distributing caps, T-shirts, or campaign buttons. The purpose of these items is to provide your supporters with a way of declaring their intentions. This can also dishearten union supporters, perhaps to the point they will abandon their pro-union efforts.

One of the fundamental things we have learned while participating in over 3,500 NLRB elections is that particularly during the latter stages of a campaign, some voters — often as many as 5% to 10% — decide how to vote based on their perception of who will win. These are the ultimate fence sitters. All they care about is being on the winning side. For these individuals, bandwagon items may be the best campaign tool available, but only if *you are sure over 50% of the voting group will wear them!*

There are things you can do to make support for management appear greater than it actually is. For example, allow supervisors and other non-voting personnel to wear campaign specialty items. Nothing is more frustrating to a union organizer than to see employees who seemed to be sure votes refuse to wear a union button or shirt; or worse, to see them show up wearing a management item.

The distribution and wearing of these and other campaign paraphernalia is legal so long as the items are inexpensive, which generally means less than about $15 each.

As a campaign director, you should be aware of several points regarding bandwagon specialty items:

1. The primary purpose of distributing these items is to create a bandwagon effect. For example, if you have 100 eligible voters and 70 are

wearing Vote No buttons or employer T-shirts, most voters will assume management is going to win the election. Some may vote for management just to be with a winner.

2. If the item distributed has some utilitarian value, such as a T-shirt or cap, voters who do not feel strongly one way or the other might wear them. Though it is rare to see strong union supporters or strong management supporters wear articles supporting the opposition, it is common for those without strong feelings to wear anything that is free or something everyone else is wearing.

3. Some people will wear campaign items to irritate another person.

4. Items must be distributed in a way so that management cannot record who accepted the items. In a recent case, an employer ordered 1,000 Vote No T-shirts and gave them to a supply clerk for distribution. Following the employer's instructions, the clerk kept a list of employees who took the shirts. The NLRB stated, "Such employer record keeping of the employees' anti-union sentiments enables (the employer) to discern leanings of employees, and to direct pressure at particular employees in its campaign efforts." The Board said employees could assume their names were being recorded to discern their sentiments about unionization, which interferes with an election. For this reason, items should be made openly available to all employees with no record kept of who accepted the items and who refused.

There is always the possibility that early in a campaign, the union will distribute campaign paraphernalia to voters. Your decision must then be whether to respond. The danger in not responding is that voters will form the wrong impression. However, there is a greater danger in responding and not getting adequate support.

If you are considering the distribution of campaign paraphernalia, you should time the distribution, if possible, so the positive effect doesn't wear off before election day. For example, if you distribute T-shirts — an item that can't be worn every day — the effect created on the day the shirts are distributed may be superb, but will never be as good on subsequent days unless certain days are designated when everyone will show their support by wearing the shirts. If you decide to use shirts, it would be ideal to distribute them two days before the election and have as many people as possible wear them the day before the election. Caps or buttons, which can be worn every day, do not pose this problem.

Be aware that if the union distributes campaign paraphernalia, management supporters will want something similar to announce their position. It would be wise to have your items selected and ordered early in the campaign so you can use them as soon as possible, should the need arise.

Other Items

Besides the specialty items already discussed, there are others that don't easily fall into any category, but can be extremely effective. For example, the union-free fortune cookies mentioned at the beginning of this chapter make excellent campaign items, particularly on the day before the election. Since management has made its last major appeal to the voting group the previous day, the day before the election is almost anticlimatic. To maintain a good level of interest and to add some levity while still making statements about the union, many employers use fortune cookies. Most employers place a large supply of cookies in the cafeteria or break room and let employees take as many as they want. Some voters try to collect every fortune. Typical fortunes include:

"Union dues buy no shoes"
"Union like bowler — always want strikes"
"Shortest strike always too long"
"Dollar in pocket better than sign in hand"
"Picket line never leads to pay window"

Obviously, you cannot expect fortune cookies to sway most voters, but they are humorous and create attention, thereby making it more difficult for the union to gain any last minute advantage.

Bumper stickers are another fun specialty item. You can buy or have stickers made that say almost anything. The one I like best says, "I don't brake for union organizers!" Some of the campaign specialty items available from the Labor Relations Institute are shown on the following pages.

Bumper Stickers • Fortune Cookies • Popcorn Bags

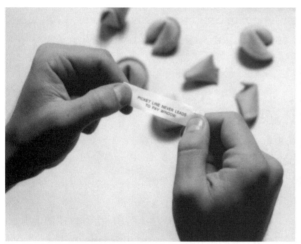

Strike Computers

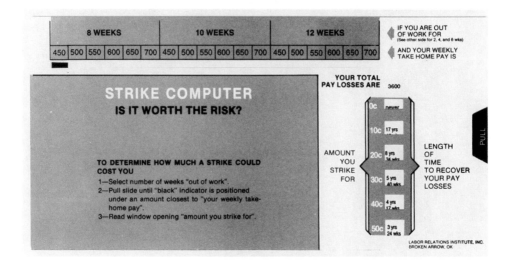

	8 WEEKS						10 WEEKS						12 WEEKS						IF YOU ARE OUT OF WORK FOR (See other side for 2, 4, and 6 wks)
450	500	550	600	650	700	450	500	550	600	650	700	450	500	550	600	650	700	AND YOUR WEEKLY TAKE HOME PAY IS

STRIKE COMPUTER

IS IT WORTH THE RISK?

TO DETERMINE HOW MUCH A STRIKE COULD COST YOU

1—Select number of weeks "out of work".
2—Pull slide until "black" indicator is positioned under an amount closest to "your weekly take-home pay".
3—Read window opening "amount you strike for".

YOUR TOTAL PAY LOSSES ARE 3600

AMOUNT YOU STRIKE FOR

0c	never
10c	17 yrs
20c	8 yrs 34 wks
30c	5 yrs 40 wks
40c	4 yrs 17 wks
50c	3 yrs 24 wks

LENGTH OF TIME TO RECOVER YOUR PAY LOSSES

PULL

LABOR RELATIONS INSTITUTE, INC.
BROKEN ARROW, OK

Campaign Segment One: Preparation & Training

During any election campaign, including NLRB representation elections, face-to-face contact with voters is very important. In his book, *Man of the House,* former Speaker of the House of Representatives Tip O'Neill relates an interesting story.

"The second political lesson I learned from my first campaign came from Mrs. O'Brien, our elocution and drama teacher in high school, who lived across the street. The night before the election she said to me, 'Tom, I'm going to vote for you tomorrow even though you didn't ask me to.'

"I was shocked. 'Why, Mrs. O'Brien,' I said, 'I've lived across from you for eighteen years. I cut your grass in the summer. I shovel your walk in the winter. I didn't think I had to ask for your vote.'

"'Tom,' she replied, 'let me tell you something: people like to be asked.'

"She gave me the lesson of my life, which is why I've been telling this story for 50 years. But it's true, people do like to be asked — and they also like to be thanked."

Face-to-face, direct campaigning is one of the most important aspects of any election campaign. And the best person to conduct this type of campaigning is a voter's immediate supervisor. But most supervisors are usually uncomfortable in this role. They are not politicians. In fact, they probably hate politicians. Yet, for the next few weeks, they have to campaign for the votes of the employees under their supervision. You must do everything possible to make them at least reasonably comfortable in this new role.

To accomplish this objective, supervisors must become involved in the earliest stages of campaign strategy and planning. They must be included in whatever fine tuning is necessary during the campaign. Most importantly, they must be given the proper initial training and ongoing assistance that will make them comfortable and confident in their new role as an effective campaigner.

Developing an Effective Supervisory Training Program

All the elements necessary to develop a successful supervisory training program are included in this book. In addition, a video training program for supervisors and management is available from the Labor Relations Institute. If you are using the video program, this chapter will provide additional information and will help you develop exercises for supervisors during the training process.

The video training program is by far the most effective training method. In eight hours of intensive instruction, the supervisory force becomes familiar with the topics and information to be included in the campaign; they come to clearly understand what they can and cannot do during the campaign period; literature distribution techniques are discussed; and supervisors discover the best ways to persuade voters to reject the union on election day. If the video is not to be used and you wish to develop your own training program, this chapter is especially important.

PART ONE

- Explain the legal requirements the union had to meet to file a petition for election (30% legal minimum, 60% to 65% realistic minimum).

- Focus of the union campaign is to maintain the support of card signers. Focus for management is to change the minds of card signers.

- Keys to management victory: captive audience meetings using either speeches or video presentations; effective literature; active and persuasive supervision.

- Show Video 1 of the *NLRB Representation Election Campaign Program* or discuss key elements of Chapter 9.

- Have each supervisor analyze voters as discussed in Chapter 2. Discuss collective results.

PART TWO

- Review materials to be used during the campaign. A list of these materials is found under Campaign Research in Chapter 2.

- Explain the importance of timing the campaign to retain voter interest and to peak that interest on election day.

- Have supervisors assist in developing a campaign calendar. Consider the materials available and the importance of timing.

- Show Video 2 or discuss key elements of Chapter 10.

PART THREE

- Review Chapter 3, Guidelines for Supervisors & Managers During a Union Organizing Effort.

- Discuss the most common types of management action likely to cause unfair labor practice charges filed by the union.

- Administer the "Can You Say It?" test in Chapter 3.

- Discuss the correct answers for the test.

- Show Video 3 or discuss key elements of Chapter 11.

PART FOUR

- Discuss the importance of campaign literature described in Chaper 5.

- Discuss rules that cover the distribution of campaign literature for both management and the union.

- Review the importance of supervisory follow-up after the distribution of campaign literature.

- Have your supervisors practice the distribution of campaign literature and active follow-up.

- Show Video 4 or discuss key elements of Chapter 12.

- Discuss personality-centered campaigns versus issue-oriented campaigns.

- Discuss the importance of focusing on issues.

- Discuss voting procedures.

- Show Video 5 or discuss key elements of Chapter 13.

The Importance of Effective Supervision

Remember that every successful campaign consists of three critical elements: frequent captive audience meetings, effective campaign literature, and persuasive and articulate supervisors. Top management and outside sources can help with captive audience meetings and even literature development, but ineffectual supervisors can be fatal to your campaign.

If your supervisory employees are functioning properly in their role as articulate spokespersons — and the other necessary elements of the campaign are in place — you have an excellent chance of winning. Even if supervisors neither help nor hurt your campaign, your chances of victory are very good if the other two elements are strong. But a negative impact by supervisors can undo all your other efforts.

Consider this possibility: You conduct frequent and persuasive captive audience meetings; your literature is outstanding and receives full distribution; but in their daily discussions with the voting group, supervisors indicate a lack of enthusiasm for your message. Maybe they indicate to voters that they don't fully agree with what you are saying, or worse, they tell voters they don't believe your message and can understand why employees may want a union. If supervisors or any members of management are perceived to be even mildly sympathetic to the union, all your good campaigning could be for nothing.

It is essential that supervisors be positive and supportive. Though not every supervisor can be a champion campaigner, they should all give their full support. Anything less is unacceptable. Because supervisors are not covered by the National Labor Relations Act, they can legally be dismissed or transferred during a campaign.

To be the kind of campaigners you want, supervisors must be given the right ammunition with which to battle the union onslaught. It's easy to tell a person to go fight the good fight, but if they are outgunned, they will probably be shot down. Fortunately, you have the ammunition; and you probably have supervisors who are willing to take the campaign directly to voters. This is why they must be properly trained and fully armed.

Campaign Segment Two:
How Unions Work
Big business, not charity

During this early campaign segment, your objective is to introduce the voting group to the many disadvantages of union membership by presenting a range of ideas and issues for voters to consider without discussing any specific issue in detail. Later in the campaign, each of these subjects will be fully addressed.

This segment should encourage employees to consider the issue of unionization more seriously. It is easy for voters to listen only to an organizer and to think that union membership sounds like a good deal. But once they get all the facts, most will see that by supporting a union, they could get more than they bargained for.

Specific goals to be reached in Segment Two are:

1. Cause voters, perhaps for the first time, to consider that union membership has distinct disadvantages.

2. Cause management supporters to become more vocal in opposition to the union and give them several specific counter arguments to union propaganda.

3. Cause the union to begin moving from an offensive to a defensive position, particularly if it is using open group meetings.

4. Begin to involve first line supervisors in the campaign process.

In each of the remaining campaign segments, the cornerstone will be the captive audience video/speech. Therefore, your literature must be coordinated with material covered in the meetings. There are a number of ways to schedule

Segment Two. Some employers simply put the captive audience video/speech pre-sentation in the middle of the segment and then begin to address specific issues in Segment Three. In that case, no literature would be distributed during this segment. Other employers begin the segment with an introductory handout followed by a captive audience meeting. Some conduct a captive audience meeting during the first part of the segment, then follow with a question-and-answer handout. There are no fixed rules for Segment Two.

If each of your campaign segments are going to be at least five days long, you should plan to use literature during Segment Two. Whether you use literature or not, it is important to follow-up the captive audience meeting with active supervisory involvement with the voting group. This is critical, since at this point in the campaign you must assume you are behind in the vote count. Remember, a union usually will not file a petition unless it has signed authorization cards from at least 60% of the voting group.

By the latter part of this segment, you need answers to the following questions:

• Has the information presented to the voting group changed the minds of any employee or group of employees?

• Which issues addressed in the captive audience meeting were particularly relevant to voters?

• How are union supporters responding to the introduction of management's campaign?

To be sure the supervisory group is interacting with voters, it is wise to schedule a handout following the captive audience presentation. The distribution of a handout will force supervisors to see each employee on an individual basis, affording them the opportunity to discuss unionization and to answer questions. If you have not done so already, review with supervisors the rules on interrogation discussed in Chapter 3 and Chapter 8 before instructing them to discuss union-related issues with voters. Following the distribution of the handout and discussions with employees under their supervision, each supervisor should have a better feel for management's present position and which issues should be most productive.

Before drafting your handout(s) and developing the calendar for this segment, decide on the content of the captive audience presentation. If you are using the LRI video program, review the video *How Unions Work — Big business, not charity.* If you are giving a speech at the first captive audience meeting instead of showing the video, a sample draft of a captive audience speech follows.

Draft of Captive Audience Speech

Unions. We read about them in newspapers, hear about them on television, but most of us don't really know much about what they are, what they do, or how they work. Since a union is now trying to become your legal representative, you need more information about how a union really works.

First, let's look at some facts about unions. A union is a business. It doesn't make or sell a product but, like any other business, it needs to make money to operate. How do unions make their money? Simple: they charge dues to their members. The amount of money charged each member multiplied by the number of members equals the amount of money each union makes. This means that the more members a union has and the more money it can charge each member, the more money the union has to spend. If it starts to lose members, it makes less money.

Let's look at what's happened to union membership over the last few years and see why unions are working so hard to sign up new members. In general, unions aren't doing very well. In 1954, they represented over 32% of the workforce in the United States. That number gradually declined between 1955 and 1975. Then, between 1975 and today, the number has decreased dramatically so now unions represent only about 15% of all employees. And today, among those who are not employed by government, the percentage belonging to unions is even lower — around 11%. This means only about one worker in ten chooses to be a union member. Remember, fewer members means fewer dues and less money.

Why is union membership decreasing? There are a lot of reasons, including layoffs in unionized industries, plant closings where unions used to represent employees, lost elections, and decertifications (this is when union members kick their union out). So unions are rapidly losing members and now have fewer and fewer people from whom they can collect dues. If they want to stay in business, they need to increase their membership.

How do unions spend the money they collect in dues? Let's take a look at **[name of the union seeking representation]** and find out. **[Insert figures from the union's actual LM-2. The remainder of this paragraph illustrates how you can present this information. If you do not have the union's LM-2, skip this paragraph.]** Each year, every union has to file a form with the United States

Department of Labor stating how much money it received and how that money was spent. The form is like your income tax return and is called an LM-2. Last year the [name of union] collected over $6 million in dues from their members during the year. It spent over five hundred thousand dollars, or 8.3 cents of every dollar collected from its members, for office expenses. Three hundred thousand dollars, or 6.2 cents of every dollar collected from its members, went for publicity. Eight hundred and fifty thousand dollars, or 13.9 cents of every dollar, went for benefits to union officials for things like cars and expense accounts. Two hundred and sixty-four thousand dollars, or 1.7 cents of every dollar collected from its members, went for miscellaneous expenses. Over $1 million, or 17.3 cents of every dollar collected, went to pay the union's taxes. And finally, how much do you think the union bosses spent on their own salaries? Over $3 million, or 50.5 cents of every dollar collected from members, went to pay the salaries of union officers and employees, and the salaries of the union bosses and the special friends of the union bosses. What all this adds up to is that 97.9 cents of every dollar the union collected from its members went to benefit the union.

But what about the remaining two cents? Maybe you're thinking it was finally spent on some of the members. Not according to the [name of union's] LM-2 which shows the amount spent on behalf of individual members was zero. Not one penny. Nothing.

Unions are having such a difficult time because they're a thing of the past. Years ago, employees didn't mind putting control of their future in the hands of an outside third party. They didn't mind being told when they should go on strike or that the union decided not to process their grievance. But today, things are different. Employees want control over their working lives. The problem is unions haven't changed. They still believe the same conditions that existed in 1930 or 1940 still exist today. They think today's workers and today's employers are exactly like the workers and employers of the past. Labor unions have failed to adjust to changing conditions. Since they haven't adapted, they're becoming extinct.

What about unionized employers? Well, they're in trouble too. In unionized industries with restrictive work rules, the union isn't really interested in the employer's success. This attitude makes it difficult, if not impossible, to compete in the world marketplace. But in non-union companies, where everyone is free to work together as a team, the future is bright. That's one of the reasons why so many large, predominantly union-free employers are successful. Employees who say "no" to unions are actually helping to ensure a more secure job future. So rejecting the union is not only a good idea from a personal standpoint, it's also one of the best ways to ensure long-term job security.

Continuing stories about corruption in organized labor have also made it tough for unions to sign up new members. Employees are no longer willing to trust their working lives to individuals who are only interested in feathering their own nests. Stories about union corruption and unions being controlled by criminals are not fiction. In fact, *Fortune* magazine published an article titled "The 50 Biggest Mafia Bosses. The Crime Business: Who runs it, how they manage it, who profits and loses." **[A copy of this article is available from LRI.]** It lists prominent Mafia bosses and tells where they get their money. Of the top 50 leaders of organized crime in the United States, 18 get a substantial part of their income from unions.

Why is all of this important to you? The union wants you to vote for it in a National Labor Relations Board election. To have an election, the union is required by law to obtain signed authorization cards from at least 30% of the employees in the group it is seeking to represent. A union authorization card is a legal document. If you read the fine print, you will find most authorization cards are really membership applications to the union. If you sign the card, you've designated the union your collective bargaining representative. When the union has the required number of signed cards, the cards are given to the National Labor Relations Board and a petition for an election is filed. The Board then notifies the employer that the union has filed a petition and that an election will be held. However, and this is very important, the election will be by secret ballot. Everyone in the eligible unit can vote, whether or not they signed a card. And you can vote whatever way you choose. You can vote against the union, even if you've signed a card.

Now that you know why the union works so hard to sign up new members, let's examine the question of your personal decision about how you will vote in the upcoming election. The National Labor Relations Act is the law that regulates union activities. It gives you the legal right to vote for or against the union. Before you make that decision, let's look at some more facts about unions, important facts that you need to know.

When a union is trying to win the votes of potential new members, a paid organizer is usually assigned to the campaign. This organizer may stand outside our property handing out union literature; or they may try to form committees of current employees to help win votes. The organizer can legally promise employees anything: higher wages, better benefits, improved working conditions, shorter hours, anything to get employees to vote for the union. These promises are not illegal. But don't forget that a union organizer is a salesperson. Their future and pay are determined by their ability to recruit new members. To win your vote, an organizer may tell you only the things you want to hear. Because the union needs new members so badly, it may even try to deceive you. Some typical union tricks include:

- Asking you to attend a union "informational" meeting where you're pressured to support the union.

- Telling you that you're the only one in your group who hasn't decided to get with the team and support the union. This usually isn't true.

- Using fellow employees to pressure you to support the union. Some standard approaches include: "Do me a favor, help us get the union in." It could prove to be a very expensive favor.

[Depending on your individual situation, the following paragraph is optional.]

Because many employees are more likely to trust each other rather than an outsider, unions have come up with a trick to take advantage of this. The new tactic is called apprentice organizing. Thousands of people are trained to sell the union, just as if they were professional organizers, then sent out to find jobs in non-union workplaces. After an undercover organizer goes to work for the targeted employer, they begin working for their real boss — the union. They suggest to their fellow employees that a union might be able to solve problems or complaints. Before you know it, the professional organizer shows up to cash in on the groundwork done by the apprentice. Unions are training thousands of their employees to do this, so remember, what sounds like a spur-of-the-moment suggestion that unionization could solve your problems was possibly planted by an apprentice organizer.

Repeated requests to support the union are made in the hope that eventually employees will be worn down, but stand up for your rights. If you don't want to support the union, don't do it.

Unfortunately, employees are often told by union pushers that if they don't support the union, their work relationship will suffer. Sometimes this approach is even more direct and threatening. Those threats may be illegal and you should bring them to management's attention. We will take all appropriate actions to deal with them.

Remember, if the union wins an election designating it your collective bargaining representative, it wins one right and one right only: the right to negotiate with this organization. Nothing more, nothing less. The truth is, a union organizer can promise everything, but can't guarantee anything. For proof of this, ask an organizer or someone who is pushing the union to give you a written guarantee that the union will get employees a certain amount of pay increase or a particular benefit, or that there will be no strikes. To really put the organizer to a test, ask if the union will make up the difference if it's unable to keep these promises.

If a union becomes the collective bargaining representative of a group of employees, this means management and the union would sit down at the bargaining table and negotiate. The union can ask for all the things the organizer promised, but management is not obligated to give anything other than what it feels it can afford or what it is willing to give. It's a lot like the game *Wheel of Fortune,* but when the wheel stops, union-represented employees can't be sure of what they'll wind up with. It could be more; it could be less; or they could wind up with the same things they started with, plus paying union dues. The union knows this is true, that's why it won't guarantee you anything.

As voters, you should be very careful about believing what an organizer promises you. The National Labor Relations Board, the government agency that regulates union organizing attempts, has stated, "Collective bargaining is potentially hazardous for employees, and as a result of such negotiations, employees could possibly wind up with less benefits after unionization than before." **[The actual case containing this statement is available from LRI.]** You can clearly see that designating the union your collective bargaining representative is really a roll of the dice, but a roll that has very high stakes.

Another important point voters often forget when considering union membership is the obligation members have to their union. All members are obligated to abide by the constitution and bylaws of the union they join. On the surface, this may not sound important. But when you consider the restrictions and obligations that union constitutions place on members, it becomes very important. For example, did you know that union constitutions contain pages and pages of restrictions on their members' rights? Did you know that the Constitution of the United States is only seven pages long, while the constitution of most unions is over 100 pages of very fine print? What's in all those pages? Let's take a look at the constitution of the **[name of union]** and find out.

[At this point in the speech, use provisions from the union's constitution. The rest of this section illustrates how you can present this information. If you do not have access to the union's constitution, you may wish to skip this section.]

One provision talks about union dues. It states that dues can be increased from time to time at the union convention.

A provision covering assessments states that whenever the union needs extra money, it can assess its members whatever amount is needed.

Another provision talks about fines. It says a union member can be fined whenever the union thinks the member has stepped out of line.

There's a provision about trials. That's right, trials. It says a union member can be put on trial.

Many provisions talk about rules and regulations. One of them says that if a member doesn't like the union and tries to get rid of it, they can be put on trial and fined. Another says that if the union calls a strike and a member continues to work, the member can be put on trial and fined. And the United States Supreme Court has upheld the right of a union to fine its members.

These are just a few examples, and this constitution is **[number of pages]** long. **[Actual number of pages]** full of rules, regulations, and restrictions.

When you hear the word "union," maybe the first thing you think about is strikes. Unions are famous for calling strikes. How does this happen? As we said earlier, if a union becomes the representative of a group of employees, it sits down with management and the two sides bargain. If they can't agree, there are very few things the union can do to try to make management accept its demands. One of those things — and the most frequently used tactic — is to call members out on strike.

There are things about union strikes you should know, things no union organizer will tell you. First, if you go on strike for more money or better benefits, you receive no paycheck and your employee benefits are terminated. No paycheck, no benefits.

Second, in most states you cannot receive unemployment compensation. No unemployment compensation. **[New York and Rhode Island are the exceptions. If you are conducting your campaign in either of these states, leave out this subject.]**

And third, you can be permanently replaced. No matter what the union organizer may tell you, if you go out on economic strike, management has the right to hire permanent replacements to fill the jobs of striking union members.

When the strike is over, those replacements can keep their jobs as long as they want them. The National Labor Relations Board has stated, "An employer may permanently replace economic strikers." If that isn't enough reason to avoid strikes, there's the violence that often goes along with a strike. Friends become enemies, tempers flare, damage is done — damage that sometimes can never be repaired.

Union organizers frequently try to convince voters that strikes are rare, but let's look at the record. According to the United States Department of Labor and the Bureau of Labor Statistics, the government agencies responsible for monitoring union activities, strikes are a relatively common occurrence. According to the Department of Labor, in the ten-year period between 1986 and 1996, unionized employees missed over 69 million work days because of strikes. Think about that: 69 million work days. And this figure includes only strikes that involved 1,000 or more employees. Strikes involving less than 1,000 employees aren't included. So as you can see, with a union, strikes are a very real possibility that you should consider when deciding how to vote.

What about job security? Union organizers try to get voters to support the union by promising that everyone will be provided greater job security. Let's look at some facts. Union membership has declined dramatically in recent years. We've all seen television reports and newspaper articles about plants closing and massive layoffs. What you might not realize is that many of the employers that have closed or had big layoffs were unionized. So does belonging to a union really provide job security?

And there are other ways that unions can fail to deliver on the promise of job security. In states where it's legal, most union contracts contain a "union shop clause" that requires every employee to join the union and remain a member or be fired. This is important to unions because they don't believe in letting individual employees make up their own minds. Unions know that without this provision, many employees would not join and therefore never pay dues.

So what can the union really do for you? Strikes, dues, fines, assessments, constitutions and bylaws that restrict your rights as an individual — but the union can't guarantee you any improvements. Our position on the union issue is very clear: We do not want a union here. We feel more can be accomplished if we continue to work together, one-on-one, without union stewards and officials, and without you paying union dues, fines, and assessments. We don't believe the union is in your best interest or the best interest of this organization. Our futures are all better served by working together toward a common goal, without interference from a union whose interests are elsewhere.

But management doesn't decide the issue of unionization. You decide. No one, either management or the union, has the right to interfere with your free choice. Support yourself. Support your future. Vote "no!"

Literature Preparation

As you can see, a number of important subjects are covered in this segment, more than you could possibly expand on in any reasonably brief handout. Your goal should not be to cover all the issues in detail — that will be done during the next four segments. Instead, you simply want to introduce each subject and cause voters to begin thinking about those issues.

One of the primary purposes of the handout(s) for this segment is to allow first line supervisors to begin to feel comfortable discussing the union issue with their employees. Therefore, the handout(s) should not be too long or complex. You want to keep it simple.

Let's examine the subjects covered in the video/speech captive audience presentation and determine what would be appropriate for campaign literature:

1. Information on the decline of union membership in the United States. (A sample handout on this subject is shown as Exhibit 9-A.)

2. How the union spends the money it collects in dues. If you have a copy of the LM-2 for the union attempting to organize your employees, you can make this information union-specific.

3. Information from the *Fortune* article or the report of the President's Commission on Organized Crime. The *Fortune* article was published in the November 10, 1986, edition and is probably available at your local library. If not, it is available from LRI. The report of the President's Commission on Organized Crime is titled, "The Edge: Organized Crime, Business, and Labor Unions." It was published by the U.S. Government Printing Office and is available from the Superintendent of Documents.

4. Information about the union's constitution and bylaws. Again, if you have a copy of the constitution of the union you are campaigning

against, you can be very specific.

5. Union strike history. If you have the strike history of the union seeking representation, you can create an effective union-specific handout.

These five specific pieces of information could generate several pieces of literature. However, you may want to be less specific and create a handout that contains more general information. (Exhibits 9-B and 9-C are examples of literature you could consider for this segment.)

These sample handouts can be used exactly as is, amended, combined, or altered to suit the status of your campaign. You can also use your own literature. Do not, however, yield to the temptation to try to say too much too quickly. Remember, this is the introductory segment. Voters should begin to think about the disadvantages of union membership and supervisors should begin to feel comfortable discussing election issues with employees. But you should not attempt to win the election during this first segment

To determine the best schedule for Segment Two, examine both your captive audience presentation and your proposed handout(s). Does the literature summarize one or more points made in the captive audience presentation? Does it contain a local example to illustrate a point? Another consideration should be the comfort level of your supervisors when discussing the union issue with employees. Finally, you should consider the work schedule of the voting group. You don't want to hold the captive audience meeting or to distribute the handout(s) just before the end of the work week when employees will probably be planning their weekend rather than listening to your message.

Under normal circumstances, consider holding the captive audience meeting on Tuesday and distributing literature on Thursday. This order should be reversed if the literature introduces the captive audience presentation and you feel supervisors are ready to begin discussions with voters. If there will be multiple handouts, the first should be introductory and the second should summarize one or more points made in the captive audience presentation. Finally, if you are going to mail letters to the home that summarize information presented during the week, select a mailing date.

During Segment Two, specialty items are generally not needed. The start of the campaign and the novelty of captive audience meetings — particularly if you are using video — combined with the distribution of literature and increased attention from supervisors is more than enough to maintain voter attention and involvement.

When you have finished scheduling all planned activities for Segment Two, meet with your supervisors and review the segment in detail. These review sessions, held at least weekly, should be conducted throughout the campaign. At these sessions examine the following items originally discussed in Chapter 2:

1. Assess the current position of the voting group by individuals. Have you gained any ground during this segment and if so, how much?

2. Are there key union supporters whose position has softened during the segment? If so, why, and how can you capitalize on this opportunity?

3. What issues have been most persuasive? Can you develop additional information to exploit these issues further?

4. Review plans and strategy for the next segment.

The calendar for Segment Two should now look something like this:

Monday — Open, no activity

Tuesday — **Handout**, distributed by supervision

Wednesday — Open, no activity

Thursday — **Captive audience meeting — Show video** *How Unions* **Work —** *Big business, not charity* or deliver speech

Friday — Letter to homes that summarizes communications during the week (optional) — Meet with supervision to review the week, update voting assessment, analyze support areas, and examine issues

Preparatory work for Segment Two is now complete. It's time to turn attention to Segment Three.

Exhibit 9-A

Don't Be A Loser. Stay Union-Free!

Organized labor loses a lot more than it wins. Today, unions represent only 14.5% of the national labor force. If this trend continues—and nothing appears likely to change it—by the year 2000, unions will represent only 13% of all employees.

% of Workforce Unionized	
1993	15.8%
1994	15.5%
1995	14.9%
1996	14.5%

Fewer and fewer employees are joining the union team. Today, unions are winning less than 50% of all representation elections. Look at the decreasing number of elections unions have recently won.

Elections Won by Unions	
1993	1,451
1994	1,436
1995	1,353
1996	1,321

Even more revealing, unions are being decertified—thrown out—in record numbers by their own membership. Just look at the number of members recently lost because people got sick and tired of their union and voted it out.

Decertification Elections 1993-1996	
Total Elections	2,196
Elections Lost by Unions	1,519
Members Lost	53,340

If unions were as effective as they claim to be, membership would be growing and no one would ever vote to get rid of their union. The facts speak for themselves: union representation is a losing game.

NO

Vote ✓

Exhibit 9-B

Heads, the union wins...
Tails, you lose

Union Initiation Fee – Heads, the union wins
This is what it costs new employees to join the union.

Monthly Union Dues – Tails, you lose
Both the local and the international union would have their hands in your pocket, every month.

Special Assessments – Heads, the union wins
You could be forced to pay additional money for a pet union project or to support a strike you never heard of.

Union Fines – Tails, you lose
If you disagreed with the union or broke a union rule, you could be fined, put on trial, and forced to pay.

Strikes – Tails, you lose again
First, you would lose your wages and benefits. You could not collect unemployment insurance. But your house payment, car payment, and other bills would continue.

Super Seniority – Heads, the union wins
Stewards and other union officials would be the last to be laid off, even if they had less seniority than you.

Individual Freedoms – Tails, you lose
You would lose the right to take complaints directly to the company or to make special requests.

Teamwork – Tails, you lose
Unions are only good at putting up barriers, not tearing them down.

NO

Vote ☑

Exhibit 9-C

IN THE UNION, BREAKING UP
IS HARD TO DO

There's no such thing as trying out the union for a little while.
Organizers encourage employees to "just try the union out for a while," but once the union is voted in, it's usually there to stay.

The union is hard to get rid of if you later change your mind.
Employees who want to throw their union out—this is called decertication—must raise funds, get legal help, secure signatures, and campaign—all within a limited time. Their employer can't help them in any way—that's against the law. Then there's the threat of union harassment, trials, and fines.

The union would not take a decertification effort lying down.
Most union constitutions state that this is a crime. Here's an example: *"Sec. 1. Any member may be penalized for committing one or more of the following offenses:...(d) advocating or attempting to bring about the withdrawal from the International Union of any local union or any member or group of members."*

Each year, disappointed members vote to get rid of their union.
Thousands of union members become so dissatisfied that they are willing to run the risk. From 1993 through 1996, more than *53,000 people succeeded in returning to their union-free status*. The experiences of those former union members need to be considered when you decide how to vote.

Once they're in, they're in

NO

Vote ✓

Campaign Segment Three:
Collective Bargaining
The union gamble

The third segment of the campaign is devoted to the collective bargaining process. The objective of this segment is to insure that the voting group clearly understands what collective bargaining is and how it works. Adequate understanding of this process can make collective bargaining a strong issue for management.

Unions often cleverly lead voters to believe that collective bargaining is a one-way street only going in the union's direction. The union would like the voting group to think collective bargaining always begins at the level of current wages, benefits, and working conditions and can only be negotiated up from there. This is not true. Whenever an employer and a union enter into contract negotiations *all wages, benefits, and working conditions become subjects for bargaining.* Though the union can ask for improvements in all these areas, management can propose that levels remain the same or even be reduced. If the union does not agree with management's proposals, it has only two choices: accept management's last offer or strike in an attempt to win all or part of its demands.

There are many recent examples of unions accepting "concessionary agreements." These agreements happen when a union accepts less in a current contract than existed in previous agreements. There are also numerous examples of unions accepting less in first contracts than employees had received before union representation.

The goal of Segment Three of the campaign is to insure that employees in the voting group clearly understand the principle of collective bargaining. It's also important they realize that if the union wins the election, all present wage rates, benefit levels, and working conditions will be subjected to the collective bargaining process.

It will be helpful to show specific examples of unionized employees who have suffered reductions as a result of collective bargaining. If you have been able to identify local examples of concessionary agreements, these should be examined to determine their applicability to your campaign.

Before drafting your handout(s) and developing the calendar for this segment, decide on the content of the captive audience presentation. If you are using the LRI video program, review the video *Collective Bargaining — The union gamble*. If you are giving a speech instead of showing the video, a sample draft of a captive audience speech follows.

Draft of Captive Audience Speech

Collective bargaining — You might have heard a lot about it during this campaign. What is collective bargaining? And what, if anything, is its importance to you and to the union that's trying to become your collective bargaining representative?

First, if the union became your legally elected representative, the National Labor Relations Act requires both management and the union to sit down together and negotiate over wages, hours, and working conditions. The key word is "negotiate." When a union wins a National Labor Relations Board representation election, all it wins is the right to negotiate with the employer — nothing more, nothing less. The union can try to make you believe anything, promise you anything; but the truth is, all it wins is the right to negotiate.

Some of you might think that if the union won the election and started bargaining with management, all wages and benefits you currently have would be the starting point and everything would be negotiated up from there. That simply isn't true. While no one can predict what the outcome of negotiations would be, the fact is all wages, benefits, and other terms and conditions of employment — those you have now, as well as those the union has promised or implied you would get — are subject to negotiations.

During an organizing campaign, the union's main tactic is the "big promise." No one would vote for a union or agree to pay dues if they didn't believe they would get more money, better benefits, or improved working conditions. Certainly no one would vote for a union if they thought they could suffer a wage decrease or lose benefits. So it's the organizer's job to convince employees that voting for the union will only improve their working lives and is a good investment. Some organizers go so far as to *guarantee* improved wages, benefits, or working conditions. The fact is, the only thing a union gets when it wins an election is the right to negotiate.

Following an election victory, a union is certified as the collective bargaining representative of the voting unit for at least one year. During that year, management must meet with the union for the purpose of bargaining. At these meetings, the union can make proposals. If management doesn't agree with those proposals, it can reject them and make counterproposals, even if those counterproposals contain lower wages, fewer benefits, and less favorable working conditions than existed before the election. Management is not legally required to sign a union contract at all, even after negotiating at great length and making every effort to reach an agreement. No employer is ever forced to agree to union demands it considers unfair or unreasonable. Any change in wages, benefits, or working conditions depends strictly on the outcome of negotiations. What the union or those supporting the union have promised or implied have no bearing on the outcome of those negotiations.

As we said, no one can predict what the outcome of collective bargaining might be. Today many contracts result in concessionary agreements in which a union settles for lower wages and fewer benefits. These kinds of agreements are not just the exception, they're common. This means unions are now settling for less and less, not just in first contracts, but in other contract negotiations as well. A report done for the Federal Reserve Bank of New York shows that during a recent seven-year period, 22% to 44% of union members had their wages frozen or cut during collective bargaining negotiations. In 1993 through 1995, over 2,600,000 union members saw their wages frozen or cut during negotiations. Think about that for a minute. The union wants you to vote for it, and yet many of the members it already represents are suffering either wage freezes or cuts. It just doesn't make sense to pay dues, fees, and possible fines and assessments for nothing. Even in contracts where employees receive so-called "raises," often these raises only increase pay rates to the level they were before the union came in.

If the union was to win the election, it would sit down with management at the bargaining table and negotiate. The union would probably ask for all the things it has promised or implied that you would receive if it won. But make no mistake about it, management is free to say "no" to any union demand it feels is not in the best interest of this organization or you, the employees. It's really like the television game show *Wheel of Fortune*. When the wheel stops, you could end up with more, you could get the same thing you started with, or you could end up with less.

The union knows that if voters are aware of these facts, they will probably vote "no." Therefore, you've probably been told negotiations begin with a base of your current wages and benefits and can only be negotiated up from there. So that you have no misunderstanding about what the facts are, here is some information you should consider: The National Labor Relations Board has stated on many occasions that collective bargaining is a two-way street. In one case the board said, "There is, of course, no obligation on the part of an employer to contract to continue all existing benefits, nor is it an unfair labor practice to offer reduced benefits..." [Case: Midwestern Instruments 133 NLRB 115]

Even more to the point, the board has declared, "Collective bargaining is potentially hazardous for employees, and as a result of such negotiations, employees could possibly wind up with less benefits after unionization than before." [Case: Coach & Equipment Sales 228 NLRB 51]

This means the union cannot guarantee anything will improve if it wins the election. In fact, there's no guarantee you would be able to keep the same things you have now. Your wages and benefits could go down. This is the truth, regardless of what the union tells you.

Let's look at a few more facts. When a union is conducting an organizing campaign, one or more organizers are assigned to try to sell employees on the idea the union is their best chance for gaining improvements in wages, benefits, and working conditions. "Sell" is exactly the right word because that's what a union organizer is, a salesperson. Organizers are paid employees of the union. Their job is to convince employees to vote "yes" in a representation election. Some organizers work on commission, so the more members they recruit, the more money they make. Like other salespersons, an organizer attempts to convince you to buy their product by pointing out only the supposed good points about unions in general and their union in particular. It's very similar to buying a used car. You'll never hear a car salesman point out any of the car's bad features, right? Union organizers are the same. They only tell you things they think you want to hear, even if they know you're about to get stuck with a lemon. Let's look at some of the things unions say or imply to win the support of voters.

Higher wages. This is probably the most frequently-used union campaign tactic: the illusion that with a union, employees will make more money. First, if a union wins an election, all it gains is the right to negotiate with management. Nothing else. During negotiations, a union can ask for more money, but management can say "no." There's no law that requires management to increase wages or even to keep wages at their current level. So can the union guarantee you higher wages? No.

Better benefits. This is another popular campaign promise. What we said about higher wages holds true here. The union can talk about better benefits, but the truth is it can only ask, and management can say "no" or propose reduced benefit levels. So is the union able to provide you better benefits than you currently have? No.

What about better working conditions? Again, a union can promise improvements, but it can't guarantee them. In fact, many employees feel their working conditions got worse after a union was voted in, particularly when it comes to getting problems solved. With a union, all problems must go through a network of stewards, committeepersons, and other union officials. This means red tape, delays, and that decisions about your personal problems could be made for political reasons rather than based on the facts of your individual case. So will the union improve working conditions? No.

You may be asking yourself how this could happen? How could a union agree to a contract that provides less than employees had before the union came in? Remember, collective bargaining is a matter of negotiation. When negotiations begin, there are three parties involved: management, the union, and you — the employees. Each wants the best possible deal. Management wants to operate its business economically. Employees want to obtain the best levels of pay, benefits, and working conditions. And the union wants to protect its financial position by assuring that all members pay dues.

When the union submits its proposals to management, it always asks for dues checkoff and, where legal, a union security clause. The dues checkoff provision requires the employer to deduct union dues from the paychecks of employees and give that amount in a lump sum to the union each month. This insures the union will get its money without going through a collection process and without facing members who may be unhappy with the union. The union security clause requires all eligible employees to become and remain members of the union to keep their jobs. If anyone doesn't pay their dues, the union can force the employer to fire them. These two clauses are very important to unions. Without them, a union would not be assured of collecting dues from all members.

When the union submits its proposal, management can say "Yes, we accept this," or "No, we don't accept it." Since collective bargaining is a situation of give-and-take, many unions give away benefits members had before union representation in exchange for things like dues checkoff and a union security clause. This is one way employees can end up with less as a result of contract negotiations. But there are many others.

You may be saying to yourself, "Well, maybe the union can ask us to accept a contract that contains less wages, fewer benefits, and less desirable working conditions in order to get some of the things it wants, but we don't have to accept the proposed contract. We can always go on strike to get what we want." That's true. However, you'll soon be receiving important information in a future meeting that shows you why strikes are not a good idea.

Remember, the union can legally promise anything. It can glorify the benefits of membership by telling you only one side of the story. But today the union pitch is falling on deaf ears. The facts speak more loudly and clearly than ever before. The union can promise, but it can't deliver. More and more employees are rejecting unions in representation elections. According to National Labor Relations Board statistics, employees consistently say "no" to unions. Year after year, organized labor loses over half of all NLRB representation elections conducted in the United States. An even more compelling statistic concerns decertification elections. These are elections where unionized employees have defied their union and voted to kick it out. During a recent two-year period, unionized employees, when given the opportunity, voted over 70% of the time to get rid of their union. Think about that. Those who know the most about union membership, when given the opportunity, got rid of their union over 70% of the time. Of course, unions do everything possible to prevent decertification elections since they lose by an overwhelming margin.

Though the union can legally promise you anything, delivering on those promises is another story, and unfortunately a story you won't be told until it's too late. Here is the truth: the union can't guarantee you anything. This is because collective bargaining is a process of give-and-take, and recently unions have been giving away more than they've taken. Think about it. What can a union really do for you? Vote "no."

Literature Preparation

The thrust of the collective bargaining segment is that negotiations do not start at the base of current wage rates and benefit levels. Through collective bargaining negotiations, the terms and conditions of employment could stay the same, improve, or decline. If you currently have an unusual benefit that employees appreciate, take time to discuss that benefit and to review local union-negotiated labor agreements that do not contain this benefit. Clearly, if the union has been unable to obtain this same benefit for its members, what is the value of union representation for your employees?

Another good presentation is to list all current benefits, then ask employees which of those benefits they would be willing to trade away so the union could obtain a dues checkoff provision or, where legal, a union security clause, or super-seniority for union officials, or any one of a number of other contract provisions that do not benefit employees.

Remember, during this discussion you cannot state or imply that if the union wins the election, current wage rates or benefit levels would automatically be lost or reduced. But you can state that they would become part of the collective bargaining process and that no one can predict what the outcome of this process would be.

Let's now consider some possible handouts that address the collective bargaining issue. Exhibit 10-A is a standard collective bargaining handout that explains the process. It includes statistics that can easily be updated. There is a quote from the NLRB stating that employees could wind up with less after negotiations than before. This flyer requires no local or regional examples and is not union-specific. It is ready to use by simply updating the statistics, if necessary.

Exhibit 10-B is a copy of a handout used in a campaign. It shows what can be accomplished with a little digging to find a same-union contract that provides lower wages and fewer benefits than non-unionized employees currently enjoy. As originally used in a campaign, the handout was printed on a legal size sheet (8 and one-half by 14 inches). Imagine the impact this flyer had when voters realized they already enjoyed a better deal than this union had been able to negotiate for employees at another local company. To develop this piece of literature, the campaign director obtained a same-union contract from a company within one mile of his firm. The campaign director made a detailed comparison of the wage rates and benefit levels between the two companies. This comparison showed the wage and benefit levels at the unionized firm were far less desirable. The handout helped convince voters that collective bargaining at the unionized facility had accomplished far less than union-free cooperation.

Exhibit 10-C is a highly effective example of a longer handout. As originally used in a campaign, the flyer was printed in two colors and was relatively expensive. It shows how a specific situation can be graphically presented to the voting group. In this case, the campaign director knew of a situation where the union had been decertified. He was able to get written statements about the union from several employees at the formerly unionized facility that were derogatory. Highlights from those statements were put together to produce the handout. To enhance credibility, all of the unedited statements were also included. This piece was particularly effective because the information was relevant — same-union, even same-employer — and, although it was several pages long, it was easy to read. By making some minor alterations, such as deleting the letter and statements about fellow employees, and referring to unions generically, rather than the Machinists union, you could easily use this handout in your campaign. More appropriate, however, would be a similar handout concerning a local decertification or same-union situation. Remember, long handouts have the virtue of making their point even if voters do not read the entire piece.

To determine the best schedule for Segment Three, examine the captive audience presentation and any union-specific or area-specific literature you wish to distribute. This literature should usually be distributed after the captive audience meeting. If you are going to use cartoons or posters, this segment is a good time to begin. While most employers will schedule only two events during this segment, some use as many as five. When you are finished scheduling all planned activities for Segment Three, meet with your supervisors and examine the campaign's present status.

1. Assess the current position of the voting group by individuals. Have you gained any ground during this segment and if so, how much?

2. Are there key union supporters whose position has softened? If so, why, and how can you capitalize on this opportunity?

3. What issues have been most persuasive? Can you develop additional information to exploit these issues further?

4. Review plans and strategy for the next segment.

The following is a calendar for Segment Three that includes multiple events. Your actual calendar could contain fewer events depending on your overall strategy.

Monday — **Poster or cartoon**

Tuesday — **Wage and benefits flyer** distributed by supervision — **Remove poster or cartoon**

Wednesday — **Captive audience meeting** — **Show video** *Collective Bargaining — The union gamble*

Thursday — **Machinists-type handout** (Exhibit 10-C) distributed by supervision

Friday — **Letter to homes that summarizes week's activities** — **Meet with supervision to review week, update voting assessment, analyze support areas, and examine issues**

The preparatory work for Segment Three is now complete. It's time begin work on Segment Four.

Exhibit 10-A

COLLECTIVE BARGAINING

a situation of
GIVE

and TAKE

Exhibit 10-A

COLLECTIVE
BARGAINING a situation of give and take

Don't be misled into thinking that if the union wins the election and starts bargaining with your employer, all wages and benefits you currently have will be the starting point and everything will be negotiated up from there. THIS IS SIMPLY NOT TRUE.

All wages, benefits and other terms and conditions of employment – those you have now, as well as those the union wants – are subject to negotiations. As a result, your wages and benefits could go up, they could go down, or they could stay the same.

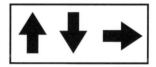

The National Labor Relations Board (the government agency that regulates union elections) has said:
"Collective bargaining is potentially hazardous for employees and as a result of such negotiations employees could possibly wind up with less benefits after unionization than before."
Coach & Equipment Sales, 228 NLRB 51

Do you want the union to do your talking?

If the union wins this election, it wins the right to negotiate with the company over your wages, benefits and working conditions. **No longer will you have the right** to talk directly to management about your wages or your individual abilities. The union would do your talking for you.

Exhibit 10-A

What happens if negotiations break down?

Though the law requires that the company and the union meet and negotiate in good faith, it does not require either the company or the union to give in to the demands of the other. If the union makes demands that management finds unreasonable and cannot agree to, the union has no alternative but to either accept what is offered or go on strike.

Your benefits can be used as bargaining chips.

Unions have a record of giving away benefits employees already enjoy in exchange for something that's only important to the union, such as dues check-off, a union security clause or super-seniority. **DUES CHECK-OFF** is the way a union makes sure members pay dues – by having them deducted directly from a person's paycheck. A **UNION SECURITY CLAUSE** requires all employees to belong to the union and pay dues or lose their jobs. **SUPER-SENIOR-ITY** provisions give artificial seniority to union officials so that in case of a layoff, those union officials keep their jobs while other employees with more service are let go.

The union can give away what you already have.

Many collective bargaining negotiations result in what are called **concessionary agreements** in which unions settle for lower wages and fewer benefits for members. These agreements are common. Unions are settling for less and less, and not just in first contracts, but in other contract negotiations as well. According to the Department of Labor, wages and benefits rose an average of only **3.8%** in the first year of collective bargaining contracts negotiated during the 4th quarter of 1991. During that year, 391,000 unionized workers had their cost-of-living adjustment clauses discontinued. Approximately 558,000 workers accepted **pay freezes**, and about 11,000 took **pay cuts**. [If your company's pay increases have been greater than 3.8%, tell employees that and explain the difference in terms of cents per hour.]

Look at what these unionized employees lost.

A good example of what can happen occurred at the [put in local example if applicable] Aerospace Division of AVCO Manufacturing Company after a union won the election and began bargaining with the company...When negotiations were over, employees <u>lost</u> their <u>sick leave</u>; had their insurance <u>benefits</u>, retirement program and shift differential <u>reduced</u>; and had gone from a merit pay review program that allowed them to earn more money, to a flat rate increase.

Exhibit 10-A

PROMISES, PROMISES

The union will glorify the "benefits" of union membership, but this is only one side of the story. Remember, it is legal for the union to make promises and try to lead you to believe that with representation you will have more money or better benefits. But today, these empty union promises are falling on deaf ears. The facts speak more loudly and more clearly than ever before. **Unions can promise, but they can no longer deliver.** A majority of employees reject unions in representation elections. According to National Labor Relations Board statistics for union representation elections, **unions now lose 53.2%** of these elections. In addition, more and more employees are decertifying unions (kicking them out) where they are already in. NLRB statistics show that in elections held during 1990 to get rid of unions, **employees voted more than 76% of the time to return to their union-free status.**

Employees aren't buying what unions are selling.

Unions represent fewer employees as a percentage of the workforce than at any time in the last 40 years. In **1954**, unions represented **32.5%** of the workforce. **Today**, less than **16%** of the workforce is unionized. So if unions are such a good deal, or if they can deliver on all their promises and successfully negotiate higher wages and better benefits, why isn't union membership growing?

You deserve more than empty promises.

Remember, the union can legally promise you anything, but delivering on those promises is another story – unfortunately a story the union won't tell you until it's too late. THE UNION CANNOT GUARANTEE ANYTHING. Collective bargaining is a give and take process, and today unions are giving up more than they are taking.

THINK ABOUT IT. WHAT CAN THE UNION REALLY DO FOR YOU? **NO** ☑

Exhibit 10-B

For many years, the employees of Armstrong Brothers Tool Co., a company in the metal manufacturing industry with about 50 employees located in the Industrial Park less than 1 mile from our plant, have been represented by the Allied Industrial Workers union. When you compare the wages, benefits and other terms and conditions of employment contained in the AIW contract at Armstrong Brothers with the wages and benefits you presently have here at Andrew, you get a very clear picture of who has the best deal. Examine the following comparisons and see for yourself.'

	ARMSTRONG BROTHERS	ANDREW ARKANSAS
SHIFT PREMIUM:	15¢ per hour	30¢ per hour
VACATIONS:	1 yr. - 1 wk. 3 yrs. - 2 wks. 8 yrs. - 3 wks.	6 mos. - 1 wk. 1 yr. - 2 wks. 6-9 yrs. - 2 wks. plus (DOS)' 10-15 yrs. - 3 wks. 16-25 yrs. - 3 wks. to 5 wks. (DOS)' '(Depending on service)
HOLIDAYS:	10	10
JURY DUTY PAY:	Regular pay minus jury duty pay	Regular pay plus jury duty pay
GRIEVANCE PROCEDURE:	Step 1: Employee presents problem - company has 3 days to answer. 3 days Step 2: Union has 3 days to appeal answer, meeting within 3 days after appeal. Answer within 3 days after meeting. 9 days Step 3: Union has 5 days to appeal answer, meeting within 5 days after appeal. Answer within 5 days after meeting. 15 days TOTAL: 27 days If the union does not accept the company's answer, they must go on strike.	Open door policy: try to solve problems and complaints as quickly as possible.
AVERAGE WAGE RATE:	$6.50 per hour	$7.30 per hour
UNION DUES CHECK-OFF:	Yes	No
PAID SICK DAYS:	No	Yes
PAID PERSONAL DAYS:	No	Yes
DENTAL INSURANCE:	No	Yes
PAY FOR FIRST 7 DAYS OF WORKER'S COMP. INJURY:	No	Yes
LONG TERM DISABILITY:	No	Yes
PROFIT SHARING:	No	Yes
STOCK PURCHASE:	No	Yes
MATCHED SAVINGS:	No	Yes
CHRISTMAS BONUS:	No	Yes
EDUCATIONAL ASSISTANCE:	Yes	Yes
SCHOLARSHIP PROGRAM:	No	Yes

As you can see, the employees at Armstrong Brothers, represented by the AIW, have not been able to do nearly as well as the employees of Andrew Arkansas, without a union.

Do the Allied Industrial Workers provide better pay? NO!

Do the Allied Industrial Workers provide better benefits? NO!

Do the Allied Industrial Workers provide better job security? NO!

VOTE NO DECEMBER 19

The actual Armstrong Brothers contract is available for you to see in the Personnel Office.

Exhibit 10-C

Machinists Union

KICKED OUT

by the
Employees of Mercury Marine
at Orlando, Florida
and St. Cloud, Florida

THIS IS A TRUE STORY
IT ACTUALLY HAPPENED

Exhibit 10-C

For several weeks now we have been furnishing you with information we believed necessary for you to make a decision on March 7, 1980 based on facts not propaganda, rumors or promises.

Mercury Marine is not anti-union, we are PRO-EMPLOYEE. We have unions in other locations, therefore we feel we know both sides of the question and sincerely believe that your interests can be best served by us working together to make Stillwater a better place for all of us to work. We do not believe the union will accomplish this.

This same international union once represented the employees at Orlando and St. Cloud, Florida, but the employees did not get what they were promised from the union. We thought it very important that you benefit from these employees experience. In an effort to fulfill my committment to you to get you the truth, I went to Florida and asked employees at these locations for statements in writing of their opinion of the I. A. M. and the benefits they received as dues paying members.

These employees learned the hard way that there are two sides to union membership - what the union tells you and the way it really is.

Union membership is not free. It costs you money. Please evaluate what the union sold your fellow employees at Orlando and St. Cloud. Decide for yourself if you think it's worth it.

Remember - these folks learned the hard way. The union has made the same promises to you - the same old promises that were made to these employees.

BOB

Exhibit 10-C

YOU KNOW THE UNION PROMISES

SOME OF YOUR FELLOW EMPLOYEES BELIEVED THEM

LOOK AT WHAT THEY SAY

Exhibit 10-C

HIGHER WAGES??

"We were supposed to get raises to wage rates in Fond Du Lac, but we didn't."

"I paid $7.50-$8.00 a month to lose money.

"We lost a pay raise."

"All a union can do is cost us money."

"Our annual raise was delayed by seven months while the union negotiated a contract."

"They failed miserably to bring about additional benefits, pay raises, etc. as they had promised."

"One employee I know of lost enough money in one month to make their house payment - all due to the union."

"We were dissatisfied with the negotiated raises. Our rate of wage increase was going down instead of up."

"The union promised raises they couldn't deliver."

"We had more before the union came in than after."

Exhibit 10-C

BETTER BENEFITS??

"The union said we would have more and better benefits, but the contract was ridiculous!"

"The only ones that benefited were the stewards."

"They promise sick days and dental plan. When they got in our plant and we asked about these things, their answer was "Don't bother us with penny-anny things like this".

"They promise to make things better for you but they will do nothing for you except make things harder on you!"

"They failed miserably to bring about additional benefits."

"When it came right down to the bare facts the union did not get us any more raise, insurance, sick pay, vacation, or holidays. . ."

"When the first contract was negotiated and signed, the employees lost some of the benefits that we already had."

"We were promised in union meetings that we would have dental insurance, but we never did get it."

"It promised to up wages, better benefits, better working conditions, and etc. . .the rest of the story is the joke."

Exhibit 10-C

MORE JOB SECURITY??

"The union said that seniority would rate very high, but that didn't happen."

"The regular hourly employees were hurt, they were reclassified down and they lost money."

"Seniority did not mean anything."

"Our seniority really didn't help us either."

"They also had a cut back in seniority due to the unions fine definition of seniority."

"When we had a layoff which ordinarily would have been by seniority, the union officers were not laid off regardless of seniority."

Exhibit 10-C

YOU WILL HAVE YOUR OWN LODGE AND MAKE YOUR OWN DECISIONS??

"This union kept employees confused."

"Although the union officials said it was our organization, they always told us what to do."

"They said they were going to have a local lodge here, but that never happened."

"We would go to the union meetings expecting to get our questions answered and would go away more confused than ever."

"The union did not answer some of the grievances presented to it by the people."

"The union promised to have a local lodge in St. Cloud, Florida, but it was never done."

Exhibit 10-C

HERE ARE THE ACTUAL LETTERS FROM THE EMPLOYEES FROM ST. CLOUD AND ORLANDO. READ WHAT THEY HAVE TO SAY THEN DECIDE FOR YOURSELF:

WHO IS TELLING THE TRUTH?

MERCURY MARINE

OR

THE UNION?

THE ORIGINALS ARE AVAILABLE FOR YOU TO SEE IN BILL RILEY'S OFFICE.

Exhibit 10-C

TO WHOM IT MAY CONCERN:

In my opinion Mercury employees don't need a union. I don't feel
that there is any benefit for us, to help us, that a union can
provide. Our employee benefits at Mercury excel those of most
other companies. All a union can do is cost us money and in many
cases, cause a rift between friendships, which makes for harder
working conditions.

Sincerely,

Jean Brown

TO WHOM IT MAY CONCERN:

I have been employed with Mercury Marine at Plant #7 for 9 years,
and the year of 1974-75 our plant went union, and all employees
that were here during this time can tell anyone this was the most
miserable two years they had ever worked. I really learned a lot
about this union. They make all kinds of promises and the sad part
about it, what ever they promise you 9 out of 10 times, the company
is going to give you the same thing or more, so why should we pay
anyone else to get something that we are already going to get. This
union kept employees confused and also took money from them for dues,
insurance, and a few more things. I think the union stinks and I'll
feel this way as long as I am employed with the company because the
9 years I have worked with the company, it has been super.

Ike Paul
Q.C. Tech.

The promises that the union made were not fulfilled. For example,
the union said that seniority would rate very high, but that didn't
happen. The union said that we would have more and better benefits,
but the contract was ridiculous!

The union we got was weak and they didn't do a thing for us. I
personally lost friends over the union issue and we lost a pay raise,
too. Everybody was at each others throat. Personally, I don't want
to pay someone else for nothing while I'm working.

I would never allow a union in again.

Ida Platt
Morematic Operator

Exhibit 10-C

Mercury pays us a decent wage. Our benefits are <u>good</u>.

The union was voted in here but some of the people were unhappy with it. It wasn't long before it was <u>voted</u> out. Why pay union dues for something we already have. Some of the people who wanted the union felt they were paying dues for nothing. Unions sometimes make promises they can't keep without a strike. When on strike you will never get back what you lose.

Mary Cochrane

The union did harm to us here because it resulted in some employees losing money. One employee family I know of lost enough money in one month to make their house payment - all due to the union.

The regular hourly employees were hurt. They were reclassified down and they lost money. The union couldn't do anything about it.

The union always had their meetings at night. They expected us on second shift to take time off work and attend their meetings. Although the union officials said it was our organization, they always told us what to do.

I would suggest a no vote, it didn't do us any good here.

Paul E. Crooks

TO WHOM IT MAY CONCERN:

The attempt to unionize Plant 7 was, in my opinion, a real failure. The short time they were in there was nothing but dissatisfaction.

They failed miserably to bring about additional benefits, pay raises, etc. as they had promised.

As a machinist I've found Mercury Marine a more than fair employer. I'd certainly rely on their promises rather than a union. Mercury keeps their promises. The union didn't.

Mike Slavik

Exhibit 10-C

The union promised raises they couldn't deliver. We were
supposed to get raises to wage rates in Fond du Lac, but we
didn't. We weren't getting anything out of the contract.

They said they were going to have a local lodge here, but that
never happened.

The only ones that benefited were the stewards who got the
higher paying jobs.

We were only given two hours to qualify for the higher pay when
we were transferred to a higher paying job. If you didn't qualify
in two hours, they would put you back to your old job.

Hard feelings were made between friends over the union and the
tension in the plant was, at times, so thick you could cut it
with a knife.

> Ruth Pietarila

In my view I think the union is something that wants your
support, but doesn't do a thing for you.

> Michael Corbett
> Mercury Employee

When the union was here at Plant #7, the harmony in the plant
went to pot and there was plenty of backstabbing. Grievances
were written on everything and the membership dues were increased
from when they started.

The union took too long to get organized and when they did, they
didn't do what they said they would. Personally, I don't like
giving my money to anybody just so I can go to work.

> John Vaillancourt
> Maintenance Mechanic Leadman

In June, 1974 the IAM union was voted to represent the employees
at Plant 7 in St. Cloud.

When the first contract was negotiated and signed, the employees lost
some of the benefits that we already had previously been given by
Mercury Marine.

I attended one union meeting where I joined the union, however, I
did not sign a card for the company to deduct dues from my pay check.
The company started taking money out of my check anyway for union
dues. When I asked why, the company produced a signed card that I
authorized the company to deduct dues from my pay check. This card
had to be a forgery because I did not sign it. Consequently, dues
were taken out of my pay for almost three years against my wishes.
This union cost me money and benefits along with creating bad
relations between many friends at Plant 7.

> Lois Seley

Exhibit 10-C

TO WHOM IT MAY CONCERN:

I hope you people at Stillwater, Oklahoma don't make the same
mistake we did.

We voted the IAM in our plant. They promised us everything but
nothing was ever accomplished. We had nobody to turn to with
our problems. It was one of the most trying times of my life.
We would go to the union meetings expecting to get our questions
answered and would go away more confused than ever.

I was one of the lucky ones and got laid off. I was glad because
I couldn't stand the pressure any more. When I returned to work
the union had been voted out and everything was back to normal.

My personal opinion is, if you feel you need a union, seek
another organization.

> Dorothy Gadd
> Dept. 544
> St. Cloud, Fla.

TO WHOM IT MAY CONCERN:

I'm under the understanding you're trying to get a union in your
plant. Please believe me you are making one big mistake. All
the union did for us was promises and promises and alot of lying.
They promise sick days and dental plan. Then when they got in our
plant and we asked about these things, their answer was "Don't
bother us with penny anny things like this". The relationship
we had between management and employees all came to an end. They
caused us alot of problems that we are still living with today,
so people please stop and think before you make the same mistake.

Your job and company is too important to bring something like that
in between you. Believe me, I know from experience all they do is
talk and make big brags and take your money. People, you work too
hard for your money to hand to people like that. They promise to
make things better for you but they will do nothing for you except
make things harder on you. Please think twice.

> Glenda Huffman

Exhibit 10-C

Dear Co-Worker,

I have been an employee of MERCURY MARINE, Plant #7 at St. Cloud, Florida for 9½ years. I started as a material handler progressed to a group leader and then in February of 1977 became a foreman. I have really and truly enjoyed every aspect of each job I have had while employed here except one!, and that being going thru a union election and certification. This union promised employees everything under the sun while it was campaigning to get in. It promised to up wages, better benefits, better working conditions, and etc. It also wanted employees to believe that with a union steward in your corner company discipline was just a joke. Well, barely enough people were deceived to the idea and this union was elected to represent the employees of Plant #7. The rest of the story is the joke. The certification did accomplish many things, it caused people to become grouped up against themselves and management, kept bitter feelings and hostility brewing constantly, caused management to become more strict and prompt when dealing with company rules and regulations, but one thing it did not accomplish was living up to the promises and changes it had raved about while campaigning to get in the door. About the only thing the people were sure of was how much the monthly dues were and where to send your money.

After a couple of years of nothing but lies and unkept promises the people of Plant #7 decided to vote the union out and get back on the right course led by only management. It has been three years since the union was disposed of and I can say honestly that in talking to the employees that at one time were union supporters not the first one has ever spoken of the union in a supporting way. Everyone has admitted to being misled and wrong in their support to elect the union into our plant.

You people in Stillwater and myself have one thing in common, that being the privilege of working with Mr. Bob Wood. Mr. Wood hired me in June of 1970. I worked for him in different capacities until he moved to Stillwater. He will always be a person I will admire and respect with great dignity. He is a person who will not cheat or deceive anyone for any reason whatsoever. I say this because I know that one of the unions strongest weapons in their war for election is to make management personnel look like dirt in the eyes of their employees. The caliber of person that Mr. Wood is has become vanishing breed upon the American horizon. He stands for truth and the betterment of himself, family, community and fellow employees. I stand tall and proud in believing that anything Mr. Wood tells or promises his employees will be the honest truth as he knows it. This is a man you can put your trust with and one who will appreciate every ounce of effort that you put into your job.

Alan Backer
Foreman, Plant #7, St. Cloud

Exhibit 10-C

To Plant #14:

Dear Co-Workers: I have been at Plant #7 for over 10 years.
When the subject of a union came up I was very much against it
as our wages & benefits are the best there are in our area. But
never the less the union officials painted a very nice picture
of how much better everything would be if the union was voted in.
By the time the union made it known that they wanted to come into
our plant we were due a raise in salary which was postponed until
the union and company negotiated (about 18 mo.) and we got a minimum
raise. When we had a layoff which ordinarily would have been by
seniority the union officers were not layed off regardless of
seniority. There was a change in our plant that is hard to believe.
Before we were like a big happy family, afterwards there was hard
feelings and have never been the same as of now.

So I am sincerely telling you that I would advise you to vote <u>no</u>.
It will only cost you money and friends; also a big change in the
company too.

I am sincerely hoping that you'll think this over.

Josephine Borowill

I thought, along with many others, that the union was some outside
people coming in to communicate with management. They would make
everything a bed of roses. Only to find out later that the union
is the people, the same people who think they can't communicate so
they vote a union in, pay dues and still have to do their own
communicating. You also find out its twice as hard because of
the tension among everyone concerned. Your promised things, but
later find out the only way to get them is by paying the price of
giving something else up. You learn the hard lesson of "You don't
need to pay a middle man to do what you can do yourself, if you go
about it right."

If you're considering joining a union, think hard about it. We
learned the hard way.

I'm happy to say we have good open communication now. It's a good
attitude among us all and we have <u>no</u> union. We all work together
as a team. Try it, without paying dues to someone outside of your-
selves, you'll be money ahead.

Selma Austin
#7 Mercury Marine
St. Cloud, Florida

Exhibit 10-C

You are only wasting your time and the company's that you
could have in your pocket or elsewhere.

Say No!
Robert Derosier

Here at Plant #7 our annual raise was delayed by seven months
while the union negotiated a contract. The union did little
to improve benefits, which were already excellent.

During the time the union was here we lost the informal work
atmosphere. People that had been friends before the union
quit talking to one another and a strain developed during
working hours. We were unable to talk to anybody in management
without being looked at with suspicion. We have now regained
a congenial atmosphere and we have added benefits since the union
was out.

The union settled few grievances and the only thing we saw was
a monthly deduction for union dues from our checks which soon
increased in amount without warning.

Virginia Hancock

I have been employed with Mercury Marine since April 2, 1972.
I have seen many improvements, none came about as a result of
the union. We have had more results from our grievance committee
of which we didn't pay any dues or go on any strike without a
paycheck.

While the union was in our Plant (7) we went one year without a
cost of living raise. The girls who payed union dues didn't
receive anything that they wouldn't have received anyway. They
also had cut back in seniority due to the unions fine definition
of seniority. I strongly believe the union did not and would not
help Mercury employees.

Sincerely,
Faye Johnson

Exhibit 10-C

The union we had didn't hold up their side of the agreement. We ended up paying out more money because of that. Our seniority didn't really help us either, but we continued to pay union dues.

The union promised to have a local lodge in St. Cloud, Florida, but it was never done.

The Negotiating Committee even agreed to a contract that provided pay at the same rate for two hours when we were transferred to a higher paying job. Before the union, we used to be paid the higher rate immediately upon transfer to a higher job.

We were promised in union meetings that we would have dental insurance, but we never did get it.

We were promised in union meetings that we would get sick pay, but we didn't get that.

We were promised in union meetings that we would get cost of living increases, but we never got that.

There would be no way I would work under a union agreement now, and I was originally very highly supportive of the union here.

I paid $7.50-$8.00 a month to lose money. I can't think of anything that was done for us by the union. You'll lose money in the long run.

Betty Putnam

I was for the union at first and it did get in at Plant 7.

However, it did cause problems among the people and to me was not worth any of it, plus paying dues, protecting those that did not belong but would vote the union in.

I am content without a union and we're treated just fine.

Claive Lidik

Exhibit 10-C

The people of St. Cloud, Plant 7 of Mercury Marine voted that
they wanted a union to represent them here. There was a lot of
favoritism being shown at that time; as well as some unfavorable
working conditions. So I joined the union.

I attended the meetings regularly. But, I soon discovered that
the contract they made with the company was just as unfair as
the practices that I was unhappy with previously.

The benefits and raises we received were not obtained for us
by the union; but given to us on a regular basis by the company.
Also, the union did not answer some of the grievances presented
to it by the people. And the most unfair practice of all was
the way in which we were recalled from lay off. Seniority did
not mean anything.

All in all, I felt that the union people just wanted the money
we paid in dues each month without really doing anything to help
us.

> Marjorie Ritter
> Line Leader
> Mercury Marine
> Plant 7

TO WHOM IT MAY CONCERN:

I have heard that the Stillwater plant is trying to get a union
in. I advise strongly against it. Plant 7 in St. Cloud, Florida
had the same union and believe me, they promise you everything,
but don't do anything except cause an uproar among the employees.
When they got in at Plant #7, I quit work for the period of time
they were here, and then I came back to work at Plant #7. I've
been back four years now but if a union should try to get back in
I would quit again.

> Gnera Nunn

Remember, you get all the benefits for free now. All it costs
you is good honest work. Why pay some union to get you what they
claim they can when all you have to do is go to work and get it
for free. Now you are thinking - I'm not getting it for free,
I'm working for it - Yes, of course you are but if you didn't
need money you wouldn't be working in the first place. So stop
and think if I have to work and who doesn't today, I may as well
work for a company who is giving me all the benefits for free and
not join a union that's going to take my money, which by the way
could maybe buy some gas for work or food for my table.

Believe me I've been there when $5.00 more on my pay check looks
darn good.

> Thank you

By the way, we no longer have a union here. We voted it out. It
was the same union that wants in your plant - Think.

> Connie Gessner

Campaign Segment Four:
Union Constitutions & Bylaws
Mechanisms of control

Segment Four of the campaign will focus voter attention on the negatives of union membership as illustrated through the constitution of the union seeking representation. Any time you can prove the negative aspects of union membership using the union's own words, your argument will be virtually indisputable.

A copy of the union's constitution provides the framework for developing literature for this segment. Most union constitutions are 100-plus pages long. Many of those pages contain procedural items of little or no interest to your campaign or the voting group. But other sections of the constitution contain provisions that dramatically illustrate the negative aspects of union membership. A helpful hint: Unions frequently put provisions that cover things such as trials and punishment under strange headings in the index, so a brief scan of the entire constitution might be necessary to uncover gems that could be used in this section of the campaign. In addition, all union constitutions are slightly different, so an examination of your particular constitution may reveal items you will want to use that are not covered in this chapter.

First, examine the index or the table of contents to see if you can readily identify those sections of primary interest. You will be looking for provisions that cover the following areas (remember to look for other provisions of interest in the particular constitution you are examining):

1. *Membership* — In this section there is usually a provision about joining and resigning from the union. Look for a discussion of how

much it costs to join and a statement about the money that must accompany an application. There could also be references to the cumbersome procedures for resigning from the union.

2. *Organization and Governing Power* — This provision often states that the International Union (also called the International) has supreme power to regulate the activities of the union and the locals.

3. *Conventions* — This section discusses how delegates are selected for the union convention. Frequently, the number of people eligible to vote in your election will be smaller than the number required to have even one delegate represent them at the union's convention.

4. *Duties & Authority of the Officers or Executive Board of the Union* — This provision could contain statements about the few individuals who have the power to punish members for violating the constitution.

5. *Initiation Fees & Dues* — This provision talks about how much money it costs to join the union and remain a member, as well as how the union can increase dues, change the collection procedure, etc.

6. *Strikes* — This section describes how strikes are called, the amount of money provided union members during a strike, and prohibitions on returning to work during a strike. Because the strikes section is several pages long, you might ask voters to consider why the union talks so much about this subject in its constitution if strikes are seldom called.

7. *Duties of Members* — Here a union constitution talks about employees giving up the right to deal directly with their employer.

8. *Trials of Officers & Members* — This revealing section contains the union's trial procedures. There may be additional rules and regulations regarding penalties, legal representation, and the filing of charges.

9. *Obligations of Members* — This information may also be found in trial procedures. Look for prohibitions on members who violate loyalty oaths or attempt to decertify the union.

10. *Discipline & Improper Conduct* — Here you will find the various ways members can be disciplined and the many things the union considers improper conduct.

11. *Meetings* — This section discloses the different types of union meetings, how they are conducted, and requirements for a quorum.

After carefully examining the union's constitution, list the relevant items you want to communicate to your employees. The list will probably be long, so plan on producing a larger handout than normal. Next, identify the one or two provisions you believe will have the greatest impact with your voting group. You may want to prepare a special handout covering just these one or two provisions.

Before drafting your handout(s) and developing the calendar for this segment, decide on the content of the captive audience presentation. If you are using the LRI video program, review the video *Union Constitutions & Bylaws — Mechanisms of control.* If you are giving a speech instead of showing the video, a sample draft of a captive audience speech follows.

Draft of Captive Audience Speech

When considering how to vote in this election, it's important that you understand the rules and obligations that come with union representation. All international unions have constitutions and most local unions have bylaws, which are more rules and regulations on top of the international union constitution. Union rules and regulations control many areas of a member's working life. Through its constitution, the union establishes and enforces the activities of its members. This means union members lose many of the rights they would normally have as employees and give those rights to their union. Also, the activities of members are strictly governed by the many provisions of the union constitution and local union bylaws. All union members are required to abide by the constitution and bylaws of the union they join.

Some people may think this isn't important. But when you carefully consider the restrictions and obligations placed on members by union constitutions and bylaws, it becomes very important. **[If you have a copy of the constitution of the union conducting your campaign, find specific provisions and discuss them with voters. The following text is provided as a guide for preparing your remarks for this section.]** Let's look at some provisions in the constitution for the **[name of union]** and see how you could be affected.

The constitution is 101 pages long, and all of it in very small print. Now, compare that with the Constitution of the United States of America, the document that grants us the basic freedoms we enjoy as citizens. The U.S. Constitution is seven pages long, and this includes all the amendments that have been added since it was adopted over 200 years ago. Why does the Constitution of the United States require only seven pages, while union's constitution requires over 100 pages? One reason might be that the U.S. Constitution grants freedoms, while many provisions of the union constitution take freedoms away. In other words, it must take more words to tell people what they can't do than it does to tell them what rights and freedoms they enjoy.

As a union member, you would lose many of the rights you have now as union-free employees and would give those rights to the union. Here's a typical example: Article 26 of the union's constitution says, "All members by becoming members of this International Union thereby vest the proper officers and committees with the authority to act for and on their behalf in the settlement and adjustment of grievances and controversies..." This implies that if you have a problem, you must use a union committeeperson or a union steward to talk to your supervisor for you. It doesn't say that you have a choice. What's the reason for a provision like this? It's simple: Because the union is a political organization, all the union stewards, all the union committee people, and all the other union officers have to be politicians. Their job is to keep getting re-elected. The way they do this is by making you believe they can do something for you that you can't do for yourself. By keeping you from talking directly to your supervisor about a problem, they can create this impression. But you give up the right to speak for yourself.

You would also give up the right to settle whatever problems you may have with management and give that right to the union. Some people might think this isn't such a bad deal since they would have someone speaking for them. The problem is the union may decide not to process your complaint; it has that right. Here's a provision taken directly from the bylaws of a local union: "Every member, by virtue of his membership in the Local Union, authorizes his Local Union to act as his exclusive bargaining representative...and to act for him and have final authority in presenting, processing and adjusting any grievance, difficulty, or dispute. The Local Union and its officers, representatives, and agents may decline to process any grievance, complaint, difficulty, or dispute..."

Think about that. You're paying dues and assessments, you're subject to trials and fines for violating the union's constitution, but the union decides if it wants to process your complaint.

This is just the tip of the iceberg. A union's constitution is so important to the union that it contains a section describing what can happen to members who violate one of its provisions. In this particular constitution, the section is titled Local Union Trials of Local Union Officers and Members. That's right, trials. This is a long section — six pages — so I won't read it all. Let me summarize. It says that if a member is charged with a violation of any provision of the constitution or with conduct unbecoming a member of the union, the member can be put on trial, just like a criminal. If you appear at your trial, the only person who can represent you is another member of the same local union; you're prevented from having a lawyer. If you don't appear at your trial, you're automatically found guilty.

In the last paragraph of the section on trials there's a list of things the union considers serious offenses. Here are just a few of them:

1. "Violation of a specific provision of the constitution." Remember, this constitution is 101 pages long, and you can be charged with a violation of any provision.

2. "Violation of the oath of loyalty to the local and the international union." That's right! You have to take a loyalty oath.

3. "Secession, or fostering the same." This means trying to get rid of the union if you don't like it. Unions know that when their own members have the opportunity to vote on whether to keep the union, they usually vote it out over 70% of the time. That's why union constitutions state that trying to get rid of the union is a crime. If the union is as good as it would have you believe, why would it even worry about members trying to get rid of it?

4. "Abuse of fellow members or officers by written or oral communications." I guess this means saying anything negative. Makes you wonder if the union ever heard of free speech.

5. "Disobedience to the rules, regulations, mandates, and decrees of the Local Union or of the officers of the International Union." I don't think this needs any further comment.

6. "Working in an establishment where a sanctioned strike is in progress, or returning to work during a sanctioned strike." This means if the union calls a strike you don't agree with and you want to continue to work to support yourself and your family, you're in violation of the union's constitution and can be disciplined.

How do unions treat members who violate a provision of their constitution? A union called a strike against Archer-Daniels-Midland Corporation, located in Decatur, Illinois. A union member named Riley, who needed his job and his paycheck, crossed the picket line and returned to work. The strike lasted 100 days before it was finally settled. After the strike was over, Mr. Riley was put on trial. The union accused him of violating its constitution by crossing the picket line and fined him $64 for every day he worked during the strike — a total of $6,400. Believe it or not, the court forced Mr. Riley to pay. Union members must obey the provisions of their union's constitution, even if they never read all the fine print.

Another interesting part of the constitution concerns the amount of money the union charges members. Seven pages are needed for this section, so let me summarize. The first part talks about initiation fees. This is the fee the union charges new members. The initiation fee is $45.00. Sometimes a union waves this fee in an attempt to win more votes. This to done to make the union sound like a good deal; but the union knows it's worth giving up initiation fees if it can win the election and collect dues every month. In addition, it would collect initiation fees from everyone hired in the future. The bottom line is this: Any union that requires members to pay an initiation fee is simply charging a person for their job.

This section goes on to talk about monthly dues. It says monthly dues shall be a minimum of $11.00 per month, but can be higher. The next paragraph talks about the union's strike fund. It says whenever the strike fund gets too low, the union will assess each member an additional amount of money until the fund is replenished.

The next paragraph says if a member fails to pay his or her dues to the union by the 10th of the month, that member will lose their membership and can only be reinstated by paying another initiation fee.

The following paragraph says "no member will be credited with dues until all fines, assessments, and other indebtedness against him or her are paid in full." This means that if you owe a fine or assessment to the union, any money you pay will go against that charge, not against dues. And remember, if you don't pay your dues on time, you have to pay another initiation fee. In other words, the union's going to get your money whether you're coming or going.

The constitution goes on to talk about where the dues money goes. Out of the minimum $11.00 monthly dues, $6.75 goes to the International Union — the big money boys at union headquarters; $4.15 goes to the union's regional office. This leaves — are you ready? — 10 cents per member for the local union. So here's the split: out of your $11.00, $10.90 would go to the union's national and regional offices. Ten cents would go to the local. The union can talk all it wants about members having a say in what happens in their local, but when it comes to money, the local union gets only a dime out of every $11.00 collected.

The next couple of paragraphs talk about assessments. This is the amount of money the union can charge you over and above initiation fees and monthly dues.

Here's a statement you might find interesting: "No Local Union shall have the right to pay any bills before it pays its full obligation to the International Union each month." This is another example that shows where a union's priorities really are.

While unions make members abide by all kinds of rules and regulations, what kind of standards do union leaders live by? Are they the kind of people you want representing you? In an earlier presentation, we talked about the article in *Fortune* magazine that listed the 50 biggest Mafia bosses. The article begins with this statement: "Crime pays. Annual gross income from the rackets will probably exceed $50 billion this year. This makes the Mob's business greater than all U.S. iron, steel, copper, and aluminum manufacturing combined...These figures were compiled for the President's Commission on Organized Crime."

Remember, this article stated that eight of the top twelve Mafia bosses get at least part of their money either directly or indirectly from unions.

I'll read just a few more paragraphs to give you an idea of how a corrupt union can hurt both employers and employees.

"A common racketeer strategy is to control a union so that it willingly signs cut-rate sweetheart contracts with Mob-run companies and threatens to strike competitors. Underworld leaders have used unions to influence and infiltrate many legitimate businesses." This means that if a union is controlled by the wrong people, it can encourage a strike at a legitimate business, like ours, just to help one of our competitors and maybe drive us out of business.

Another paragraph in the *Fortune* article states that Mafia influence "in union affairs reaches right to the top." It describes one case where a Mafia leader hand-picked a person to be president of a large international union. When the person the Mafia chose was sent to prison, the justice department found the Mob continued to control the union.

So unions establish rules, regulations, constitutions and bylaws to restrict the rights of their members, but at the same time some union officials — or people who control those officials — violate the law. This is not right, but it happens.

Think about it. This union wants you to vote for it in the election. That's why it's spending time and money trying to get your vote. It wants you to become a member, pay dues, and abide by its constitution and bylaws. If you vote to support the union, you're placing your future and the future of this organization in the hands of people you don't really know. If you feel the things we've talked about today are things you would not be comfortable with, like dues, fines, assessments, trials, restrictions on your freedom of speech, restrictions on solving your own problems, how dues money would be spent, and the type of people who control some unions, vote "no."

Literature Preparation

Opening this campaign segment with a simple handout that delivers a clear message can have good results. Some employers have prepared a handout with a cover headline that states, "The Union Constitution — What's In It For Me?" The inside of the handout is left entirely blank to make the point that there is nothing in the constitution to protect employees' rights. A red dot is printed on the last page of the handout with the statement, "Blow on this dot. When it turns blue, union promises will come true." (An example of this handout is shown as Exhibit 11-A.)

Other employers have taken a single provision from the union constitution that they believe will have high impact with their voting group and have prepared a handout covering that provision.

Another effective handout is called "Rules of the Road." This format takes several provisions from the constitution and includes comments in the margin.

(An example of this handout is shown as Exhibit 11-B.)

At this point in your campaign, consider accelerating the number of events per segment to at least three. When you are finished scheduling all planned activities for Segment Four, meet with your supervisors and examine the campaign's present status.

1. Assess the current position of the voting group by individuals. Have you gained any ground during this segment and if so, how much?

2. Are there key union supporters whose position has softened during the segment? If so, why, and how can you capitalize on this opportunity?

3. What issues have been most persuasive? Can you develop additional information to exploit these issues further?

4. Review plans and strategy for the next segment.

The following calendar includes five events, however, you should select the number most appropriate for your campaign.

Monday — **Poster or cartoon**

Tuesday — **The Union Constitution — What's In It For Me?** handout distributed by supervisors — **Remove poster or cartoon**

Wednesday — **Captive audience meeting** — **Show video** *Union Constitutions & Bylaws — Mechanisms of control*

Thursday — **Rules of the Road** handout distributed by supervision

Friday — **Letter to homes that summarizes communications during this week** — **Meet with supervision to review week, update voting assessment, analyze support areas, and examine issues**

The preparatory work for Segment Four is now complete. It's time to begin work on Segment Five.

Exhibit 11-A

the UNION CONSTITUTION

Exhibit 11-A

Blow on this dot.

When it turns blue, union promises will come true.

Exhibit 11-B

I B E W

RULES OF
THE ROAD

Exhibit 11-B

Before you vote, be sure you understand what the IBEW's constitution really says.

Becoming a member of the International Brotherhood of Electrical Workers carries with it serious obligations. If you become a member, you cannot choose to support or withdraw from those obligations whenever you want. You must follow specific rules, regulations, and procedures that are often very complicated and hard to understand.

The Electrical Workers constitution is 106 pages long. One hundred and six pages of fine print that will affect every aspect of your working life. It is not a document that describes a member's rights and liberties, but a set of rules, regulations, and obligations that members must obey.

Has the union told you about all the regulations that members must follow? Have you been given a copy of the Electrical Workers constitution or the local union bylaws? Even if you have, these documents are so long and complicated that most people don't read them or don't fully understand what they say. This *Rules of the Road* handout will show you why the Electrical Workers either haven't given you a copy of their constitution or hope that you won't read it.

As we look through the IBEW's constitution, we will find some interesting provisions that you need to know about before you decide how to vote. Incidentally, if the union won't give you a copy of the constitution, notify your supervisor. We will be happy to provide a copy for you to review.

Exhibit 11-B

THIS IS WHAT THE UNION SAYS

IBEW Constitution, Page 6

Ready reference for monthly dues payments to the International office through Local Unions or to the International secretary by members holding participating withdrawal card status...

Effective January 1, 1994
"A" MEMBERS
$19.30 Monthly

Reinstatement fees are required of all members who fall three or more months in arrears. Reinstatement fees for "A" members are $30.00.

ARTICLE 3, Section 8

The annual compensation of officers and senior representatives shall be:
I.P. $120,000
I.S. $106,000
I.T. $27,000
I.V.P. $74,000
I.E.C.Chairman................................... $27,000
I.E.C.Members $23,500
Senior Representative....................... $54,000

Thereafter, salaries of the International President, International Secretary, International Vice Presidents and Senior Representatives shall be increased annually on October 1.

ARTICLE 4, Section 3, Paragraph 13

When negotiating agreements with any national or international labor organization, or association of employers, or with any company, corporation or firm doing an inter-state, or inter-provencial business in electrical work, it is imperative that the I.P. have the authority to negotiate and enter into these agreements, or withdraw from these agreements, as circumstances so require.

BUT IS THIS WHAT IT MEANS?

Even before the first article in the IBEW's constitution the union clearly states what is most important – **your money**. And this is just for the International Union; the Local Union will require additional monthly dues. If you ever fell behind in dues, you would have to pay the IBEW again for the privilege of re-joining the union.

It takes a lot of **union bosses** to control the IBEW, and they don't come cheap. In the fiscal year ending June 30, 1996, the union paid these people **$1,924,410** in salaries and **$536,191** in expenses. Over $2,400,000 of the members' dues money was spent just for these union "fat cats." And every October 1st, they get a **raise**, no matter what!

The IBEW can tell you that you will have a say during contract negotiations, but the International president is the **only** person who has the power "to negotiate and enter into these agreements."

Page 3

Exhibit 11-B

THIS IS WHAT THE UNION SAYS

ARTICLE 13, Sections 1, 2, & 4

Any L.U. hereinafter organized shall pay to the I.S. five dollars ($5.00) for each "A" member admitted as a charter member. The five dollar ($5.00) fee shall be divided with three dollars ($3.00) paid to the General Fund and two dollars ($2.00) paid to the Pension Benefit Fund.

L.U.s already organized shall pay to the I.S. fifty percent (50%) of the admission fees collected from all new members...

L.U.s shall pay the I.S. one-half of the ten dollars ($10.00) reinstatement fee collected from "A" members in arrears. "BA" members shall pay a three dollars ($3.00) reinstatement fee, one-half of which shall be sent to the I.S. All members, before reinstatement, shall pay all arrearages to date of reinstatement.

ARTICLE 16, Section 16

Each L.U. shall establish the amount of its admission fee subject to approval of the I.P. Such fees must be stated in the L.U. bylaws; and in case of a dispute, the fees recorded in the bylaws shall be conclusive of the correct amount.

ARTICLE 21, Section 4

Each applicant admitted, shall, in the presence of members of the IBEW, repeat and sign the following obligation:
"I,_____, in the presence of members of the International Brotherhood of Electrical Workers, promise and agree to conform to and abide by the Constitution and laws of the IBEW and its local unions. I will further the purposes for which the IBEW is instituted. I will bear true allegiance to it and will not sacrifice its interests in any manner."

BUT IS THIS WHAT IT MEANS?

As soon as it was voted in, you would **owe** the IBEW money.

Then **everyone** hired gets hit up for money.

If you were to fall behind in your dues and wanted to be reinstated, the IBEW would **hit you again** for money.

Now it's the Local Union's turn to go after your **paycheck**.

Here are *Webster's* definitions for a couple of key words in the IBEW loyalty oath –
obligation: in law, (a) an agreement by which the *obligor* is bound under penalty of law to make payment or perform services for the benefit of the *obligee*; (b) the bond, contract, or other written document setting forth the terms of this agreement.
allegiance: the relationship of a vassal to his feudal lord.

Page 4

Exhibit 11-B

THIS IS WHAT THE UNION SAYS

ARTICLE 22, Sections 1 & 2

No member is entitled to notice of the monthly or quarterly dues of his L.U., nor of arrearages, but must take notice when payments are due.

When a member's working card has expired, he at once, without notice, stands suspended from all L.U. benefits.

ARTICLE 26, Section 1

Any member may be penalized for committing any one or more of the following offenses:
(1) Violation of any provision of this Constitution and the rules herein, or the bylaws, working agreements, or rules of a L.U.
(2) Having knowledge of the violation of any provision of this Constitution, or the bylaws or rules of a L.U., yet failing to file charges against the offender or to notify the proper officers of the L.U.
(4) Engaging in activities designed to bring about a withdrawal or secession from the IBEW of any L.U. or of any member or group of members, or to cause dual unionism or schism within the IBEW.

ARTICLE 26, Sections 2 & 5

All charges, except against officers and representatives of L.U.s, shall be heard and tried by the L.U. Executive Board which shall act as the trial board in accordance with Article XVIII. A majority vote of the board shall be sufficient for decision and sentence.

...He [the accused] must, upon request, be allowed an IBEW member to represent him.

BUT IS THIS WHAT IT MEANS?

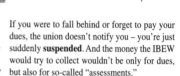

If you were to fall behind or forget to pay your dues, the union doesn't notify you – you're just suddenly **suspended**. And the money the IBEW would try to collect wouldn't be only for dues, but also for so-called "assessments."

The IBEW's constitution alone is **106 pages** long with scores of provisions. But if a member violates even one of those provisions, they're in **trouble** with the union.

Personal loyalty and friendship take a backseat to union loyalty; so if a friend violates any of the IBEW's many rules and regulations, you had better be ready to turn into a **snitch** or you're in trouble too.

If you were to become dissatisfied with the union and tried to get it voted out, you would be in serious trouble. (Here's the **truth** about "trying the union out for a while" to see if you like it.)

If you were accused of violating any of the union's rules, you would be put on **trial**. Officials of the Local Union would **decide your fate**, not an impartial jury.

If you wanted someone to represent you, it would have to be **another member** of the IBEW, not a lawyer. Does this seem fair?

Page 5

Exhibit 11-B

THIS IS WHAT THE UNION SAYS	**BUT IS THIS WHAT IT MEANS?**

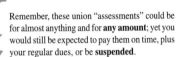

ARTICLE 19, Section 2

All assessments imposed shall be charged by the F.S. against the member as regular dues and must be paid within the time required to protect the member's continuous good standing and benefits.

Remember, these union "assessments" could be for almost anything and for **any amount**; yet you would still be expected to pay them on time, plus your regular dues, or be **suspended**.

ARTICLE 12, Section 4

(d) *Prohibition of Work*. It is a condition for admission to pension benefits, including vested pension right and the continuation thereof, that the member shall not perform any work of any kind coming under the IBEW's jurisdiction either for compensation or gratis for anyone...

If you retired, then needed extra money to make ends meet, this provision would **prevent** you from working at your trade, even for free! You could go to work as a greeter at Wal-Mart for minimum wage, but not as a skilled worker doing the job you were trained for. Maybe this wouldn't be a problem for a retired IBEW union boss living on a big pension, but it makes no sense for regular retired people who sometimes need extra money.

Page 6

Exhibit 11-B

PROTECT YOURSELF
PROTECT YOUR FUTURE

Campaign Segment Five:
Job Security & Strikes
Your future in the union's hands

S egment Five of the campaign covers the subjects of job security and strikes. Traditionally, these issues are management's strongest. The biggest concern most employees have relative to the prospect of unionization is what would happen to them in case of a strike. There are so many horror stories about union strikes, it is impossible to say one example is better or worse than another. The point you want to emphasize is that when employees engage in an economic strike, many things can happen, and almost all of them are bad. The job security and strike issue is also highly emotional. Employees who tend to make their voting decisions based on emotions will probably support management if you make an effective presentation.

During this segment, focus attention on the fact that union strikes can and do happen. When they occur, the consequences for employees are often negative. If you have acquired the strike history of the union that is attempting to organize your employees, you will know the number of strikes this union has called, how many employees were involved in each strike, the employers that were struck, and how long the strikes lasted. When planning how to best use this information, consider several points. First, if the number of strikes called by the union during the last two or three years is substantial — 50 per year or more — an introductory handout based on this fact alone is effective. Second, look at the number of man-days members of this union have lost because of strikes (strike duration x number of members involved). You may decide this number is more impressive than the total number of strikes. Third, determine whether any strikes were called by this union in your geographic area. Time spent finding a local "horror story" may prove to be the best time you will invest in the entire campaign. If possible, find an employee or former employee of the affected company who will agree to give a testimonial.

It is always best if your strike message is union- and/or area-specific. If you are recounting a strike "horror story," try to use events that are as current as possible. Strike history data and newspaper clippings are excellent sources for powerful and factual information during this critical campaign segment. Union constitutions also contain useful information regarding rules that members must observe during a strike.

Before drafting your handout(s) and developing the calendar for this segment, decide on the content of the captive audience presentation. If you are using the LRI video program, review the video *Job Security & Strikes — Your future in the union's hands.* If you are giving a speech instead of showing the video, a sample draft of a captive audience speech follows.

Draft of Captive Audience Speech

Whenever the subject of unions is mentioned, one of the first things people think of is strikes. Unions are famous for calling strikes. All of us have heard about strikes and the violence that often accompanies them. During a union organizing campaign, there's a lot of misinformation about strikes: how they start, what happens to union members during a strike, what the rights of strikers and their employer are, and how strikes finally end. Today I want to give you the facts about union strikes.

First, let's see how strikes begin. As we discussed in the presentation on collective bargaining, a union and an employer must sit down to negotiate a contract. Whether it's a first contract or any subsequent contract, both sides are free to make whatever proposals or demands they want. If management says "no" to any of the union's demands or the union says "no" to any of management's demands, the union must decide whether to accept management's offer or try to force management to accept the union's position. If the union decides to force its position, there are very few things it can do to make management meet its demands. However, one of those things — and the most frequently-used tactic — is to call unionized employees out on strike.

Strikes have been used by unions since the beginning of the organized labor movement and continue to be used today. Often, during organizing campaigns, unions try to convince voters that strikes seldom happen. Here are the facts:

According to the United States Department of Labor and the Bureau of Labor Statistics, union strikes are a relatively common occurrence. During a recent 10-year period, over 68 million workdays were lost due to strikes; and that figure doesn't even include striking workforces of less than 1,000 people.

Consider the number of times you've recently heard or read about strikes and related violence. The Greyhound strike, for example, when shots were fired into buses loaded with innocent passengers. Or the Pittston mine workers whose union was fined hundreds of thousands of dollars for sponsoring strike-related violence against the company. [If available, substitute current area- and union-specific strike information.] As you can see, with a union, strikes are always a very real possibility, and something you should consider when deciding how to vote.

Many organizers tell voters that as union members they couldn't be forced on strike unless they approved it first. This is very misleading. Most union constitutions state that a strike can be approved by a simple majority of the members present at a sanctioned strike vote. What about those who aren't present for a strike vote? [If the union's constitution contains this type of provision, consider citing the article and page numbers and distributing copies of the highlighted provision.]

Thousands of union members first hear of a strike when they go to work and are greeted by a picket line. They were either overlooked or deliberately excluded from the strike vote. Even if you didn't attend the strike meeting, or if you voted "no," you would still have to honor the strike or be faced with angry pickets and union trials and fines. So voting for the union means you could be involved in a strike that's called without your knowledge. Are you willing to take that chance with your future?

There are other things you need to know about union strikes, things the union organizer may not tell you. If you go on strike for more money, better benefits, or improved working conditions, two things happen. First, you get no paycheck. Second, your benefits are terminated. No paycheck, no benefits. If a union organizer is honest, they'll tell you the same thing.

The organizer might also tell you that if you go on strike, you receive union strike benefits. Well, it's a good idea to find out just what these benefits really are. Strike benefits for [name of union] are only $_____ a week, and to get them you have to spend several hours on the picket line each week. Also, benefits usually don't begin until you've been on strike at least two weeks. Imagine how hard it would be to support yourself and your family on $_____ a week with no employee benefits. Even worse, imagine how tough it would be if these so-called strike benefits were canceled by the union. It can happen. It happened at Greyhound. Striking bus drivers who had been getting $50 a week since the strike started suddenly lost all benefits. Union bosses said they needed the money to continue the union's legal fight.

It's a violation of many union constitutions for members to take part-time work during a strike to support their families. If the union organizer tries to deny any of this, ask the organizer to sign a guarantee that states: "I, (name of union organizer), guarantee that if any employee of this company is forced out of work because of a strike, the union will pay their regular salary and continue their current benefits until the strike is settled and all employees can return to work." If the organizer won't sign this pledge — and I promise you they won't — you can be sure a strike by the union will cost you money, maybe a lot of money.

Also, in almost every state [**New York and Rhode Island are the exceptions**], employees on strike cannot receive unemployment compensation. This means you receive no money for the first two weeks of a strike, and only $____ per week from the union after that, and you wouldn't be eligible for unemployment.

Not only would you suffer severe economic hardship, there's a chance your job could be gone when the strike is settled. If you go out on strike, management has the legal right to hire a permanent replacement to fill your job.

Let's take a closer look at an actual strike: how it started, what happened during the strike, and how it ended. [**A local or same-union strike would be a preferable example.**] During negotiations for a new contract, the union that represented the hourly employees of Liberty Glass Company in Sapulpa, Oklahoma, made demands the company found impossible to accept. The union called its members out on strike. Incidentally, this strike wasn't over higher wages; it was over operational provisions of the labor agreement.

The strike began, as most strikes normally do, with the union placing picketers around the plant. The first newspaper article about the strike stated, "Glass workers early today staged picket lines in front of the Liberty Glass Company plant as the first full day of a strike for improved benefits began. About 350 union members are involved in the strike. The local union president said negotiations over the company's benefit package, not wages, prompted the strike."

In time, the company exercised its legal right and began hiring permanent replacements for the striking workers. The National Labor Relations Board has stated, "An employer may permanently replace economic strikers." Here's what the newspaper reported: "Glass workers walking picket lines today were joined by a second group outside the doors of Liberty Glass Company — dozens of job seekers hoping for positions the strikers had left. The job applicants were responding to advertisements the company placed in local and area newspapers...”

After this strike had gone on for over five weeks, things got out of control when mass picketing and demonstrations began. The newspaper reported that over 100 people marched for two hours in front of the Liberty Glass Company plant carrying makeshift signs, in spite of the march being a violation of a judge's ban on picketing activity. A union spokesman declined to say what effect the march would have on a settlement effort. An attorney for management stated the company's position remained firm and had actually hardened since the strike started.

Negotiations continued with no settlement. Then the situation literally exploded. An automobile owned by a Liberty Glass Company employee was destroyed by a firebomb. Police found a beer bottle with the remains of what appeared to be a cloth wick inside the burned car. The Liberty Glass employee, who was home at the time of the firebombing, told police he had been followed after work several times by strikers and he believed they had firebombed his car. According to the newspaper, the firebombing was only the latest in a series of similar incidents reported to police involving either Liberty Glass security guards or employees. Four bottles, believed filled with gasoline, had been thrown into a parking lot across from the plant. Federal agents were brought in to assist with specialized arson and bomb investigation procedures.

By this time, several employees had become so dissatisfied with their union they either crossed the picket line and returned to work or filed complaints against the union with the National Labor Relations Board. The newspaper reported “a determination in several grievances filed by several parties in the six-week-long Liberty Glass Company strike may be forthcoming, a National Labor Relations Board investigator said today. The investigator said he hoped for decisions in at least one and possibly more grievances...The most recent grievance was filed by seven glassworkers who broke ranks with the union and returned to work. The workers say they have been threatened by the union for returning to work...”

Soon after this, the arrests began. Two counts of assault were filed against a man identified as a member of the striking glass worker's union in connection with incidents at Liberty Glass. The man named in the complaints reportedly tried to drive his vehicle into a truck carrying several electricians into the Liberty Glass Company plant. Police were still investigating an incident in which a shot was fired at a guardhouse window. Police were also investigating an incident in which a Liberty Glass employee was almost struck by a car near the company.

But the violence didn't stop; it got worse. Again, according to the newspaper, several bullets were fired into the home of a Liberty Glass Company employee, narrowly missing two children. This was only one in a number of violent acts reported at the Liberty Glass plant or at the homes of employees.

Even though the union members were unhappy and violence continued, the union held out and kept members on strike. What was the union doing to help these members? Apparently not much. The newspaper reported that "Representatives of two glass workers unions in Oklahoma brought an estimated $1,000 worth of food to strike headquarters in a show of support for the 114-day-old strike against Liberty Glass Company. The president of the Liberty Glass union expressed his gratitude for the help and said it gets bleak out there sometimes when you have people losing their homes and their cars."

That bears repeating. The union president said, "IT GETS BLEAK OUT THERE SOMETIMES WHEN YOU HAVE PEOPLE LOSING THEIR HOMES AND THEIR CARS." Doesn't it seem incredible that a union would allow that to happen to its members? Incidentally, the $1,000 worth of food amounted to about $2.85 for each union member on strike.

Now the strike was five months old and the violence continued. According to the newspaper, someone even tried to burn down the plant. The story stated: "Fire that damaged a large metal warehouse at Liberty Glass early this morning has been termed possible arson by investigators. Firemen battled smoke and flames inside the building for five hours before controlling the fire shortly before dawn. The fire chief said the fire was being listed as suspicious and probably was set by an arsonist."

There were many other acts of violence reported during this strike. A newspaper article stated that "armed security guards ringed Liberty Glass Company facilities after a near riot erupted Thursday that ended with injury to five persons. Two men who have been employees of Liberty Glass for sixteen years and ten years respectively were arrested with more arrests expected. The sheriff's department reported that the five were injured when they were struck over the head, body and arms by union members swinging baseball bats, bed slats and hammer handles. Several weapons were seized at the scene of the fight. The sheriff stated that the incident was a near riot situation involving a small number of unarmed Liberty Glass employees and security guards and fifteen or twenty strikers."

Another article described an incident in which a three-year-old child suffered head injuries when a driver leaving the union strike headquarters forced a Liberty Glass employee off the road and into a utility pole.

So, in summary, the union called a strike. The strike wasn't over wages, but over something important only to the union. Many employees, dissatisfied with the union, crossed the picket line and returned to their jobs — jobs they needed to support their families. Their decision wasn't respected by the union, which threatened these employees with fines, firebombs, gunshots into their homes, riots, and injury at work.

The Liberty Glass strike lasted 21 months. Twenty-one months of aggravation, violence, no pay, no benefits, and no unemployment compensation for strikers. As the union president said, people lost their homes, their cars, and probably all of their life savings. After all these sacrifices, how did the strike end? This final newspaper story gave a good summary. "The Liberty Glass strike is over. The union has been voted out by the employees by a margin of 269 to 4. Union officials refused to comment about the election but a company spokesman commented about the issues. He stated the major issue in the strike was not money. The company had met the so-called industry wage package and actually granted wages over the industry rate for certain skilled jobs. The company spokesman stated, 'We did it to avoid a strike, but the international union had goals of its own.'"

That's an important statement: "THE INTERNATIONAL UNION HAD GOALS OF ITS OWN." It shows how the wishes of employees can be overruled by the desires of a large union. But that isn't the end of the story. Those union members who stayed out on strike had no jobs to return to. They had been permanently replaced. After being on strike for over 21 months with no wages, no benefits and no unemployment, their union was voted out. The union officials still had jobs and paychecks; they also had NO COMMENT.

There it is. An inside look at a union strike. It really happened. You might be saying to yourself well, maybe it happened there, but something like that could never happen here. That's exactly what the employees of Liberty Glass once thought. They were hard-working family people, just like you, but they lost control of their working lives. They turned their futures over to a union.

I'm not saying that if the union wins this election there will automatically be a strike, or that if a strike occurs, the things that happened in this case will happen here. But union strikes can happen and things can get out of control. One way to make certain you never have to go through the same things the employees of Liberty Glass suffered is to never put yourself in the position where a union could call you out on strike. How do you do that? Simple. Vote "no."

Literature Preparation

Campaign literature is a good way to introduce the subject of strikes and to begin informing voters that with union representation comes the very real possibility of being called out on strike. Consider a handout with bowling ball and pins artwork on the cover and a headline that states, "ONLY THIS KIND OF STRIKE IS FUN." Inside are photos of union picket lines and the headline, "NOT THIS KIND!" The copy documents how many union members have recently been on strike and the average number of days out of work. (An example of this handout is shown as Exhibit 12-A.)

Another option for an introductory handout is a simple flyer about a specific strike called by the union that's seeking representation. The description of the strike should be brief since the most powerful handout will follow the captive audience presentation. Newspapers published by unions are a good source for strike stories. Most employers whose employees are represented by a union receive and save copies of these newspapers.

After the captive audience meeting, be prepared to follow-up with possibly the most powerful handout of your campaign. If you have a local strike example or a good same-union example, use it. A reminder: the more relevant you make a handout, the more effective it will be in persuading voters to reject the union. However, it is not always possible to find a good local or same-union example. This is not a disaster. Different location, different union examples can be very successful.

The Liberty Glass strike described in the captive audience speech is a classic example of employees who suffered through a long and costly union strike. It makes an excellent piece of campaign literature. (This handout is shown as Exhibit 5-C.)

The flyer titled "John Bean Plant Closed" describes a company that went out of business as a result of a strike. It's another good example of how a strike situation can be developed into an effective flyer. (This handout is shown as Exhibit 12-B.)

Strike histories are not the only way to illustrate that a union's actions can threaten job security. The flyer shown in Exhibit 12-C reproduces an actual unfair labor practice charge filed against a union by one of its members. In this particular case, the union threatened the employee with discharge unless she paid her dues.

The strike computer shown in Chapter 7 also makes an excellent handout to be distributed at the end of this segment's captive audience meeting. Explain how the computer works, then let the voting group do their own calculations.

Segment Five should include at least three events. However, as many as five events could be scheduled if you have sufficient information. *This is not the time to hold back!*

When you are finished scheduling all planned activities for Segment Five, meet with your supervisors and examine the campaign's present status.

1. Assess the current position of the voting group by individuals. Have you gained any ground during this segment and if so, how much?

2. Are there key union supporters whose position has softened during the segment? If so, why, and how can you capitalize on this opportunity?

3. What issues have been most persuasive? Can you develop additional information to exploit these issues further?

4. Review plans and strategy for the next segment.

The following is a five-event calendar. At the least, you should schedule three events for this segment.

Monday — **Poster or cartoon**

Tuesday — **"Strike That's Fun"** handout distributed by supervisor — **Remove poster or cartoon**

Wednesday — **Captive audience meeting — Show the video** *Job Security & Strikes — Your future in the union's hands* **— Distribute strike computer at the conclusion of the captive audience meeting**

Thursday — **Relevant local strike** handout or **"Liberty Glass on Strike"** handout distributed by supervisor

Friday — **Letter to home that summarizes communications during this segment — Meet with supervision to review week, update voting assessment, analyze support areas, and examine issues**

The preparatory work for Segment Five is now complete. It's time to begin work on Segment Six.

Exhibit 12-A

ONLY THIS KIND OF STRIKE IS FUN

Exhibit 12-A

NOT THIS KIND!

The UNION kind of STRIKE can cost you money, even your job.

Union organizers want you to believe that strikes are rare. THIS ISN'T TRUE. Figures from the Department of Labor prove that strikes still happen. In fact, the total number of union members affected by strikes has recently increased.

Year	Members on Strike	Year	Members on Strike
1996	120,753	1997	333,832

During these two years, striking union members were out of work an average of **34 DAYS — 34 DAYS WITH NO PAYCHECK OR COMPANY BENEFITS.**

One of the strikes that ended in 1996 had gone on for 635 DAYS.

Members who follow their union out on strike can lose more than their wages and benefits—sometimes they lose their jobs. **EMPLOYERS CAN LEGALLY HIRE PERMANENT REPLACEMENTS FOR ECONOMIC STRIKERS.**

Good customers often stop doing business with companies that have gone through a strike. Once a strike is settled, the result can be a need for fewer employees. We aren't saying that a strike will happen if the union is voted in, but we are saying that strikes would always be a *possibility*.

Who doesn't lose during a union strike?

Union bosses and other union officials continue to draw high salaries and receive lavish benefits, while union members and their families are expected to sacrifice for as long as a strike continues.

Protect your future and your economic security... Vote **NO**

Exhibit 12-B

HARASSMENT

LOST WAGES

DEMANDS

JOHN BEAN

TROUBLE

PLANT

VIOLENCE

FINES

CLOSED

STRIKES

DUES

PROMISES

PICKETS

VANDALISM

Exhibit 12-B

IT HAPPENED IN LANSING,

MICHIGAN.

THIS IS THE <u>TRUE</u> STORY

OF A UNION STRIKE AT

AN AGRICULTURAL MACHINERY

DIVISION PLANT.

READ THE <u>FACTS</u> BEFORE

IT HAPPENS HERE.

THIS IS HOW IT ALL BEGAN . . .

THE UNION WON A LABOR BOARD
ELECTION AT THE AGRICULTURAL
MACHINERY DIVISION PLANT.

THE UNION MAKE DEMANDS
BUT THE COMPANY SAID
<u>NO!</u>

Exhibit 12-B

SO THE UNION CALLED A

**S
T
R
I
K
E**

John Bean Shut Down By Strike

About 400 members of United Auto Workers Local 724 went on strike Friday against the John Bean Co., a division of Food Manufacturing Corp., shutting down the food processing plant

Union officials said the strike was called in a dispute over a new contract. They said talks had stalled on money matters...

The union pulled the employees out on **STRIKE!**

Although many of the employees did not want to go on strike they were afraid not to. They had voted for the union and now they were stuck with it. The union led them to believe that there would be no strike but they all ended up on the picket line.

Exhibit 12-B

THE STRIKE WENT

ON

AND

ON

AND

ON

Exhibit 12-B

THE UNION KEPT EMPLOYEES
ON THE PICKET LINE FOR
SIX MONTHS.

THE STRIKERS WENT WITHOUT
THEIR WAGES FOR SIX
MONTHS. THEIR FAMILIES
SUFFERED.

BUT THE UNION ORGANIZERS
WERE NOT HURT BY THE
STRIKE.

Exhibit 12-B

AND <u>WHERE</u> <u>WERE</u> <u>THE</u>
<u>UNION</u> ORGANIZERS ???

THE <u>UNION</u> <u>ORGANIZERS</u> WERE STILL DRAWING <u>THEIR</u> FAT PAYCHECKS -- SO <u>THEY</u> <u>DIDN'T</u> <u>CARE</u>·THEIR FAMILIES STILL HAD ENOUGH MONEY TO EAT, AND PAY THEIR BILLS- IT WAS THE <u>EMPLOYEES</u> AND THE <u>EMPLOYEES'</u> FAMILIES WHO <u>SUFFERED</u>!!!

Exhibit 12-B

IT WAS THE LONGEST EVER IN THE CITY

Strike At John Bean Longest Ever in City

The strike at the John Bean Division of FMC is now in its 112th day—the l o n g e s t industrial plant strike in Lansing's history. The longest previous strike, against General Motors installations in 1946, lasted 110 days...

Exhibit 12-B

VANDALISM

AND

TROUBLE

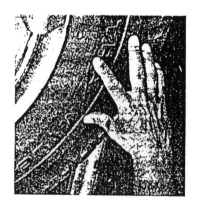 

Picketing
At Issue

Lawyers for John Bean Division of FMC were scheduled to
return to Circuit Court this afternoon to ask for a court order
restraining members of striking UAW Local 724 from mass
picketing...

Exhibit 12-B

WHAT DID VOTING FOR THE UNION GET THEM??

WHAT DID THE STRIKE AND VIOLENCE GET FOR THOSE EMPLOYEES??

TURN THE PAGE AND SEE. . .

Exhibit 12-B

PLANT CLOSED

ate Journal (Lansing, MI), July 6

The last six John Bean production workers shaking hands are (from left) Joe Krchmar, Frank Linley, Albert Verhille, Ed Cole, Eddie Sylvester and Jay Earls.

By MARK NIXON
Staff Writer

"I'm going out for a beer, then head for the employment office."

Frank Linley spoke solemnly, betraying only a flicker of bitterness he holds for John Bean, the company that employed him for 14 years.

LINLEY'S JOB was phased out Friday, one of the last painful steps before the company becomes a part of Lansing manufacturing history after 60 years in operation.

Linley and five other long-term veterans of the John Bean factory filed out one-by-one into the sunny factory parking lot Friday punctually at 3:30 p.m. It was the normal quitting time after an eight-hour day. But this time, there would be no Monday morning grind to return to next week.

They were survivors of layoffs that gnawed away at the ranks of John Bean production workers, which once stood as high as 230 only a year ago. The six spent the past few months crating machinery and parts for shipment to the new operation in Arkansas.

Last year, the company said lower taxes in Arkansas plus labor difficulties (Bean had a six-month strike in 1968, the city's longest) contributed to the decision to leave Lansing.

Linley, until Friday the unit chairman for the UAW local, is now left without a membership to govern. "It's just one of those things . . . I'll just get in the unemployment line with the rest of them," he said.

Finish of Shift Means End of Job

Why company leaves Lansing

After the union caused all the trouble—where did the employee go with all the union's help?

EVERY EMPLOYEE LOST HIS JOB

THEY LEARNED THE HARD WAY

WHERE UNIONS WIN
—EMPLOYEES LOSE

Exhibit 12-B

THOSE WORKERS DIDN'T
BELIEVE IT COULD HAPPEN
TO THEM—BUT IT DID!

THINK

(BEFORE IT'S TOO LATE)

DON'T LET THIS
HAPPEN HERE.

VOTE NO!

Exhibit 12-C

THE UNION DOESN'T WANT YOU TO SEE WHAT'S INSIDE THIS FLYER

CONFIDENTIAL

Exhibit 12-C

Union Harasses Member

UNITE[D] [ST]ATES OF AMERICA
NATIONAL LABOR RELATIONS BOARD
CHARGE AGAINST LABOR ORGANIZATION
OR ITS AGENTS

	NOT WRITE IN THIS SPACE
Case	Date Filed
36-CB-1752	10-15-92

INSTRUCTIONS: File an original and 4 copies of this charge and an additional copy for each organization, each local, and each individual named in Item 1 with the NLRB Regional Director of the region in which the alleged unfair labor practice occurred or is occurring.

1. LABOR ORGANIZATION OR ITS AGENTS AGAINST WHICH CHARGE IS BROUGHT

a. Name
UFCW Local 555

b. Union Representative to contact
DAN DUGAN

c. Telephone No.
503-684-3822

d. Address (street, city, state and ZIP code)
7045 S.W. SANDBURG RD. P.O. Box 23555
TIGARD, OREGON 97223

e. The act... (section 8(b), subsection(s) (list subsection))

2. Basis of the Charge (set forth a clear and concise statement of the facts constituting the alleged unfair labor practices)

On April 11th 1992, Dan Dugan came into
Albertsons and started thinking me on the job
About Union dues. He gave me a final discharge
Slip and said that I didn't pay my union due
by April 29th 1992, that I would be discharged.
To my Knowledge, our dept was not bargaind
in to the union, but he stire Kept harassing
me at home, he would call me. I had to
borrow the money from a friend just to
pay the union plus I paid other dues.
And late fees. Now I would like to have
all the money returned, plus late fees,
until we are bargaind in.

3. Name of Employer
ALBERTSONS

4. Telephone No.
206-574-6105

5. Location of establishment (street, city, state and ZIP code)
9915 N.E. HAZEL DELL AVE. VANCOUVER, WA.
98685

6. Employer representative to contact

7. Type of establishment (factory, mine, wholesaler, etc.)
GROCERY

8. Identify principal product or service

9. Number of workers employed

10. Full name of party filing charge
BRENDA LOUISE Frazier

11. Address of party filing charge (street, city, state and ZIP code)
10316 N.E. Stutz Rd. Apt. B VANCOUVER, WA.
98685

12. DECLARATION
I declare that I have read the above charge and that the statements therein are true to the best of my knowledge and belief.

By (signature) Brenda Louise Frazier
LOBBY CLERK
(title, if any)

Address 10316 N.E. Stutz Rd. Apt. B Vancuv. WA.
98685

12. Telephone No.
206-574-7027

Date 9-30-92

WILLFUL FALSE STATEMENTS ON THIS CHARGE CAN BE PUNISHED BY FINE AND IMPRISONMENT (U.S. CODE, TITLE 18, SECTION 1001)

Each year, thousands of charges are filed against unions by their own members

This Unfair Labor Practice charge filed by a union member says her union....

△ **Harassed her on the job about union dues**

△ **Threatened to have her discharged if she didn't pay what the union said she owed**

△ **Continued to harass her at home**

Desperate, the member borrowed money from a friend to stop the union threats.

This case shows what's most important to the union—YOUR MONEY! One of the union's main objectives in collective bargaining negotiations is to get what's called a Dues Checkoff provision. THIS REQUIRES UNION DUES TO BE AUTOMATICALLY DEDUCTED FROM YOUR PAYCHECK. The purpose of this provision is clear: Regardless of your own financial needs, the union always gets its money first.

If the union says you owe money, watch out!

Vote NO

Campaign Segment Six:
Election Day
Participation & choice

The final segment of the campaign will probably be the hardest. This is when the pressure becomes most intense and you find out if you win or lose. NLRB elections have no draws; if the election ends in a tie, you're declared the winner. If the union receives 50% plus one vote, it wins.

Election week is always a short week for campaigning. If the election is held on Friday, you have only three days to campaign. If the election is held on Wednesday or Thursday, you have only one or two days respectively to campaign. You will not campaign heavily on election day, or for at least part of the day before election day, since this is the insulated period. For all practical purposes, you have three days at most to campaign. Two days before the election, you will present the 24-hour captive audience presentation. At this time you will inform employees about voting procedures. A handout describing these procedures should be distributed. This is also the time when you should distribute your most powerful handout.

Occasionally, it is possible to lengthen your campaign period during the final week, but this must be done before a date and time for the election is established. In smaller voting units with no more than two shifts, the time of the election is often set in the late afternoon. If only one shift will be voting, the election will take place during the latter part of the shift. If two shifts are voting, the election will take place during the latter part of the first shift and the early part of the second shift. As an example, if the polls open at 2:30 PM on a Friday, the insulated period would not begin until 2:30 PM, Thursday. This would give you most of Thursday to campaign. If you have three shifts or a large workforce, it is more difficult to extend the campaign week.

Before drafting your handout(s) and developing the calendar for this final segment, decide on the content of the captive audience presentation. If you are using the LRI video program, review the video *Election Day — Participation & choice*. If you are giving a speech instead of showing the video, a sample draft of a captive audience speech follows.

Draft of Captive Audience Speech

During the past few weeks, you've received information about the upcoming union election. Now the time has come to evaluate all this information and to decide a very important question: Union versus union-free — Which is best for you?

We've made our position on the union issue clear. We don't want a union here. More can be accomplished if we continue to work together, one-on-one, without union stewards and officers, and without you being forced to pay union dues, fines, and assessments.

But management doesn't decide the issue of unionization. You, the employees, decide. No one from either management or the union has the right to interfere with your free choice.

I know many of you have questions about how the election will be conducted. First, a time and place has already been established for conducting the election. This is shown on the Notice of Election form that's been posted. [**State voting times and places.**] When you enter the voting area, you'll see several people seated at a table. These people will include a representative of the National Labor Relations Board. This is the person designated by the United States government to conduct the election. Also at the table will be two or more people — possibly your co-workers — who have been designated to observe the election and to make sure that only eligible voters are given ballots and allowed to vote. Both management and the union are each allowed to select an equal number of observers.

When you walk up to the table, tell the National Labor Relations Board agent your name and, if required, your employee number. The NLRB agent and the election observers will then check your name off the official list of eligible voters. This is done so no one other than you can vote under your name and so no one can vote twice.

If you're an eligible voter, the National Labor Relations Board agent will give you a ballot. The ballot does not list your name or employee number, or have any other way of identifying you. It's a completely secret ballot.

The ballot you receive simply asks you to "mark the square of your choice." Two boxes are shown and each is clearly identified.

Next, you go into a voting booth. After you've marked the ballot, fold it so no one can see how it's marked and leave the voting booth. You drop the folded ballot into a sealed ballot box. No one, except the National Labor Relations Board agent, can open the ballot box. Your ballot is mixed in with all the other ballots cast by your fellow employees.

When the allotted time for voting is over, the polls are closed. The National Labor Relations Board agent will then open the ballot box and count the ballots while representatives of management and the union watch. After all votes have been counted, the National Labor Relations Board agent announces the winner. The ballots are then sealed and become the property of the United States government.

It is extremely important that every eligible voter cast a ballot. The winner of the election will be decided by a majority of those who vote. By not voting, you're putting your future into the hands of others who may not be voting in your best interest. Therefore, it is crucial that every eligible employee vote.

In this, our last meeting, I want to review with you some of the things we've talked about during the past several weeks, and emphasize those points you need to consider before casting one of the most important votes of your working life. We know union membership has been on the decline, and in recent years has fallen drastically. In 1954, unions represented over 32% of the workforce in this country. That number gradually fell between 1955 and 1975. Then, between 1975 and today, the number has decreased dramatically, so now unions represent only about 15% of the total workforce. This means that today less than one worker in six chooses to become a union member. That's why unions are trying so hard to get new members. **[If available, include union-specific numbers for membership decline.]**

The union has probably told you there's nothing to lose by voting "yes" in this election because you can always decide later to vote the union out if you don't like what it does. Voting out a union is not as easy as it sounds. Remember, it's a violation of the union constitution to kick the union out, and violations can lead to trials and fines. This means the union can intimidate members into taking no action against it. The union isn't like a politician who has to run for re-election every few years. In fact, the union never has to run for re-election; for all practical purposes, once it gets in, you're stuck with it.

Here are some things you should ask yourself: If unions are a good deal, why hasn't union membership grown instead of fallen? Why are more and more people who have the facts and know both sides of the issue saying "no" to supporting a union? Maybe most important, why do unions lose nearly 70% of the decertification elections conducted? These are elections where employees who are currently represented by a union have the opportunity to decide whether to remain members.

You can learn a lot from the answers to these questions. Employees who have tried unions have learned — in many cases the hard way — that unions aren't the answer to their problems. Many unionized workers will tell you that their union actually causes more problems than it solves. This is especially true when it comes to resolving individual complaints. Remember, with a union, all your individual problems must go through a network of stewards, committeepersons, and other union officials. This means red tape, delays, and decisions made for political reasons rather than based on the facts of your individual case.

In one of our earlier presentations, we talked about the collective bargaining process and how it works. Collective bargaining simply means that when a union wins an election, the law requires both management and the union to negotiate over wages, hours, and working conditions. The key word is *negotiate*. In negotiations, the union can ask management for anything it wants; and it's perfectly legal for management to say "no."

If a union wins an election and starts bargaining, all wages and benefits employees currently have become a part of the negotiations, as well as those things the union may want. Remember, the National Labor Relations Board has said collective bargaining is a two-way street. The board has stated, "...there is, of course, no obligation on the part of an employer to contract to continue all existing benefits, nor is it an unfair labor practice to offer reduced benefits..." This means there's no guarantee that after negotiations employees will wind up with what they currently have. Even more to the point, the board has said, "Collective bargaining is potentially hazardous for employees, and as a result of such negotiations, employees could possibly wind up with less benefits after unionization than before."

At best, collective bargaining is a risky proposition. It's a lot like the game show *Wheel of Fortune*. When the wheel stops, you could wind up with more, you could wind up with the same thing you already have, or you could wind up with less. This is the way collective bargaining really works, regardless of what the union has told you.

Are there other reasons to say "no" to the union? Absolutely!

In our discussion about union constitutions and bylaws, we looked at a provision from the union's constitution that said, "All members by becoming members of this International Union thereby vest the proper officers and committees with the authority to act for and on their behalf in the settlement and adjustment of grievances." Then, this provision was in another section of the constitution: "Every member, by virtue of his membership in the Local Union, authorizes his Local union to act as his exclusive bargaining representative...and to act for him and have final authority in presenting, processing, and adjusting any grievance, difficulty, or dispute. The Local Union and its officers, representatives, and agents may decline to process any grievance, complaint, difficulty or dispute..." **[If possible, use the constitution of the union attempting to represent your employees.]**

This means the union has the absolute right to decide what's best for you; to talk for you, act for you, and to tell you exactly what to do. The union also has the right to tell you to jump in the lake. Maybe that's one of the reasons why union members, when given the opportunity, kick their union out nearly 70% of the time.

But that's not all the union's constitution does. It also typically contains provisions that cover things such as trials of members, fines, assessments, initiation fees, strikes, and dues. Minimum monthly dues are $11.00. Out of that $11.00, $6.75 goes to the international union and $4.15 goes to the union's regional office. That leaves ten cents per member for the local union. Surely there are better ways to use your money than paying union dues. **[If possible, use specific union constitution.]**

What about job security? That's another so-called union selling point. The truth is unions don't provide job security. The union won't help us sell our products or get more customers — and that's what keeps us in business and provides jobs. Sometimes, unions contribute to job insecurity. If you don't believe that, ask employees in unionized industries who have lost their jobs because their unionized employer was no longer competitive. Or ask union members who have lost jobs because their union had them fired for not paying dues. These people and hundreds of thousands of others now know that unions don't provide job security.

Right now, you enjoy more job security than any union could possibly offer. Here's just one reason why I say this: Many customers send us a form that asks if our business is covered by a union labor agreement and, if so, when this agreement expires. Why would a customer want to know this information? Simple. Customers depend on us. If we had a labor contract in effect, there would always be a possibility of a strike when the contract expires. Customers assume that if we had a strike, they wouldn't be able to get what they need from us on time. What do many customers do when faced with this possibility? They decide to find another company that does the same things we do and start doing business with that company as well as with us. This gives the customer some insurance against the chance we could go on strike. So right now, without a union contract, we're probably able to get a higher percentage of our customers' business. This provides each of you greater job security. So unions don't really guarantee job security — another excellent reason you should vote "no."

What else could happen if you were ever forced out on strike by the union? First, you would not receive a paycheck. Second, there would be no employee benefits. Third, in most states you cannot receive unemployment compensation. And, no matter what the union organizer may tell you, you can be permanently replaced. If you go out on economic strike, management has the right to hire replacement workers to fill your job. When the strike is over, replacement employees can keep those jobs as long as they want. Finally, you need to consider the strong-arm tactics unions often use against members who disagree with a strike.

As if all those weren't enough reasons to reject the union, let me read you a short quote about unions being controlled by criminals. "We thought we knew a few things about trade union corruption, but we didn't know the half of it, one-tenth of it, or the one-hundredth of it. We didn't know, for instance, that we had unions where a criminal record was almost a prerequisite to holding office under the national union." Who do you think said this? Well, it was none other than George Meany, the former president of the AFL-CIO.

Don't think that organized crime's involvement in union activities can't harm you personally — it could easily cost you thousands of dollars. A few years ago, a *Reader's Digest* article described the way union pension and insurance programs are being plundered by the Mafia. One union member who contributed to a union-operated pension fund for 14 years retired to poverty; he and his wife lived on only his social security check and the free meals they received from their church. The Mafia-controlled union had stolen all the money he had paid into the pension fund and couldn't care less about this retired union member's welfare. The article went on to state that the assets of one-third of the union pension funds in existence are controlled by organized crime.

Many union benefit programs are scams for the Mob as well. Dental and medical plans sometimes use low-paid, unqualified physicians and dentists who do poor work, then inflate the cost to provide big payoffs for the union bosses. Are these the types of people you want to associate with? Do you want them to control your money and your future? I think all of you work too hard for your money to have it squandered by a bunch of crooks. [**You can probably obtain a copy of the *Reader's Digest* article at your local library. If not, it is available from LRI.**]

The union has probably been making you a lot of promises. But promises are not guarantees. Can the union guarantee you higher pay? No. Only management can increase your pay.

What about better benefits? No. Only management can provide more or better benefits.

Job security? No. The union can't provide you greater job security; that has to come through both you and management working together for a common goal.

By voting to support the union, would you become a member of a growing and well-respected organization? No. Organized labor is shrinking as people become more aware of how unions really operate and how little they do for their members.

What about freedom from strikes? No. Though it's impossible to say for sure whether we would ever have a strike here if the union won the election, the one thing we definitely know is that if a majority of you say "no" to the union on election day, we'll never have to worry about that possibility.

What about the freedom to speak for yourself? No. Union constitutions prevent members from speaking for themselves or solving their own problems.

What about freedom from dues, fines, and assessments? No. All union members must pay dues to their union, and there are even provisions in union constitutions that allow unions to put members on trial who don't pay their dues and to impose fines and assessments.

Here's the bottom line: We don't need a union here. Instead, we need greater teamwork and mutual respect. The enemy isn't management. The real enemy, as far as your working life is concerned, is the competition. We all need to do what will enable us to stay competitive. As you've seen, bringing in a union clearly isn't the answer. The union has nothing to offer that you can't get without paying dues, fines, and assessments. It has nothing to offer that you can't get right now by dealing directly with management. On election day, vote for yourself, vote for your future — vote "no."

Literature Preparation

All the issues are now before the voters. Through discussions with supervisors and managers, you should know where you stand with the voting group and what the most effective issue has been. Hopefully, you have a clear picture of this situation at least one week before the 24-hour presentation. This will help insure that your choice of a final handout is correct. Since this handout will be your most important, let's examine its objectives.

1. The final handout should be dramatic.

2. It should concentrate on the point you expect will achieve the greatest results. Generally, this is management's strongest issue or the union's weakest.

3. The handout can be longer than normal, but must be easy to read.

4. The handout should swing any remaining undecided voters to the management side.

Several handouts included in this book, particularly the longer ones, were originally used as the final piece of campaign literature. Each is different, which emphasizes the point that every campaign is different. The following literature was originally used as final handouts:

1. Machinists Union Kicked Out (Chapter 10)

2. Rules of the Road (Chapter 11)

3. Liberty Glass On Strike (Chapter 5)

4. John Bean Plant Closed (Chapter 12)

Another effective handout that fits in this category is titled "Steelworkers Union Causes Plant Shutdown." (This is shown as Exhibit 13-A.) Generic variations of each of these handouts can be used, but the most effective approach is to find a local or same-union example and to format the information as suggested.

Assuming you will have a Friday election with the polls opening at 7:00 AM, here is a typical election week calendar.

1. Monday — Distribute a **Question-and-Answer** handout that responds to any questions you feel may remain in the minds of voters (See Chapter 15). If you have decided to handle questions and answers in a booklet format, this is an excellent opportunity to do so. Consider mailing a question-and-answer booklet to voters' homes. Time the mailing for Monday delivery.

2. Tuesday — Distribute the final, dramatic handout — the **Bombshell.** This handout should be distributed early in the shift to allow employees to discuss its content. Final literature is often several pages long and may include newspaper articles or letters. However, as shown in the examples, if a voter does not want to read the fine print or any backup material included in the handout, they will still get important information by reading the headlines or large print. If you believe voters will want to read every word of the handout, it is a good idea to distribute it before a lunch break. Since this is your most important piece of literature, do everything possible to insure that it is read. Some employers hold a special captive audience meeting to distribute the final handout, giving voters an oral explanation of the handout and allowing them time to read it and ask questions.

3. Wednesday — Make the final captive audience presentation. At the conclusion of the 24-hour meeting, distribute a short handout that describes voting procedures. (An example of this handout is shown as Exhibit 13-B.) This is also the time to distribute any bandwagon items.

4. Thursday — Insulated period. Fortune cookies can be distributed in break areas. Supervisors make a final request for votes. **NO GROUP MEETINGS. ALL COMMUNICATIONS TAKE PLACE ON AN INDIVIDUAL BASIS!** A final word about the insulated period: Captive audience meetings are illegal during this period. What constitutes a captive audience meeting? Calling a group of employees

into a conference room to discuss campaign issues would be a violation; but there are other more subtle incidents that could qualify as a captive audience discussion. For example, if a supervisor is engaged in a discussion with several employees in the employees' work area, that also might be ruled a captive audience meeting. To be safe, your campaign director should advise all members of management and supervision to refrain from any group discussions with eligible voters during this period. Answering questions one-on-one is acceptable.

5. Friday — Election.

Some employers elect to alter the Monday through Wednesday schedule, depending on the contents of the final piece of literature. If you believe the final handout is truly a "bombshell" and will have a greater impact on voters than the captive audience presentation, you may elect to switch the Tuesday/Wednesday schedule, conducting the captive audience meeting on Tuesday and distributing the bombshell handout on Wednesday. Some employers make the final captive audience meeting a video/speech and distribute the bombshell handout. Your decision should be based on what you believe will be most effective with your voting group.

No controversial campaign literature can be distributed during the insulated period. If you adhere to the suggested schedule, there should be no problem. You can, however, engage in mild campaigning during this time. All campaign activity should stop at least two hours prior to the polls opening. Examples of mild campaigning include:

- Having cookies or cakes available in the lunch room decorated with the "Vote No" message.

- Taking the amount of money an employee would pay annually in dues, purchasing goods with that money, and displaying those goods with an appropriate sign. For example, if the annual dues for an average employee would be $300, you could purchase $300 worth of groceries and display them with a sign.

- Giving a free "Vote No" T-shirt, button, or cap to any employee who is interested. These items should be readily available in an area that cannot be monitored to determine who is and who is not supporting management. Do not give away any item that has a substantial value. Keep the value of an item at less than $15; and be sure all items are campaign oriented. Because bandwagon items are intended to show that management is a winner, do not risk an open display of support unless you are certain substantially more than half the eligible voters will wear the items.

These suggested ideas can also be used at other times during the campaign.

Exhibit 13-A

Steelworkers Union

cause

PLANT SHUTDOWN

in

Kellogg, Idaho

Battle of Bunker Hill
lost by workers

This is a True Story - it
actually happened!

Exhibit 13-A

YOU KNOW THE UNION PROMISES

SOME
EMPLOYEES BELIEVED THEM

LOOK AT WHAT
REALLY HAPPENED!

Exhibit 13-A

HOW IT HAPPENED

August, 1981	Gulf Chemical and Resources Co. of Houston, announced the closing of the Bunker Hill operation. Bunker Hill was reported to be losing 40 million dollars yearly. 2,100 Employees would be out of a job.
	Gulf looked for a buyer for Bunker Hill.
November, 1981	A local investment group became interested and negotiations for an option to buy were initiated. An option was worked out until December 31, 1981.
December, 1981	Purchase option extended to January 15, 1982.
	Purchase option extended to 5:00 p.m. January 18, 1982.
January, 1982	January 11, 1982 — Investment group agreed to purchase Bunker Hill. Conditions set a deadline extended to January 22, 1982
	January 14, 1982 — Steelworkers union recommended rejection of proposed new contract with purchasers.

Exhibit 13-A

Since January, 1982

January 17, — Membership voted 695 to 506 to **ACCEPT** the new proposal.

January 18, 1982 — International Steelworkers Union refused to sign the contract.

January 20, 1982 — Investment group withdrew it's option to buy and dropped further attempts to save the Facility because of the unwillingness of the International arm of Steelworkers of America to sign a Labor Agreement.

President of Steelworkers rejected petition of some 1300 employees — denied Governors request and ignored Senators, and Representatives pleas.

THE FACILITY IS CLOSED AND NO-ONE IN THE AREA EXPECTS THAT THE TOTAL FACILITY WILL EVER RE-OPEN.

THE FOLLOWING LETTERS FROM EMPLOYEES, CITIZENS AND NEWS ARTICLES TELL THE STORY.

IT HAPPENED IN KELLOGG — DON'T GIVE IT A CHANCE TO HAPPEN HERE.

Exhibit 13-A

Friday, June 18, 1982
Kellogg, Idaho

TO WHOM IT MAY CONCERN,

I am an unemployed Bunker Hill worker, along with over 2,000 others, due to the action of the United Steelworkers Union, who do not and did not honor the vote and wishes of the members of Local 7854, plus the craft unions.

Gulf Resources decided to close Bunker Hill last year. A group of investors got together and presented a package and had an option to buy Bunker Hill. True, the offer was not the same or even the best, but it was one chance to keep our jobs, our homes, our families fed and clothed.

On 17th of January 1982, we were to vote on accepting or rejecting the contract proposed. The membership of all the Unions (Steelworkers & Crafts) voted 695 to about 508 to accept.

When that happened, when we went against the desires of the Union, the entire governing board of the local resigned, putting control in the hands of the International who **would not honor** the wishes of the men and women.

We lost our U. S. Constitutional rights in our vote that day. They allowed us to vote, but then because it did not go their way, they said our vote was no good and they would tell us what was good for us.

To my knowledge, neither the International nor the local union has helped with the finding of jobs or money to help us. I have not received any.

In ending, I would say this to you, keep control of your own lives and destiny. Keep control of your own money. **Do not** let **control** of **either** leave your town. Once they have control, you will be dictated to and told what to do.

Do not let control out of your hands.

Ward L. Clark
ex - Bunker Hill Worker

Exhibit 13-A

June 17, 1982

I might be working today at Bunker Hill if the
USWA had respected the wishes of their membership. As a USWA member, I was present at the
union meeting last fall when the membership
was told that we could vote on whether or not
to accept a wage and benefit reduction in an
effort to keep the Bunker Hill mine and smelter
from being permanently closed.

A majority of the union members voted to accept
the cuts in order to keep working.

The local USWA officers almost immediately resigned, and were reinstated to their original
positions under regional and national USWA control. In other words, they were no longer responsible to the local membership. The vote was then
declared to be an advisory vote only and therefore ignored. The USWA representatives refused
to sign the wage and benefit reduction agreements.

The investor group's option-to-purchase expired
and the Bunker Hill Company closed its' doors.

Bob Ridout
P. O. Box 975
Osburn, Idaho

Exhibit 13-A

Letters to the editor

Retain your choice

Editor:

Everybody wins on a "yes" vote at Bunker Hill; everyone loses on a "no" vote.

A "yes" vote creates 1,500 jobs. A "no" vote destroys 1,500 jobs.

Anyone dissatisfied with the job can quit or take a better job that becomes available.

Anyone who stays on the job, or anyone who must stay to protect his home and other assets, can.

Everyone will be able to make the best individual choice for himself or herself. Nobody will be forced out of a job or a home by someone else's decision.

The jobs, the pay, and all the other conditions of employment will have to be competitive with other available work, or it will be impossible for Bunker Hill to maintain a work force.

Every industry, workman and union in the nation is being faced with the same problem we have here, and each must adjust to it.

Capital is the only thing in this world capable of creating a job.

The Valley is fortunate to have $100 million made available to give everyone a chance to make that adjustment.

Don't let the labor pros decide the issue for you on Saturday.

A secret ballot is the only way you can defend your interests. Pittsburgh is far, far away; its interests may be entirely different than the interests of you and your community.

Vote "yes" and you retain a choice; vote "no" and we all take a very cold bath right now!

These opinions are strictly my own.

PIATT HULL
Wallace

Boarded-up homes?

Editor:

Are we — the people of Kellogg, the real people, the life blood — going to be so stupid as to let some union officials from back East dictate to us and lose our white knights that we all have been praying for day and night for the past six months?

After hearing Mr. Hagadone's proposal yesterday to the people of Kellogg, I say thank God for millionaires like him and all the rest of the investors that are willing and have enough guts in these precarious times to bail us out of the closure of Bunker Hill.

Because if we vote not to take what they are offering, then we might just as well board up our homes and our businesses and say goodbye to Kellogg.

MILDRED LINHART
Kellogg

Please vote acceptance

Editor:

I would like to ask the union members to please vote to accept the investment group's proposal.

If they reject it, they are dooming many Valley people to an economic death. If they accept it, we will at least have a chance to live here if we choose.

Even if they don't like the agreement, it would buy them time in which to hunt for jobs elsewhere.

Please remember that your vote affects not only your jobs, but those of many other workers in the Valley.

LOIS SCHLAEFER
Pinehurst

'Yes' vote sought

Editor:

I am a taxpaying resident in Kellogg and a former Bunker Hill worker, and I helped get the Steelworkers union started in the district.

I can't vote on the current proposed Bunker Hill deal, but I would like to see a "yes" vote, even though it appears to be not fair at this time to the union members. If the Bunker Hill can get operating again, things can be changed.

We don't want to have to send our products to foreign countries. Why don't we try to keep the jobs in this country? The outcome of this situation not only affects the workers, but everyone in the Silver Valley and the entire country.

WILBUR HENNINGS
Kellogg

Jobs are few

Editor:

The question on all of our minds today is, "Can we live on and with what the proposed investors are offering?"

None of us wants to take a cut in pay or benefits. But let's be realistic. Things are bad all over; we are not the only ones facing the loss of jobs.

We have been looking in other places for jobs. Face the facts; they are few and far between. Let me ask you a question: What about all you have worked for — your homes, cars, trucks, etc.?

If you think that a job is going to drop in your lap, you're mistaken. I you think if you turn down thi proposal that some miraculous thing is going to happen and the old Bunker Hill will be back to the way it was you'd better think again.

Who is going to buy the homes we have worked so hard for, because the economy around is going to be blown to bits? How many of us can afford to keep up with house payments, look for work elsewhere and try to make a living?

These are all questions that each one of us will have to answer for ourselves. Let's hope that the decision each one of us makes is one that each can live with.

ED AND KATHY NUSTAD
Pinehurst

Wants to stay

Editor's note: The following letter is addressed to hourly employees of The Bunker Hill Co.

Editor:

I am one of you. I was in the first group laid off from the zinc plant in September. Since then I have had two interviews, but still no job.

I would like all of you to know that jobs for the unskilled in this area of our country are practically nonexistent. For four months my family and I have lived on unemployment and food stamps. I am frustrated and ashamed that I have not found employment. I have also discovered that principle and pride are not edible.

Why this letter to all of you ex-employees? Because we must not be swayed by those who would have us vote "no" to the proposal offered by the Bunker Hill investment group. If the proposal is not for you, please vote "yes" for those of us who wish to remain in the Valley. You can move on and seek employment elsewhere.

If you guys vote "no," what option do I have to remain in the Valley?

CHUCK FRENCH JR.
Kellogg

Exhibit 13-A

Kellogg in chains?

Various petitions, hard hats and posters at the Steelworkers Hall in Kellogg help tell the story of the plight of Bunker Hill workers trying to salvage their jobs. Members of United Steelworkers of America Local 7854, representing most workers at Bunker Hill, have recently made attempts to revoke their union charter in order to help negotiate a purchase of the sprawling Bunker Hill operations in Kellogg.

KEN photo by Mike Green

Exhibit 13-A

The Kellogg Evening News

SMELTER CITY OF THE COEUR D'ALENES — WORLD'S LARGEST LEAD-SILVER MINE

FIFTY-SEVENTH YEAR — NO. 213   KELLOGG, IDAHO, TUESDAY, JANUARY 12, 1982   25 CENTS PER COPY

Simplot says 'Yes;' unions to get proposal

By JIM FISHER
KEN Staff Writer

Officials of the J.R. Simplot Co. and three businessmen who hold a purchase option for The Bunker Hill Co. last night announced Simplot will join in trying to exercise the option and buy the Kellogg mining and smelting company.

The group of investors seeking to acquire the troubled company from Gulf Resources & Chemical Corp. met Monday in Boise to hammer out plans for the purchase, and last evening emerged with what could be the best news for the Silver Valley since Gulf Resources' Aug. 25 announcement that it would close its Kellogg subsidiary.

In addition to enlisting Simplot's agreement to become the major investor in Bunker Hill, the group last night received yet another extension on its purchase option from Gulf Resources Chairman Robert H. Allen. The extension, which extends the option deadline to 5 p.m. Jan. 22, was needed to allow banks arranging financing for the purchase time to formulate an agreement following a union vote on proposed work force, wage and benefit concessions, it was announced.

That vote, if one is called at special union meetings Saturday, will be held between 8 a.m. and 8 p.m. Sunday at Steelworkers Hall

in Kellogg, said Ken Flatt, president of United Steelworkers of America Local 7854, the largest Bunker Hill union.

"It is going to be difficult to make this thing work," Jack R. Simplot, chairman of the Simplot board, said in a prepared release, "but I am confident we have a bright future ahead, and with the cooperation and encouragement of all people involved, we will put Bunker back on its feet."

The group of investors proceeding with the purchase plans comprises Simplot, Harry F. Magnuson of Wallace, Duane B. Hagadone of Coeur d'Alene, J. William Pfeiffer of La Jolla, Calif., Sunshine Mining Co. and Coeur d'Alene Mines Corp.

"That represents the total investor package," the Evening News was told today by Hagadone.

Simplot's role in the new company will comprise the majority interest, Magnuson confirmed today.

Four conditions remain

The group said four conditions remain to be met before the purchase option can be exercised. Those conditions are:

—Acceptance of a new labor agreement by the Bunker Hill unions.

—Clarification of limitations on Bunker Hill liabilities the investors will face.

—Limitations of certain environmental regulations and potential environmental liabilities.

—Approval of acceptable financing for the acquisition by unidentified banks.

Hagadone said today the group had originally planned to take its proposal to the unions as the last step in the deal, but the reluctance by banks to proceed short of labor acceptance of a concession plan had forced a change in the schedule.

Hagadone said the banks' reluctance was based on an earlier rejection of a concession proposal by one company union, the International Brotherhood of Electrical Workers, prior to the shutdown announcement.

The new proposal will be presented to union officials at 1 p.m. Wednesday in Coeur d'Alene.

"It can't be a negotiated proposal," Hagadone said today, explaining that union members will be asked to approve a plan already drafted by the investor group.

Regarding what the proposal may include, Hagadone said, "We're certainly going to ask for more than the 30 percent" wage cut that was key to the request rejected earlier. He ex-

plained that even with major labor concessions, designed to increase Bunker Hill's productivity, "We look at '82 and '83 to be pretty tough years."

Following the two lean years, Hagadone said the group expects the company and its work force "to start making some money."

Of the union vote, he said, "It will be important and I don't underestimate the problems."

Asked this morning why the list of conditions includes environmental safeguards, considering the five-year regulatory agreements already obtained from the Environmental Protection Agency and the Occupational Safety and Health Administration, Magnuson said, "The environmental and legal people just thought there should be some clarification on those matters."

Magnuson said company liabilities arising from lawsuits over alleged lead poisoning of Kellogg-area residents in the past had been disposed of in the option agreement itself.

Ownership split undecided

One issue remaining unsettled among the investors is the percentage interest each will assume in the new company, other than that

Simplot will have the majority interest. Once that is decided the group will form a new company to operate Bunker Hill, the investors said.

Dennis Wheeler, president of Coeur d'Alene Mines Corp. said this morning his company has been involved in the purchase negotiations for about five weeks. "This isn't something that just dropped out of the air," he said.

Wheeler said he could not say what share Coeur d'Alene Mines would assume in the new company.

Efforts to secure agreement from enough investors to make a go of the Bunker Hill bailout have been anything but easy.

"For almost 2½ months, Duane Hagadone and I have been working on this thing," he said. "She's been an uphill battle all the way. She's really been a tough one."

That battle now moves to the field of the Bunker Hill unions, who will learn tomorrow what will be asked of them.

Platt, contacted last evening after word of Simplot's decision was received, said he does not know what the group will ask for, but he added "I'm positive they (the investors) do....I don't know whether I'm elated, or have the weight of the world on my shoulders."

If anyone, Simplot can, Evans says

BOISE, Idaho (AP) — Gov. John Evans said Tuesday it's "the best news of the year" that the J.R. Simplot Co. is joining the effort to save the beleaguered Bunker Hill Co. at Kellogg.

"If anybody can do it, Jack Simplot can do it," said Evans at a news conference. Hours before the Boise-based Simplot financial empire announced it will join an investor group trying to purchase the Bunker Hill operation at Kellogg.

Evans said Simplot telephoned him Tuesday morning "and he's very optimistic about it. Jack told me he's optimistic about the ore reserve and optimistic that we can have a profitable operation there for the next 100 years.

"He's excited about it, and we are too," said Evans. "We will be doing all the things required to help." He didn't go into specifics, but said the state would offer "all the help and support necessary" to wrap up the deal.

Bunker Hill Investment team

The group of investors now proceeding with plans to purchase the Bunker Hill Co. in Kellogg are shown above following a meeting in Boise Monday. The group, which represents the total investment team, includes, from left, E. Vint Howard, executive vice president of Sunshine Mining Co.; J. William Pfeiffer of La Jolla, Calif., one of the original three purchase option holders; Harry F. Magnuson of Wallace, a fellow option holder; Jack R. Simplot, chairman of the board of J.R. Simplot Co.; Duane B. Hagadone of Coeur d'Alene, the third original op-

tion holder; Scott Simplot, executive vice president of J.R. Simplot Co.; Dale Dunn, president of J.R. Simplot Co.; and Dennis Wheeler of Wallace, president of Coeur d'Alene Mines Corp. The group will present its proposed labor concessions to Bunker Hill union officials Wednesday for a Sunday membership vote, and then seek to arrange financing by the new 5 p.m. Jan. 22 option deadline.

Exhibit 13-A

The Kellogg Evening News

SMELTER CITY OF THE COEUR D'ALENES - WORLD'S LARGEST LEAD-SILVER MINE

FIFTY-SEVENTH YEAR — NO. 215   KELLOGG, IDAHO, THURSDAY, JANUARY 14, 1982   25 CENTS PER COPY

Bunker union recommends rejection of wage cuts

Hopes for a revival of the Bunker Hill Co. sagged this afternoon, when union representatives announced they would go to their membership and recommend that the rank and file turn down a wage cut proposal that potential Bunker Hill purchasers asked for.

Representatives for an investor group with an option to purchase Bunker Hill met with union officials Wednesday and today to discuss the wage and benefit cuts.

At a news conference in Coeur d'Alene this afternoon, Ken Flatt, president of United Steelworkers Local 7854, representing most Bunker Hill workers, said he is still going to go to his membership on Saturday with the proposal, but he will recommend that the proposal be turned down.

Flatt said the investor team told union officials, "If our membership would reject this they (the investor group) would not enter into a purchase."

The main point of contention seems to be the provisions for seniority in the investors' proposal.

Flatt said, "It would give the company full rights of assignment with disregard to seniority."

Duane Hagadone, a Coeur d'Alene newspaper publisher and one of the original members of the investment team, said "The changes in the work rules have to be done to increase productivity. The management of The Bunker Hill Co. has to be put back in the hands of management. This is critical."

The union contingent contends that negotiators for the investor group "walked out" of the meeting between the two groups this morning.

Duane Hagadone also held a news conference in Coeur d'Alene this afternoon.

Hagadone said his group left the meeting only after business had been completed.

He said the investors answered 14 written questions, submitted by the unions on Wednesday, and told the unions that they would not negotiate points of the proposal.

The proposal calls for a 25 percent reduction in wages, based on wages as of Dec. 31, 1981. Graduated increases for the next four years would be included in the five-year agreement.

Workers would get a 5 percent increase the second year and a 15 percent increase over each previous year for the last three years of the agreement.

Gulf Resources and Chemical Corp., parent company of Bunker Hill, has predicted a $40 million loss for next year, but Hagadone said the losses will more likely run about $54 million next year, based on current metal prices.

Hagadone said he expected a workforce of about 1,500 when the facilities were operating at full capacity, compared to a former workforce of 2,100.

To a certain degree, Hagadone said, the workers have to accept the credibility of the investor group.

"I feel it is a fair proposal and it is a fair contract," Hagadone said.

Employees on a monthly salary would be asked to take a 15 percent reduction in pay, Hagadone said. He said that figure was fair because studies have shown that over the last five years, increases in hourly wages have been 50 percent higher than those for salaried employees.

This is because of cost of living adjustments, Hagadone said.

Hagadone urged members of the community to get a copy of the proposal and read it.

"Take the effort to get a copy of the agreement and take the time to understand it," Hagadone said.

The Kellogg Evening News

SMELTER CITY OF THE COEUR D'ALENES - WORLD'S LARGEST LEAD-SILVER MINE

FIFTY-SEVENTH YEAR — NO. 216   KELLOGG, IDAHO, FRIDAY, JANUARY 15, 1982   25 CENTS PER COPY

Union members to review new labor agreement

By DOUG BARKER
KEN Staff Writer

Members of United Steelworkers of America Local 7854, and other Bunker Hill unions, will probably have until Sunday to study a wage and benefit concession proposal put to them by an investor group with an option to buy The Bunker Hill Co.

Two Steelworkers meetings are scheduled for Saturday to decide if the union membership will vote on the proposal Sunday. The Saturday meetings — open for all but membership votes to spouses and the press — are set for 10 a.m. and 6 p.m. at the Kellogg Junior High School gym.

Talks between union officials representing Bunker Hill workers and the investor group ended Thursday morning. Both sides called news conferences in Coeur d'Alene Thursday afternoon to give their views concerning the proposal.

Officials of the seven Bunker Hill unions said they would recommend rejection of the proposal to their members. Duane Hagadone, a member of the investor group, said the contract is fair and urged everyone in the Valley to study the proposal and understand it.

The proposal would be a five-year labor agreement between Local 7854 and Bunker Holdings Inc., the name given to the investor group.

The unions are most concerned with management, seniority and no-strike clauses of the new agreement — things they say are non-economic and therefore unnecessary.

Hagadone says the clauses are critical to putting the management of the Bunker Hill Co. "back in the hands of management.", . .

Exhibit 13-A

The Kellogg Evening News

SMELTER CITY OF THE COEUR D'ALENES — WORLD'S LARGEST LEAD-SILVER MINE

FIFTY-SEVENTH YEAR — NO. 217   KELLOGG, IDAHO, MONDAY, JANUARY 18, 1982   25 CENTS PER COP'

Bunker Hill pact in limbo after vote, resignations

By DOUG BARKER
KEN Staff Writer

The leadership of United Steelworkers of America Local 7854 was in the process of being re-appointed this afternoon, after resigning Sunday evening following the local membership's acceptance of a five-year labor agreement put to them by a group of investors seeking to purchase The Bunker Hill Co.

The vote was 516 to 506 in favor of accepting the controversial labor agreement, which was opposed by union leadership.

Control of the local, which represents most of the union workers at Bunker Hill, is now in the hands of the international headquarters of the Steelworkers, located in Pittsburgh, Pa.

The vote is now being called an "advisory vote," and Robert Petris, director of the USWA's District 38 covering the western states, issued a statement this morning saying the international will take the advisory vote into consideration when it negotiates with the investor group.

The investor group, however, has said it will not negotiate.

The international is an administrative control of the local union and has appointed International Staff Representative Lavern Mellon as the administrator.

The international has frozen the assets of the union and now owns Steelworkers Hall, where Local 7854 is headquartered, and all the local's assets.

Mellon said the international had authority to take the action by virtue of the resignation of Flatt and the executive board Sunday night. The constitution of the international union gives it the authority, according to Mellon.

Because of the void created by the resignation of Flatt and his executive board, the international had to step in, Mellon said.

This afternoon Mellon was in the process of re-appointing Flatt and the executive board to their previous positions, to be paid and directed from Pittsburgh.

"Kenny (Flatt) is now president of the local again; Larry (Hansen) is secretary; Bob (Allen) is the treasurer," Mellon said.

Mellon said he had not been able to contact all of the executive board yet, but had re-appointed several of them.

At press time it was unclear what this would mean concerning the vote taken Sunday.

Investor spokesman Duane B. Hagadone scheduled a news conference in Coeur d'Alene for 1 p.m. this afternoon, presumably to discuss the latest wrinkle in efforts to buy the company by Bunker Holdings Inc. The group is working to exercise its purchase option for Bunker Hill by the 5 p.m. Friday, Jan. 22, deadline.

The most recent chapter of the 'almost unbelievable saga of The Bunker Hill Co. began to unfold Saturday with a packed house of union members at the Kellogg Junior High School gym.

This was the weekend of what came to be known simply as "The Vote."

The memberships of United Steelworkers of America Local 7854 and the six craft unions at Bunker Hill crowded into the gym before 10 a.m. for the first of two scheduled meetings that day. The purpose of the meetings was to discuss a labor agreement proposal made to Bunker Hill union employees by a group of investors who are trying to purchase Bunker Hill.

Earlier in the week the union hierarchy had met with the investors and said in a loud, public voice that they would recommend that the rank-and-file turn the proposal down.

In effect, union officials said, the proposal destroyed the union. They also said that the investors group refused to bargain with them and in fact walked out of talks.

Union members woke up in a near-blizzard Saturday morning, but the weather did not keep many of them away.

On Friday, Local 7854 President Ken Flatt said spouses of union members and members of the media would be allowed to sit in on the meetings. But when reporters showed up they were told the plans had changed and they would not be allowed to remain inside the hall, out of concern for freedom of expression without later repercussions. Spouses were allowed to stay.

About a dozen reporters, including three Spokane television stations waited outside, along with union men who needed a smoke.

Inside, the union membership was examining the proposal and a point-by-point comparison of the present labor-management agreement and the proposed agreement.

The meeting broke up at about noon, and most of the membership filed out quietly. A few, however, threw the proposals on the ground, and one man set fire to his.

One man shouted, "There ain't gonna be no forced labor camp around here."

After the meeting reporters were allowed into the school to talk to union officials.

Flatt called reporters together and said that in the wee hours of Saturday morning the investor group had agreed to meet with union officials that afternoon to negotiate on the proposal.

Prior to this, Hagadone, one of the investors and the spokesman for the group, said the points of the proposal were not negotiable.

Flatt said the meeting would 'take place at 2 p.m. at an undisclosed location.

Scott Spencer, a lawyer from the Steelworkers headquarters in Pittsburgh, said that negotiations like this were governed by a strict rule of secrecy, and nothing from the meeting would be disclosed. However, details from the original investor proposal were public record.

Flatt said the morning meeting of the membership had not been adjourned; it had been recessed and could be called back in order quickly if he had something new to take to his membership.

Sunday morning most of the radios in the Valley were tuned to KWAL, to listen Hagadone answer questions concerning the proposal.

Before he began answering questions, Hagadone gave his account of what happened at the Saturday meeting between the investors and the unions.

Hagadone said Flatt and he had agreed who was to be at the meeting, but Flatt came later and asked if the meeting could be postponed until 9 p.m. so that another representative of the international union organization could attend the meeting.

Hagadone said he told Flatt before the meeting that if there were areas of agreement on the three major points of difference to be discussed, the investors would submit a "letter of understanding" to the union. But Hagadone said it was not really a negotiating session.

Hagadone said he told Flatt that if the groups were to meet it would have to be right away, not that evening.

When the meeting started, Hagadone said a representative from Pittsburgh told him that even if the three major sticking points could be ironed out, the international union would not sign the agreement.

Hagadone said he asked the international representative what purpose there was in a meeting if that was the case, and the meeting was effectively over at that point.

Grim-faced union employees of The Bunker Hill Co. review the proposed labor agreement, presented by investors seeking to buy the troubled company, at a union meeting Saturday.

Exhibit 13-A

The Kellogg Evening News

SMELTER CITY OF THE COEUR D'ALENES – WORLD'S LARGEST LEAD-SILVER MINE

FIFTY-SEVENTH YEAR — NO. 219 | KELLOGG, IDAHO, WEDNESDAY, JANUARY 20, 1982 | 25 CENTS PER COPY

Bunker Hill purchase falls through

By DOUG BARKER
KEN Staff Writer

All hopes for saving The Bunker Hill Co. were washed away this morning when Bunker Holdings Inc., a group of investors seeking to buy the company, announced it had withdrawn its purchase option and would drop any further attempts to save the facility.

The Silver Valley got the news just as it had the original closure announcement on Aug. 25, — by radio.

Duane B. Hagadone, spokesman for the investors, told a news conference that unwillingness of the international arm of the United Steelworkers of America to sign a labor agreement, and the tenuous nature of labor agreements signed by newly-elected officers of USWA Local 7854, forced the investors to terminate their option.

The membership of Local 7854 voted [illegible] Sunday to accept the labor agreement proposed by the investors.

That evening local President Ken Flatt and the executive board for the local resigned, allowing the international arm of the union to seize control of Steelworkers Hall and the assets of the local.

Lloyd McBride, president of USWA in Pittsburgh, Pa., appointed Lavern Melton, a USWA international staff worker from Wallace, to be the administrator of Local 7854 and all its holdings.

Melton re-appointed Flatt and most of the board on Monday. The union had been left without officers just long enough for the international to claim the right of takeover.

Tuesday morning the local membership elected new officers, and it was these officers who finally signed the Steelworkers' labor agreement on Tuesday.

Meanwhile, officials of the international, who had been in the Kellogg area, dropped out of sight. [illegible]

[illegible]

Towles orders pact executed by union

[illegible]

Union members gather after Bunker announcement

[illegible]

Delegation leaves for Spokane

Workers seek to revoke union charter

[illegible]

By MIKE GREEN
KEN Staff Writer

[illegible]

Bunker news casts pall over governor's office

BOISE, Idaho (AP) — [illegible]

Exhibit 13-A

The Kellogg Evening News

SMELTER CITY OF THE COEUR D'ALENES — WORLD'S LARGEST LEAD-SILVER MINE

FIFTY-SEVENTH YEAR   NO. 220   KELLOGG, IDAHO, THURSDAY, JANUARY 21, 1982   25 CENTS PER COPY

Craig: No deal set over pact

By The Associated Press
and the KEN staff

BOISE — Rep. Larry Craig, R-Idaho, said he has been advised by Robert Petris, District 38 director for the United Steelworkers of America, that the union will not sign an agreement covering Bunker Hill Co. workers unless there are changes in it.

The agreement, in which Bunker Hill workers accept 25 percent wage cuts, apparently is the key to keeping the mining-smelting complex at Kellogg in operation. An investor group announced Wednesday it was pulling out of negotiations to buy Bunker Hill because union officials would not sign the agreement.

The agreement was approved by union members Sunday night.

Craig flew to Spokane Wednesday night to meet with Petris and other union officials. He said Petris expressed some concern over wording of the agreement.

"It's possible that the agreement can be changed to meet their concerns," Craig told a Boise news conference.

After meeting with the union officials, Craig said he was left with the impression that the national union is worried that it might set a bad precedent for future negotiations. The union objections to the agreement, he said, "go far beyond concern for the local people."

He said it appears the union officials are trying more to protect the interests of the national union than to work to save jobs at Bunker Hill. "I have to think that's the case," he said.

Craig said he would be "extremely cautious" about predicting when negotiations might result, or if they will resume at all.

"I don't want to raise expectations. They have been raised too many times before and then dashed," he said.

He said he has no indications that the investor group would become interested in Bunker Hill again, even if the union contract is approved, "but anything's possible."

Later today, Craig sent a telegram, which was signed and endorsed by the three other members of Idaho's congressional delegation, to USWA President Lloyd McBride, asking him to direct Petris to sign the agreement "on behalf of the community of Kellogg, Idaho."

"Only you can take the necessary action to expedite the employees' attempt to maintain their jobs," the telegram said.

"It is not for us we ask. It is not for you we ask, but rather for the 2,100 employees that we ask."

The telegram was co-signed by Sens. James McClure and Steve Symms and Rep. George Hansen.

Receiving the bad news

Coffee customers line the front counter at Dick and Floyd's Liberty Billiards in Kellogg Wednesday as they listen to Duane B. Hagadone announce over the radio his investor group has terminated its option agreement to purchase The Bunker Hill Co. from Gulf Resources & Chemical Corp. Most people in the Silver Valley huddled around the radio to listen to the five news conference broadcast from Coeur d'Alene, as well as other news conferences, union announcements and question and-answer sessions conducted by Hagadone. Events relating to the attempted purchase of Bunker Hill occurred so rapidly during the past week that some news already was old by the time newspapers were received in homes.

KEN photo by Mike Green

Exhibit 13-A

Politicians blame unions for breakdown

By The Associated Press

Idaho congressional and legislative leaders Wednesday blamed national union officials for thwarting efforts to keep the struggling Bunker Hill Co. in operation.

An investor group headed by Wallace businessman Harry Magnuson, Coeur d'Alene businessman Duane Hagadone and potato magnate J.R. Simplot of Boise attempted to buy Bunker Hill for $15 million in future profits, but the deal hinged largely on the acceptance of contract concessions by union officials, Hagadone said.

Local union members approved the concessions in a 695-506 vote Sunday, but the national leaders for five of seven international unions rejected the local unions' efforts.

Sen. Steve Symms, R-Idaho, said union leaders outside of Idaho helped cause Bunker Hill's downfall.

He said the union members voted to accept the labor proposal to save jobs and keep Bunker Hill alive, but "they're being denied that chance by union bosses in Pittsburgh."

Symms charged that top union officials did not have an interest in the "human tragedy" of people losing their jobs.

In a press release issued by his office, Sen. James McClure, R-Idaho, said he was "extremely disappointed" that the agreement between the unions and the investment group had fallen through.

McClure said that although the economic impact of the Bunker Hill closure would be hardest felt by the firm's employees, the effects of the closure would have a rippling effect on the Silver Valley and much of northern Idaho.

Second District Rep. George Hansen, R-Idaho, said local union members in the Kellogg area should have the "final say as to what affects their lives."

"I certainly hoped that with arguments within the unions, the will of the local people who are directly concerned for their jobs would prevail," Hansen said. "It would be unfortunate if outsiders made the decisions that would affect people who will be out of work."

Lt. Gov. Phil Batt, a gubernatorial candidate, said he was "deeply disappointed" over the breakdown of negotiations between the unions and the investment group.

"It's too bad that Idaho's people were not able to shape their own destiny," Batt said.

Idaho Senate Majority Leader Jim Risch criticized national leaders for not honoring the local union members' vote.

"It's extremely unfortunate that the national unions wouldn't honor the locals' vote," he said. "They are putting people out of work that want to work. Their actions deteriorate people's opinions of unions, especially on the national level. People generally support a democratic system of majority vote, but that wasn't done here."

Another gubernatorial candidate, Idaho House Speaker Ralph Olmstead, said he sympathized with union members who voted in favor of the contract concessions.

"They voted that they wanted and needed to work, but it turns out their votes were meaningless because of the obstacles between union officials from out of state and their prospective employers," Olmstead said.

"The workers might have lost their last opportunity to retain their employment because of the incomprehensible, stubborn attitude of those out-of-state union officials," Olmstead said.

"It's about time we passed a right-to-work law in our state," he said. "Had we such a law, this disaster would not have occurred."

Suit filed against USWA International

WALLACE, Idaho (AP) — A Coeur d'Alene lawyer said today he is representing more than 200 union members in a multimillion-dollar class-action suit against the United Steelworkers of America International Union.

Thomas Mitchell said he would file the suit in District Court in Wallace on behalf of more than 200 workers. He said the suit would allege the workers were unfairly represented by the steelworkers in its handling of the Sunday vote by members of Bunker Hill Co.'s bargaining units.

Mitchell said the suit will ask for a temporary restraining order, plus damages "for failing to do what was mandated by the vote."

Bunker Hill union members voted affirmatively 695-506 Sunday on what many said they thought was a labor-management agreement proposal from investors wishing to buy Bunker Hill.

United Steelworers representatives said when the ballot results were announced that the vote was an "advisory vote" and it only authorized union leaders to enter negotiations with the investors.

Investors, however, said their proposal was non-negotiable.

Mitchell said the labor organization's actions were a "breach of the union's duty of fair representation of its members."

the suit seeks more than $250,000 for each person named in the suit.

Repeated attempts to reach steelworkers officials for comment were unsuccessful.

Mitchell said every member of United Steelwoekers Local 7854, the bargaining unit representing 1,400 of the 1,700 unionized employees, would be represented in the suit.

Exhibit 13-A

Sign or let members go, Evans asks union chief

The attempt to convince the president of the United Steelworkers of America to ratify a proposed labor-management agreement that would have allowed some 1,500 laid off workers of The Bunker Hill Co. to return to their jobs was joined today by Gov. John Evans.

The governor announced at a morning news conference in Boise that he had sent a telegram to the Pittsburgh, Pa., office of Lloyd McBride, urging McBride to take one of two options on the agreement. Those options are, in Evans' words, "that you accept the majority vote of your own members and ratify the contract offer presented by the investors," or "that you grant the local union freedom to act as a local and remove the international charter."

"We have serious problems here in Idaho," the governor began his telegram. He then mentioned not only the loss of jobs at Bunker Hill, but also the state's sagging timber and construction industries. As a result, "Idaho has the highest unemployment it has experienced in 20 years," Evans said.

"A search has been going on for two years to find a purchaser for Bunker Hill," the governor wired McBride. "In all that time, only one group of Idaho investors has come forward with an offer. That contract offer was accepted in a democratic vote by some 60 percent of the local union members. That decision was reaffirmed in a petition signed by over 1,300 members.

"I understand the concerns of the international union. However, my responsibility and my overriding concern is for the people of the state of Idaho and jobs for Idahoans. We must keep the Bunker Hill operation open and let those people get back to work.

"It is vital that you take immediate action to allow this to happen."

Gaetha Lloyd, an aide to Evans, told the Evening News this afternoon no response to the telegram had yet been received, but that McBride had told the governor he would consider the message and respond as soon as possible.

McBride rejects plea to sign pact

PITTSBURGH (AP) — Despite pleas from two Idaho congressmen, United Steelworkers of America officials have rejected concessions sought by investors hoping to take over the Bunker Hill Co. in northern Idaho.

Rep. Larry Craig and Sen. Steve Symms, both Republicans, accused the union Tuesday of blocking an agreement that could revive the company.

Gulf Resources and Chemical Corp., Bunker Hill's parent firm, announced plans in August to close the mining and smelting company. But Idaho investors said they were interested in buying the facility if the union would agree to wage reductions and other concessions.

Steelworkers president Lloyd McBride on Tuesday rejected the proposals, which would have freed the prospective owners of any obligation to honor past work rules or methods of operation.

The investors also wanted to determine the order in which furloughed workers would be recalled, erase 80 union grievances against Gulf Resources and disregard benefit claims assured under the current contract.

Robert Petris, a Steelworkers leader in the West, said the investors did not offer to negotiate.

"They can't give us a document and say, 'That's it, take it or leave it.' We've never been able to sit down to discuss and review the document," he said.

The congressmen delivered 6,000 signatures supporting the concessions and said union members voted in favor of the plan. But Petris said the vote only advised USW leaders to continue considering the proposals.

Craig said the meeting was a "last-ditch" plea to save Bunker Hill, where the last of 2,100 employees are about to be laid off.

"What we wanted to impress on Mr. McBride today was the impact of what their actions could mean for the state of Idaho and for those citizens in that valley," he said.

The investor group, which included Duane Hagadone of Coeur d'Alene, Idaho, had offered Bunker Hill unions a new wage and benefit agreement. The union membership voted to accept the agreement, despite drastically reduced wages and benefits.

However, international union officials refused to sign the documents as time ran out on the investors' option to buy.

A meeting has been scheduled for Thursday in Spokane, Wash., by the Federal Mediation and Conciliation Service. Hagadone said Monday he sees no need for it.

Bill Edwards, a spokesman for the steelworkers, said after the meeting here that the union still urged the investors to negotiate.

"This is still America and we still have the right to negotiate. We're not under martial law." He characterized the investors' agreement as a "Hitler-like ultimatum" and said their refusal to bargain "created a panic-like siege mentality" in the mining district of northern Idaho.

Hagadone said if the unions adopted the investors' wage contract, he "would do everything within my power to get that group back together again."

But, he said, he spoke only for himself and has not spoken with the other investors to find out their opinions on a revival.

Exhibit 13-A

AND - AFTER ALL THIS . . . HERE'S WHAT HAPPENED

All laid off Bunker hourly workers to be terminated next week

By DOUG BARKER
KEN Staff Writer

All Bunker Hill Co. hourly employees now on lay-off status will be terminated from the company's employ on Feb 3, the company announced today.

The non-salaried workers will be covered by medical and dental insurance for 60 days after that.

Gerald Turnbow, vice-president of public and employee relations for Bunker Hill, sent letters explaining the terminations to union officials representing both local and international organs of the United Steelworkers of America and the AFL-CIO craft unions at Bunker Hill.

The letters are dated Jan. 26.

Some 300 hourly workers are still employed at Bunker Hill, doing mostly maintenance work, Turnbow said.

He said Bunker Hill would retain the same relationship with the unions it always has. "Only now there are more of them," he said, as apparent reference to the group of dissident Steelworkers now trying to form a union called the Silver Valley People's Union.

Turnbow addressed one of the letters to its president, Ronald Byrd. A letter was also addressed to Byrd as president of USWA Local 7854. Byrd was elected to head the local at a meeting of union dissidents last week.

In the letter, Turnbow said Bunker Hill has maintained layoff status, as opposed to termination, for about 1,500 workers "hoping

that someone would purchase our facilities in Kellogg and keep them in operation."

When the workers are laid off they may receive medical and dental insurance benefits.

Workers who are terminated in the future will also get the 60-day extension of medical and dental insurance benefits.

Turnbow added, "There is now no reason to believe our facilities will continue in operation. Therefore, Bunker Hill intends to move ahead with its shutdown plans."

In the letter addressed to Ken Flatt and Ronald Byrd, both of whom are acting as president of Local 7854, and Bill Thompson, staff representative for the USWA International, Turnbow says it is addressed to all

three men because there is confusion over who now represents the bargaining unit described in the present labor agreement for Bunker Hill.

"We are confused," Turnbow says, "because of the apparent schism in the Union, and possible desertion by the Steelworkers."

According to an attorney for the National Labor Relations Board, the word "schism" comes up in rules governing attempts at decertifying a union.

Terry Jensen of the NLRB told the Evening News that in most cases a union can only be decertified at the end of a labor agreement, but there is an exception to that rule.

A "schism" in the highest ranks of the union may be grounds for an attempt at

decertification, Jensen said.

However, that process is very rare, Jensen said, adding that in over eight years he worked for the NLRB he has not seen it pass.

Thursday the Coeur d'Alene Press, owned by Duane B. Hagadone, one of a group of who held an option to buy Bunker reported that Hagadone said his group would reconsider a purchase of Bunker Hill if union problem could be overcome.

The paper said, however, that Hagadone questioned if the company's closure had gone too far.

The newspaper quoted Hagadone as saying, "We've done all the work and got it to position. But personally, I don't know how it could be saved."

Dissidents seek labor support

Leaflets soliciting support for dissident members of United Steelworkers of America Local 7854 were passed out at the Sunshine Mine Thursday. The leaflets were written by a group of Steelworkers led by Ron Byrd, the man elected as president of Local 7854 after the USWA International took administrative control of the union local. Among other things, the leaflets asked, "Does your union work for you or does it work for national?" Plans also call for the leaflets to be handed out at the other two unions in the district — the Lucky Friday and the Galena. Shown here handing the leaflets to Sunshine worker going on shift are Penny and Debbie Lloyd.

Exhibit 13-A

For several weeks now we have been furnishing you with information we believed necessary for you to make a decision on June 25, 1982 based on facts not propaganda, rumors or promises.

Broderick & Bascom is not anti-union, we are PRO-EMPLOYEE. We feel we know both sides of the question and sincerely believe that your interests can be best served by us working together to make Sedalia a better place for all of us to work. We do not believe the union will accomplish this.

This same international union once represented the employees at Bunker Hill Kellogg, Idaho, but the employees did not get what they were promised from the union. We thought it very important that you benefit from these employees disaster. In an effort to fullfill our committment to you to get you the truth, we went to Idaho and got the true story from the source, people that were employees of the mine and residents of Kellogg, Idaho.

These employees learned the hard way that there are two sides to union membership - what the union tells you and the way it really is.

Union membership is not free. It costs you money. Please evaluate what the union sold employees at Kellogg. Decide for yourself if you think it's worth it.

Remember - these folks learned the hard way. The union has made the same promises to you - the same old promises that were made to these employees.

Exhibit 13-B

Your
Secret
Weapon

VOTE

X

NO

Nobody knows how you vote!
The federal government guarantees your
secret ballot. Nobody will ever know
how you vote!

Exercise
Your
Right

VOTE

X

NO

Your
ballot is a
secret
weapon

USE IT!

VOTE NO

The United States government
guarantees that your ballot is
cast in secret. No snoopers can
learn how you vote. The laws of
this country protect your right
to vote in secret!

Exhibit 13-B

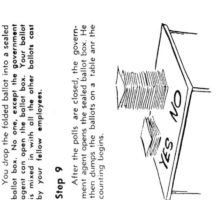

Step 1

You are ready to vote in an NLRB election. You see sitting at the desk a U. S. Government NLRB Agent, a Company representative and a Union representative.

Step 2

You give them your name and clock number. That's for the purpose of finding out if you are eligible to vote. (If you were hired on or before Jan. 17, 1980, you will be eligible to vote.)

Step 3

The three representatives will check your name off the official list of eligible voters. This is done so no one else can vote under your name . . . and so no one can vote twice.

Step 4

The government agent will then hand you a ballot. THE BALLOT DOES NOT LIST YOUR NAME OR CLOCK NUMBER . . . NOR DOES IT HAVE ANY OTHER MEANS OF IDENTIFI- CATION. In other words, it's a completely secret ballot!

Step 5

The ballot you receive simply asks you to "mark the square of your choice." It then provides two boxes — each of which is identified — so you can make your choice. There are absolutely no markings which could associate you with the ballot.

Step 6

You go into the voting booth which has a curtain. The curtain is there to give you privacy . . . and to prevent anyone from seeing how you mark your ballot.

Step 7

After you have marked your ballot, you fold it so no one can see how it is marked and leave the voting booth.

Step 8

You drop the folded ballot into a sealed ballot box. No one, except the government agent can open the ballot box. Your ballot is mixed in with all the other ballots cast by your fellow employees.

Step 9

After the polls are closed, the govern- ment agent opens the sealed ballot box. He then dumps the ballots on a table anr the counting begins.

Step 10

The government agent counts the votes while Company and Union representatives watch. After all the votes have been count- ed, the government agent announces the "winner." The ballots are then sealed and become the property of the U. S. Government.

Response Literature

"Treating your adversary with respect is giving him an advantage to which he is not entitled."

SAMUEL JOHNSON

During most union organizing campaigns, the union will make a statement that is so outrageous it demands a response. At other times, the union may focus its attack on an area where you believe you are vulnerable. In either case, you may feel a response is necessary to keep the campaign on course. At other times, the union may distribute literature that contains false or misleading information. It may be to your advantage to point out the inaccuracy to voters, thereby damaging the union's credibility. Whatever the reason, there will likely be a time during the campaign when a piece of literature needs to be produced to respond to union statements. There is, however, one cardinal rule: **Do not use response literature unless absolutely necessary or unless you can use it to strengthen your campaign. Frequent use of response literature means you are allowing the union to dictate the issues. This is usually a FATAL mistake.**

If you decide to produce a response handout, be sure it meets the following requirements:

1. It should make a clear and unmistakable point, and one that is entirely supported by facts. In most response documents, you will be calling the union — more specifically the union organizer and/or the organizing committee — a liar, so you must be accurate.

2. Response literature should be more dramatic than conventional literature; maybe larger with a different headline format, etc. Do not make response literature look like your normal campaign handouts.

3. Make your response in such a way that it closes the door on the issue at hand. If the union offers a response to your response, you're back where you started. Do not allow yourself to be trapped in a no-win situation.

4. The decision to distribute a response handout must be made without emotion. Sometimes during a campaign, the union will talk about members of management in uncomplimentary or even insulting terms. Unflattering cartoons might be used. Though your first instinct may be to respond, delay that decision until your anger subsides. Often, these personal attacks on management infuriate voters as well and cost the union support. If this is the case, no response is needed.

5. Be certain that your response will not cause you to deviate substantially from your campaign calendar.

6. If it is possible to time your response for a more appropriate segment of the campaign, you should consider doing so. For example, if you are in the collective bargaining segment and the response you are considering is on the subject of strikes, is it possible to delay your response until the segment in which you plan to discuss strikes? Examine what you want to say in your response; you may find you've already said it in your planned message.

7. Do not engage in mudslinging unless you can make a specific point and then move the campaign back to high ground. However, this is easier said than done.

8. If there are multiple union statements that deserve a response, it may be more effective to handle all of them in a single response handout distributed during the latter stages of the campaign.

Since you cannot know in advance if response literature will be needed, this type of material will have to be prepared quickly. If you cannot delay your response until the time you have scheduled to discuss the subject, respond as soon as possible. If the union has damaged your campaign, the sooner this is repaired, the better.

When drafting response literature, clearly identify the handout as a response. A good way to do this is by quoting the statement that you wish to dispute. This also applies when you need to dispute multiple statements. Consider reproducing part of a union handout with the disputed statement or statements circled.

Let's look at how a piece of response literature was used effectively in a campaign. Management had scored a point with voters on the issue of strikes. The union apparently felt this had swayed votes and issued a handout that stated the vast majority of contracts it negotiated had been settled without strikes. The union proudly said 97% of its contracts were settled without strikes.

Management had no way to determine if the 97% figure was correct, but it had the union's strike history. A response handout was produced using a 22 by 18 inch sheet of paper folded to a final size of 11 by 9 inches. The cover of the handout stated, "The union tells you they have a record to be proud of in any league." The handout then unfolded to 11 by 18 inches with the statement, "Here it is...in their words." After this headline was a reproduction of a portion of the union's own flyer. Management's handout then unfolded to its full 22 by 18 inch size. The last headline said, "Here's the record they're so proud of...506 strikes in 5 years." Listed in very small print was each of the 506 strikes.

Obviously no voter read the entire list; but the point of the handout was not for every word to be read. Instead, it was to make a dramatic, indisputable point. When voters unfolded the large sheet of paper and saw all 506 strikes listed, this drove home the reality of strikes and effectively destroyed the union's claim that most of its contracts were settled without work interruptions.

Here's another example of a successful response flyer: During a campaign, the union had made a number of statements that were either untrue or misleading. Management had not responded to any of these statements since, individually, they had not damaged the campaign. Also, responding to each union statement would have substantially altered the campaign schedule. However, during the latter stages of the campaign, management decided an important point could be made if it took many of the untrue union statements and drafted a dramatic response flyer. A montage was made using portions of the union handouts that contained statement's management wanted to dispute. The flyer printed on 11 by 17 inch paper folded in half. The 8 1/2 by 11 inch cover contained a cartoon and the headline "Does the union lie?...Is a 40 pound gnat fat?" Inside, the handout quoted each false union statement, followed by the facts. (This flyer is shown as Exhibit 14-A.)

Occasionally, management can anticipate union promises and can plan response literature in advance. This is possible by examining previous campaigns conducted by the same union or organizer. "Warranty Coupons" are a good example of this type of handout. A Warranty Coupon booklet is a small multiple-page handout that contains a number of coupons. Each coupon is printed with a statement or a promise that unions typically make to voters, but cannot guarantee. The booklet advises voters that to protect themselves from rash promises and irresponsible union organizers, they should get certain things guaranteed in writing before deciding how to vote. Each coupon has a place for the union organizer to sign and date the guarantee. Typical guarantees include:

1. I guarantee you will get a pay raise of ___ cents per hour in the very first contract my union negotiates with your employer. If this pay raise is not negotiated, my union will pay you the difference.

2. I guarantee that my union will pay you your regular straight time hourly rate of pay in the event you lose any time from work because of labor trouble or strikes.

3. I guarantee that despite provisions in the International Constitution, you will never be put on trial, fined, or levied any assessments by my union.

4. I guarantee that there will be no layoffs at this facility as long as my union is the collective bargaining representative of the employees.

5. I guarantee that my union will pay for the support of you and your family and all of their expenses in the event you are thrown out of work because of strikes called by the union.

6. I guarantee that once you become a member of my union, you will not be required to abide by the Constitution and Bylaws of the union because I have not given you a copy of these documents or explained what they mean.

7. I guarantee you will not be held back from pay increases or promotions if you prove you can do more than another member who has

more seniority than you.

8. I guarantee that if you are called out on strike, management cannot hire a permanent replacement for you and that you will get your job back at the end of the strike.

9. I guarantee that should a strike be called and you choose to work during the strike, you will not be fined, put on trial, or harassed in any way by my union or by union members for crossing the picket line.

Dozens of different Warranty Coupon statements or guarantees can be used; however, the more personalized they are to your campaign, the more effective they will be. Pre-printed Warranty Coupon booklets are available for purchase from LRI.

These handouts show the kind of effective and imaginative response literature that can be based on union statements or issues. Remember, the objective is to run the campaign according to *your* schedule, while talking about your issues. This is usually possible, particularly if videos are used in conjunction with effective literature. In most campaigns, the union will spend all its time just trying to counter your arguments.

Exhibit 14-A

Does The Union Lie?

Is A 40 Pound Gnat **Fat**?

Exhibit 14-A

During the course of this campaign, you have received a lot of information from both the company and the union. The company literature has contained only the truth; still, the union has accused management of trying to win your vote by lying. Though there has never been any proof offered that we have told you anything but the truth, the union accusations continue.

It is now time to set the record straight. It is time to prove who is telling the truth and who is not. The following are some of the lies the union has told you during this campaign. After each union lie is the truth. And remember, these are only some of the lies the union has been telling you.

UNION LIE: "In the twelve month period ending last October, the average hourly rate in each of the three [unionized] plants increased about 10%."

THE TRUTH: In 1978, the wage rates in those three plants increased 8.4%, and 7.1% in 1979. But here in Stillwater, our rates increased 10.4% in 1978, and 7.3% in 1979. In both years the percentage increases here in Stillwater were higher than those in our Wisconsin plants with Machinists contracts.

UNION LIE: If the union wins the election, "Stillwater employees will have their own lodge and run their own affairs."

THE TRUTH: The union constitution is 183 pages long and contains many, many restrictions. All Machinists lodges must conform to these restrictions or else. Incidentally, the Machinists union promised employees in Orlando and St. Cloud the same thing, but it never happened.

UNION LIE: If the union wins the election, your benefits will only go up.

Exhibit 14-A

THE TRUTH: All wages, benefits and other terms and condition of employment are subject to negotiations. These things can stay the same, they can go up, or they can go down. You don't automatically have anything. Everything must be negotiated.

UNION LIE: With a union, you will have more job security.

THE TRUTH: Satisfied customers provide orders – and as a result, jobs for all of us. No union can provide that. In fact, the union may have you fired if you don't "cough up" your dues on time.

UNION LIE: The company has started rumors that the plant will shut down if we go union.

THE TRUTH: No such rumor was ever started in this plant. Over the past three years, the Stillwater plant has steadily grown and there is every expectation that this will continue.

UNION LIE: The company put pressure on the Redwood West to cancel the union meeting.

THE TRUTH: The union's failure to pay the room deposit caused the reservation to be cancelled.

UNION LIE: The Machinists union hardly every goes on strike.

THE TRUTH: The Machinists union has called at least 666 strikes in the last three years. Over 260,000 people were put out of work because of these strikes.

Remember, the Company has told you the TRUTH.

Exhibit 14-A

On our own,
we've got a good thing going!

Union
NO

Questions & Answers

"Men are never so likely to settle a question rightly as when they discuss it freely."

THOMAS BABINGTON

Expect the voting group to have questions about such things as the organizing process, the various campaign issues, voting procedures, and how unionization would affect them and their employer. It is the responsibility of management — and good campaign strategy — to provide voters with answers to these questions. The format you select for doing this depends on your campaign strategy. Many campaign directors prefer to develop a booklet that answers several questions at the same time. Others prefer to issue a small weekly handout that answers only a few questions pertaining to the subject being discussed during that campaign segment. Some personalize this approach by preparing supervisors to raise questions with individual employees that will enable them to provide conversational answers in a one-on-one setting. There are advantages and disadvantages to each method.

The advantage of the booklet format is that it lends itself to an informative presentation that is usually perceived by the voting group as being educational, rather than campaign propaganda. Another advantage is that it makes an excellent piece for mailing to the home. This helps to involve a voter's family. The primary disadvantage is that a booklet is several pages long, relatively expensive to produce, and there is always the danger it will not be read. Another disadvantage is that booklets have to be prepared early in the campaign and cannot be amended to respond to questions that arise after the booklet is printed.

The primary advantage of a brief handout every week is that questions and answers can relate to a particular campaign segment, it can be read quickly, and this format is inexpensive to produce. The primary disadvantage is that another handout per segment will be added and may cause voters to tire of campaign literature more quickly than normal.

The one-on-one approach has the great advantage of sparking positive communication between supervisors and voters; it encourages the participation of employees who might not be comfortable speaking out during a general question-and-answer session. The only potential disadvantage is if supervisors are not fully prepared to discuss specific campaign issues.

There is no single best way to answer employee questions. The format you select should be based on what you feel would work best with your voting group. You may even elect to answer questions with bulletin board notices instead of using handouts, mailing pieces, or personal contact. The important thing is that employee questions must be answered. You do not, however, have to answer only those questions that are asked. Answer any other questions you think would be of interest to voters.

The following questions and answers are presented in a booklet format to illustrate how such a booklet could be produced. These are questions typically asked by voters. After each question is a possible management answer. With some adjustment, these answers can be made employer- and/or industry-specific.

What About Unions?

This booklet has been specially prepared for you, whether you are:

- For unions
- Against unions
- Haven't decided
- Don't care
- Can't be represented by a union anyway

Do you know the answers to these questions about union representation? If you are undecided about supporting the union, this may help you decide. No one should fail to read this. Unionization would affect you, regardless of how you feel about a union or your position within this organization.

Q. Is management against unionization?

A. Yes, but not for the reasons the union would have you believe. The union does not understand our business; it does not understand the present economic conditions in our industry. The union seems to believe all we have to do to raise wages and benefits is to pass those increased costs on to our customers in the form of higher prices. If it was really that easy, we would have done it already. We believe any rise in price to the customer at this time will result in less business. This can mean fewer jobs.

Furthermore, as you know, our customers depend on us. When we are awarded a contract, we must be able to fulfill it without interruptions. A union always brings the threat of work stoppages or strikes. If union demands resulted in such a work stoppage or strike, we believe this would spell the beginning of the end of our business. Customers could always turn to someone else whose employees have not placed themselves in the hands of a union.

We are pro-company and pro-employee. As you study the questions and answers that follow, we hope you will come to feel as we do: The union is not, cannot, and will not be a good thing for you or this organization.

Q. Do I have to join the union to hold a job?

A. (Right-to-Work version) Because we are located in a Right-to-Work state, a union security clause cannot be included in a labor contract. This clause would force a person to join and remain a member to keep their job. Though this is illegal in our state — which means you may choose not to join the union — if the union was voted in, you would still have to follow all rules and regulations contained in the labor contract; management would have to treat you the same as if you were a union member. Also, the union would probably start harassing you to join so it could collect more dues.

A. (non-Right-to-Work version) Most labor contracts in non-Right-to-Work states, like ours, contain a union security clause that forces everyone in the bargaining unit to join and remain a member of the union to keep their job. If this clause was in the contract, you would have no choice but to become a "member in good standing" with the union. This means paying dues.

Q. What happens when I sign a union authorization card?

A. This card is not as innocent as you might think. It means you are making an application to become a union member and subject to all the union's rules and regulations. It is not — as the union would have you believe — simply a poll to determine how employees feel. In most cases, it is a binding application for membership between you and the union. Would you sign any other document without knowing all the facts? As a member, you must pay dues, pay union fines for stepping out of line and pay special assessments for union pet projects, even if you don't agree with them. A union authorization card can also be used by the union to claim that it represents you. And remember, if an election is held, you do not have to sign a card to vote.

Q. If I don't want to join the union, but the union organizer keeps pestering me, what can I do?

A. You can just say "No." Or you can report it to your supervisor. Union salespeople are pretty smooth. They know how to get in your front door, but you are not obligated to talk to them.

Q. If I join the union, won't I gain the right to decide what my wages and other benefits will be?

A. If the union ever gets voted in, management and the union would negotiate over wages and benefits. Negotiate does not mean agree — it only means we would try to agree. Let's be realistic: How could any employer stay in business if employees had the right to decide for themselves what they would be paid? Management decides what it can afford to pay and what is fair. With or without a union, we can only pay what is in the best interests of both this organization and its employees.

Q. But *my* best interest is in getting more pay!

A. We understand that and know how important your wages, benefits, and job security are to you. We take great pride in what we are able to do for our employees — and not how little we can get by with, as the union wants you to believe. We are always looking for ways to improve the work environment: the way we work, the equipment we own, and the wages and benefits we offer. We will continue to seek improvement in all areas, including wages and benefits, whether you belong to a union or not.

It's easy for the union to discount this. In fact, it will *have* to if it hopes to win your support. But that cannot change the fact we have increased wages and added benefits (insurance, hospitalization, pension plan, profit sharing, educational assistance, etc.) without any outside third party representing employees. We've done these things because they were the right things to do, and we intend to continue this policy.

By contrast, today's economic conditions have resulted in many unionized companies negotiating substantial wage and benefit *reductions* with the unions that represent employees.

Q. Don't unions often get higher wages and better benefits for members?

A. This is another tired union argument that has no basis in fact. Since 1992, union wage increases have averaged only 3% or less. This is the lowest rate of increase since 1986. For all union contacts negotiated in 1996, the average wage/benefit increase was again only 3%. Last year, we gave you an increase of ___%.

Q. I've heard that some employers raise wages when there's union activity. Doesn't this prove the union's claim that management could be giving us a better deal?

A. First, it's illegal for an employer to grant a wage increase during a union campaign unless increases are normally given at that same time. Second, most employers grant wage increases based on their wage policy and the success of the business. You should understand that during an organizing drive the union will try to use any raise given as propaganda, claiming it was only done because of union activity.

Q. Can't the union guarantee me job security?

A. If it could, it would also have to guarantee that we will stay in business. If the union representative has guaranteed to do that, please send them around to apply for a job. The real answer is "no." Job security comes from our ability to get and keep customers.

Q. Can't the union guarantee I won't be fired?

A. No. To protect you, we already have strict rules and regulations against improper discharge. With or without the union, no one here is ever discharged without good cause. Under our policy, any discharge action must be reviewed by someone in higher authority than your immediate supervisor, unless the cause for discharge is so aggravated there can be no question of it being proper. As to layoffs due to lack of work, the union cannot prevent this under any circumstances.

Q. Doesn't the union protect employees who are in trouble with their boss?

A. We understand that disagreements may arise from time to time, but they are generally worked out between the employee and the employee's immediate supervisor. If an employee develops a serious problem with their supervisor, the personnel department is available to help. Management approaches these matters on a fair and reasonable basis. A union neither adds to nor detracts from this management function. The union would not become involved in this, nor would it afford any so-called protection.

Q. Don't I need the union's help in pleading my grievances?

A. Turning your complaint over to a third party doesn't guarantee better results. In fact, a union agent may be more concerned with union policy than your personal welfare. The union wants you to believe you are working for unreasonable people. Do you honestly believe this is true? Also, many union grievance procedures are so complicated it can take more than six months for a grievance to be settled.

Q. If the union gets in, can it get rid of that supervisor I don't get along with?

A. The union has nothing whatsoever to say about supervisors. If you honestly have a complaint about one, that's what the personnel department is here for; and you can go right to the top.

Q. Wouldn't the union give me seniority rights?

A. If you mean would the union contract require that all promotions, layoffs, recalls, and other job rights be based on *no other yardstick except seniority,* regardless of other circumstances, we can only say that the union contracts we've seen do not do this.

We appreciate and give full recognition to employees with long service, while also providing opportunities for those with less service. We do not believe a completely arbitrary system is good. Strict seniority, without considering ability, does not seem fair. Yes, seniority is always considered, provided ability and merit are equal, but the first consideration is the quality of work our people perform.

Q. Getting back to negotiations — How long do these negotiations last?

A. No one can say. If management and the union don't agree, negotiations could go on a long time.

Q. Who negotiates for the union?

A. A union business agent or representative who is not an employee of this organization and who usually has no firsthand knowledge of our problems or of you, the employees.

Q. What can the union do if it can't agree with management?

A. The union has one alternative — to call you out on strike.

Q. If I go on strike, what happens then?

A. You would receive no pay and no benefits.

Q. If I go on strike, could I lose my job?

A. Management is legally free to hire permanent replacements for anyone on economic strike.

Q. If there were a strike, would this organization continue to operate?

A. Management has the right to continue to operate during a strike. We also have an obligation to continue servicing our customers.

Q. If the strike was later called off, but I had been replaced, would I get my job back?

A. By law, management cannot be forced to re-hire you. Your best hope would be to have your name put on a re-hire list so you could be called back as jobs become available.

Q. What are the chances of a strike?

A. No one knows. Unions like to claim that it's a small percentage of the total hours industry works. But this percentage figure isn't much consolation to someone who's forced out on strike and trying to live without a paycheck.

Q. Who calls for a strike?

A. You will have to read the union's constitution and local bylaws to determine this. Usually it is a small group because only a few union members attend union meetings. You could be called out on strike even though you're happy with your own situation and the majority of all employees did not vote for the strike.

Q. Do striking employees get unemployment compensation?

A. No. [Check your state law before giving this answer. Currently, New York and Rhode Island are the exceptions.]

Q. I've seen stories about union strike violence on TV and in newspapers. Why hasn't the union told me anything about this?

A. Quoting a union organizer from a newspaper interview: "Talk the union up. Play down strikes and violence." That's why during an organizing drive the union only talks about its promises and tries never to mention unpleasant things like strikes and violence. However, we all know that with a union the threat of a strike is always present. On occasion, violence erupts. From 1975 to 1995, over 8,500 incidents of property damage or personal injury occurred during union strikes.

Q. What else can the union do if it can't reach agreement with management after long negotiations?

A. The union can quit representing you anytime it feels like it.

Q. Nevertheless, don't unions get wage increases for their members?

A. It's misleading to think a union "gets" anything for anybody. The law merely requires that the union and management negotiate. The law also says management cannot grant any wage increase or benefit, *even when it wants to*, without first negotiating the increase with the union. All this red tape can give the impression that the union got something for its members. If management was free to grant wage and benefit increases without consulting a union, employees would soon come to realize they don't really need a union in the first place.

Q. What assurances do I have that I'm getting the best possible deal without the union?

A. Think about this: Our organization, along with others in this area, is competing for your job skills. An employer who is indifferent to wages, benefits, and working conditions isn't able to attract the best employees. We don't claim to have every conceivable benefit that anyone could dream up, or the highest wages and the shortest hours of anyone in any industry, anywhere. But we know we offer a good program and we help employees who want to help themselves.

Q. What happens to my wages and other benefits if the union is voted in?

A. Let's go back further. Once the union claims it has 30% of the employees signed up, management cannot grant any wage increases or improve any benefit programs unless those changes had been planned before the union started its campaign. If the union wins an election, your wages and benefits then become negotiable. Your present wage rate and benefits would be as much a subject of negotiations as any new things the union asks for. That's not our idea, it's the law.

Q. I heard that if I support the union, I won't have less than I have now, and it could be more. Is that true?

A. Don't believe everything you hear from the union. Bargaining over a union contract doesn't necessarily start from a base of present benefits. All wage rates and benefits are subject to bargaining. The union may trade away some present benefit for something it especially wants. For example, the union could bargain away a present employee benefit in exchange for getting management to deduct union dues from your paycheck. In fact, the National Labor Relations Board has stated, "*. . . there is, of course, no obligation on the part of an employer to contract to continue all existing benefits, nor is it an unfair labor practice to offer reduced benefits.*" This quote is not meant to imply anything other than to inform you of the facts.

Q. The union contract thing still isn't clear. Doesn't a union contract protect me?

A. A contract sets forth the wages and benefits extended to you by your employer, plus the rules you work under. With or without a union contract, all benefits are only as good as this organization's ability to stay in business. Under a union contract, there is generally no bending of the rules to take care of special circumstances. This is another reason we don't believe a union improves anything. By its very nature and purpose, a union sets a certain group of employees apart from the rest of the organization.

Q. Why don't I just join the union and try it out for a while? Maybe it can really do something.

A. A union is not something you just "try out." Once voted in, the procedure to get rid of a union is so involved that, for all practical purposes, it would be here to stay. If you wanted to get it out, you would have to do this on your own. You would probably face discipline from the union, as spelled out in its constitution. Management is prohibited by law from giving any assistance.

Q. But isn't the union more interested in us than management is?

A. Why should strangers have an interest in you? Their real interest is to perpetuate the union by getting you to join and pay dues. Remember, it's the union organizer's job to sign you up. If organizers aren't successful at this, they're out of a job. Is it any wonder that organizers say and do almost anything to get your vote?

Further, unions do not encourage individual achievement. This is borne out by the fact that union members have been fined for increased production. Also, there are union contracts that provide if a person is promoted to a supervisory position, that person loses all their service for seniority purposes. Applying this to our situation, after years of service, an employee could be promoted to supervisor, then moved back to their previous position. Under such a contract, this person would be considered a new employee for purposes of seniority. By discouraging those who wish to advance to positions of greater responsibility, a union seems to be more interested in keeping someone in the union and collecting dues than in helping employees to advance.

Q. Doesn't the union provide me insurance, a pension, burial expenses, and other benefits?

A. You will have to check the union constitution, but if it does, you pay for those things, either as a special payment or out of your dues.

Q. If it wins, will supervisors be represented by the union?

A. Definitely not.

Q. Don't most people belong to a union?

A. No. Government statistics show that less than 15% of America's workforce is represented by a union. Union membership as a percentage of the total workforce is in a long-term decline. Is it any wonder the union looks hungrily at our company?

Q. Management makes a lot of statements and the union makes a lot of statements. The union says it's giving me the facts — and management says it's giving me the facts. Who can I believe?

A. Employees are expected to realize that the union organizer is a salesperson. You must take it upon yourself to determine whether the union is telling the truth. In other words, "Let the buyer beware."

The law requires management to give voters the straight story, and it severely limits what management can say. We cannot make promises; we cannot make threats. The union can say and promise practically anything and get away with it. The union is like a politician who has to get elected *just once* to have a permanent job.

Please remember, we will be working together for a long time, no matter what happens. The union organizer, on the other hand, has no obligation to you. If they aren't successful, they just move on to greener pastures. Who do you think is more likely to tell you the truth?

Q. What are my rights as an employee during a union organizing campaign?

A. Everyone should make it their personal mission to know the truth and get the facts. Union officials can give out leaflets, hold meetings, and make promises to you regarding higher pay and better benefits. As we've stated, however, the union cannot guarantee these things. Instead, those items must be negotiated.

Management can also give you leaflets and hold meetings to tell you the facts, but it is against the law for us to make any promises to you during the campaign.

Employees who are voting in the election have the right to talk about the union and distribute union literature during lunch periods or during breaks in any non-work areas, such as the parking lot, lunch room, or rest rooms, or in any non-work areas during non-work times.

Q. Why doesn't management tell us what will happen if the union loses the election?

A. The law that allows the union to make promises to employees during an organizing campaign says it is illegal for management to do the same. This may not seem fair, but it's the law. The union is allowed to make promises because it is assumed voters will realize these promises are just campaign talk.

Q. Is it legal for a union organizer to visit me at my home?

A. Yes, but the decision to let the organizer into your home is entirely yours. A union organizer has no legal right to enter your home.

Q. I don't care about the union one way or the other. Why should I bother to vote?

A. You're going to be affected whether you vote or not. The election is decided by a majority of those voting. The outcome of the election is important to everyone. If the union wins, you would be represented by it, whether you want to be or not. So don't let someone else make a decision that affects your future. Please vote. Your vote could decide the outcome.

Q. How much does it cost to belong to a union and what is the money used for?

A. Union dues average about two hours pay per month. These dues are used for a variety of things. First, a union has a lot of expenses: salaries and expenses for a large staff; salaries and expenses for organizers (like the people who are trying to win your support in this election); office buildings and cars for union employees; and other expenses. In addition to dues, a union can charge employees assessments if it runs low on money, and employees can be fined for violating the union's constitution.

Q. Can the union increase its dues?

A. Yes, the union can always increase dues. You can usually find a provision in the union's constitution that provides for dues increases. Unions may also require special contributions for such things as strike funds, political campaigns, building funds, and other special projects.

Election Day Conduct

Preparation for election day actually begins during the earliest stages of the campaign when you agree to a date and time for the election. In this section, however, we will only focus on the preparations you need to make and the actions you need to take to insure that the election is conducted properly.

Several days before the election, you should give thought to selecting your election observers. While the election is being conducted, no member of management or supervision will be allowed in the voting area. A representative of the National Labor Relations Board conducts the election. However, both management and the union may select an equal number of observers — usually one or two per voting location — to observe the election. Their function is to make sure only eligible voters are allowed to cast a ballot and that no one votes twice. They may challenge any person they believe is not an eligible voter. You may select anyone who is not a member of management or supervision. It is best to select your observers from members of the voting group. The union will do this also.

Virtually every eligible voter feels that being selected as an observer is an honor, so make your selection carefully. Some who are not selected might be disappointed. Make sure that your decision is popular and widely accepted. If your election is conducted in two or more session's — for example, one session for first shift, another for second shift — you may select different observers for each session.

When choosing your observers, keep these things in mind:

1. Management observers should be people who have worked actively and openly against union representation.

2. They should be well-recognized and well-liked by their fellow employees.

3. They should personally know as many of the voters as possible.

After choosing your observers, inform them of their selection and be sure they are willing to act in this capacity. Inform them of their general or specific duties and of the things they cannot do as observers. You will receive instructions for election observers from the NLRB before the election. (These instructions are also shown at the end of this chapter.)

Early on the morning of the election or the evening before, be sure the voting place and areas just outside the voting place where employees may have to stand while waiting to vote are free of campaign literature, signs, posters, or any other election material. If the voting area has windows or glass doors that would allow non-voting employees or members of management to observe the election, those windows or doors should be papered over. Any doors leading into the voting area that will not be used by voters should be locked or blocked with a sign that reads "Election In Progress — Do Not Enter."

Approximately 30 minutes to one hour before the election is scheduled to begin, an agent of the NLRB will arrive for a pre-election conference. One or more representatives of the union are allowed to participate in this conference, as well as one or more representatives of management and the observers. You are required to allow the union representatives on your property during this period. However, you do not have to allow them to walk around and visit with voters. The best procedure is to be pleasant, but escort the union representative(s) to the voting area where the pre-election conference will take place, then escort them out after the conference is over.

At the pre-election conference, the Board agent will ask if there are any changes or alterations to be made to the Excelsior list, review the duties of the observers, set up the voting booth and ballot box, and prepare for the voting.

If the election is to be held in more than one session, the same procedure repeats at the beginning of the second session.

When voting is over, the individuals who participated in the pre-election conference are allowed to observe the counting of the ballots. Others will probably want to observe — voters, members of management and supervision, and perhaps other union representatives — but with few exceptions, these requests should be denied. If the union only brings two or three additional people to observe the counting, that should not constitute a problem. In addition, the president of your organization or two to three management officials may want to observe. That, too, should not be a problem. You should, however, keep the number of people in the room to a reasonably small group.

As the ballots are counted, you may keep track of how you are doing by using a small counter. Each board agent uses his or her own method of counting ballots. Most separate the ballots by Yes or No votes, placing them in two stacks. After the ballots have been stacked, the Board agent will count each stack. If, by using the counter, you keep track of the No ballots being put in the stack, you will know when you reach 50% of the eligible voters. When you reach this point, you have won the election. If any ballots have been challenged, they will only become meaningful if they could affect the outcome of the election.

After the ballots have been counted, the Board agent will ask the observers to sign a Certification on Conduct of Election. This statement says that the balloting was fairly conducted, that all eligible voters were given an opportunity to cast their ballot in secret, and that the ballot box was protected. On occasion, union representatives refuse to sign, but this is nothing to worry about.

The Board agent will then present a Tally of Ballots form to both management and the union for each party to sign. This form certifies that the tabulation of ballots, as counted by the Board agent, is correct.

When you win, do not allow any management representatives to engage in any type of celebration in the voting area. Congratulate the union representatives on a good campaign and escort them out of the building. Management representatives who engage in a celebration in the presence of union representatives could cause the union to return next year, not because of employee interest, but because the union wants to get even. Once the union officials have left, you can celebrate!

Instructions for Election Observers

(as issued by the NLRB)

DUTIES (General):

    1. Act as checkers and watchers.

    2. Assist in identification of voters.

    3. Challenge voters and ballots.

    4. Otherwise assist agents of the Board.

THINGS TO DO (Specific):

    1. Identify voters.

    2. Check off the name of the person applying to vote. A check is put before the name by one representative; another check is put after the name by the other representative.

    3. See that only one voter occupies a booth at any one time.

    4. See that each voter deposits a ballot in the ballot box.

    5. See that each voter leaves the voting area immediately after depositing their ballot.

    6. Report any conflict regarding the right to vote to the agent of the Board at your table.

    7. Remain in the voting area until all ballots are counted to check on the fairness of the count, if ballots are counted at that time. If they are not counted immediately, you will be informed as to when and where ballots will be counted.

    8. Report any irregularities to the Board agent as soon as noticed.

9. Challenge of Voters — An agent of the Board or an authorized observer may question eligibility of a voter. A challenge MUST be made before the voter's ballot has been placed in the ballot box.

10. Wear your observer badge at all times during the conduct of the election.

11. BE ON TIME. (One-half hour before the time for the opening of the polls.)

THINGS NOT TO DO (Specific):

1. Give any help to any voter. Only an agent of the Board can assist voters.

2. Electioneer any place during the hours of the election.

3. Argue regarding the election.

4. Leave the polling place without the agent's consent.

5. Use intoxicating liquors.

6. Keep any list of those who have or have not voted.

As an official representative of your organization, you should enter upon this task with a fair and open mind. Conduct yourself so that no one can find fault with your actions during the election. You are here to see that the election is conducted in a fair and impartial manner, so that each eligible voter has a fair and equal chance to express themselves freely and in secret.

NATIONAL LABOR RELATIONS ACT
Also cited NLRA or the Act; 29 U.S.C. §§ 151–169
[Title 29, Chapter 7, Subchapter II, United States Code]

FINDINGS AND POLICIES

Section 1. [§ 151.] The denial by some employers of the right of employees to organize and the refusal by some employers to accept the procedure of collective bargaining lead to strikes and other forms of industrialstrife or unrest, which have the intent or the necessary effect of burdening or obstructing commerce by (a) impairing the efficiency, safety, or operation of the instrumentalities of commerce; (b) occurring in the current of commerce; (c) materially affecting, restraining, or controlling the flow of raw materials or manufactured or processed goods from or into the channels of commerce, or the prices of such materials or goods in commerce; or (d) causing diminution of employment and wages in such volume as substantially to impair or disrupt the market for goods flowing from or into the channels of commerce.

The inequality of bargaining power between employees who do not possess full freedom of association or actual liberty of contract and employers who are organized in the corporate or other forms of ownership association substantially burdens and affects the flow of commerce, and tends to aggravate recurrent business depressions, by depressing wage rates and the purchasing power of wage earners in industry and by preventing the stabilization of competitive wage rates and working conditions within and between industries.

Experience has proved that protection by law of the right of employees to organize and bargain collectively safeguards commerce from injury, impairment, or interruption, and promotes the flow of commerce by removing certain recognized sources of industrial strife and unrest, by encouraging practices fundamental to the friendly adjustment of industrial disputes arising out of differences as to wages, hours, or other working conditions, and by restoring equality of bargaining power between employers and employees.

Experience has further demonstrated that certain practices by some labor organizations, their officers, and members have the intent or the necessary effect of burdening or obstructing commerce by preventing the free flow of goods in such commerce through strikes and other forms of industrial unrest or through concerted activities which impair the interest of the public in the free flow of such commerce. The elimination of such practices is a necessary condition to the assurance of the rights herein guaranteed.

It is declared to be the policy of the United States to eliminate the causes of certain substantial obstructions to the free flow of commerce and to mitigate and eliminate these obstructions when they have occurred by encouraging the practice and procedure of collective bargaining and by protecting the exercise by workers of full freedom of association, self-organization, and designation of representatives of their own choosing, for the purpose of negotiating the terms and conditions of their employment or other mutual aid or protection.

DEFINITIONS

Sec. 2. [§ 152.] When used in this Act [subchapter]—

(1) The term "person" includes one or more individuals, labor organizations, partnerships, associations, corporations, legal representatives, trustees, trustees in cases under title 11 of the United States Code [under title 11], or receivers.

(2) The term "employer" includes any person acting as an agent of an employer, directly or indirectly, but shall not include the United States or any wholly owned Government corporation, or any Federal Reserve Bank, or any State or political subdivision thereof, or any person subject to the Railway Labor Act [45 U.S.C. § 151 et seq.], as amended from time to time, or any labor organization (other than when acting as an employer), or anyone acting in the capacity of officer or agent of such labor organization.

[Pub. L. 93–360, § 1(a), July 26, 1974, 88 Stat. 395, deleted the phrase "or any corporation or association operating a hospital, if no part of the net earnings inures to the benefit of any private shareholder or individual" from the definition of "employer."]

(3) The term "employee" shall include any employee, and shall not be limited to the employees of a particular employer, unless the Act [this subchapter] explicitly states otherwise, and shall include any individual whose work has ceased as a consequence of, or in connection with, any current labor dispute or because of any unfair labor practice, and who has not obtained any other regular and substantially equivalent employment, but shall not include any individual employed as an agricultural

laborer, or in the domestic service of any family or person at his home, or any individual employed by his parent or spouse, or any individual having the status of an independent contractor, or any individual employed as a supervisor, or any individual employed by an employer subject to the Railway Labor Act [45 U.S.C. § 151 et seq.], as amended from time to time, or by any other person who is not an employer as herein defined.

(4) The term "representatives" includes any individual or labor organization.

(5) The term "labor organization" means any organization of any kind, or any agency or employee representation committee or plan, in which employees participate and which exists for the purpose, in whole or in part, of dealing with employers concerning grievances, labor disputes, wages, rates of pay, hours of employment, or conditions of work.

(6) The term "commerce" means trade, traffic, commerce, transportation, or communication among the several States, or between the District of Columbia or any Territory of the United States and any State or other Territory, or between any foreign country and any State, Territory, or the District of Columbia, or within the District of Columbia or any Territory, or between points in the same State but through any other State or any Territory or the District of Columbia or any foreign country.

(7) The term "affecting commerce" means in commerce, or burdening or obstructing commerce or the free flow of commerce, or having led or tending to lead to a labor dispute burdening or obstructing commerce or the free flow of commerce.

(8) The term "unfair labor practice" means any unfair labor practice listed in section 8 [section 158 of this title].

(9) The term "labor dispute" includes any controversy concerning terms, tenure, or conditions of employment, or concerning the association or rep-resentation of persons in negotiating, fixing, maintaining, changing, or seek-ing to arrange terms or conditions of employment, regardless of whether the disputants stand in the proximate relation of employer and employee.

(10) The term "National Labor Relations Board" means the National Labor Relations Board provided for in section 3 of this Act [section 153 of this title].

(11) The term "supervisor" means any individual having authority, in the interest of the employer, to hire, transfer, suspend, lay off, recall, promote, discharge, assign, reward, or discipline other employees, or respon-sibly to direct them, or to adjust their grievances, or effectively to

rec-ommend such action, if in connection with the foregoing the exercise of such authority is not of a merely routine or clerical nature, but requires the use of independent judgment.

(12) The term "professional employee" means—

(a) any employee engaged in work (i) predominantly intellectual and varied in character as opposed to routine mental, manual, mechanical, or physical work; (ii) involving the consistent exercise of discretion and judgment in its performance; (iii) of such a character that the output produced or the result accomplished cannot be standardized in relation to a given period of time; (iv) requiring knowledge of an advanced type in a field of science or learning customarily acquired by a prolonged course of specialized intellectual instruction and study in an institution of higher learning or a hospital, as distinguished from a general academic education or from an apprenticeship or from training in the performance of routine mental, manual, or physical processes; or

(b) any employee, who (i) has completed the courses of specialized intellectual instruction and study described in clause (iv) of paragraph (a), and (ii) is performing related work under the supervision of a professional person to qualify himself to become a professional employee as defined in paragraph (a).

(13) In determining whether any person is acting as an "agent" of another person so as to make such other person responsible for his acts, the question of whether the specific acts performed were actually authorized or subsequently ratified shall not be controlling.

(14) The term "health care institution" shall include any hospital, convalescent hospital, health maintenance organization, health clinic, nursing home, extended care facility, or other institution devoted to the care of sick, infirm, or aged person.

[Pub. L. 93–360, § 1(b), July 26, 1974, 88 Stat. 395, added par. (14).]

NATIONAL LABOR RELATIONS BOARD

Sec. 3. [§ 153.] (a) [Creation, composition, appointment, and tenure; Chairman; removal of members] The National Labor Relations Board (hereinafter called the "Board") created by this Act [subchapter] prior to its amendment by the Labor Management Relations Act, 1947 [29 U.S.C. § 141 et seq.], is continued as an agency of the United States, except that the Board shall consist of five instead of three members, appointed by the President by and with the advice and consent of the

Senate.

Of the two additional members so provided for, one shall be appointed for a term of five years and the other for a term of two years. Their successors, and the successors of the other members, shall be appointed for terms of five years each, excepting that any individual chosen to fill a vacancy shall be appointed only for the unexpired term of the member whom he shall succeed. The President shall designate one member to serve as Chairman of the Board. Any member of the Board may be removed by the President, upon notice and hearing, for neglect of duty or malfeasance in office, but for no other cause.

(b) [Delegation of powers to members and regional directors; review and stay of actions of regional directors; quorum; seal] The Board is authorized to delegate to any group of three or more members any or all of the powers which it may itself exercise. The Board is also authorized to delegate to its regional directors its powers under section 9 [section 159 of this title] to determine the unit appropriate for the purpose of collective bargaining, to investigate and provide for hearings, and determine whether a question of representation exists, and to direct an election or take a secret ballot under subsection (c) or (e) of section 9 [section 159 of this title] and certify the results thereof, except that upon the filling of a request therefor with the Board by any interested person, the Board may review any action of a regional director delegated to him under this paragraph, but such a review shall not, unless specifically ordered by the Board, operate as a stay of any action taken by the regional director. A vacancy in the Board shall not impair the right of the remaining members to exercise all of the powers of the Board, and three members of the Board shall, at all times, constitute a quorum of the Board, except that two members shall constitute a quorum of any group designated pursuant to the first sentence hereof. The Board shall have an official seal which shall be judicially noticed.

(c) [Annual reports to Congress and the President] The Board shall at the close of each fiscal year make a report in writing to Congress and to the President summarizing significant case activities and operations for that fiscal year.

(d) [General Counsel; appointment and tenure; powers and duties; vacancy] There shall be a General Counsel of the Board who shall be appointed by the President, by and with the advice and consent of the Senate, for a term of four years. The General Counsel of the Board shall exercise general supervision over all attorneys employed by the

Board (other than administrative law judges and legal assistants to Board members) and over the officers and employees in the regional offices. He shall have final authority, on behalf of the Board, in respect of the investigation of charges and issuance of complaints under section 10 [section 160 of this title], and in respect of the prosecution of such complaints before the Board, and shall have such other duties as the Board may prescribe or as may be provided by law. In case of vacancy in the office of the General Counsel the President is authorized to designate the officer or employee who shall act as General Counsel during such vacancy, but no person or persons so designated shall so act (1) for more than forty days when the Congress is in session unless a nomination to fill such vacancy shall have been submitted to the Senate, or (2) after the adjournment sine die of the session of the Senate in which such nomination was submitted.

[The title "administrative law judge" was adopted in 5 U.S.C. § 3105.]

Sec. 4. [§ 154. Eligibility for reappointment; officers and employees; payment of expenses] (a) Each member of the Board and the General Counsel of the Board shall be eligible for reappointment, and shall not engage in any other business, vocation, or employment. The Board shall appoint an executive secretary, and such attorneys, examiners, and regional directors, and such other employees as it may from time to time find necessary for the proper performance of its duties. The Board may not employ any attorneys for the purpose of reviewing transcripts of hearings or preparing drafts of opinions except that any attorney employed for assignment as a legal assistant to any Board member may for such Board member review such transcripts and prepare such drafts. No administrative law judge's report shall be reviewed, either before or after its publication, by any person other than a member of the Board or his legal assistant, and no administrative law judge shall advise or consult with the Board with respect to exceptions taken to his findings, rulings, or recommendations. The Board may establish or utilize such regional, local, or other agencies, and utilize such voluntary and uncompensated services, as may from time to time be needed. Attorneys appointed under this section may, at the direction of the Board, appear for and represent the Board in any case in court. Nothing in this Act [subchapter] shall be construed to authorize the Board to appoint individuals for the purpose of conciliation ormediation, or for economic analysis.

[The title "administrative law judge" was adopted in 5 U.S.C. § 3105.]

(b) All of the expenses of the Board, including all necessary traveling and subsistence expenses outside the District of Columbia incurred by the members or employees of the Board under its orders, shall be allowed and paid on the presentation of itemized vouchers therefor approved by the Board or by any individual it designates for that purpose.

Sec. 5. [§ 155. Principal office, conducting inquiries throughout country; participation in decisions or inquiries conducted by member] The principal office of the Board shall be in the District of Columbia, but it may meet and exercise any or all of its powers at any other place. The Board may, by one or more of its members or by such agents or agencies as it may designate, prosecute any inquiry necessary to its functions in any part of the United States. A member who participates in such an inquiry shall not be disqualified from subsequently participating in a decision of the Board in the same case.

Sec. 6. [§ 156. Rules and regulations] The Board shall have author-ity from time to time to make, amend, and rescind, in the manner prescribed by the Administrative Procedure Act [by subchapter II of chapter 5 of title 5], such rules and regulations as may be necessary to carry out the provisions of this Act [subchapter].

RIGHTS OF EMPLOYEES

Sec. 7. [§ 157.] Employees shall have the right to self-organization, to form, join, or assist labor organizations, to bargain collectively through representatives of their own choosing, and to engage in other concerted activities for the purpose of collective bargaining or other mutual aid or protection, and shall also have the right to refrain from any or all such activities except to the extent that such right may be affected by an agreement requiring membership in a labor organization as a condition of employment as authorized in section 8(a)(3) [section 158(a)(3) of this title].

UNFAIR LABOR PRACTICES

Sec. 8. [§ 158.] (a) [Unfair labor practices by employer] It shall be an unfair labor practice for an employer—

(1) to interfere with, restrain, or coerce employees in the exercise of the rights guaranteed in section 7 [section 157 of this title];

(2) to dominate or interfere with the formation or administration of any labor organization or contribute financial or other support to it: Provided, That subject to rules and regulations made and published by the Board pursuant to section 6 [section 156 of this title], an employer shall not be prohibited from permitting employees to confer with him during working hours without loss of time or pay;

(3) by discrimination in regard to hire or tenure of employment or any term or condition of employment to encourage or discourage membership in any labor organization: Provided, That nothing in this Act [sub-chapter], or in any other statute of the United States, shall preclude an employer from making an agreement with a labor organization (not established, maintained, or assisted by any action defined in section 8(a) of this Act [in this subsection] as an unfair labor practice) to require as a condition of employment membership therein on or after the thirtieth day following the beginning of such employment or the effective date of such agreement, whichever is the later, (i) if such labor organization is the representative of the employees as provided in section 9(a) [section 159(a) of this title], in the appropriate collective-bargaining unit covered by such agreement when made, and (ii) unless following an election held as provided in section 9(e) [section 159(e) of this title] within one year preceding the effective date of such agreement, the Board shall have certified that at least a majority of the employees eligible to vote in such election have voted to rescind the authority of such labor organization to make such an agreement: Provided further, That no employer shall justify any discrimination against an employee for nonmembership in a labor organization (A) if he has reasonable grounds for believing that such membership was not available to the employee on the same terms and conditions generally applicable to other members, or (B) if he has reasonable grounds for believing that membership was denied or terminated for reasons other than the failure of the employee to tender the periodic dues and the initiation fees uniformly required as a condition of acquiring or retaining membership;

(4) to discharge or otherwise discriminate against an employee because he has filed charges or given testimony under this Act [subchapter];

(5) to refuse to bargain collectively with the representatives of his employees, subject to the provisions of section 9(a) [section 159(a) of this title].

(b) [Unfair labor practices by labor organization] It shall be an unfair labor practice for a labor organization or its agents—

(1) to restrain or coerce (A) employees in the exercise of the rights guaranteed in section 7 [section 157 of this title]: Provided, That this paragraph shall not impair the right of a labor organization to prescribe its own rules with respect to the acquisition or retention of membership therein; or (B) an employer in the selection of his representatives for

the purposes of collective bargaining or the adjustment of grievances;

(2) to cause or attempt to cause an employer to discriminate against an employee in violation of subsection (a)(3) [of subsection (a)(3) of this section] or to discriminate against an employee with respect to whom membership in such organization has been denied or terminated on some ground other than his failure to tender the periodic dues and the initiation fees uniformly required as a condition of acquiring or retaining membership;

(3) to refuse to bargain collectively with an employer, provided it is the representative of his employees subject to the provisions of section 9(a) [section 159(a) of this title];

(4)(i) to engage in, or to induce or encourage any individual employed by any person engaged in commerce or in an industry affecting commerce to engage in, a strike or a refusal in the course of his employment to use, manufacture, process, transport, or otherwise handle or work on any goods, articles, materials, or commodities or to perform any services; or (ii) to threaten, coerce, or restrain any person engaged in commerce or in an industry affecting commerce, where in either case an object thereof is—

(A) forcing or requiring any employer or self-employed person to join any labor or employer organization or to enter into any agreement which is prohibited by section 8(e) [subsection (e) of this section];

(B) forcing or requiring any person to cease using, selling, handling, transporting, or otherwise dealing in the products of any other producer, processor, or manufacturer, or to cease doing business with any other person, or forcing or requiring any other employer to recognize or bargain with a labor organization as the representative of his employees unless such labor organization has been certified as the representative of such employees under the provisions of section 9 [section 159 of this title]: Provided, That nothing contained in this clause (B) shall be construed to make unlawful, where not otherwise unlawful, any primary strike or primary picketing;

(C) forcing or requiring any employer to recognize or bargain with a particular labor organization as the representative of his employees if another labor organization has been certified as the representative of such employees under the provisions of section 9 [section 159 of this title];

(D) forcing or requiring any employer to assign particular work to employees in a particular labor organization or in a particular trade,

craft, or class rather than to employees in another labor organization or in another trade, craft, or class, unless such employer is failing to conform to an order or certification of the Board determining the bargaining representative for employees performing such work:
Provided, That nothing contained in this subsection (b) [this subsection] shall be construed to make unlawful a refusal by any person to enter upon the premises of any employer (other than his own employer), if the employees of such employer are engaged in a strike ratified or approved by a representative of such employees whom such employer is required to recognize under this Act [subchapter]: Provided further, That for the purposes of this paragraph (4) only, nothing contained in such paragraph shall be construed to prohibit publicity, other than picketing, for the purpose of truthfully advising the public, including consumers and members of a labor organization, that a product or products are produced by an employer with whom the labor organization has a primary dispute and are distributed by another employer, as long as such publicity does not have an effect of inducing any individual employed by any person other than the primary employer in the course of his employment to refuse to pick up, deliver, or transport any goods, or not to perform any services, at the establishment of the employer engaged in such distribution;

(5) to require of employees covered by an agreement authorized under subsection (a)(3) [of this section] the payment, as a condition precedent to becoming a member of such organization, of a fee in an amount which the Board finds excessive or discriminatory under all the circumstances. In making such a finding, the Board shall consider, among other relevant factors, the practices and customs of labor organizations in the particular industry, and the wages currently paid to the employees affected;

(6) to cause or attempt to cause an employer to pay or deliver or agree to pay or deliver any money or other thing of value, in the nature of an exaction, for services which are not performed or not to be performed; and

(7) to picket or cause to be picketed, or threaten to picket or cause to be picketed, any employer where an object thereof is forcing or requiring an employer to recognize or bargain with a labor organization as the representative of his employees, or forcing or requiring the employees of an employer to accept or select such labor organization as their collective-bargaining representative, unless such labor organization is currently certified as the representative of such employees:

(A) where the employer has lawfully recognized in accordance with this Act [subchapter] any other labor organization and a question concerning representation may not appropriately be raised under section 9(c) of this Act [section 159(c) of this title],

(B) where within the preceding twelve months a valid election under section 9(c) of this Act [section 159(c) of this title] has been conducted, or

(C) where such picketing has been conducted without a petition under section 9(c) [section 159(c) of this title] being filed within a reasonable period of time not to exceed thirty days from the commencement of such picketing: Provided, That when such a petition has been filed the Board shall forthwith, without regard to the provisions of section 9(c)(1) [section 159(c)(1) of this title] or the absence of a showing of a substantial interest on the part of the labor organization, direct an election in such unit as the Board finds to be appropriate and shall certify the results thereof: Provided further, That nothing in this subparagraph (C) shall be construed to prohibit any picketing or other publicity for the purpose of truthfully advising the public (including consumers) that an employer does not employ members of, or have a contract with, a labor organization, unless an effect of such picketing is to induce any individual employed by any other person in the course of his employment, not to pick up, deliver or transport any goods or not to perform any services. Nothing in this paragraph (7) shall be construed to permit any act which would otherwise be an unfair labor practice under this section 8(b) [this subsection].

(c) [Expression of views without threat of reprisal or force or promise of benefit] The expressing of any views, argument, or opinion, or the dissemination thereof, whether in written, printed, graphic, or visual form, shall not constitute or be evidence of an unfair labor practice under any of the provisions of this Act [subchapter], if such expression contains no threat of reprisal or force or promise of benefit.

(d) [Obligation to bargain collectively] For the purposes of this section, to bargain collectively is the performance of the mutual obligation of the employer and the representative of the employees to meet at reasonable times and confer in good faith with respect to wages, hours, and other terms and conditions of employment, or the negotiation of an agreement or any question arising thereunder, and the execution of a written contract incorporating any agreement reached if requested by either party, but such obligation does not compel either party to agree to a proposal or require the making of a concession: Provided, That where there is in effect a collective-bargaining contract covering employees in an industry affecting commerce, the duty to bargain collectively shall also mean that no party to such contract shall terminate or modify such contract, unless the party desiring such termination or modification—

(1) serves a written notice upon the other party to the contract of the proposed termination or modification sixty days prior to the expiration date thereof, or in the event such contract contains no expiration date, sixty days prior to the time it is proposed to make such termination or modification;

(2) offers to meet and confer with the other party for the purpose of negotiating a new contract or a contract containing the proposed modifications;

(3) notifies the Federal Mediation and Conciliation Service within thirty days after such notice of the existence of a dispute, and simultaneously therewith notifies any State or Territorial agency established to mediate and conciliate disputes within the State or Territory where the dispute occurred, provided no agreement has been reached by that time; and

(4) continues in full force and effect, without resorting to strike or lockout, all the terms and conditions of the existing contract for a period of sixty days after such notice is given or until the expiration date of such contract, whichever occurs later:

The duties imposed upon employers, employees, and labor organizations by paragraphs (2), (3), and (4) [paragraphs (2) to (4) of this subsection] shall become inapplicable upon an intervening certification of the Board, under which the labor organization or individual, which is a party to the contract, has been superseded as or ceased to be the representative of the employees subject to the provisions of section 9(a) [section 159(a) of this title], and the duties so imposed shall not be construed as requiring either party to discuss or agree to any modification of the terms and conditions contained in a contract for a fixed period, if such modification is to become effective before such terms and conditions can be reopened under the provisions of the contract. Any employee who engages in a strike within any notice period specified in this subsection, or who engages in any strike within the appropriate period specified in subsection (g) of this section, shall lose his status as an employee of the employer engaged in the particular labor dispute, for the purposes of sections 8, 9, and 10 of this Act [sections 158, 159, and 160 of this title], but such loss of status for such employee shall terminate if and when he is reemployed by such employer. Whenever the collective bargaining involves employees of a health care institution, the provisions of this section 8(d) [this sub-section] shall be modified as follows:

(A) The notice of section 8(d)(1) [paragraph (1) of this subsection] shall be ninety days; the notice of section 8(d)(3) [paragraph (3) of this subsection] shall be sixty days; and the contract period of section 8(d)(4) [paragraph (4) of this subsection] shall be ninety days.

(B) Where the bargaining is for an initial agreement following certification or recognition, at least thirty days' notice of the existence of a dispute shall be given by the labor organization to the agencies set forth in section 8(d)(3) [in paragraph (3) of this subsection].

(C) After notice is given to the Federal Mediation and Conciliation Service under either clause (A) or (B) of this sentence, the Service shall promptly communicate with the parties and use its best efforts, by mediation and conciliation, to bring them to agreement. The parties shall participate fully and promptly in such meetings as may be undertaken by the Service for the purpose of aiding in a settlement of the dispute.

[Pub. L. 93–360, July 26, 1974, 88 Stat. 395, amended the last sentence of Sec. 8(d) by striking the words "the sixty-day" and inserting the words "any notice" and by inserting before the words "shall lose" the phrase, "or who engages in any strike within the appropriate period specified in subsection (g) of this section." It also amended the end of paragraph Sec. 8(d) by adding a new sentence "Whenever the collective bargaining . . . aiding in a settlement of the dispute."]

(e) [Enforceability of contract or agreement to boycott any other employer; exception] It shall be an unfair labor practice for any labor organization and any employer to enter into any contract or agreement, express or implied, whereby such employer ceases or refrains or agrees to cease or refrain from handling, using, selling, transporting, or otherwise dealing in any of the products of any other employer, or cease doing business with any other person, and any contract or agreement entered into heretofore or hereafter containing such an agreement shall be to such extent unenforceable and void: Provided, That nothing in this subsection (e) [this subsection] shall apply to an agreement between a labor organization and an employer in the construction industry relating to the contracting or subcontracting of work to be done at the site of the construction, alteration, painting, or repair of a building, structure, or other work: Provided further, That for the purposes of this subsection (e) and section 8(b)(4)(B)[this subsection and subsection (b)(4)(B) of this section] the terms "any employer," "any person engaged in commerce or an industry affecting commerce," and "any person" when used in relation to the terms "any other producer, processor, or manufacturer," "any other employer," or "any other person" shall not include persons in the relation of a jobber, manufacturer, contractor, or subcontractor working on the goods or premises of the jobber or manufacturer or performing parts of an integrated process of production in the apparel and clothing industry: Provided further, That nothing in this Act [subchapter] shall prohibit the enforcement of any agreement which is within the foregoing exception.

(f) [Agreements covering employees in the building and construction industry] It shall not be an unfair labor practice under subsections (a) and (b) of this section for an employer engaged primarily in the building and construction industry to make an agreement covering employees engaged (or who, upon their employment, will be engaged) in the building and construction industry with a labor organization of which building and construction employees are members (not established, maintained, or assisted by any action defined in section 8(a) of this Act [subsection (a) of this section] as an unfair labor practice) because (1) the majority status of such labor organization has not been established under the provisions of section 9 of this Act [section 159 of this title] prior to the making of such agreement, or (2) such agreement requires as a condition of employment, membership in such labor organization after the seventh day following the beginning of such employment or the effective date of the agreement, whichever is later, or (3) such agreement requires the employer to notify such labor organization of opportunities for employment with such employer, or gives such labor organization an opportunity to refer qualified applicants for such employment, or (4) such agreement specifies minimum training or experience qualifications for employment or provides for priority in opportunities for employment based upon length of service with such employer, in the industry or in the particular geographical area: Provided, That nothing in this subsection shall set aside the final proviso to section 8(a)(3) of this Act [subsection (a)(3) of this section]: Provided further, That any agreement which would be invalid, but for clause (1) of this subsection, shall not be a bar to a petition filed pursuant to section 9(c) or 9(e) [section 159(c) or 159(e) of this title].

(g) [Notification of intention to strike or picket at any health care institution] A labor organization before engaging in any strike, picketing, or other concerted refusal to work at any health care institution shall, not less than ten days prior to such action, notify the institution in writing and the Federal Mediation and Conciliation Service of that intention, except that in the case of bargaining for an initial agreement following certification or recognition the notice required by this subsection shall not be given until the expiration of the period specified in clause (B) of the last sentence of section 8(d) of this Act [subsection (d) of this section]. The notice shall state the date and time that such action will commence. The notice, once given, may be extended by the written agreement of both parties.

[Pub. L. 93–360, July 26, 1974, 88 Stat. 396, added subsec. (g).]

REPRESENTATIVES AND ELECTIONS

Sec. 9 [§ 159.] (a) [Exclusive representatives; employees' adjustment of grievances directly with employer] Representatives designated or selected for the purposes of collective bargaining by the majority of the employees in a unit appropriate for such purposes, shall be the exclusive representatives of all the employees in such unit for the purposes of collective bargaining in respect to rates of pay, wages, hours of employment, or other conditions of employment: Provided, That any individual employee or a group of employees shall have the right at any time to present grievances to their employer and to have such grievances adjusted, without the intervention of the bargaining representative, as long as the adjustment is not inconsistent with the terms of a collective-bargaining contract or agreement then in effect: Provided further, That the bargaining representative has been given opportunity to be present at such adjustment.

(b) [Determination of bargaining unit by Board] The Board shall decide in each case whether, in order to assure to employees the fullest freedom in exercising the rights guaranteed by this Act [subchapter], the unit appropriate for the purposes of collective bargaining shall be the employer unit, craft unit, plant unit, or subdivision thereof: Provided, That the Board shall not (1) decide that any unit is appropriate for such purposes if such unit includes both professional employees and employees who are not professional employees unless a majority of such professional employees vote for inclusion in such unit; or (2) decide that any craft unit is inappropriate for such purposes on the ground that a different unit has been established by a prior Board determination, unless a majority of the employees in the proposed craft unit votes against separate representation or (3) decide that any unit is appropriate for such purposes if it includes, together with other employees, any individual employed as a guard to enforce against employees and other persons rules to protect property of the employer or to protect the safety of persons on the employer's premises; but no labor organization shall be certified as the representative of employees in a bargaining unit of guards if such organization admits to membership, or is affiliated directly or indirectly with an organization which admits to membership, employees other than guards.

(c) [Hearings on questions affecting commerce; rules and regulations] (1) Whenever a petition shall have been filed, in accordance with such regulations as may be prescribed by the Board—

(A) by an employee or group of employees or any individual or labor organization acting in their behalf alleging that a substantial number of employees (i) wish to be represented for collective bargaining and that their employer declines to recognize their representative as the representative defined in section 9(a) [subsection (a) of this section], or (ii) assert that the individual or labor organization, which has been certified or is being currently recognized by their employer as the bargaining representative, is no longer a representative as defined in section 9(a) [subsection (a) of this section]; or

(B) by an employer, alleging that one or more individuals or labor organizations have presented to him a claim to be recognized as the representative defined in section 9(a) [subsection (a) of this section]; the Board shall investigate such petition and if it has reasonable cause to believe that a question of representation affecting commerce exists shall provide for an appropriate hearing upon due notice. Such hearing may be conducted by an officer or employee of the regional office, who shall not make any recommendations with respect thereto. If the Board finds upon the record of such hearing that such a question of representation exists, it shall direct an election by secret ballot and shall certify the results thereof.

(2) In determining whether or not a question of representation affecting commerce exists, the same regulations and rules of decision shall apply irrespective of the identity of the persons filing the petition or the kind of relief sought and in no case shall the Board deny a labor organization a place on the ballot by reason of an order with respect to such labor organization or its predecessor not issued in conformity with section 10(c) [section 160(c) of this title].

(3) No election shall be directed in any bargaining unit or any subdivision within which, in the preceding twelve-month period, a valid election shall have been held. Employees engaged in an economic strike who are not entitled to reinstatement shall be eligible to vote under such regulations as the Board shall find are consistent with the purposes and provi-

sions of this Act [subchapter] in any election conducted within twelve months after the commencement of the strike. In any election where none of the choices on the ballot receives a majority, a runoff shall be conducted, the ballot providing for a selection between the two choices receiving the largest and second largest number of valid votes cast in the election.

(4) Nothing in this section shall be construed to prohibit the waiving of hearings by stipulation for the purpose of a consent election in conformity with regulations and rules of decision of the Board.

(5) In determining whether a unit is appropriate for the purposes specified in subsection (b) [of this section] the extent to which the employees have organized shall not be controlling.

(d) [Petition for enforcement or review; transcript] Whenever an order of the Board made pursuant to section 10(c) [section 160(c) of this title] is based in whole or in part upon facts certified following an investigation pursuant to subsection (c) of this section and there is a petition for the enforcement or review of such order, such certification and the record of such investigation shall be included in the transcript of the entire record required to be filed under section 10(e) or 10(f) [subsection (e) or (f) of section 160 of this title], and thereupon the decree of the court enforcing, modifying, or setting aside in whole or in part the order of the Board shall be made and entered upon the pleadings, testimony, and proceedings set forth in such transcript.

(e) [Secret ballot; limitation of elections] (1) Upon the filing with the Board, by 30 per centum or more of the employees in a bargaining unit covered by an agreement between their employer and labor organization made pursuant to section 8(a)(3) [section 158(a)(3) of this title], of a petition alleging they desire that such authorization be rescinded, the Board shall take a secret ballot of the employees in such unit and certify the results thereof to such labor organization and to the employer.
(2) No election shall be conducted pursuant to this subsection in any bargaining unit or any subdivision within which, in the preceding twelve-month period, a valid election shall have been held.

PREVENTION OF UNFAIR LABOR PRACTICES
Sec. 10. [§ 160.] (a) [Powers of Board generally] The Board is empowered, as hereinafter provided, to prevent any person from engaging in any unfair labor practice (listed in section 8 [section 158 of this title]) affecting commerce. This power shall not be affected by any other means of adjustment or prevention that has been or may be established by agree

ment, law, or otherwise: Provided, That the Board is empowered by agreement with any agency of any State or Territory to cede to such agency jurisdiction over any cases in any industry (other than mining, manufacturing, communications, and transportation except where predominately local in character) even though such cases may involve labor disputes affecting commerce, unless the provision of the State or Territorial statute applicable to the determination of such cases by such agency is inconsistent with the corresponding provision of this Act [subchapter] or has received a construction inconsistent therewith.

(b) [Complaint and notice of hearing; six-month limitation; answer; court rules of evidence inapplicable] Whenever it is charged that any person has engaged in or is engaging in any such unfair labor practice, the Board, or any agent or agency designated by the Board for such purposes, shall have power to issue and cause to be served upon such person a complaint stating the charges in that respect, and containing a notice of hearing before the Board or a member thereof, or before a designated agent or agency, at a place therein fixed, not less than five days after the serving of said complaint: Provided, That no complaint shall issue based upon any unfair labor practice occurring more than six months prior to the filing of the charge with the Board and the service of a copy thereof upon the person against whom such charge is made, unless the person aggrieved thereby was prevented from filing such charge by reason of service in the armed forces, in which event the six-month period shall be computed from the day of his discharge. Any such complaint may be amended by the member, agent, or agency conducting the hearing or the Board in its discretion at any time prior to the issuance of an order based thereon. The person so complained of shall have the right to file an answer to the original or amended complaint and to appear in person or otherwise and give testimony at the place and time fixed in the complaint. In the discretion of the member, agent, or agency conducting the hearing or the Board, any other person may be allowed to intervene in the said proceeding and to present testimony. Any such proceeding shall, so far as practicable, be conducted in accordance with the rules of evidence applicable in the district courts of the United States under the rules of civil procedure for the district courts of the United States, adopted by the Supreme Court of the United States pursuant to section 2072 of title 28, United States Code [section 2072 of title 28].

(c) [Reduction of testimony to writing; findings and orders of Board] The testimony taken by such member, agent, or agency, or the

Board shall be reduced to writing and filed with the Board. Thereafter, in its discretion, the Board upon notice may take further testimony or hear argument. If upon the preponderance of the testimony taken the Board shall be of the opinion that any person named in the complaint has engaged in or is engaging in any such unfair labor practice, then the Board shall state its findings of fact and shall issue and cause to be served on such person an order requiring such person to cease and desist from such unfair labor practice, and to take such affirmative action including reinstatement of employees with or without backpay, as will effectuate the policies of this Act [subchapter]: Provided, That where an order directs reinstatement of an employee, backpay may be required of the employer or labor organization, as the case may be, responsible for the discrimination suffered by him: And provided further, That in determining whether a complaint shall issue alleging a violation of section 8(a)(1) or section 8(a)(2) [subsection(a)(1) or (a)(2) of section 158 of this title], and in deciding such cases, the same regulations and rules of decision shall apply irrespective of whether or not the labor organization affected is affiliated with a labor organization national or international in scope. Such order may further require such person to make reports from time to time showing the extent to which it has complied with the order. If upon the preponderance of the testimony taken the Board shall not be of the opinion that the person named in the complaint has engaged in or is engaging in any such unfair labor practice, then the Board shall state its findings of fact and shall issue an order dismissing the said complaint. No order of the Board shall require the reinstatement of any individual as an employee who has been suspended or discharged, or the payment to him of any backpay, if such individual was suspended or discharged for cause. In case the evidence is presented before a member of the Board, or before an administrative law judge or judges thereof, such member, or such judge or judges, as the case may be, shall issue and cause to be served on the parties to the proceeding a proposed report, together with a recommended order, which shall be filed with the Board, and if no exceptions are filed within twenty days after service thereof upon such parties, or within such further period as the Board may authorize, such recommended order shall become the order of the Board and become affective as therein prescribed.

[The title "administrative law judge" was adopted in 5 U.S.C. § 3105.]

(d) [Modification of findings or orders prior to filing record in court] Until the record in a case shall have been filed in a court, as hereinafter provided, the Board may at any time, upon reasonable notice and in such manner as it shall deem proper, modify or set aside, in whole or in part, any finding or order made or issued by it.

(e) [Petition to court for enforcement of order; proceedings; review of judgment] The Board shall have power to petition any court of appeals of the United States, or if all the courts of appeals to which application may be made are in vacation, any district court of the United States, within any circuit or district, respectively, wherein the unfair labor practice in question occurred or wherein such person resides or transacts business, for the enforcement of such order and for appropriate temporary relief or restraining order, and shall file in the court the record in the proceeding,as provided in section 2112 of title 28, United States Code [section 2112 of title 28]. Upon the filing of such petition, the court shall cause notice thereof to be served upon such person, and thereupon shall have jurisdiction of the proceeding and of the question determined therein, and shall have power to grant such temporary relief or restraining order as it deems just and proper, and to make and enter a decree enforcing, modifying and enforcing as so modified, or setting aside in whole or in part the order of the Board. No objection that has not been urged before the Board, its member, agent, or agency, shall be considered by the court, unless the failure or neglect to urge such objection shall be excused because of extraordinary circumstances. The findings of the Board with respect to questions of fact if supported by substantial evidence on the record considered as a whole shall be conclusive. If either party shall apply to the court for leave to adduce additional evidence and shall show to the satisfaction of the court that such additional evidence is material and that there were reasonable grounds for the failure to adduce such evidence in the hearing before the Board, its member, agent, or agency, the court may order such additional evidence to be taken before the Board, its member, agent, or agency, and to be made a part of the record. The Board may modify its findings as to the facts, or make new findings, by reason of additional evidence so taken and filed, and it shall file such modified or new findings, which findings with respect to question of fact if supported by substantial evidence on the record considered as a whole shall be conclusive, and shall file its recommendations, if any, for the modification or setting aside of its original order. Upon the filing of the record with it the jurisdiction of the court shall be exclusive and its judgment and decree shall be final, except that the same shall be subject to review by the appropriate United States court of appeals if application was made to the district court as hereinabove provided, and by the Supreme Court of the United States upon writ of certiorari or certification as provided in section 1254 of title 28.

(f) [Review of final order of Board on petition to court] Any person aggrieved by a final order of the Board granting or denying in whole or in part the relief sought may obtain a review of such order in any United States court of appeals in the circuit wherein the unfair labor practice in question was alleged to have been engaged in or wherein such person resides or transacts business, or in the United States Court of Appeals for the District of Columbia, by filing in such court a written petition praying that the order of the Board be modified or set aside. A copy of such petition shall be forthwith transmitted by the clerk of the court to the Board, and thereupon the aggrieved party shall file in the court the record in the proceeding, certified by the Board, as provided in section 2112 of title 28, United States Code [section 2112 of title 28]. Upon the filing of such petition, the court shall proceed in the same manner as in the case of an application by the Board under subsection (e) of this section, and shall have the same jurisdiction to grant to the Board such temporary relief or restraining order as it deems just and proper, and in like manner to make and enter a decree enforcing, modifying and enforcing as so modified, or setting aside in whole or in part the order of the Board; the findings of the Board with respect to questions of fact if supported by substantial evidence on the record considered as a whole shall in like manner be conclusive.

(g) [Institution of court proceedings as stay of Board's order] The commencement of proceedings under subsection (e) or (f) of this section shall not, unless specifically ordered by the court, operate as a stay of the Board's order.

(h) [Jurisdiction of courts unaffected by limitations prescribed in chapter 6 of this title] When granting appropriate temporary relief or a restraining order, or making and entering a decree enforcing, modifying and enforcing as so modified, or setting aside in whole or in part an order of the Board, as provided in this section, the jurisdiction of courts sitting in equity shall not be limited by sections 101 to 115 of title 29, United States Code [chapter 6 of this title] [known as the "Norris-LaGuardia Act"].

(i) Repealed.

(j) [Injunctions] The Board shall have power, upon issuance of a complaint as provided in subsection (b) [of this section] charging that any person has engaged in or is engaging in an unfair labor practice, to petition any United States district court, within any district wherein the unfair labor practice in question is alleged to have occurred or wherein such person resides or transacts business, for appropriate temporary relief or restraining order. Upon the filing of any such petition the court shall cause notice thereof to be served upon such person, and thereupon shall have jurisdiction to grant to the Board such temporary relief or restraining order as it deems just and proper.

(k) [Hearings on jurisdictional strikes] Whenever it is charged that any person has engaged in an unfair labor practice within the meaning of paragraph (4)(D) of section 8(b) [section 158(b) of this title], the Board is empowered and directed to hear and determine the dispute out of which such unfair labor practice shall have arisen, unless, within ten days after notice that such charge has been filed, the parties to such dispute submit to the Board satisfactory evidence that they have adjusted, or agreed upon methods for the voluntary adjustment of, the dispute. Upon compliance by the parties to the dispute with the decision of the Board or upon such voluntary adjustment of the dispute, such charge shall be dismissed.

(l) [Boycotts and strikes to force recognition of uncertified labor organizations; injunctions; notice; service of process] Whenever it is charged that any person has engaged in an unfair labor practice within the meaning of paragraph (4)(A), (B), or (C) of section 8(b) [section 158(b) of this title], or section 8(e) [section 158(e) of this title] or section 8(b)(7) [section 158(b)(7) of this title], the preliminary investigation of such charge shall be made forthwith and given priority over all other cases except cases of like character in the office where it is filed or to which it is referred. If, after such investigation, the officer or regional attorney to whom the matter may be referred has reasonable cause to believe such charge is true and that a complaint should issue, he shall, on behalf of the Board, petition any United States district court within any district where the unfair labor practice in question has occurred, is alleged to have occurred, or wherein such person resides or transacts business, for appropriate injunctive relief pending the final adjudication of the Board with respect to such matter. Upon the filing of any such petition the district court shall have jurisdiction to grant such injunctive relief or temporary restraining order as it deems just and proper, notwithstanding any other provision of law: Provided further, That no temporary restraining order shall be issued without notice unless a petition alleges that substantial and irreparable injury to the charging party will be unavoidable and such temporary restraining order shall be effective for no longer than five days and will become void at the expiration of such period: Provided further, That such officer or regional attorney shall not apply for any restraining order under section 8(b)(7) [section 158(b)(7) of this title] if a charge against the employer under section 8(a)(2) [section 158(a)(2) of this title] has been filed and after the preliminary investigation, he has reasonable cause to believe that such charge is true and that a complaint should issue. Upon filing of any such petition the courts shall cause notice thereof to be served upon any person involved in the charge and such person, including the charging party, shall be given an opportunity to appear by counsel and present any relevant testimony: Provided further, That for the purposes of this subsection district courts shall be deemed to have jurisdiction of a labor organization (1) in the district in which such organization maintains its principal office, or (2) in any district in which its duly authorized officers or agents are engaged in promoting or protecting the interests of employee members. The service of legal process upon such officer or agent shall constitute service upon the labor organization and make such organization a party to the suit. In situations where such relief is appropriate the procedure specified herein shall apply to charges with respect to section 8(b)(4)(D) [section 158(b)(4)(D) of this title].

(m) [Priority of cases] Whenever it is charged that any person has engaged in an unfair labor practice within the meaning of subsection (a)(3) or (b)(2) of section 8 [section 158 of this title], such charge shall be given priority over all other cases except cases of like character in the office where it is filed or to which it is referred and cases given priority under subsection (l) [of this section].

INVESTIGATORY POWERS

Sec. 11. [§ 161.] For the purpose of all hearings and investigations, which, in the opinion of the Board, are necessary and proper for the exercise of the powers vested in it by section 9 and section 10 [sections 159 and 160 of this title]—

(1) [Documentary evidence; summoning witnesses and taking testimony]
The Board, or its duly authorized agents or agencies, shall at all reasonable times have access to, for the purpose of examination, and the right to copy any evidence of any person being investigated or proceeded against that relates to any matter under investigation or in ques-

tion. The Board, or any member thereof, shall upon application of any party to such proceedings, forthwith issue to such party subpoenas requiring the attendance and testimony of witnesses or the production of any evidence in such proceeding or investigation requested in such application. Within five days after the service of a subpoena on any person requiring the production of any evidence in his possession or under his control, such person may petition the Board to revoke, and the Board shall revoke, such subpoena if in its opinion the evidence whose production is required does not relate to any matter under investigation, or any matter in question in such proceedings, or if in its opinion such subpoena does not describe with sufficient particularity the evidence whose production is required. Any member of the Board, or any agent or agency designated by the Board for such purposes, may administer oaths and affirmations, examine witnesses, and receive evidence. Such attendance of witnesses and the production of such evidence may be required from any place in the United States or any Territory or possession thereof, at any designated place of hearing.

(2) [Court aid in compelling production of evidence and attendance of witnesses] In case on contumacy or refusal to obey a subpoena issued to any person, any United States district court or the United States courts of any Territory or possession, within the jurisdiction of which the inquiry is carried on or within the jurisdiction of which said person guilty of contumacy or refusal to obey is found or resides or transacts business, upon application by the Board shall have jurisdiction to issue to such person an order requiring such person to appear before the Board, its member, agent, or agency, there to produce evidence if so ordered, or there to give testimony touching the matter under investigation or in question; and any failure to obey such order of the court may be punished by said court as a contempt thereof.

(3) Repealed.

[Immunity of witnesses. See 18 U.S.C. § 6001 et seq.]

(4) [Process, service, and return; fees of witnesses] Complaints, orders and other process and papers of the Board, its member, agent, or agency, may be served either personally or by registered or certified mail or by telegraph or by leaving a copy thereof at the principal office or place of business of the person required to be served. The verified return by the individual so serving the same setting forth the manner of such service shall be proof of the same, and the return post office receipt or telegraph receipt therefor when registered or certified and mailed or when telegraphed as aforesaid shall be proof of service of the same. Witnesses summoned before the Board, its member, agent, or agency, shall be paid the same fees and mileage that are paid witnesses in the courts of the United States, and witnesses whose depositions are taken and the persons taking the same shall severally be entitled to the same fees as are paid for like services in the courts of the United States.

(5) **[Process, where served]** All process of any court to which application may be made under this Act [subchapter] may be served in the judicial district wherein the defendant or other person required to be served resides or may be found.

(6) **[Information and assistance from departments]** The several departments and agencies of the Government, when directed by the President, shall furnish the Board, upon its request, all records, papers, and information in their possession relating to any matter before the Board.

Sec. 12. [§ 162. Offenses and penalties] Any person who shall willfully resist, prevent, impede, or interfere with any member of the Board or any of its agents or agencies in the performance of duties pursuant to this Act [subchapter] shall be punished by a fine of not more than $5,000 or by imprisonment for not more than one year, or both.

LIMITATIONS

Sec. 13. [§ 163. Right to strike preserved] Nothing in this Act [subchapter], except as specifically provided for herein, shall be construed so as either to interfere with or impede or diminish in any way the right to strike or to affect the limitations or qualifications on that right.

Sec. 14. [§ 164. Construction of provisions] (a) [Supervisors as union members] Nothing herein shall prohibit any individual employed as a supervisor from becoming or remaining a member of a labor organization, but no employer subject to this Act [subchapter] shall be compelled to deem individuals defined herein as supervisors as employees for the purpose of any law, either national or local, relating to collective bargaining.

(b) **[Agreements requiring union membership in violation of State law]** Nothing in this Act [subchapter] shall be construed as authorizing the execution or application of agreements requiring membership in a labor organization as a condition of employment in any State or Territory in which such execution or application is prohibited by State or Territorial law.

(c) [Power of Board to decline jurisdiction of labor disputes; assertion of jurisdiction by State and Territorial courts] (1) The Board, in its discretion, may, by rule of decision or by published rules adopted pursuant to the Administrative Procedure Act [to subchapter II of chapter 5 of title 5], decline to assert jurisdiction over any labor dispute involving any class or category of employers, where, in the opinion of the Board, the effect of such labor dispute on commerce is not sufficiently substantial to warrant the exercise of its jurisdiction: Provided, That the Board shall not decline to assert jurisdiction over any labor dispute over which it would assert jurisdiction under the standards prevailing upon August 1, 1959.

(2) Nothing in this Act [subchapter] shall be deemed to prevent or bar any agency or the courts of any State or Territory (including the Commonwealth of Puerto Rico, Guam, and the Virgin Islands) from assuming and asserting jurisdiction over labor disputes over which the Board declines, pursuant to paragraph (1) of this subsection, to assert jurisdiction.

Sec. 15. [§ 165.] Omitted.
[Reference to repealed provisions of bankruptcy statute.]

Sec. 16. [§ 166. Separability of provisions] If any provision of this Act [subchapter], or the application of such provision to any person or circumstances, shall be held invalid, the remainder of this Act [subchapter], or the application of such provision to persons or circumstances other than those as to which it is held invalid, shall not be affected thereby.

Sec. 17. [§ 167. Short title] This Act [subchapter] may be cited as the "National Labor Relations Act."

Sec. 18. [§ 168.] Omitted.
[Reference to former sec. 9(f), (g), and (h).]

INDIVIDUALS WITH RELIGIOUS CONVICTIONS

Sec. 19. [§ 169.] Any employee who is a member of and adheres to established and traditional tenets or teachings of a bona fide religion, body, or sect which has historically held conscientious objections to joining or financially supporting labor organizations shall not be required to join or financially support any labor organization as a condition of employment; except that such employee may be required in a contract between such employee's employer and a labor organization in lieu of periodic dues and initiation fees, to pay sums equal to such dues and initiation fees to a nonreligious, nonlabor organization charitable fund exempt from taxation under section 501(c)(3) of title 26 of the Internal Revenue Code [section 501(c)(3) of title 26], chosen by such employee from a list of at least three such funds, designated in such contract or if the contract fails to designate such funds, then to any such fund chosen by the employee.

If such employee who holds conscientious objections pursuant to this section requests the labor organization to use the grievance-arbitration procedure on the employee's behalf, the labor organization is authorized to charge the employee for the reasonable cost of using such procedure.

[Sec. added, Pub. L. 93–360, July 26, 1974, 88 Stat. 397, and amended, Pub. L. 96–593, Dec. 24, 1980, 94 Stat. 3452.]

A guide to basic law and procedures under the

NATIONAL LABOR RELATIONS ACT

This is a revised edition of a pamphlet originally issued in 1962. It provides a basic framework for a better understanding of the National Labor Relations Act and its administration.

A special chart that arranges systematically the types of cases in which an employer or a labor organization may be involved under the Act, including both unfair labor practice cases and representation election proceedings, appears in the booklet.

U.S. GOVERNMENT PRINTING OFFICE

WASHINGTON, D.C.   1997

For sale by the Superintendent of Documents, U.S. Government Printing Office
Washington, D.C. 20402

A guide to basic law and procedures

under the

NATIONAL LABOR RELATIONS ACT

Prepared in the Office of the General Counsel
NATIONAL LABOR RELATIONS BOARD

Table of Contents

Foreword

The Regional Offices of the National Labor Relations Board have found that, more than six decades after its enactment, there is still a lack of basic information about the National Labor Relations Act. Staff members have expressed a need for a simply stated explanation of the Act to which anyone could be referred for guidance. To meet this demand, the basic law under the Act has been set forth in this pamphlet in a nontechnical way so that those who may be affected by it can better understand what their rights and obligations are.

Any effort to state basic principles of law in a simple way is a challenging and unenviable task. This is especially true about labor law, a relatively complex field of law. Anyone reading this booklet must bear in mind several cautions.

First, it must be emphasized that the Office of the General Counsel does not issue advisory opinions and this material cannot be considered as an official statement of law. It represents the view of the Office of the General Counsel as of the date of publication only. It is important to note that the law changes and advances. In fact, it is the duty of the Agency to keep its decisions abreast of changing conditions, yet within the basic statute. Accordingly, with the passage of time no one can rely on these statements as absolute until and unless a check has been made to see whether the law may have been changed substantially or specifically.

Furthermore, these are broad general principles only and countless subprinciples and detailed rules are not included. Only by evaluation of specific fact situations in the light of current principles and with the aid of expert advice would a person be in a position to know definitely where the proposed conduct may fit under the statute. No basic primer or text can constitute legal advice in particular fact situations. This effort to improve basic education about the statute should not be considered as such. Many areas of the statute remain untested. Legal advisers and other experts can find the total body of "Board law" reported in other Agency publications.

One other caution: This material does not deal with questions arising under other labor laws, but only with the National Labor Relations Act. Laws administered by other Government agencies, such as the Labor-Management Reporting and Disclosure Act of 1959, the Employee Retirement Income Security Act, the Occupational Safety and Health Act, the Railway Labor Act, the Fair Labor Standards, Walsh-Healey and Davis-Bacon Acts, Title VII of the Civil Rights Act of 1964, Americans with Disabilities Act, the Federal Mine Safety and Health Act, and the Veterans' Preference Act, are not treated herein.

Lastly, this material does not reflect the view of the National Labor Relations Board as the adjudicating agency that in the end will decide each case as it comes before it.

It is hoped that with this cautionary note this booklet may be helpful to those in need of a better basic understanding of the National Labor Relations Act.

Summary of the Act

A Guide to Basic Law and Procedures Under the National Labor Relations Act

It is in the national interest of the United States to maintain full production in its economy. Industrial strife among employees, employers, and labor organizations interferes with full production and is contrary to our national interest. Experience has shown that labor disputes can be lessened if the parties involved recognize the legitimate rights of each in their relations with one another. To establish these rights under law, Congress enacted the National Labor Relations Act. Its purpose is to define and protect the rights of employees and employers, to encourage collective bargaining, and to eliminate certain practices on the part of labor and management that are harmful to the general welfare.

Purpose of the Act

The National Labor Relations Act states and defines the rights of employees to organize and to bargain collectively with their employers through representatives of their own choosing or not to do so. To ensure that employees can freely choose their own representatives for the purpose of collective bargaining, or choose not to be represented, the Act establishes a procedure by which they can exercise their choice at a secret-ballot election conducted by the National Labor Relations Board. Further, to protect the rights of employees and employers, and to prevent labor disputes that would adversely affect the rights of the public, Congress has defined certain practices of employers and unions as unfair labor practices.

What the Act provides

The law is administered and enforced principally by the National Labor Relations Board and the General Counsel acting through 52 regional and other field offices located in major cities in various sections of the country. The General Counsel and the staff of the Regional Offices investigate and prosecute unfair labor practice cases and conduct elections to determine employee representatives. The five-member Board decides cases involving charges of unfair labor practices and determines representation election questions that come to it from the Regional Offices.

How the Act is enforced

The rights of employees, including the rights to self-organization and collective bargaining that are protected by Section 7 of the Act, are presented first in this guide. The Act's provisions concerning the requirements for union-security agreements are covered in the same section, which also includes a discussion of the right to strike and the right to picket. The obligations of collective bargaining and the Act's provisions for the selection of employee representatives are treated in the next section. Unfair labor practices of employers and of labor organizations are then presented in separate sections. The final section, entitled "How the Act Is Enforced," sets forth the organization of the NLRB; its authority and limitations; its procedures and powers

How this material is organized

1

in representation matters, in unfair labor practice cases, and in certain special proceedings under the Act; and the Act's provisions concerning enforcement of the Board's orders.

The Rights of Employees
The Section 7 Rights

The rights of employees are set forth principally in Section 7 of the Act, which provides as follows:

Sec. 7. Employees shall have the right to self-organization, to form, join, or assist labor organizations, to bargain collectively through representatives of their own choosing, and to engage in other concerted activities for the purpose of collective bargaining or other mutual aid or protection, and shall also have the right to refrain from any or all of such activities except to the extent that such right may be affected by an agreement requiring membership in a labor organization as a condition of employment as authorized in section 8(a)(3).

Examples of the rights protected by this section are the following:

Examples of Section 7 rights

- Forming or attempting to form a union among the employees of a company.
- Joining a union whether the union is recognized by the employer or not.
- Assisting a union to organize the employees of an employer.
- Going out on strike to secure better working conditions.
- Refraining from activity on behalf of a union.

Union Security

The Act permits, under certain conditions, a union and an employer to make an agreement, called a union-security agreement, that requires employees to make certain payments to the union in order to retain their jobs. A union-security agreement cannot require that applicants for employment be members of the union in order to be hired, and such an agreement cannot require employees to join or maintain membership in the union in order to retain their jobs. Under a union-security agreement, individuals choosing to be dues-paying nonmembers may be required, as may employees who actually join the union, to pay full initiation fees and dues within a certain period of time (a "grace period") after the collective-bargaining contract takes effect or after a new employee is hired. However, the most that can be required of nonmembers who inform the union that they object to the use of their payments for non-representational purposes is that they pay their share of the union's costs relating to representa-tional activities (such as collective bargaining, contract administration, and grievance adjustment).

Union-security agreements

The grace period, after which the union-security agreement becomes effective, cannot be less than 30 days except in the building and construction industry. The Act allows a shorter

2

grace period of 7 full days in the building and construction industry (Section 8 (f)). A union-security agreement that provides a shorter grace period than the law allows is invalid, and any employee discharged because he or she has not complied with such an agreement is entitled to reinstatement.

Under a union-security agreement, employees who have religious objections to becoming members of a union or to supporting a union financially may be exempt from paying union dues and initiation fees. These employees may, however, be required to make contributions to a nonreligious, nonlabor tax exempt organization instead of making payments to a union. Unions representing such employees may also charge them the reasonable cost of any grievances processed at the employees' request.

Requirements for union-security agreements

For a union-security agreement to be valid, it must meet all the following requirements:

1. The union must not have been assisted or controlled by the employer (see Section 8(a)(2) under "Unfair Labor Practices of Employers" on pp. 19–20).

2. The union must be the majority representative of the employees in the appropriate collective-bargaining unit covered by such agreement when made.

3. The union's authority to make such an agreement must not have been revoked within the previous 12 months by the employees in a Board election.

4. The agreement must provide for the appropriate grace period.

Prehire agreements in the construction industry

Section 8(f) of the Act allows an employer engaged primarily in the building and construction industry to sign a union-security agreement with a union without the union's having been designated as the representative of its employees as otherwise required by the Act. The agreement can be made before the employer has hired any employees for a project and will apply to them when they are hired. As noted above, however, the union-security provisions of a collective-bargaining contract in the building and construction industry may become effective with respect to new employees after 7 full days. If the agreement is made while employees are on the job, it must allow existing employees the same 7-day grace period to comply. As with any other union-security agreement, the union involved must be free from employer assistance or control.

Collective-bargaining contracts in the building and construction industry can include, as stated in Section 8(f), the following additional provisions:

1. A requirement that the employer notify the union concerning job openings.

2. A provision that gives the union an opportunity to refer qualified applicants for such jobs.

3. Job qualification standards based on training or experience.

4. A provision for priority in hiring based on length of service with the employer, in the industry, or in the particular geographic area.

These four hiring provisions may lawfully be included in collective-bargaining contracts which cover employees in other industries as well.

Finally, pursuant to Section 14(b) of the Act, individual States may prohibit, and some States have prohibited, certain forms of union-security agreements.

Section 7 of the Act states in part, "Employees shall have the right . . . to engage in other concerted activities for the purpose of collective bargaining or other mutual aid or protection." Strikes are included among the concerted activities protected for employees by this section. Section 13 also concerns the right to strike. It reads as follows:

Nothing in this Act, except as specifically provided for herein, shall be construed so as either to interfere with or impede or diminish in any way the right to strike, or to affect the limitations or qualifications on that right.

It is clear from a reading of these two provisions that: the law not only guarantees the right of employees to strike, but also places limitations and qualifications on the exercise of that right. See, for example, restrictions on strikes in health care institutions, page 41.

The lawfulness of a strike may depend on the object, or purpose, of the strike, on its timing, or on the conduct of the strikers. The object, or objects, of a strike and whether the objects are lawful are matters that are not always easy to determine. Such issues often have to be decided by the National Labor Relations Board. The consequences can be severe to striking employees and struck employers, involving as they do questions of reinstatement and back pay.

It must be emphasized that the following is only a brief outline. A detailed analysis of the law concerning strikes, and application of the law to all the factual situations that can arise in connection with strikes, is beyond the scope of this material. Employees and employers who anticipate being involved in strike action should proceed cautiously and on the basis of competent advice.

The Right to Strike

Lawful and unlawful strikes

4

Employees who strike for a lawful object fall into two classes "economic strikers" and "unfair labor practice strikers." Both classes continue as employees, but unfair labor practice strikers have greater rights of reinstatement to their jobs.

Strikes for a lawful object

If the object of a strike is to obtain from the employer some economic concession such as higher wages, shorter hours, or better working conditions, the striking employees are called economic strikers. They retain their status as employees and cannot be discharged, but they can be replaced by their employer. If the employer has hired bona fide permanent replacements who are filling the jobs of the economic strikers when the strikers apply unconditionally to go back to work, the strikers are not entitled to reinstatement at that time. However, if the strikers do not obtain regular and substantially equivalent employment, they are entitled to be recalled to jobs for which they are qualified when openings in such jobs occur if they, or their bargaining representative, have made an unconditional request for their reinstatement.

Economic strikers defined

Employees who strike to protest an unfair labor practice committed by their employer are called unfair labor practice strikers. Such strikers can be neither discharged nor permanently replaced. When the strike ends, unfair labor practice strikers, absent serious misconduct on their part, are entitled to have their jobs back even if employees hired to do their work have to be discharged.

Unfair labor practice strikers defined

If the Board finds that economic strikers or unfair labor practice strikers who have made an unconditional request for reinstatement have been unlawfully denied reinstatement by their employer, the Board may award such strikers back pay starting at the time they should have been reinstated.

A strike may be unlawful because an object, or purpose, of the strike is unlawful. A strike in support of a union unfair labor practice, or one that would cause an employer to commit an unfair labor practice, may be a strike for an unlawful object. For example, it is an unfair labor practice for an employer to discharge an employee for failure to make certain lawful payments to the union when there is no union-security agreement in effect (Section 8(a)(3)). A strike to compel an employer to do this would be a strike for an unlawful object and, therefore, an unlawful strike. Strikes of this nature will be discussed in connection with the various unfair labor practices in a later section of this guide.

Strikes unlawful because of purpose

Furthermore, Section 8(b)(4) of the Act prohibits strikes for certain objects even though the objects are not necessarily unlawful if achieved by other means. An example of this would be a strike to compel Employer A to cease doing business with Employer B. It is not unlawful for Employer A voluntarily to stop doing business with Employer B, nor is it unlawful for a union merely to request that it do so. It is, however, unlawful for the union to strike with an object of forcing the employer to do so. These points will be covered in more detail in the explanation of Section 8(b)(4).In any event, employees who participate in an unlawful strike may be discharged and are not entitled to reinstatement.

Strikes unlawful because of timing—Effect of no-strike contract

A strike that violates a no-strike provision of a contract is not protected by the Act, and the striking employees can be discharged or otherwise disciplined, unless the strike is called to protest certain kinds of unfair labor practices committed by the employer. It should be noted that not all refusals to work are considered strikes and thus violations of no-strike provisions. A walkout because of conditions abnormally dangerous to health, such as a defective ventilation system in a spray-painting shop, has been held not to violate a no-strike provision.

Same—Strikes at end of contract period

Section 8(d) provides that when either party desires to terminate or change an existing contract, it must comply with certain conditions. (See p. 8.) If these requirements are not met, a strike to terminate or change a contract is unlawful and participating strikers lose their status as employees of the employer engaged in the labor dispute. If the strike was caused by the unfair labor practice of the employer, however, the strikers are classified as unfair labor practice strikers and their status is not affected by failure to follow the required procedure.

Strikes unlawful because of misconduct of strikers

Strikers who engage in serious misconduct in the course of a strike may be refused reinstatement to their former jobs. This applies to both economic strikers and unfair labor practice strikers. Serious misconduct has been held to include, among other things, violence and threats of violence. The U.S. Supreme Court has ruled that a "sitdown" strike, when employees simply stay in the plant and refuse to work, thus depriving the owner of property, is not protected by the law. Examples of serious misconduct that could cause the employees involved to lose their right to reinstatement are:

• Strikers physically blocking persons from entering or leaving a struck plant.
• Strikers threatening violence against nonstriking employees.
• Strikers attacking management representatives.

The Right to Picket

Likewise the right to picket is subject to limitations and qualifications. As with the right to strike, picketing can be prohibited because of its object or its timing, or misconduct on the picket line. In addition, Section 8(b)(7) declares it to be an unfair labor practice for a union to picket for certain objects whether the picketing accompanies a strike or not. This will be covered in more detail in the section on union unfair labor practices.

Collective Bargaining and Representation of Employees

Collective Bargaining

Collective bargaining is one of the keystones of the Act. Section 1 of the Act declares that the policy of the United States is to be carried out "by encouraging the practice and procedure of collective bargaining and by protecting the exercise by workers of full freedom of association, self-organization, and designation of representatives of their own choosing, for the purpose of negotiating the terms and conditions of their employment or other mutual aid or protection."

Collective bargaining is defined in the Act. Section 8(d) requires an employer and the representative of its employees to meet at reasonable times, to confer in good faith about certain matters, and to put into writing any agreement reached if requested by either party. The parties must confer in good faith with respect to wages, hours, and other terms or conditions of employment, the negotiation of an agreement, or any question arising under an agreement.

Duty to bargain imposed on both employer and union

These obligations are imposed equally on the employer and the representative of its employees. It is an unfair labor practice for either party to refuse to bargain collectively with the other. The obligation does not, however, compel either party to agree to a proposal by the other, nor does it require either party to make a concession to the other.

Section 8(d) provides further that when a collective-bargaining agreement is in effect no party to the contract shall end or change the contract unless the party wishing to end or change it takes the following steps:

Bargaining steps to end or change a contract

1. The party must notify the other party to the contract in writing about the proposed termination or modification 60 days before the date on which the contract is scheduled to expire. If the contract is not scheduled to expire on any particular date, the notice in writing must be served 60 days before the time when it is proposed that the termination or modification take effect.

2. The party must offer to meet and confer with the other party for the purpose of negotiating a new contract or a contract containing the proposed changes.

3. The party must, within 30 days after the notice to the party, notify the Federal Mediation and Conciliation Service of the existence of a dispute if no agreement has been reached by that time. Said party must also notify at the same time any State or Territorial mediation or conciliation agency in the State or Territory where the dispute occurred.

4. The party must continue in full force and effect, without resorting to strike or lockout, all the terms and conditions of the existing contract until 60 days after the notice

to the other party was given or until the date the contract is scheduled to expire, whichever is later.

(In the case of a health care institution, the requirement in paragraphs 1 and 4 is 90 days, and in paragraph 3 is 60 days. In addition, there is a 30-day notice requirement to the agencies in paragraph 3 when a dispute arises in bargaining for an initial contract.)

The requirements of paragraphs 2, 3, and 4, above, cease to apply if the NLRB issues a certificate showing that the employees' representative who is a party to the contract has been replaced by a different representative or has been voted out by the employees. Neither party is required to discuss or agree to any change of the provisions of the contract if the other party proposes that the change become effective before the provision could be reopened according to the terms of the contract.

Examples of violations of Section required

As has been pointed out, any employee who engages in a strike within the notice period loses status as an employee of the struck employer. This loss of status ends, however, if and when that individual is reemployed by the same employer.

The Employee Representative

Section 9(a) provides that the employee representatives that have been "designated or selected for the purposes of collective bargaining by the majority of the employees in a unit appropriate for such purposes, shall be the exclusive representatives of all the employees in such unit for the purposes of collective bargaining."

What is an appropriate bargaining unit

A unit of employees is a group of two or more employees who share a community of interest and may reasonably be grouped together for purposes of collective bargaining. The determination of what is an appropriate unit for such purposes is, under the Act, left to the discretion of the NLRB. Section 9(b) states that the Board shall decide in each representation case whether, "in order to assure to employees the fullest freedom in exercising the rights guaranteed by this Act, the unit appropriate for the purposes of collective bargaining shall be the employer unit, craft unit, plant unit, or subdivision thereof."

This broad discretion is, however, limited by several other provisions of the Act. Section 9(b)(1) provides that the Board shall not approve as appropriate a unit that includes both professional and nonprofessional employees, unless a majority of the professional employees involved vote to be included in the mixed unit.

Section 9(b)(2) provides that the Board shall not hold a proposed craft unit to be inappropriate simply because a different unit was previously approved by the Board, unless a majority of the employees in the proposed craft unit vote against being represented separately.

Section 9(b)(3) prohibits the Board from including plant guards in the same unit with other employees. It also prohibits the Board from certifying a labor organization as the representative of a plant guard unit if the labor organization has members who are nonguard employees or if it is "affiliated directly or indirectly" with an organization that has members who are nonguard employees.

Generally, the appropriateness of a bargaining unit is determined on the basis of a community of interest of the employees involved. Those who have the same or substantially similar interests concerning wages, hours, and working conditions are grouped together in a bargaining unit. In determining whether a proposed unit is appropriate, the following factors are also considered:

1. Any history of collective bargaining.
2. The desires of the employees concerned.
3. The extent to which the employees are organized. Section 9(c)(5) forbids the Board from giving this factor controlling weight.

How the appropriateness of a unit is determined

Finally, with regard to units in the health care industry, the Board also is guided by Congress' concern about preventing disruptions in the delivery of health care services, and its directive to minimize the number of appropriate bargaining units.

A unit may cover the employees in one plant of an employer, or it may cover employees in two or more plants of the same employer. In some industries in which employers are grouped together in voluntary associations, a unit may include employees of two or more employers in any number of locations. It should be noted that a bargaining unit can include only persons who are "employees" within the meaning of the Act. The Act excludes certain individuals, such as agricultural laborers, independent contractors, supervisors, and persons in managerial positions, from the meaning of "employees." None of these individuals can be included in a bargaining unit established by the Board. In addition, the Board, as a matter of policy, excludes from bargaining units employees who act in a confidential capacity to an employer's labor relations officials.

Who can or cannot be included in a unit

Once an employee representative has been designated by a majority of the employees in an appropriate unit, the Act makes that representative the exclusive bargaining agent for all employees in the unit. As exclusive bargaining agent it has a duty to represent equally and fairly all employees in the unit without regard to their union membership or activities. Once a collective-bargaining representative has been designated or selected by its employees,

Duties of bargaining representative and employer

9

it is illegal for an employer to bargain with individual employees, with a group of employees, or with another employee representative.

Section 9(a) provides that any individual employee or a group of employees shall have the right at any time to present grievances to their employer and to have such grievances adjusted without the intervention of the bargaining representative provided:

1. The adjustment is not inconsistent with the terms of any collective-bargaining agreement then in effect.

2. The bargaining representative has been given the opportunity to be present at such Adjustment.

How a Bargaining Representative Is Selected

The Act requires that an employer bargain with the representative selected by its employees. The most common method by which employees can select a bargaining representative is a secret-ballot representation election conducted by the Board.

Petition for certification of representatives

The NLRB can conduct such an election only when a petition has been filed requesting one. A petition for certification of representatives can be filed by an employee or a group of employees or any individual or labor organization acting on their behalf, or it can be filed by an employer. If filed by or on behalf of employees, the petition must be supported by a substantial number of employees who wish to be represented for collective bargaining and must state that their employer declines to recognize their representative. If filed by an employer, the petition must allege that one or more individuals or organizations have made a claim for recognition as the exclusive representative of the same group of employees.

Petition for decertification election

The Act also contains a provision whereby employees or someone acting on their behalf can file a petition seeking an election to determine if the employees wish to retain the individual or labor organization currently acting as their bargaining representative, whether the representative has been certified or voluntarily recognized by the employer. This is called a decertification Election.

Union-security deauthorization

Provision is also made for the Board to determine by secret ballot whether the employees covered by a union-security agreement desire to withdraw the authority of their representative to continue the agreement. This is called a union-security deauthorization election and can be brought about by the filing of a petition signed by 30 percent or more of the employees covered by the agreement.

10

If you will refer to the "Types of Cases" on pages 22 and 23 of this booklet you may find it easier to understand the differences between the six types of petitions that can be filed under the Act.

Purpose of investigation and hearing

The same petition form is used for any kind of Board election. When the petition is filed, the NLRB must investigate the petition, hold a hearing if necessary, and direct an election if it finds that a question of representation exists. The purpose of the investigation is to determine, among other things, the following:

1. Whether the Board has jurisdiction to conduct an election.
2. Whether there is a sufficient showing of employee interest to justify an election.
3. Whether a question of representation exists.
4. Whether the election is sought in an appropriate unit of employees.
5. Whether the representative named in the petition is qualified.
6. Whether there are any barriers to an election in the form of existing contracts or prior Elections.

Jurisdiction to conduct an election

The jurisdiction of the NLRB to direct and conduct an election is limited to those enterprises that affect commerce. (This is discussed in greater detail at pp. 42–46.) The other matters listed above will be discussed in turn.

Expedited elections under Section 8(b)(7)(C)

First, however, it should be noted that Section 8(b)(7)(C) provides, among other things, that when a petition is filed within a reasonable period, not to exceed 30 days, after the commencement of recognitional or organizational picketing, the NLRB shall "forthwith" order an election and certify the results. This is so if the picketing is not within the protection of the second proviso to Section 8(b)(7)(C). When an election under Section 8(b)(7)(C) is appropriate, neither a hearing nor a showing of interest is required, and the election is scheduled sooner than under the ordinary procedure.

Showing of interest required

Regarding the showing of interest, it is the policy to require that a petitioner requesting an election for either certification of representatives or decertification show that at least 30 percent of the employees favor an election. The Act also requires that a petition for a union-security deauthorization election be filed by 30 percent or more of the employees in the unit covered by the agreement for the NLRB to conduct an election for that purpose. The showing of interest must be exclusively by employees who are in the appropriate bargaining unit in which an election is sought.

Existence of question of representation

Section 9(c)(1) authorizes the NLRB to direct an election and certify the results thereof, provided the record shows that a question of representation exists. Petitions for certification of representatives present a question of representation if, among other things, they are based on a demand for recognition by the employee representative and a denial of recognition by the employer. The demand for recognition need not be made in any particular form; in fact, the filing of a petition by the representative itself is considered to be a demand for recognition. The NLRB has held that even a representative that is currently recognized by the employer can file a petition for certification and that such petition presents a question of representation provided the representative has not previously been certified.

A question of representation is also raised by a decertification petition that challenges the representative status of a bargaining agent previously certified or currently recognized by the employer. However, a decertification petition filed by a supervisor does not raise a valid question of representation and must be dismissed.

Who can qualify as bargaining representative

Section 2(4) of the Act provides that the employee representative for collective bargaining can be "any individual or labor organization." A supervisor or any other management representative may not be an employee representative. It is NLRB policy to direct an election and to issue a certification unless the proposed bargaining agent fails to qualify as a bona fide representative of the employees. In determining a union's qualifications as bargaining agent, it is the union's willingness to represent the employees rather than its constitution and bylaws that is the controlling factor. The NLRB's power to certify a labor organization as bargaining representative is limited by Section 9(b)(3) which prohibits certification of a union as the representative of a unit of plant guards if the union "admits to membership, or is affiliated directly or indirectly with an organization which admits to membership, employees other than guards."

Bars to Election

The NLRB has established the policy of not directing an election among employees presently covered by a valid collective-bargaining agreement except in accordance with certain rules. These rules, followed in determining whether or not an existing collective-bargaining contract will bar an election, are called the NLRB contract-bar rules. Not every contract will bar an election. Examples of contracts that would not bar an election are:

Existing collective-bargaining contract

- The contract is not in writing, or is not signed.
- The contract has not been ratified by the members or the union, if such is expressly required.

- The contract does not contain substantial terms or conditions of employment sufficient to stabilize the bargaining relationship.
- The contract can be terminated by either party at any time for any reason.
- The contract contains a clearly illegal union-security clause.
- The bargaining unit is not appropriate.
- The union that entered the contract with the employer is no longer in existence or is unable or unwilling to represent the employees.
- The contract discriminates between employees on racial grounds.
- The contract covers union members only.
- The contracting union is involved in a basic internal conflict at the highest levels with resulting unstabilizing confusion about the identity of the union.
- The employer's operations have changed substantially since the contract was executed.

Time provisions

Under the NLRB rules a valid contract for a fixed period of 3 years or less will bar an election for the period covered by the contract. A contract for a fixed period of more than 3 years will bar an election sought by a contracting party during the life of the contract, but will act as a bar to an election sought by an outside party for only 3 years following its effective date. A contract of no fixed period will not act as a bar at all.

When a petition can be filed if there is an existing contract

If there is no existing contract, a petition can bring about an election if it is filed before the day a contract is signed. If the petition is filed on the same day the contract is signed, the contract bars an election, provided the contract is effective immediately or retroactively and the employer has not been informed at the time of execution that a petition has been filed. Once the contract becomes effective as a bar to an election, no petition will be accepted until near the end of the period during which the contract is effective as a bar. Petitions filed not more than 90 days but over 60 days before the end of the contract-bar period will be accepted and can bring about an election. These time periods for filing petitions involving health care institutions are 120 and 90 days, respectively. Of course, a petition can be filed after the contract expires. However, the last 60 days of the contract-bar period is called an "insulated" period. During this time the parties to the existing contract are free to negotiate a new contract or to agree to extend the old one. If they reach agreement in this period, petitions will not be accepted until 90 days before the end of the new contract-bar period.

Effect of certification

In addition to the contract-bar rules, the NLRB has established a rule that when a representative has been certified by the Board, the certification will ordinarily be binding for at least

1 year and a petition filed before the end of the certification year will be dismissed. In cases in which the certified representative and the employer enter a valid collective-bargaining contract during the year, the contract becomes controlling, and whether a petition for an election can be filed is determined by the Board's contract-bar rules.

Section 9(c)(3) prohibits the holding of an election in any collective-bargaining unit or subdivision thereof in which a valid election has been held during the preceding 12-month period. A new election may be held, however, in a larger unit, but not in the same unit or subdivision in which the previous election was held. For example, if all the production and maintenance employees in Company A, including draftsmen in the company's engineering office, are included in a collective-bargaining unit, an election among all the employees in the unit would bar another election among all the employees in the unit for 12 months. Similarly, an election among the draftsmen only would bar another election among the draftsmen for 12 months. However, an election among the draftsmen would not bar a later election during the 12-month period among all the production and maintenance employees including the draftsmen.

It is the Board's interpretation that Section 9(c)(3) prohibits only the holding of an election during the 12-month period, but does not prohibit the filing of a petition. Accordingly, the NLRB will accept a petition filed not more than 60 days before the end of the 12-month period. The election cannot be held, of course, until after the 12-month period. If an election is held and a representative certified, that certification is binding for 1 year and a petition for another election in the same unit will be dismissed if it is filed during the 1-year period after the certification. If an election is held and no representative is certified, the election bars another election for 12 months. A petition for another election in the same unit can be filed not more than 60 days before the end of the 12-month period and the election can be held after the 12-month period expires.

The Representation Election

Section 9(c)(1) provides that if a question of representation exists, the NLRB must make its determination by means of a secret-ballot election. In a representation election employees are given a choice of one or more bargaining representatives or no representative at all. To be certified as the bargaining representative, an individual or a labor organization must receive a majority of the valid votes cast.

An election may be held by agreement between the employer and the individual or labor organization claiming to represent the employees. In such an agreement the parties would

Effect of prior election

When a petition can be filed if there has been a prior election

Consent-election agreements

14

state the time and place agreed on, the choices to be included on the ballot, and a method to determine who is eligible to vote. They would also authorize the NLRB Regional Director to conduct the election.

If the parties are unable to reach an agreement, the Act authorizes the NLRB to order an election after a hearing. The Act also authorizes the Board to delegate to its Regional Directors the determination on matters concerning elections. Under this delegation of authority the Regional Directors can determine the appropriateness of the unit, direct an election, and certify the outcome. Upon the request of an interested party, the Board may review the action of a Regional Director, but such review does not stop the election process unless the Board so orders. The election details are left to the Regional Director. Such matters as who may vote, when the election will be held, and what standards of conduct will be imposed on the parties are decided in accordance with the Board's rules and its decisions.

To be entitled to vote, an employee must have worked in the unit during the eligibility period set by the Board and must be employed in the unit on the date of the election. Generally, the eligibility period is the employer's payroll period just before the date on which the election was directed. This requirement does not apply, however, to employees who are ill, on vacation, or temporarily laid off, or to employees in military service who appear in person at the polls. The NLRB rules take into consideration the fact that employment is typically irregular in certain industries. In such industries eligibility to vote is determined according to formulas designed to permit all employees who have a substantial continuing interest in their employment conditions to vote. Examples of these formulas, which differ from case to case, are:

- In one case, employees of a construction company were allowed to vote if they worked for the employer at least 65 days during the year before the "eligibility date" for the election.

- In another case longshoremen who worked at least 700 hours during a specified contract year, and at least 20 hours in each full month between the end of that year and the date on which the election was directed, were allowed to vote.

- Radio and television talent employees and musicians in the television film, motion picture, and recording industries have been held eligible to vote if they worked in the unit 2 or more days during the year before the date on which the election was directed.

Who determines election matters

Who may vote in a representation election

When strikers may be allowed to vote

Section 9(c)(3) provides that economic strikers who have been replaced by bona fide permanent employees may be entitled to vote in "any election conducted within 12 months after the commencement of the strike." The permanent replacements are also eligible to vote at the same time. As a general proposition, a striker is considered to be an economic striker unless found by the NLRB to be on strike over unfair labor practices of the employer. Whether the economic striker is eligible to vote is determined on the facts of each case.

When elections are held

Ordinarily, elections are held within 30 days after they are directed. Seasonal drops in employment or any change in operations that would prevent a normal work force from being present may cause a different election date to be set. Normally an election will not be conducted when unfair labor practice charges have been filed based on conduct of a nature which would have a tendency to interfere with the free choice of the employees in an election, except that, in certain cases, the Board may proceed to the election if the charging party so requests.

Conduct of elections

NLRB elections are conducted in accordance with strict standards designed to give the employee voters an opportunity to freely indicate whether they wish to be represented for purposes of collective bargaining. Election details, such as time, place, and notice of an election, are left largely to the Regional Director who usually obtains the agreement of the parties on these matters. Any party to an election who believes that the Board election standards were not met may, within 7 days after the tally of ballots has been furnished, file objections to the election with the Regional Director under whose supervision the election was held. In most cases, the Regional Director's rulings on these objections may be appealed to the Board for decision.

An election will be set aside if it was accompanied by conduct that the NLRB considers created an atmosphere of confusion or fear of reprisals and thus interfered with the employees' freedom of choice. In any particular case the NLRB does not attempt to determine whether the conduct actually interfered with the employees' expression of free choice, but rather asks whether the conduct tended to do so. If it is reasonable to believe that the conduct would tend to interfere with the free expression of the employees' choice, the election may be set aside. Examples of conduct the Board considers to interfere with employee free choice are:

- Threats of loss of jobs or benefits by an employer or a union to influence the Votes or union activities of employees.
- A grant of benefits or promise to grant benefits to influence the votes or union activities of employees.

- An employer firing employees to discourage or encourage their union activities or a union causing an employer to take such action.
- An employer or a union making campaign speeches to assembled groups of employees on company time within the 24-hour period before the election.
- The incitement of racial or religious prejudice by inflammatory campaign appeals made by either an employer or a union.
- Threats or the use of physical force or violence against employees by an employer or a union to influence their votes.
- The occurrence of extensive violence or trouble or widespread fear of job losses which prevents the holding of a fair election, whether caused by an employer or a union.

Unfair Labor Practices of Employers

The unfair labor practices of employers are listed in Section 8(a) of the Act; those of labor organizations in Section 8(b). Section 8(e) lists an unfair labor practice that can be committed only by an employer and a labor organization acting together. The "Types of Cases" chart at pages 22–23 may be helpful in getting to know the relationship between the various unfair labor practice sections of the Act.

Section 8(a)(1)— Interference with Section 7 Rights

Section 8(a)(1) forbids an employer "to interfere with, restrain, or coerce employees in the exercise of the rights guaranteed in section 7." Any prohibited interference by an employer with the rights of employees to organize, to form, join, or assist a labor organization, to bargain collectively, to engage in other concerted activities for mutual aid or protection, or to refrain from any or all of these activities, constitutes a violation of this section. This is a broad prohibition on employer interference, and an employer violates this section whenever it commits any of the other employer unfair labor practices. In consequence, whenever a violation of Section 8(a) (2), (3), (4), or (5) is committed a violation of Section 8(a)(1) is also found. This is called a "derivative violation" of Section 8(a)(1).

Employer conduct may, of course, independently violate Section 8(a)(1). Examples of such independent violations are:

Examples of violations of Section 8(a)(1)

- Threatening employees with loss of jobs or benefits if they should join or vote for a union.
- Threatening to close down the plant if a union should be organized in it.

- Questioning employees about their union activities or membership in such circumstances as will tend to restrain or coerce the employees.
- Spying on union gatherings, or pretending to spy.
- Granting wage increases deliberately timed to discourage employees from forming or joining a union.

Section 8(a)(2) makes it unlawful for an employer "to dominate or interfere with the formation or administration of any labor organization or contribute financial or other support to it." This section not only outlaws "company unions" that are dominated by the employer, but also forbids an employer to contribute money to a union it favors or to give a union improper advantages that are denied to rival unions.

Domination

A labor organization is considered dominated within the meaning of this section if the employer has interfered with its formation and has assisted and supported its operation and activities to such an extent that it must be looked at as the employer's creation instead of the true bargaining representative of the employees. Such domination is the result of a combination of factors and has been found to exist where there is not only the factor of the employer getting the organization started, but also such other factors as the employer deciding how the organization will be set up and what it will do, or representatives of management actually taking part in the meetings and activities of the organization and trying to influence its actions and policies.

Illegal assistance and support

Certain lesser kinds of employer assistance to a union may constitute unlawful "interference" even if the union is not "dominated" by the employer. For example, an employer may not provide financial support to a union either by direct payments or indirect financial aid. (But an employer does not violate this prohibition by permitting employees to confer with it and/or the union regarding grievances or other union business during working hours without loss of pay.)

When rival unions are competing to organize an employer's employees, the employer is forbidden to give the union it favors privileges it denies to the other union. It is also forbidden to recognize either union once it knows that one of the unions has filed a valid petition with the Board requesting a representation election. When an employer and a union already have an established bargaining relationship, however, the employer is required to continue bargaining with the incumbent even though a rival union is attempting to organize the employees. In these circumstances, the rival's filing of a petition does not prevent continued dealing between

18

the employer and the incumbent unless the incumbent has lost the support of a majority of the employees.

An employer violates Section 8(a)(2) by:

- Taking an active part in organizing a union or a committee to represent employees.
- Bringing pressure on employees to support a union financially, except in the enforcement of a lawful union-security agreement.
- Allowing one of several unions, competing to represent employees, to solicit on company premises during working hours and denying other unions the same privilege.
- Soliciting and obtaining from employees and applicants for employment, during the hiring procedure, applications for union membership and signed authorizations for the check-off of union dues.

Examples of violation of Section 8(a)(2)

In remedying such unfair labor practices, the NLRB distinguishes between domination of a labor organization and conduct which amounts to no more than illegal assistance. When a union is found to be dominated by an employer, the Board has announced it will order the organization completely disestablished as a representative of employees. But, if the organization is found only to have been supported by employer assistance amounting to less than domination, the Board usually orders the employer to stop such support and to withhold recognition from the organization until such time as it has been certified by the Board as a bona fide representative of employees.

Remedy in cases of domination differs from that in cases of illegal assistance and support

Section 8(a)(3) makes it an unfair labor practice for an employer to discriminate against employees "in regard to hire or tenure of employment or any term or condition of employment" for the purpose of encouraging or discouraging membership in a labor organization. In general, the Act makes it illegal for an employer to discriminate in employment because of an employee's union or other group, activity within the protection of the Act. A banding together of employees, even in the absence of a formal organization, may constitute a labor organization for purposes of Section 8(a)(3). It also prohibits discrimination because an employee has refrained from taking part in such union or group activity except where a valid union-security agreement is in effect. Discrimination within the meaning of the Act would include such action as refusing to hire, discharging, demoting, assigning to a less desirable shift or job, or withholding benefits.

As previously noted, Section 8(a)(3) provides that an employee may be discharged for failing to make certain lawfully required payments to the exclusive bargaining representative

Section 8(a)(3)— Discrimination Against Employees

The union-security exception to Section 8(a)(3)

19

under a lawful union-security agreement. For a fuller discussion of this issue, see pages 2–4, above.

Even when there is a valid union-security agreement in effect, an employer may not pay the union the dues and fees owed by its employees. The employer may, however, deduct these amounts from the wages of its employees and forward them to the union for each employee who has Voluntarily signed a dues "checkoff" authorization. Such checkoff authorization may be made irrevocable for no more than a year. But employees may revoke their checkoff authorizations after a Board-conducted election in which the union's authority to maintain a union-security agreement has been withdrawn.

The Act does not limit employer's right to discharge for economic reasons

This section does not limit an employer's right to discharge, transfer, or lay off an employee for genuine economic reasons or for such good cause as disobedience or bad work. This right applies equally to employees who are active in support of a union and to those who are not.

In situations in which an employer disciplines an employee both because the employee has violated a work rule and because the employee has engaged in protected union activity, the discipline is unlawful unless the employer can show that the employee would have received the same discipline even if he or she had not engaged in the protected union activity.

An employer who is engaged in good-faith bargaining with a union may lock out the represented employees, sometimes even before impasse is reached in the negotiations, if it does so to further its position in bargaining. But a bargaining lockout may be unlawful if the employer is at that time unlawfully refusing to bargain or is bargaining in bad faith. It is also unlawful if the employer's purpose in locking out its employees is to discourage them in their union loyalties and activities, that is, if the employer is motivated by hostility toward the union. Thus, a lockout to defeat a union's efforts to organize the employer's employees would violate the Act, as would the lockout of only those of its employees who are members of the union. On the other hand, lockouts are lawful that are intended to prevent any unusual losses or safety hazards that would be caused by an anticipated "quickie" strike. And a whipsaw strike against one employer engaged in multiemployer bargaining justifies a lockout by any of the other employers who are party to the bargaining.

Examples of violations of Section 8(a)(3)

Examples of illegal discrimination under Section 8(a)(3) include:

• Discharging employees because they urged other employees to join a

20

- Refusing to reinstate employees when jobs they are qualified for are open because they took part in a union's lawful strike.

- Granting of "superseniority" to those hired to replace employees engaged in a lawful strike.

- Demoting employees because they circulated a union petition among other employees asking the employer for an increase in pay.

- Discontinuing an operation at one plant and discharging the employees involved followed by opening the same operation at another plant with new employees because the employees at the first plant joined a union.

- Refusing to hire qualified applicants for jobs because they belong to a union. It would also be a violation if the qualified applicants were refused employment because they did not belong to a union, or because they belonged to one union rather than another.

Section 8(a)(4)—Discrimination for NLRB Activity

Section 8(a)(4) makes it an unfair labor practice for an employer "to discharge or otherwise discriminate against an employee because he has filed charges or given testimony under this Act." This provision guards the right of employees to seek the protection of the Act by using the processes of the NLRB. Like the previous section, it forbids an employer to discharge, lay off, or engage in other forms of discrimination in working conditions against employees who have filed charges with the NLRB, given affidavits to NLRB investigators, or testified at an NLRB hearing. Violations of this section are in most cases also violations of Section 8(a)(3).

Examples of violations of Section 8(a)(4)

Examples of violations of Section 8(a)(4) are:

- Refusing to reinstate employees when jobs they are otherwise qualified for are open because they filed charges with the NLRB claiming their layoffs were based on union activity.

- Demoting employees because they testified at an NLRB

Section 8(a)(5)—Refusal to Bargain in Good Faith

Section 8(a)(5) makes it illegal for an employer to refuse to bargain in good faith about wages, hours, and other conditions of employment with the representative selected by a majority of the employees in a unit appropriate for collective bargaining. A bargaining representative which seeks to enforce its right concerning an employer under this section must show that it has been designated by a majority of the employees, that the unit is appropriate, and that there has been both a demand that the employer bargain and a refusal by the employer to do so.

TYPES OF CASES

I. CHARGES OF UNFAIR LABOR PRACTICES
(C CASES)

Charge Against Employer		Charge Against Labor Organization			
Section of the Act	**C A**	*Section of the Act*	**C B**	*Section of the Act*	**C C**

Section of the Act	**C A**
8(a)(1)	To interfere with, restrain, or coerce employees in exercise of their rights under Section 7 (to join or assist a labor organization or to refrain).
8(a)(2)	To dominate or interfere with the formation or administration of a labor organization or contribute financial or other support to it.
8(a)(3)	By discrimination in regard to hire or tenure of employment or any term or condition of employment to encourage or discourage membership in any labor organization.
8(a)(4)	To discharge or otherwise discriminate against employees because they have given testimony under the Act.
8(a)(5)	To refuse to bargain collectively with representatives of its employees.

Section of the Act	**C B**
8(b)(1)(A)	To restrain or coerce employees in exercise of their rights under Section 7 (to join or assist a labor organization or to refrain).
8(b)(1)(B)	To restrain or coerce an employer in the selection of its representatives for collective bargaining or adjustment of grievances.
8(b)(2)	To cause or attempt to cause an employer to discriminate against an employee.
8(b)(3)	To refuse to bargain collectively with an employer.
8(b)(5)	To require of employees the payment of excessive or discriminatory fees for membership.
8(b)(6)	To cause or attempt to cause an employer to pay or agree to pay money or other thing of value for services which are not performed or not to be performed.

Section of the Act	**C C**
8(b)(4)(i)	To engage in, or induce or encourage any individual employed by any person engaged in commerce or in an industry affecting commerce to engage in, a strike, work stoppage, or boycott, or
(ii)	to threaten, coerce, or restrain any person engaged in commerce or in an industry affecting commerce, where in either case an object is:
(A)	To force or require any employer or self-employed person to join any labor or employer organization or to enter into any agreement prohibited by Section 8(e).
(B)	To force or require any person to cease using, selling, handling, transporting, or otherwise dealing in the products of any other producer, processor, or manufacturer; or to cease doing business with any other person, or force or require any other employer to recognize or bargain with a labor organization as the representative of its employees unless such labor organization has been so certified.
(C)	To force or require any employer to recognize or bargain with a particular labor organization as the representative of its employees if another labor organization has been certified as the representative.

Charge Against Labor Organization (continued)

Section of the Act	**C D**
8(b)(4)(i)	To engage in, or induce or encourage any individual employed by any person engaged in commerce or in an industry affecting commerce to engage in, a strike, work stoppage, or boycott, or
(ii)	to threaten, coerce, or restrain any person engaged in commerce or in an industry affecting commerce, where in either case an object is:
(D)	To force or require any employer to assign particular work to employees in a particular labor organization or in a particular trade, craft, or class rather than to employees in another trade, craft, or class, unless such employer is failing to conform to an appropriate Board order or certification.

Section of the Act	**C G**
8(g)	To strike, picket, or otherwise concertedly refuse to work at any health care institution without notifying the institution and the Federal Mediation and Conciliation Service in writing 10 days prior to such action.

22

TYPES OF CASES—Continued

1. CHARGES OF UNFAIR LABOR PRACTICES (C CASES)		2. PETITIONS FOR CERTIFICATION OR DECERTIFICATION OR REPRESENTATIVES (R CASES)		3. OTHER PETITIONS
Charge Against Labor Organization C P	**Charge Against Labor Organization and Employer** C E	**By or on Behalf of Employees** R C	**By or on Behalf of Employees** R D	**By or on Behalf of Employees** U D

1. CHARGES OF UNFAIR LABOR PRACTICES (C CASES)

Charge Against Labor Organization — C P

Section of the Act

8(b)(7) To picket, or cause or threaten the picketing of, any employer where an object is to force or require an employer to recog-Nize or bargain with a labor organization as the representative of its employees, or to force or require the employees of an em-Ployer to select such labor organization as their collective-bargaining representative, unless such labor organization is currently certified as the representative of such em-Ployees:

(A) where the employer has lawfully rec-Ognized any other labor organization and a question concerning representation may not appropriately be raised under Section 9(c).

(B) where within the preceding 12 months a valid election under Section 9(c) has been conducted, or

(C) where picketing has been conducted without a petition under Section 9(c) being filed within a reasonable period of time not to exceed 30 days from the commencement of the picketing; except where the picket-Ing is for the purpose of truthfully advising the public (including consumers) that an employer does not employ members of, or have a contract with, a labor organization, and it does not have an effect of inter-Ference with deliveries or services.

Charge Against Labor Organization and Employer — C E

Section of the Act

8(e) To enter into any contract or agreement (any labor orga-nization and any employer) whereby such employer ceases or refrains or agrees to cease or refrain from handling or dealing in any product of any other employer, or to cease doing business with any other person.

2. PETITIONS FOR CERTIFICATION OR DECERTIFICATION OR REPRESENTATIVES (R CASES)

By or on Behalf of Employees — R C

Section of the Act

9(c)(1)(A)(i) Alleging that a substantial number of employees wish to be represented for collective bargaining and their employer declines to recognize their representative.*

By or on Behalf of Employees — R D

Section of the Act

9(c)(1)(A)(ii) Alleging that a substantial number of employees assert that the certified or currently rec-Ognized bargaining representative is no longer their Representative.*

By an Employer — R M

Section of the Act

9(c)(1)(B) Alleging that one or more claims for rec-Ognition as exclusive bargaining representative have been received by the employer.*

*If an 8(b)(7) charge has been filed involving the same employer, these statements in RC, RD, and RM peti-Tions are not required.

3. OTHER PETITIONS

By or on Behalf of Employees — U D

Section of the Act

9(e)(1) Alleging the employees (30 per-cent or more of an appropriate unit) wish to rescind an existing union secu-Rity agreement.

By a Labor Organization or an Employer — R M

Board Rules

Subpart C Seeking clarification of an ex-Isting bargaining unit.

By a Labor Organization or an Employer — R M

Board Rules

Subpart C Seeking amendment of an outstanding certification of bargaining Representative.

Charges filed with the National Labor Relations Board are letter-coded and numbered. Unfair labor practice charges are classified as "C" cases and petitions for certification or decerti-Fication of representatives as "R" cases. This chart indicates the letter codes used for "C" cases, at left, and "R" cases, above, and also presents a summary of each section involved.

The duty to bargain covers all matters concerning rates of pay, wages, hours of employment, or other conditions of employment. These are called "mandatory" subjects of bargaining about which the employer, as well as the employees' representative, must bargain in good faith, although the law does not require "either party to agree to a proposal or require the making of a concession." In addition to wages and hours of work, these mandatory subjects of bargaining include but are not limited to such matters as pensions for present employees, bonuses, group insurance, grievance procedures, safety practices, seniority, procedures for discharge, layoff, recall, or discipline, and union security. Certain managerial decisions such as subcontracting, relocation, and other operational changes may not be mandatory subjects of bargaining, even though they affect employees' job security and working conditions. The issue of whether these decisions are mandatory subjects of bargaining depends on the employer's reasons for taking action. Even if the employer is not required to bargain about the decision itself, it must bargain about the decision's effects on unit employees. On "nonmandatory" subjects, that is, matters that are lawful but not related to "wages, hours, and other conditions of employment," the parties are free to bargain and to agree, but neither party may insist on bargaining on such subjects over the objection of the other party.

An employer who is required to bargain under this section must, as stated in Section 8(d), "meet at reasonable times and confer in good faith with respect to wages, hours, and other terms and conditions of employment, or the negotiation of an agreement or any question arising thereunder, and the execution of a written contract incorporating any agreement reached if requested by either party."

An employer, therefore, will be found to have violated Section 8(a)(5) if its conduct in bargaining, viewed in its entirety, indicates that the employer did not negotiate with a good-faith intention to reach agreement. However, the employer's good faith is not at issue when its conduct constitutes an out-and-out refusal to bargain on a mandatory subject. For example, it is a violation for an employer, regardless of good faith, to refuse to bargain about a subject that it believes is not a mandatory subject of bargaining, when in fact it is.

The duty of an employer to meet and confer with the representative of its employees includes the duty to deal with whoever is designated by the employees' representative to carry on negotiations. An employer may not dictate to a union its selection of agents or representatives and the employer must, in general, recognize the designated agent.

Required subjects of bargaining

Duty to bargain defined

What constitutes a violation of Section 8(a)(5)

Duty to meet and confer

The employer's duty to bargain includes the duty to supply, on request, information that is "relevant and necessary" to allow the employees' representative to bargain intelligently and effectively with respect to wages, hours, and other conditions of employment.

Duty to supply information

When there is a history of bargaining between a union and a number of employers acting jointly, the employees who are thus represented constitute a multiemployer bargaining unit. Once such a unit has been established, any of the participating employers–or the union– may retire from this multiemployer bargaining relationship only by mutual assent or by a timely submitted withdrawal. Withdrawal is considered timely if unequivocal notice of the withdrawal is given near the termination of a collective-bargaining agreement but before bargaining begins on the next agreement.

Multiemployer bargaining

Finally, the duty of an employer to bargain includes the duty to refrain from unilateral action, that is, taking action on its own with respect to matters concerning which it is required to bargain, and from making changes in terms and conditions of employment without consulting the employees' representative.

Duty to refrain from unilateral Action

An employer who purchases or otherwise acquires the operations of another may be obligated to recognize and bargain with the union that represented the employees before the business was transferred. In general, these bargaining obligations exist–and the purchaser is termed a successor employer–when there is a substantial continuity in the employing enterprise despite the sale and transfer of the business. Whether the purchaser is a successor employer is dependent on several factors, including the number of employees taken over by the purchasing employer, the similarity in operations and product of the two employers, the manner in which the purchaser integrates the purchased operations into its other operations, and the character of the bargaining relationship and agreement between the union and the original employer.

Duty of successor employers

Examples of violations of Section 8(a)(5) are as follows:

Examples of violations of Section 8(a)(5)

- Refusing to meet with the employees' representative because the employees are out on strike.
- Insisting, until bargaining negotiations break down, on a contract provision that all employees will be polled by secret ballot before the union calls a strike.
- Refusing to supply the employees' representative with cost and other data a group concerning insurance plan covering the employees.
- Announcing a wage increase without consulting the employees' representative.

- Failing to bargain about the effects of a decision to close one of the employer's plants.

Section 8(e)—Entering a Hot Cargo Agreement

Section 8(e), added to the Act in 1959, makes it an unfair labor practice for any labor organization and any employer to enter into what is commonly called a "hot cargo" or "hot goods" agreement. It may also limit the restrictions that can be placed on the subcontracting of work by an employer. The typical hot cargo or hot goods clause in use before the 1959 amendment to the Act provided that employees would not be required by their employer to handle or work on goods or materials going to, or coming from, an employer designated by the union as "unfair." Such goods were said to be "hot cargo" thereby giving Section 8(e) its popular name. These clauses were most common in the construction and trucking industries.

What is prohibited

Section 8(e) forbids an employer and a labor organization to make an agreement whereby the employer agrees to stop doing business with any other employer and declares void and unenforceable any such agreement that is made. It should be noted that a strike or picketing, or any other union action, or the threat of it, to force an employer to agree to a hot cargo provision, or to force it to act in accordance with such a clause, has been held by the Board to be a violation of Section 8(b)(4). Exceptions are allowed in the construction and garment industries, and a union may seek, by contract, to keep within a bargaining unit work that is being done by the employees in the unit or to secure work that is "fairly claimable" in that unit.

Exceptions for construction and garment industries

In the construction industry a union and an employer in the industry may agree to a provision that restricts the contracting or subcontracting of work to be done at the construction site. Such a clause contained in the agreement between the employer and the union typically provides that if work is subcontracted by the employer it must go to an employer who has an agreement with the union. A union in the construction industry may engage in a strike and picketing to obtain, but not to enforce, contractual restrictions of this nature. Similarly, in the garment industry an employer and a union can agree that work to be done on the goods or on the premises of a jobber or manufacturer, or work that is part of "an integrated process of production in the apparel and clothing industry," can be subcontracted only to an employer who has an agreement with the union. This exception, unlike the previous one concerning the construction industry, allows a labor organization in the garment industry, not only

26

to seek to obtain, but also to enforce, such a restriction on subcontracting by striking, picketing, or other lawful actions.

Section 8(b)(1)(A) forbids a labor organization or its agents "to restrain or coerce employees in the exercise of the rights guaranteed in section 7." The section also provides that it is not intended to "impair the rights of a labor organization to prescribe its own rules" concerning membership in the labor organization.

Like Section 8(a)(1), Section 8(b)(1)(A) is violated by conduct that independently restrains or coerces employees in the exercise of their Section 7 rights regardless of whether the conduct also violates other provisions of Section 8(b). But whereas employer violations of Section 8(a)(2), (3), (4), and (5) are held to be violations of Section 8(a)(1) too, the Board has held, based on the intent of Congress when Section 8(b)(1)(A) was written, that violation of Section 8(b)(2) through (7) do not also "derivatively" violate Section 8(b)(1)(A). The Board does hold, however, that making or enforcing illegal union-security agreements or hiring agreements that condition employment on union membership not only violates Section 8(b)(2) but also Section 8(b)(1)(A), because such action restrains or coerces employees in their Section 7 rights.

Union conduct that is reasonably calculated to restrain or coerce employees in their Section 7 rights violates Section 8(b)(1)(A) whether it succeeds in actually restraining or coercing employees.

A union may violate Section 8(b)(1)(A) by coercive conduct of its officers or agents, of pickets on a picket line endorsed by the union, or of strikers who engage in coercion in the presence of union representatives who do not repudiate the conduct.

Unlawful coercion may consist of acts specifically directed at an employee such as physical assaults, threats of violence, and threats to affect an employee's job status. Coercion also includes other forms of pressure against employees such as acts of a union while representing employees as their exclusive bargaining agent (see Section 9(a), p. 10). A union that is a statutory bargaining representative owes a duty of fair representation to all the employees it represents. It may exercise a wide range of reasonable discretion in carrying out the representative function, but it violates Section 8(b)(1)(A) if, while acting as the employees' statutory bargaining representative, it takes or withholds action in connection with their employment because of their union activities or for any irrelevant or arbitrary reason such as an employee's race or sex.

Unfair Labor Practices of Labor Organizations

Section 8(b)(1)(A)— Restraint and Coercion of Employees

Section 8(b)(1)(A) compared with Section 8(a)(1)

What violates Section 8(b)(1)(A)

Section 8(b)(1)(A) recognizes the right of unions to establish and enforce rules of membership and to control their internal affairs. This right is limited to union rules and discipline that affect the rights of employees as union members and that are not enforced by action affecting an employee's employment. Also, rules to be protected must be aimed at matters of legitimate concern to unions such as the encouragement of members to support a lawful strike or participation in union meetings. Rules that conflict with public policy, such as rules that limit a member's right to file unfair labor practice charges, are not protected. And a union may not fine a member for filing a decertification petition although it may expel that individual for doing so. A rule that prohibits a member from resigning from the union is unlawful. The union may not fine a former member for any protected conduct engaged in after he or she resigns.

Examples of restraint or coercion that violate Section 8(b)(1)(A) when done by a union or its agents include the following:

- Mass picketing in such numbers that nonstriking employees are physically barred from entering the plant.
- Acts of force or violence on the picket line, or in connection with a strike.
- Threats to do bodily injury to nonstriking employees.
- Threats to employees that they will lose their jobs unless they support the union's activities.
- Statement to employees who oppose the union that the employees will lose their jobs if the union wins a majority in the plant.
- Entering into an agreement with an employer that recognizes the union as exclusive bargaining representative when it has not been chosen by a majority of the employees.
- Fining or expelling members for crossing a picket line that is unlawful under the Act or that violates a no-strike agreement.
- Fining employees for crossing a picket line after they resigned from the union.
- Fining or expelling members for filing unfair labor practice charges with the Board or for participating in an investigation conducted by the Board.

The following are examples of restraint or coercion that violate Section 8(b)(1)(A) when done by a union that is the exclusive bargaining representative:

- Refusing to process a grievance in retaliation against an employee's criticism of union officers.

Examples of violations of Section 8(b)(1)(A)

28

Section 8(b)(1)(B)— Restraint and Coercion of Employers

Examples of violations of Section 8(b)(1)(B)

Section 8(b)(2)—Causing or Attempting to Cause Discrimination

- Maintaining a seniority arrangement with an employer under which seniority is based on the employee's prior representation by the union elsewhere.
- Rejecting an application for referral to a job in a unit represented by the union based on the applicant's race or union activities.

Section 8(b)(1)(B) prohibits a labor organization from restraining or coercing an employer in the selection of a bargaining representative. The prohibition applies regardless of whether the labor organization is the majority representative of the employees in the bargaining unit. The prohibition extends to coercion applied by a union to a union member who is a representative of the employer in the adjustment of grievances. This section is violated by such conduct as the following:

- Insisting on meeting only with a company's owners and refusing to meet with the attorney the company has engaged to represent the company in contract negotiations, and threatening to strike to force the company to accept its demands.
- Striking members of an employer association that bargains with the union as the representative of the employers to compel the struck employers to sign individual contracts with the union.
- Insisting during contract negotiations that the employer agree to accept working conditions that will be established by a bargaining group to which it does not belong.
- Fining or expelling supervisors for the way they apply the bargaining contract while carrying out their supervisory functions or for crossing a picket line during a strike to perform their supervisory duties.

Section 8(b)(2) makes it an unfair labor practice for a labor organization to cause an employer to discriminate against an employee in violation of Section 8(a)(3). As discussed earlier, Section 8(a)(3) prohibits an employer from discriminating against an employee in regard to wages, hours, and other conditions of employment for the purpose of encouraging or discouraging membership in a labor organization. It does allow, however, the making of union-security agreements under certain specified conditions. (See pp. 2–4, above.)

A union violates Section 8(b)(2), for example, by demanding that an employer discriminate against employees because of their failure to make certain otherwise lawful payments to the union when there is no valid union-security agreement in effect. (See pp. 2–4, above.) The section can also be violated by agreements or arrangements with employers that unlawfully condition employment or job benefits on union membership, on the performance of union

What violates Section 8(b)(2)

membership obligations, or on arbitrary grounds. Union conduct affecting an employee's employment in a way that is contrary to provisions of the bargaining contract may likewise be violative of the section. But union action that causes detriment to an individual employee in that individual's employment does not violate Section 8(b)(2) if it is consistent with nondiscriminatory provisions of a bargaining contract negotiated for the benefit of the total bargaining unit or if it is for some other legitimate purpose.

To find that a union caused an employer to discriminate, it is not necessary to show that any express demand was spoken. A union's conduct, accompanied by statements advising or suggesting that action is expected of an employer, may be enough to find a violation of this section if the union's action can be shown to be a causal factor in the employer's discrimination.

Illegal hiring hall agreements and practices

Contracts or informal arrangements with a union under which an employer gives preferential treatment to union members are violations of Section 8(b)(2). It is not unlawful for an employer and a union to enter into an agreement whereby the employer agrees to hire new employees exclusively through the union hiring hall so long as there is neither a provision in the agreement nor a practice in effect that discriminates against nonunion members in favor of union members or otherwise discriminates on the basis of union membership obligations. Both the agreement and the actual operation of the hiring hall must be nondiscriminatory; referrals must be made without reference to union membership or irrelevant or arbitrary considerations such as race. Referral standards or procedures, even if nondiscriminatory on their face, are unlawful when they continue previously discriminatory conditions of referral. However, a union may, in setting referral standards, consider legitimate aims such as sharing available work and easing the impact of local unemployment. It may also charge referral fees if the amount of the fee is reasonably related to the cost of operating the referral service.

Illegal union-security agreements

Union-security agreements that require employees to make certain lawfully required payments to the union after they are hired are permitted by this section as previously discussed. Union-security agreements that do not meet all the requirements listed on page 3 will not support a discharge. A union that attempts to force an employer to enter into an illegal union-security agreement, or that enters into and keeps in effect such an agreement, violates Section 8(b)(2), as does a union that attempts to enforce such an illegal agreement by bringing about an employee's discharge. Even when a union-security provision of a bargaining contract meets all statutory requirements so that it is permitted by Section 8(a)(3), a union may not lawfully require the discharge of employees under the provision unless the employees had been informed of the union-security agreement and of their specific obligation under it. And a union violates Section 8(b)(2) if it tries to use the union-security provisions of a contract to collect payments other than those that lawfully may be required. (See pp. 2–4, above.) Assessments, fines, and penalties may not be enforced by application of a union-security agreement.

Examples of violations of Section 8(b)(2)

Examples of violations of Section 8(b)(2) are:

- Causing an employer to discharge employees because they circulated a petition urging a change in the union's method of selecting shop stewards.
- Causing an employer to discharge employees because they made speeches against a contract proposed by the union.
- Making a contract that requires an employer to hire only members of the union or employees "satisfactory" to the union.
- Causing an employer to reduce employees' seniority because they engaged in anti-union acts.
- Refusing referral or giving preference on the basis of race or union activities in making job referrals to units represented by the union.
- Seeking the discharge of an employee under a union-security agreement for failure to pay a fine levied by the union.

Section 8(b)(3)—Refusal to Bargain in Good Faith

Section 8(b)(3) makes it illegal for a labor organization to refuse to bargain in good faith with an employer about wages, hours, and other conditions of employment if it is the representative of that employer's employees. This section imposes on labor organizations the same duty to bargain in good faith that is imposed on employers by Section 8(a)(5). Both the labor organization and the employer are required to follow the procedure set out in Section 8(d) before terminating or changing an existing contract (see p. 8).

A labor organization that is the employees' designated representative must meet at reasonable times with the employer or his designated representative, must confer in good faith on matters pertaining to wages, hours, or other conditions of employment, or the negotiation of an agreement, or any question arising under an agreement, and must sign a written agreement if requested and if one is reached. The obligation does not require the labor organization or the employer to agree to a proposal by the other party or make a concession to the other party, but it does require bargaining with an open mind in an attempt to reach agreement. So, while a union may try in contract negotiations to establish wages and benefits comparable to those

31

contained in other bargaining agreements in the area, it may not insist on such terms without giving the employer an opportunity to bargain about the terms. Likewise, a union may seek *voluntary* bargaining on nonmandatory subjects of bargaining (p. 24), such as a provision for an industry promotion fund, but may not *insist* on bargaining about such subjects or condition execution of a contract on the reaching of agreement on a nonmandatory subject.

When a union has been bargaining with a group of employers in a multiemployer bargaining unit, it may withdraw at any time from bargaining on that basis and bargain with one of the employers individually if the individual employer and the multiemployer group agree to the union's withdrawal. And even in the absence of employer consent, a union may withdraw from multiemployer bargaining by giving the employers unequivocal notice of its withdrawal near the expiration of the agreement but before bargaining on a new contract has begun.

Section 8(b)(3) not only requires that a union representative bargain in good faith with employers, but also requires that the union carry out its bargaining duty fairly with respect to the employees it represents. A union, therefore, violates Section 8(b)(3) if it negotiates a contract that conflicts with that duty, such as a contract with racially discriminatory provisions, or if it refuses to handle grievances under the contract for irrelevant or arbitrary reasons.

Section 8(b)(3) is violated by any of the following:

- Insisting on the inclusion of illegal provisions in a contract, such as a closed shop or a discriminatory hiring hall.
- Refusing to negotiate on a proposal for a written contract.
- Striking against an employer who has bargained, and continues to bargain, on a multiemployer basis to compel it to bargain separately.
- Refusing to meet with the attorney designated by the employer as its representative in negotiations.
- Terminating an existing contract and striking for a new one without notifying the employer, the Federal Mediation and Conciliation Service, and the state mediation service, if any.
- Conditioning the execution of an agreement on inclusion of a nonmandatory provision such as a performance bond.
- Refusing to process a grievance because of the race, sex, or union activities of an employee for whom the union is the statutory bargaining representative.

Examples of violations of Section 8(b)(3)

32

Section 8(b)(4)— Prohibited Strikes and Boycotts

Section 8(b)(4) prohibits a labor organization from engaging in strikes or boycotts or taking other specified actions to accomplish certain purposes or "objects" as they are called in the Act. The proscribed action is listed in clauses (i) and (ii), the objects are described in subparagraphs (A) through (D). A union commits an unfair labor practice if it takes any of the kinds of action listed in clauses (i) and (ii) as a means of accomplishing any of the objects listed in the four subparagraphs.

Proscribed action: Inducing or encouraging a strike, work stoppage, or boycott

Clause (i) forbids a union to engage in a strike, or to induce or encourage a strike, work stoppage, or a refusal to perform services by "any individual employed by any person engaged in commerce or in an industry affecting commerce" for one of the objects listed in subparagraphs (A) through (D). The words "induce and encourage" are considered by the U.S. Supreme Court to be broad enough to include every form of influence or persuasion. For example, it has been held by the NLRB that a work stoppage on a picketed construction project was "induced" by a union through its business agents who, when they learned about the picketing, told the job stewards that they (the business agents) would not work behind the picket line. It was considered that this advice not only induced the stewards to leave the job, but caused them to pass the information on to their fellow employees, and that such conduct informed the other employees that they were expected not to work behind the picket line. The world "person" is defined in Section 2(1) as including "one or more individuals, labor organizations, partnerships, associations, corporations," and other legal persons. As so defined, the word "person" is broader than the word "employer." For example, a railroad company, although covered by the Railway Labor Act, is excluded from the definition of "employer" in the National Labor Relations Act and, therefore, neither the railroad company nor its employees are covered by the National Labor Relations Act. But a railroad company is a "person engaged in commerce" as defined above and, therefore, a labor organization is forbidden to "induce or encourage" individuals employed by a railroad company to engage in a strike, work stoppage, or boycott for any of the objects in subparagraphs (A) through (D).

Proscribed action: Threats, coercion, and restraint

Clause (ii) makes it an unfair labor practice for a union to "threaten, coerce, or restrain any person engaged in commerce or in an industry affecting commerce" for any of the proscribed objects. Even though no direct threat is voiced by the union, there may nevertheless be coercion and restraint that violates this clause. For example, when a union picketed a construction job to bring about the removal of a nonunion subcontractor in violation of Section 8(b)(4)(B), the picketing induced employees of several other subcontractors to stop work. When the general contractor asked what could be done to stop the picketing, the union's business agent replied that the picketing would stop only if the nonunion subcontractor were removed from the job. The NLRB held this to be "coercion and restraint" within the meaning of clause (ii).

Section 8(b)(4)(A) prohibits unions from engaging in clause (i) or (ii) action to compel an employer or self-employed person to join any labor or employer organization or to force an employer to enter a hot cargo agreement prohibited by Section 8(e). Examples of violations of this section are:

- In an attempt to compel a beer distributor to join a union, the union prevents the distributor from obtaining beer at a brewery by inducing the brewery's employees to refuse to fill the distributor's orders.

- In an attempt to secure for its members certain stevedoring work required at an employer's unloading operation, the union pickets to force the employer to join an employer association with which the union has a contract.

- A union pickets an employer (one not in the construction and garment industries), or threatens to picket it, to compel that employer to enter into an agreement whereby the employer will only do business with persons who have an agreement with a union.

Section 8(b)(4)(B) contains the Act's secondary boycott provision. A secondary boycott occurs if a union has a dispute with Company A and, in furtherance of that dispute, causes the employees of Company B to stop handling the products of Company A, or otherwise forces Company B to stop doing business with Company A. The dispute is with Company A, called the "primary" employer, the union's action is against Company B, called the "secondary" employer, hence the term "secondary boycott." In many cases the secondary employer is a customer or supplier of the primary employer with whom the union has the dispute. In general, the Act prohibits both the secondary boycott and the threat of it. Examples of prohibited secondary boycotts are:

- Picketing an employer to force it to stop doing business with another employer who has refused to recognize the union.

- Asking the employees of a plumbing contractor not to work on connecting up air-conditioning equipment manufactured by a nonunion employer whom the union is attempting to organize.

34

- Urging employees of a building contractor not to install doors that were made by a manufacturer that is nonunion or that employs members of a rival union.
- Telling an employer that its plant will be picketed if that employer continues to do business with an employer the union has designated as "unfair."

The prohibitions of Section 8(b)(4)(B) do not protect a secondary employer from the incidental effects of union action that is taken directly against the primary employer. Thus, it is lawful for a union to urge employees of a secondary supplier at the primary employer's plant not to cross a picket line there. Section 8(b)(4)(B) also does not proscribe union action to prevent an employer from contracting out work customarily performed by its employees, even though an incidental effect of such conduct might be to compel that employer to cease doing business with the subcontractor.

In order to be protected against the union action that is prohibited under this subparagraph, the secondary employer has to be a neutral as concerns the dispute between the union and the primary employer. For secondary boycott purposes an employer is considered an "ally" of the primary employer and, therefore, not protected from union action in certain situations. One is based on the ownership and operational relationship between the primary and secondary employers. Here, a number of factors are considered, particularly the following: Are the primary and secondary employers owned and controlled by the same person or persons? Are they engaged in "closely integrated operations"? May they be treated as a single employer under the Act? Another test of the "ally" relationship is based on the conduct of the secondary employer. If an employer, despite its claim of neutrality in the dispute, acts in a way that indicates that it has abandoned its "neutral" position, the employer opens itself up to primary action by the union. An example of this would be an employer who, claiming to be a neutral, enters into an arrangement with a struck employer whereby it accepts and performs farmed-out work of that employer who would normally do the work itself, but who cannot perform the work because its plant is closed by a strike.

When employees of a primary employer and those of a secondary employer work on the same premises, a special situation is involved and the usual rules do not apply. A typical example of the shared site or "common situs" situation is when a subcontractor with whom a union has a dispute is engaged at work on a construction site alongside other subcontractors with whom the union has no dispute. Picketing at a common situs is permissible if directed solely against the primary employer. But it is prohibited if directed against secondary employers

When an employer is not protected from secondary strikes and boycotts

When a union may picket an employer who shares a site with another employer

regularly engaged at that site. To assist in determining whether picketing at a common situs is restricted to the primary employer and therefore permissible, or directed at a secondary employer and therefore violative of the statute, the NLRB and the courts have suggested various guidelines for evaluating the object of the picketing, including the following.

Subject to the qualification noted below, the picketing would appear to be primary picketing if the picketing is:

1. Limited to times when the employees of the primary employer are working on the Premises.

2. Limited to times when the primary employer is carrying on its normal business there.

3. Confined to places reasonably close to where the employees of the primary employer are working.

4. Conducted so that the picket signs, the banners, and the conduct of the pickets indicate clearly that the dispute is with the primary employer and not with the secondary Employer.

These guidelines are known as the *Moore Dry Dock* standards from the case in which they were first formulated by the NLRB. However, the NLRB has held that picketing at a common situs may be unlawful notwithstanding compliance with the *Moore Dry Dock* standards if a union's statements or actions otherwise indicate that the picketing has an unlawful objective.

Picketing contractors' gates

In some situations a company may set aside, or reserve, a certain plant gate, or entrance to its premises, for the exclusive use of a contractor. If a union has a labor dispute with the company and pickets the company's premises, including the gate so reserved, the union may be held to have violated Section 8(b)(4)(B). The U.S. Supreme Court has stated the circumstances under which such a violation may be found as follows:

There must be a separate gate, marked and set apart from other gates; the work done by the employees who use the gate must be unrelated to the normal operations of the employer, and the work must be of a kind that would not, if done when the plant were engaged in its regular operations, necessitate curtailing those operations.

However, if the reserved gate is used by employees of both the company and the contractor, the picketing would be considered primary and not a violation of Section 8(b)(4)(B).

Subparagraph (B)—Prohibited object: Compelling recognition of an uncertified union

Section 8(b)(4)(B) also prohibits secondary action to compel an employer to recognize or bargain with a union that is not the certified representative of its employees. If a union takes action described in clause (i) or (ii) against a secondary employer, and the union's object

36

is recognition by the primary employer, the union commits an unfair labor practice under this section. To establish that the union has an object of recognition, a specific demand by the union for recognition need not be shown; a demand for a contract, which implies recognition or at least bargaining, is enough to establish an 8(b)(4)(B) object.

Section 8(b)(4)(C) forbids a labor organization from using clause (i) or (ii) conduct to force an employer to recognize or bargain with a labor organization other than the one that is currently certified as the representative of its employees. Section 8(b)(4)(C) has been held not to apply when the picketing union is merely protesting working conditions that are sub-standard for the area.

Subparagraph (C)–Prohibited object: Compelling recognition of a union if another union has been certified

Section 8(b)(4)(D) forbids a labor organization from engaging in action described in clauses (i) and (ii) for the purpose of forcing any employer to assign certain work to "employees in a particular labor organization or in a particular trade, craft, or class rather than to employees in another labor organization or in another trade, craft, or class." The Act sets up a special procedure for handling disputes over work assignments that will be discussed later in this material (see p. 50).

Subparagraph (D)–Prohibited object: Compelling assignment of certain work to certain employees

The final provision in Section 8(b)(4) provides that nothing in Section 8(b)(4) shall be construed "to prohibit publicity, other than picketing, for the purpose of truthfully advising the public, including consumers and members of a labor organization, that a product or products are produced by an employer with whom the labor organization has a primary dispute and are distributed by another employer." Such publicity is not protected if it has "an effect of inducing any individual employed by any persons other than the primary employer" to refuse to handle any goods or not to perform services. The Supreme Court has held that this provision permitted a union to distribute handbills at the stores of neutral food chains asking the public not to buy certain items distributed by a wholesaler with whom the union had a primary dispute. Moreover, it has also held that peaceful picketing at the stores of a struck employer when they traded chain to persuade customers not to buy the products of a struck employer when they traded in these stores was not prohibited by Section 8(b)(4).

Publicity such as handbilling allowed by Section 8(b)(4)

Section 8(b)(5) makes it illegal for a union to charge employees who are covered by an authorized union-security agreement a membership fee "in an amount which the Board finds excessive or discriminatory under all the circumstances." The section also provides that the Board in making its finding must consider among other factors "the practices and customs

Section 8(b)(5)— Excessive or Discriminatory Membership Fees

of labor organizations in the particular industry, and the wages currently paid to the employees affected."

Examples of violations of this section include:

- Charging old employees who do not join the union until after a union-security agreement goes into effect an initiation fee of $15 while charging new employees only thirty-five.

- Increasing the initiation fee from $75 to 1250 and thus charging new members an amount equal to about 4 weeks' wages when other unions in the area charge a fee equal to about one-half the employee's first week's pay.

Section 8(b)(6) forbids a labor organization "to cause or attempt to cause an employer to pay or deliver or agree to pay or deliver any money or other thing of value, in the nature of an exaction, for services which are not performed or not to be performed."

Section 8(b)(7) prohibits a labor organization that is not currently certified as the employees' representative from picketing or threatening to picket with an object of obtaining recognition by the employer (recognitional picketing) or acceptance by his employees as their representative (organizational picketing). The object of picketing is ascertained from all the surrounding facts including the message on the picket signs and any communications between the union and the employer. "Recognitional" picketing as used in Section 8(b)(7) refers to picketing to obtain an employer's initial recognition of the union as bargaining representative of its employees or to force the employer, without formal recognition of the union, to maintain a specific and detailed set of working conditions. It does not include picketing by an incumbent union for continued recognition or for a new contract. Neither does it include picketing that seeks to prevent the employer from undermining area standards of working conditions by operating at less than the labor costs which prevail under bargaining contracts in the area.

Recognitional and organizational picketing are prohibited in three specific instances.

A. When the employer has lawfully recognized another union and a representation election would be barred by either the provisions of the Act or the Board's Rules, as in the case of a valid contract between the employer and the other union (8(b)(7)(A)). (A union is considered lawfully recognized when the employer's recognition of the union cannot be attacked under the unfair labor practice provisions of Section 8 of the Act.)

Examples of violations of Section 8(b)(5)

Section 8(b)(6)— "Featherbedding"

Section 8(b)(7)— Organizational and Recognitional Picketing by Noncertified Unions

38

B. When a valid NLRB representation election has been held within the previous 12 months (8(b)(7)(B)).

C. When a representation petition is not filed "within a reasonable period of time not to exceed thirty days from the commencement of such picketing" (8(b)(7)(C)).

Publicity picketing

Subparagraph (C) is subject to an exception, called a proviso, which permits picketing "for the purpose of truthfully advising the public (including consumers)" that an employer does not employ union members or have a contract with a labor organization. However, such picketing loses the protection of this proviso if it has a substantial effect on the employer's business because it induces "any individual employed by any other person" to refuse to pick up or deliver goods or to perform other services.

Expedited elections under Section 8(b)(7)(C)

If an 8(b)(7)(C) charge is filed against the picketing union and a representation petition is filed within a reasonable time after the picketing starts, subparagraph (C) provides for an election to be held forthwith. This election requires neither a hearing nor a showing of interest among the employees. As a consequence the election can be held and the results obtained faster than in a regular election under Section 9(c), and for this reason it is called an "expedited" election. Petitions filed more than a reasonable time after picketing begins and petitions filed during picketing protected by the 8(b)(7)(C) proviso, discussed above, are processed under normal election procedures and the election will not be expedited. The reasonable period in which to file a petition cannot exceed 30 days and may be shorter, when, for instance, picketing is accompanied by violence.

Examples of violations of Section 8(b)(7)

Examples of violations of Section 80(7) are as follows:

- Picketing by a union for organizational purposes shortly after the employer has entered a lawful contract with another union (8(b)(7)(A)).

- Picketing by a union for organizational purposes within 12 months after a valid NLRB election in which a majority of the employees in the unit voted to have no union (8(b)(7)(B)).

- Picketing by a union for recognition continuing for more than 30 days without the filing of a representation petition wherein the picketing stops all deliveries by employees of an other employer (8(b)(7)(C)).

Section 8(e)—Entering a Hot Cargo Agreement

Section 8(e) makes it an unfair labor practice for an employer or a labor organization to enter a hot cargo agreement. This section applies equally to unions and to employers. The

Section 8(g)–Striking or Picketing a Health Care Institution Without Notice

discussion of this section as an unfair labor practice of employers has been treated as a discussion of an unfair labor practice of unions as well. (See pp. 26 and 27.)

Section 8(g) prohibits a labor organization from engaging in a strike, picketing, or other concerted refusal to work at any health care institution without first giving at least 10 days' notice in writing to the institution and the Federal Mediation and Conciliation Service.

How the Act Is Enforced

The rights of employees declared by Congress in the National Labor Relations Act are not self-enforcing. To ensure that employees may exercise these rights, and to protect them and the public from unfair labor practices, Congress established the NLRB to administer and enforce the Act.

Organization of the NLRB

The NLRB includes the Board, which is composed of five members with their respective staffs, the General Counsel and staff, and the Regional, Subregional, and Resident Offices. The

The Board

General Counsel has final and independent authority on behalf of the Board, in respect to the investigation of charges and issuance of complaints. Members of the Board are appointed

The General Counsel

by the President, with consent of the Senate, for 5-year terms. The General Counsel is also appointed by the President, with consent of the Senate, for a 4-year term. Offices of the Board and the General Counsel are in Washington, D.C. To assist in administering and enforcing

The Regional Offices

the law, the NLRB has established 33 regional and a number of other field offices. These offices, located in major cities in various States and Puerto Rico, are under the general supervision of the General Counsel.

Functions of the NLRB

The Agency has two main functions: to conduct representation elections and certify the results, and to prevent employers and unions from engaging in unfair labor practices. In both kinds of cases the processes of the NLRB are begun only when requested. Requests for such action must be made in writing on forms provided by the NLRB and filed with the proper Regional Office. The form used to request an election is called a "petition," and the form for unfair labor practices is called a "charge." The filing of a petition or a charge sets in motion the machinery of the NLRB under the Act. Before discussing the machinery established by the Act, it would be well to understand the nature and extent of the authority of the NLRB.

Authority of the NLRB

The NLRB gets its authority from Congress by way of the National Labor Relations Act. The power of Congress to regulate labor-management relations is limited by the commerce clause of the United States Constitution. Although it can declare generally what the rights of employees are or should be, Congress can make its declaration of rights effective only in respect to enterprises whose operations "affect commerce" and labor disputes that "affect commerce.' The NLRB, therefore, can direct elect ions and certify the results only in the case of an employer whose operations affect commerce. Similarly, it can act to prevent unfair labor practices only in cases involving labor disputes that affect, or would affect, commerce.

"Commerce" includes trade, traffic, transportation, or communication within the District of Columbia or any Territory of the United States; or between any State or Territory and any other State, Territory, or the District of Columbia; or between two points in the same State, but through any other State, Territory, the District of Columbia, or a foreign country. Examples of enterprises engaged in commerce are:

- A manufacturing company in California that sells and ships its product to buyers in Oregon.
- A company in Georgia that buys supplies in Louisiana.
- A trucking company that transports goods from one point in New York State through Pennsylvania to another point in New York State.
- A radio station in Minnesota that has listeners in Wisconsin.

Although a company may not have any direct dealings with enterprises in any other State, its operations may nevertheless affect commerce. The operations of a Massachusetts manufacturing company that sells all of its goods to Massachusetts wholesalers affect commerce if the wholesalers ship to buyers in other States. The effects of a labor dispute involving the Massachusetts manufacturing concern would be felt in other States and the labor dispute would, therefore, "affect" commerce. Using this test, it can be seen that the operations of almost any employer can be said to affect commerce. As a result, the authority of the NLRB could extend to all but purely local enterprises.

The scope of the commerce clause is limited, however, by the first amendment's prohibition against Congress' enacting laws restricting the free exercise of religion. Because of this potential conflict, and because Congress has not clearly expressed an intention that the Act cover lay faculty in church-operated schools, the Supreme Court has held that the Board may not assert jurisdiction over faculty members in such institutions.

Although the National Labor Relations Board could exercise its powers to enforce the Act in all cases involving enterprises whose operations affect commerce, the Board does not act in all such cases. In its discretion it limits the exercise of its power to cases involving enterprises

Enterprises whose operations affect commerce

What is commerce

When the operations of an employer affect commerce

The Board does not act in all cases affecting commerce

whose effect on commerce is substantial. The Board's requirements for exercising its power or jurisdiction are called "jurisdictional standards." These standards are based on the yearly amount of business done by the enterprise, or on the yearly amount of its sales or of its purchases. They are stated in terms of total dollar volume of business and are different for different kinds of enterprises. The Board's standards in effect on July 1, 1990, are as follows:

NLRB jurisdictional standards

1. *Nonretail business:* Direct sales of goods to consumers in other States, or indirect sales through others (called outflow), of at least $50,000 a year; or direct purchases of goods from suppliers in other States, or indirect purchases through others (called inflow), of at least $50,000 a year.

2. *Office buildings:* Total annual revenue of $100,000 of which $25,000 or more is derived from organizations that meet any of the standards except the indirect outflow and indirect inflow standards established for nonretail enterprises.

3. *Retail enterprises:* At least $500,000 total annual volume of business.

4. *Public utilities:* At least $250,000 total annual volume of business, or $50,000 direct or in direct outflow or inflow.

5. *Newspapers:* At least $200,000 total annual volume of business.

6. *Radio, telegraph, television, and telephone enterprises:* At least $100,000 total annual volume of business.

7. *Hotels, motels, and residential apartment houses:* At least $500,000 total annual volume of business.

8. *Privately operated health care institutions:* At least $250,000 total annual volume of business for hospitals; at least $100,000 for nursing homes, visiting nurses associations, and related facilities; at least $250,000 for all other types of private health care institutions defined in the 1974 amendments to the Act. The statutory definition includes: "any hospital, convalescent hospital, health maintenance organizations, health clinic, nursing home, extended care facility or other institution devoted to the care of the sick, infirm, or aged person." Public hospitals are excluded from NLRB jurisdiction by Section 2(2) of the Act.

9. *Transportation enterprise, links and channels of interstate commerce:* At least $50,000 total annual income from furnishing interstate passenger and freight transportation services; also performing services valued at $50,000 or more for businesses which meet any

of the jurisdictional standards except the indirect outflow and indirect inflow of standards established for nonretail enterprises.

10. *Transit systems:* At least $250,000 total annual volume of business.

11. *Taxicab companies:* At least $500,000 total annual volume of business.

12. *Associations:* These are regarded as a single employer in that the annual business of all association members is totaled to determine whether any of the standards apply.

13. *Enterprises in the Territories and the District of Columbia:* The jurisdictional standards apply in the Territories; all businesses in the District of Columbia come under NLRB jurisdiction.

14. *National defense:* Jurisdiction is asserted over all enterprises affecting commerce when their operations have a substantial impact on national defense, whether the enterprises satisfy any other standard.

15. *Private universities and colleges:* At least $1 million gross annual revenue from all sources (excluding contributions not available for operating expenses because of limitaTions imposed by the grantor).

16. *Symphony orchestras:* At least $1 million gross annual revenue from all sources (excludIng contributions not available for operating expenses because of limitations imposed by the grantor).

17. *Law firms and legal assistance programs:* At least $250,000 gross annual revenues.

18. *Employers that provide social services:* At least $250,000 gross annual revenues.

Through enactment of the 1970 Postal Reorganization Act, jurisdiction of the NLRB was extended to the United States Postal Service, effective July 1, 1971.

In addition to the above-listed standards, the Board asserts jurisdiction over gambling casinos when these enterprises are legally operated, when their total annual revenue from gambling is at least $500,000.

Ordinarily, if an enterprise does the total annual volume of business listed in the standard, it will necessarily be engaged in activities that "affect" commerce. The Board must find, however, based on evidence, that the enterprise does in fact "affect" commerce.

The Board has established the policy that when an employer whose operations "affect" commerce refuses to supply the Board with information concerning total annual business, the Board may dispense with this requirement and exercise jurisdiction.

Finally, Section 14(c)(1) authorizes the Board, in its discretion, to decline to exercise jurisdiction over any class or category of employers when a labor dispute involving such employees is not sufficiently substantial to warrant the exercise of jurisdiction, provided that it cannot refuse to exercise jurisdiction over any labor dispute over which it would have asserted jurisdiction under the standards it had in effect on August 1, 1959. In accordance with this provision the Board has determined that it will not exercise jurisdiction over racetracks, owners, breeders, and trainers of racehorses, and real estate brokers.

In addition to the foregoing limitations, the Act states that the term "employee" shall include any employee   Except the following:

- Agricultural laborers.
- Domestic servants.
- Any individual employed by his parent or spouse.
- Independent contractors.
- Supervisors
- Individuals employed by an employer subject to the Railway Labor Act.
- Government employees, including those employed by the U.S. Government, any Government corporation or Federal Reserve Bank, or any State or political subdivision such as a city, town, or school district.

The Act does not cover certain individuals

Supervisors are excluded from the definition of "employee" and, therefore, not covered by the Act. Whether an individual is a supervisor for purposes of the Act depends on that individual's authority over employees and not merely a title. A supervisor is defined by the Act as any individual who has the authority, acting in the interest of an employer, to cause another employee to be hired, transferred, suspended, laid off, recalled, promoted, discharged, assigned, rewarded, or disciplined, either by taking such action or by recommending it to a superior; or who has the authority responsibly to direct other employees or adjust their grievances; provided, in all cases, that the exercise of authority is not of a merely routine or clerical nature, but requires the exercise of independent judgment. For example, a foreman who determined which employees would be laid off after being directed by the job superintendent to lay off four employees would be considered a supervisor and would, therefore, not be covered by the Act; a "strawboss" who, after someone else determined which employees would be laid off, merely informed the employees of the layoff and who neither directed other employees

Supervisor defined

44

nor adjusted their grievances would not be considered a supervisor and would be covered by the Act.

"Managerial" employees are also excluded from the protection of the Act. A managerial employee is one who represents management interests by taking or recommending actions that effectively control or implement employer policy.

The term "employer" includes any person who acts as an agent of an employer, but it does not include the following:

- The United States or any State Government, or any political subdivision of either, or any Government corporation or Federal Reserve Bank.
- Any employer subject to the Railway Labor Act.

NLRB Procedures

The authority of the NLRB can be brought to bear in a representation proceeding only by the filing of a petition. Forms for petitions must be signed, sworn to or affirmed under oath, and filed with the Regional Office in the area where the unit of employees is located. If employees in the unit regularly work in more than one regional area, the petition may be filed with the Regional Office of any of such regions.

Section 9(c)(1) provides that when a petition is filed, "the Board shall investigate such petition and if it has reasonable cause to believe that a question of representation affecting commerce exists shall provide for an appropriate hearing upon due notice." If the Board finds from the evidence presented at the hearing that "such a question of representation exists, it shall direct an election by secret ballot and shall certify the results thereof." When there are three or more choices on the ballot and none receives a majority, Section 9(c)(3) provides for a runoff between the choice that received the largest and the choice that received the second largest number of valid votes in the election. After the election, if a union receives a majority of the votes cast, it is certified; if no union gets a majority, that result is certified. A union that has been certified is entitled to be recognized by the employer as the exclusive bargaining agent for the employees in the unit. If the employer fails to bargain with the onion, it commits an unfair labor practice.

The procedure in an unfair labor practice case is begun by the filing of a charge. A charge may be filed by an employee, an employer, a labor organization, or any other person. Like petitions, charge forms, which are also available at Regional Offices, must be signed, sworn to or affirmed under oath, and filed with the appropriate Regional Office–that is, the Regional Office in the area where the alleged unfair labor practice was committed. Section 10 provides

45

for the issuance of a complaint stating the charges and notifying the charged party of a hearing to be held concerning the charges. Such a complaint will issue only after investigation of the charges through the Regional Office indicates that an unfair labor practice has in fact occurred.

In certain limited circumstances when an employer and union have an agreed-upon grievance arbitration procedure that will resolve the dispute, the Board will defer processing an unfair labor practice case and await resolution of the issues through that grievance arbitration procedure. If the grievance arbitration process meets the Board's standards, the Board may accept the final resolution and defer that decision. If the procedure fails to meet all the Board standards for deferral, the Board may then resume processing of the unfair labor practice issues.

An unfair labor practice hearing is conducted before an NLRB administrative law judge in accordance with the rules of evidence and procedure that apply in the U.S. district courts. Based on the hearing record, the administrative law judge makes findings and recommendations to the Board. All parties to the hearing may appeal the administrative law judge's decision to the Board. If the board considers that the party named in the complaint has engaged in or is engaging in the unfair labor practices charged, the Board is authorized to issue an order requiring such person to cease and desist from such practices and to take appropriate affirmative action.

Section 10(b) provides that "no complaint shall issue based upon any unfair labor practice occurring more than six months prior to the filing of the charge with the Board and the service of a copy thereof upon the person against whom such charge is made." An exception is made if the charging party "was prevented from filing such charge by reason of service in the armed forces, in which event the six-month period shall be computed from the day of his discharge." It should be noted that the charging party must, within 6 months after the unfair labor practice occurs, file the charge with the Regional Office and serve copies of the charge on each person against whom the charge is made. Normally service is made by sending the charge by registered mail, return receipt requested.

If the Regional Director refuses to issue a complaint in any case, the person who filed the charge may appeal the decision to the General Counsel in Washington. Section 3(d) places in the General Counsel "final authority, on behalf of the Board, in respect of the investigation of charges and issuance of complaints." If the General Counsel reverses the Regional Director's

The 6-month rule limiting issuance of complaint

Appeal to the General Counsel if complaint is not issued

46

decision, a complaint will be issued. If the General Counsel approves the decision not to issue a complaint, there is no further appeal.

To enable the NLRB to perform its duties under the Act, Congress delegated to the Agency certain powers that can be used in all cases. These are principally powers having to do with investigations and hearings.

As previously indicated, all charges that are filed with the Regional Office are investigated, as are petitions for representation elections. Section 11 establishes the powers of the Board and the Regional Offices in respect to hearings and investigations. The provisions of Section 11(1) authorize the Board or its agents to:

- Examine and copy "any evidence of any person being investigated or proceeded against that relates to any matter under investigation or in question."
- Issues subpoenas, on the application of any party to the proceeding, requiring the attendance and testimony of witnesses or the production of any evidence.
- Administer oaths and affirmations, examine witnesses, and receive evidence.
- Obtain a court order to compel the production of evidence or the giving of testimony.

The National Labor Relations Act is not a criminal statute. It is entirely remedial. It is intended to prevent and remedy unfair labor practices, not to punish the person responsible for them. The Board is authorized by Section 10(c) not only to issue a cease-and-desist order, but "to take such affirmative action including reinstatement of employees with or without back pay, as will effectuate the policies of this Act."

The object of the Board's order in any case is twofold: to eliminate the unfair labor practice and to undo the effects of the violation as much as possible. In determining what the remedy will be in any given case, the Board has considerable discretion. Ordinarily, its order in regard to any particular unfair labor practice will follow a standard form that is designed to remedy that unfair labor practice, but the Board can, and often does, change the standard order to meet the needs of the case. Typical affirmative action of the Board may include orders to an employer who has engaged in unfair labor practices to:

- Disestablish an employer-dominated union.
- Offer certain named individuals immediate and full reinstatement to their former positions or, if those positions no longer exist, to substantially equivalent positions without prejudice to their seniority and other rights and privileges, and with back pay, including interest.

Powers of the NLRB

Powers concerning investigations

The Act is remedial, not criminal

Affirmative action may be ordered by the Board

Examples of affirmative action directed to employers

- On request, bargain collectively with a certain union as the exclusive representative of the employees in a certain described unit and sign a written agreement if an understanding is reached.

Examples of affirmative action that may be required of a union that has engaged in unfair labor practices include orders to:

- Notify the employer and the employees that it has no objection to reinstatement of certain employees, or employment of certain applicants, whose discriminatory discharge, or denial of employment, was caused by the union.
- Refund dues or fees illegally collected, plus interest.
- On request, bargain collectively with a certain employer and sign a written agreement if one is reached.

The Board's order usually includes a direction to the employer or the union or both requiring them to post notices in the employer's plant or the union's office notifying the employees that they will cease the unfair labor practices and informing them of any affirmative action being undertaken to remedy the violation. Special care is taken to be sure that these notices are readily understandable by the employees to whom they are addressed.

Special Proceedings in Certain Cases

Special proceedings are required by the Act in certain kinds of cases. These include the determination of jurisdictional disputes under Section 10(k) and injunction proceedings under Section 10(l) and (j).

Whenever it is charged that any person has engaged in an unfair labor practice in violation of Section 8(b)(4)(D), the Board must hear and determine the dispute out of which the unfair labor practice arises. Section 8(b)(4)(D) prohibits unions from striking or inducing a strike to compel an employer to assign particular work to employees in one union, or in one trade or craft, rather than another. For a jurisdictional dispute to exist, there must be real competition between unions or between groups of employees for certain work. In effect, Section 10(k) provides an opportunity for the parties to adjust the dispute during a 10-day period after notice of the 8(b)(4)(D) charge has been served. At the end of this period if the parties have not submitted to the Board satisfactory evidence that they have adjusted, or agreed on a method of adjusting, the dispute, the Board is "empowered and directed" to determine which of the competing groups is entitled to have the work.

Section 10(l) provides that whenever a charge is filed alleging a violation of certain sections of the Act relating to boycotts, picketing, and work stoppages, the preliminary investigation

Examples of affirmative action directed to unions

Proceedings in jurisdictional disputes

48

of the charge must be given priority over all other types of cases in the Regional Office where it is filed. The unfair labor practices subject to this priority concerning the investigation are those defined in Section 8(b)(4)(A), (B), or (C), all three subparagraphs of Section 8(b)(7), Section 8(e) and, where appropriate, 8(b)(4)(D). Section 10(m) requires that second priority be given to charges alleging violations of Section 8(a)(3), the prohibition against employer discrimination to encourage or discourage membership in a union, and Section 8(b)(2), which forbids unions to cause or attempt to cause such discrimination.

The investigation of certain charges must be given priority

If the preliminary investigation of any of the first priority cases shows that there is reasonable cause to believe that the charge is true and that a complaint should issue, Section 10(l) further requires the Board to petition a U.S. district court to grant an injunction pending the final determination of the Board. The section authorizes the court to grant "such injunctive relief or temporary restraining order as it deems just and proper." Another provision of the section prohibits the application for an injunction based on a charge of violation of Section 8(b)(7) (the prohibition on organizational or recognitional picketing in certain situations) if a charge against an employer alleging violation of Section 8(a)(2) has been filed and the preliminary investigation establishes reasonable cause to believe that such charge is true.

Injunction proceedings under Section 10(l)

Section 10(j) allows the Board to petition a Federal district court for an injunction to temporarily prevent any unfair labor practice after a complaint has been issued and to restore the status quo, pending the full review of the case by the Board. This section does not require that injunctive relief be sought, but only makes it possible for the Board to do so in cases when it is considered appropriate.

Injunctive relief may be sought in other cases

Court Enforcement of Board Orders

If an employer or a union fails to comply with a Board order, Section 10(e) empowers the Board to petition the U.S. court of appeals for a court decree enforcing the order of the Board enjoining conduct that the Board has found to be unlawful. Section 10(f) provides that any person aggrieved by a final order of the Board granting or denying in whole or in part the relief sought may obtain a review of such order in any appropriate circuit court of appeals. When the court of appeals hears a petition concerning a Board order, it may enforce the order, remand it to the Board for reconsideration, change it, or set it aside entirely. If the court of appeals issues a judgment enforcing the Board order, failure to comply may be punishable by fine or imprisonment for contempt of court.

In the U.S. court of appeals

49

In some cases the U.S. Supreme Court may be asked to review the decision of a circuit court of appeals, particularly when there is a conflict in the views of different courts on the same important problem.

In this material the entire Act has been covered, but, of necessity, the coverage has been brief. No attempt has been made to state the law in detail or to supply you with a textbook on labor law. We have tried to explain the Act in a manner intended to make it easier to understand what the basic provisions of the Act are and how they may concern you. If it helps you to recognize and know your rights and obligations under the Act, and aids in determining whether you need expert assistance when a problem arises, its purpose will have been satisfied. More than that, the objective of the Act will have been furthered.

The objective of the National Labor Relations Act, to avoid or reduce industrial strife and protect the public health, safety, and interest, can best be achieved by the parties or those who may become parties to an individual dispute. Voluntary adjustment of differences at the community and local level is almost invariably the speediest, most satisfactory, and longest lasting way of carrying out the objective of the Act.

Efforts are being made in all our Regional Offices to increase the understanding of all parties about what the law requires of them. Long experience has taught us that when the parties fully understand their rights and obligations, they are more ready and able to adjust their differences voluntarily. Seldom do individuals go into a courtroom, a hearing, or any other avoidable contest, knowing that they are in the wrong and that they can expect to lose the decision. No one really likes to be publicly recorded as a law violator (and a loser too). Similarly, it is seldom that individuals refuse to accept an informal adjustment of differences that is reasonable, knowing that they can obtain no better result from the formal proceeding, even if they prevail.

The consequences of ignorance in these matters—formal proceedings that can be time-consuming and costly, and that are often followed by bitterness and antagonism—are economically wasteful, and usually it is accurate to say that neither party really wins. It is in an attempt to bring about more widespread awareness of the basic law and thus help the parties avoid these consequences that this material has been prepared and presented as a part of a continuing program to increase understanding of the National Labor Relations Act.

Conclusion

50

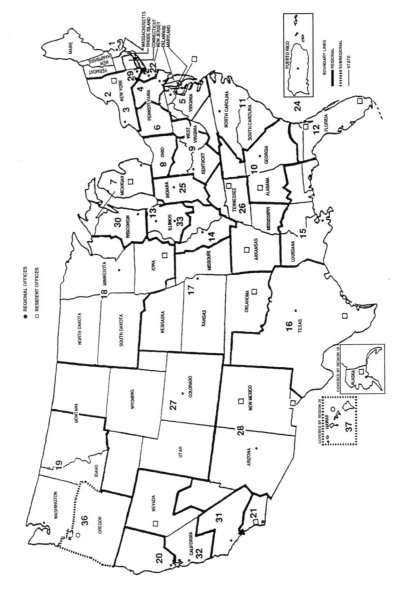

MAP SHOWING REGIONAL BOUNDARIES

● REGIONAL OFFICES

□ RESIDENT OFFICES

BOUNDARY LINES

▬▬▬ REGIONAL

••••••• SUBREGIONAL

——— STATE

NATIONAL LABOR RELATIONS BOARD DIRECTORY*

Region 1
10 Causeway Street–6th Floor
Boston MA 02222–1072
(617) 565–6700

Region 2
26 Federal Plaza–Room 3614
New York NY 10278–0104
(212) 264–0300

Region 3
111 West Huron Street–Room 901
Buffalo NY 14202–2387
(716) 846–4931

Region 4
615 Chestnut Street–7th Floor
Philadelphia PA 19106–4404
(215) 597–7601

Region 5
The Appraisers Store Building
103 South Gay Street–8th Floor
Baltimore MD 21202–4026
(410) 962–2822

Region 6
1000 Liberty Avenue–Room 1501
Pittsburgh PA 15222–4173
(412) 644–2977

Region 7
477 Michigan Avenue–Room 300
Detroit MI 48226–2569
(313) 226–3200

Region 8
1240 East 9th Street–Room 1695
Cleveland OH 44199–2086
(216) 522–3715

Region 9
550 Main Street–Room 3003
Cincinnati OH 45202–3272
(513) 684–3686

Region 10
101 Marietta Street NW–Suite 2400
Atlanta GA 30323–3301
(404) 331–2896

Region 11
Republic Square, Suite 200
4035 University Parkway
Winston-Salem NC 27106–3325
(910) 631–5201

Region 12
Enterprise Plaza–Suite 530
201 East Kennedy Boulevard
Tampa FL 33602–5824
(813) 228–2641

Region 13
200 West Adams Street–Suite 800
Chicago IL 60606–5208
(312) 353–7570

Region 14
1222 Spruce Street, Room 8.302
St. Louis MO 63103–2829
(314) 539–7770

Region 15
1515 Poydras Street–Room 610
New Orleans LA 70112–3723
(504) 589–6361

Region 16
819 Taylor Street–Room 8A24
Fort Worth TX 76102–6178
(817) 978–2921

Region 17
8600 Farley Street–Suite 100
Overland Park KS 66212–4677
(913) 967–3000

Region 18
110 South 4th Street–Room 316
Minneapolis MN 55401–2291
(612) 348–1757

52

Region 19
915 2nd Avenue–Room 2948
Seattle WA 98174–1078
(206) 220–6300

Subregional Office 36–Region 19
222 SW Columbia Street–Room 401
Portland OR 97201–6604
(503) 326–3085

Region 20
901 Market Street–Room 400
San Francisco CA 94103–1735
(415) 356–5130

Subregional Office 37–Region 20
300 Ala Moana Boulevard–Room 7318
Honolulu HI 96850–4980
(808) 541–2814

Region 21
888 Figueroa Street–9th Floor
Los Angeles CA 90017–5449
(213) 894–5200

Region 22
970 Broad Street–Room 1600
Newark NJ 07102–2570
(201) 645–2100

Region 24
La Torre de Plaza
Plaza Las Americas, Suite 1002
525 F. D. Roosevelt Avenue
Hato Rey PR 00918–1002
(787) 766–5347

Region 25
575 N. Pennsylvania Street–Room 238
Indianapolis IN 46204–1577
(317) 226–7430

Region 26
1407 Union Avenue–Room 800
Memphis TN 38104–3627
(901) 544–0018

Region 27
600 17th Street–3rd Floor, South Tower
Denver CO 80202–5433
(303) 844–3551

Region 28
234 North Central Avenue–Suite 440
Phoenix AZ 85004–2212
(602) 379–3361

Region 29
One MetroTech Center
Jay Street and Myrtle Avenue–10 Floor
Brooklyn NY 11201–4201
(718) 330–7713

Region 30
310 West Wisconsin Avenue–Suite 700
Milwaukee WI 53202–2211
(414) 297–3861

Region 31
11000 Wilshire Boulevard–Room 12100
Los Angeles CA 90024–3682
(310) 235–7352

Region 32
1301 Clay Street–Room 300N
Oakland CA 94612–5211
(510) 637–3300

Region 33
300 Hamilton Boulevard–Suite 200
Peoria IL 61602–1246
(309) 671–7080

Region 34
One Commercial Plaza–21st Floor
Hartford CT 06103–3599
(860) 240–3522

*For addresses and telephone numbers of various subregional offices please consult your local telephone directory.

53

COLLECTIVE BARGAINING UNITS
IN THE HEALTH CARE INDUSTRY

Eight bargaining units have been established in which union elections for health care employees may be conducted. Those eight units are as follows:

1. **Registered Nurse Unit** - All RNs reporting to the director of nursing are included in this unit, unless supervisory or managerial. The NLRB has generally included the following classifications within RN units...

- graduate nurses or nurse permittees
- non-nursing department nurses
- nurse anesthetists
- nurse instructors or facility nurses
- nurse practitioners

2. **Physician Unit** - All physicians, though the NLRB has not drawn clear lines between physicians and other types of doctors, such as chiropractors and osteopaths. Dentists have been included within this unit. Physicians who are not employees, but rather independent contractors, students, managers or supervisors may well be excluded.

3. **All-Other Professional Unit** - Professionals other than registered nurses and physicians are included in this unit. Positions that the NLRB has determined to be professional include...

- audiologists
- chemists
- counselors
- dieticians
- educational programmers
- medical artists
- medical technologists
- nuclear physicists
- pharmacists
- physical and occupational therapists

- psychologists
- recreational therapists
- social workers
- teachers

4. **Technical Unit** - Technical employees are generally considered to be those whose jobs require: additional education or training beyond high school; certification, registration or licensure. They are mainly distinguished from professionals by the fact their positions do not require a college degree. Some positions that the NLRB has determined to be technical are...

- biomedical engineers
- cardiopulmonary technicians
- cytotechnologists
- emergency medicine technicians
- histology technicians
- infant care technicians
- inhalation therapists
- laboratory technicians
- licensed psychiatric technicians
- licensed vocational nurses
- operating room technicians
- orthopedic technicians
- physical therapy technicians or assistants
- radiation technologists
- recreation activity specialists
- renal and dialysis technicians
- respiratory therapists

5. **Skilled Maintenance Unit** - Skilled Maintenance positions require a high school education and normally some trade or vocational school experience or completion of an apprenticeship program. The NLRB has described such a unit as including...

- automotive mechanics
- carpenters
- chief engineers
- electricians
- fireman/boiler operators
- HVAC (heating, ventilating and air conditioning)
- locksmiths
- mason/bricklayers

- operating engineers
- painters
- pipefitters
- plumbers
- sheetmetal fabricators
- welders

6. **Business Office Clerical Unit** - Positions that fit this bargaining unit are those primarily responsible for financial and billing practices, dealing with Medicare, DRGs, price schedules, insurance issues and reimbursement systems. Other positions may require selecting, completing or interpreting business forms and performing tasks on them using computers, key board terminals or typewriters. Generally, a high school diploma and specific clerical skills may be required. The NLRB has included the following positions within this category...

- accounting clerks
- administration clerks
- audit clerks
- cashiers
- computer operators, programmers and data entry clerks
- credit and collection clerks
- credit union clerks
- insurance clerks
- management engineering clerks
- personnel and payroll clerks
- planning and development clerks
- public relations and community affairs clerks
- switchboard, telephone and PBX operators
- volunteer department clerks

7. **All-Other Non-Professional Unit** - Appropriate employees for this unit are those with a high school education or less, performing unskilled jobs requiring only limited on-the-job training. Some positions within this unit typically include...

- barbers
- hotel service employees (food service, linen, housekeeping)
- material management personnel
- medical records clerks
- medical transcriptionists
- nurse aides

- patient transporters
- pharmacy aides or technicians
- porters
- recovery room technicians (if not technical)
- research aides
- unskilled workers in diagnostic and treatment areas
  (i.e., radiology assistants, laboratory assistants, dark room technicians, physical therapy aides, phlebotomists)
- utilization review coordinator
  (if degree or technical training is not required)
- ward clerks

8. **Guard Unit** - All security officers whose job requires enforcing the employer's rules to protect property and the safety of persons on the employer's premises. Other job descriptions cannot be combined with guards.

The Bargaining Unit Rule applies to "acute care hospitals," the definition of which is a short-term care hospital in which either the average length of patient stay is less than 30 days, or at least 50% of all patients are admitted to units where the average length of patient stay is less than 30 days. A facility will bear the burden of proof establishing that it is *not* an acute care hospital. Psychiatric hospitals, rehabilitation hospitals and nursing homes are excluded from the Rule.

(NOTE: You will find an extensive discussion of the Bargaining Unit Rule in the American Hospital Association's *Legal Memorandum Number Sixteen, Collective Bargaining Units in The Health Care Industry.* Legal counsel should also be sought when determining appropriate bargaining units.)

INDEX

---

investigative authority, NLRB, 397-399

issues in election campaign, 74, 76-77, 84-86, 126, 141

    see also election campaign segments

job security, 77, 79-80, 85, 317, 319, 359-360

    see also election campaign segments

LRI Online, 66-68

labor dispute, NLRA definition, 377

labor organization, NLRA definition, 377

Labor Relations Institute, 40, 83, 155, 198, 199

literature, campaign

    development, 153-160, 228-229

    distribution 149-152, 158-159, 229

        restrictions, 151

    examples, 161-194

    format, 153

    posters and cartoons, 159-160

    printer selection, 158

    question and answer booklet, 356-367

    response literature, 345-353

        guidelines, 345-347

        use of, 345

    and use of videos, 201

    see also election campaign segments

management

    campaign conduct, 86-87, 91-114, 369-371

    campaign training, 213-217

    influence, 91

    literature distribution, 150-152

    NLRA definitions, 4, 92, 456-457

    and unionization, 92, 314, 357

National Labor Relations Act, 375-401

    authority, 2

    coverage, 456

        employees, 3-4

        employers, 2, 457

    enforcement, 452-461

    summary, 413-414

    see also Guide to Basic Law and Procedures under the National Labor Relations Act

National Labor Relations Board

    annual reports, 379

    authority, 452-457

    composition, 378-379

    court enforcement, 461-462